Legal Writing: Getting It Right and Getting It Written

Fourth Edition

Mary Barnard Ray

and

Jill J. Ramsfield

AMERICAN CASEBOOK SERIES®

THOMSON
WEST

Mat #40268372

American Casebook Series and West Group are trademarks
registered in the U.S. Patent and Trademark Office.

COPYRIGHT © 1987, 1993 WEST PUBLISHING CO.
© West, a Thomson business, 2000
© 2005 Thomson/West
     610 Opperman Drive
     P.O. Box 64526
     St. Paul, MN 55164–0526
     1–800–328–9352
ISBN 0–314–15434–5

TEXT IS PRINTED ON 10% POST
CONSUMER RECYCLED PAPER

∞

To William, Kathryn, Mark, and Dennis;
To Eugenio, mio carissimo;
and to our students.

*

Acknowledgments

Our thanks go to the many contributors to this book: students, teachers, practitioners, and non-lawyers. As usual, they offered ideas for entries, pointers and practical tips, corrections on the Fourth Edition, and reflections on overall content. Special thanks to Brook Bowman for adding the ALWD section of the citation tables and to Tanya Stern for editing the Bluebook Table. Thanks to Lisa Fine for proofreading drafts, Kathy Walters and Anne Falk for persisting through all the detailed refinements. Thanks to Dennis Ray for help with formatting, and Kathryn Ray, who has grown up with this book and now helps proofread.

As always, we thank our family and friends, who supported us as we prepared this edition. Their ideas and good cheer allowed us to work creatively, free of pressure.

And, once again, we must thank each other. We rediscovered that collaboration can be creative, cathartic, and carefree. We enjoyed rediscovering the book, and we hope our collective thoughts are helpful to all readers.

*

Introduction

This book addresses many of the questions that professional legal writers face. It answers the busy lawyer's questions on the job, the law student's questions at the computer, and all legal writers' questions about the process of writing well under pressure.

This book is a desktop reference that provides quick, reliable answers to those questions when they arise during research, writing, analyzing, and editing. It addresses questions that occur to all legal writers, such as identifying the writing priorities for complaints or the proper uses of commas. It also addresses the individual writer's propensities with entries on such topics as writing blocks and perfectionism. It covers small particulars, such as whether to use *infer* or *imply*, and large issues, such as research strategies.

This book helps the legal writer resolve incidental problems, review a document efficiently, and develop an individualized approach to legal writing. For example, some writers enjoy starting a project, but bog down in the middle and then rush at the end. Some are good at organizing information but have trouble translating that organization into smooth, coherent sentences. And some are perfectionists, stopping at every sentence, enjoying the perfecting, while the clock ticks away and other projects accumulate. This book helps the legal writer even out, refine, and develop his or her approach to researching and writing.

This book also helps the legal writer develop over time. What sufficed in undergraduate studies falters in law school and may fail in practice. Year by year, lawyers must achieve more, becoming more prolific, more productive, and perhaps more profound. Such development requires a conscious effort to release old habits that are no longer useful to gain new ones that are.

New in this edition are entries that encourage legal writers to keep their voices alive, their individual choices conscious and creative, and their analytical alternatives appropriate but memorable. As much as writers may hear that they must conform to the profession's (or teacher's or supervising attorney's) norms, too much conformity can rob the writing of any life. Success often depends on staying alert and individual, but knowing when and how to meet audiences' needs. The two need not be mutually exclusive, as discussed in entries on voice, choices in legal writing, and personality in legal writing.

Also new in this edition are entries on email, a forum for writing that deserves as much conscious analysis and preparation as other media. There is also an entry on voice mail, and updates on using computers for research and writing. Legal reasoning gets more attention in this edition, too, with entries on such subjects as synthesis, stare decisis, and the canons of construction.

This book allows legal writers to examine in detail the written product and the manner of writing it. It is designed to serve as a professional resource, handbook, and style manual. We hope you find it useful.

How to Use This Book

The book covers the full range of topics that arise in legal writing, all arranged alphabetically so that you can find them quickly. It addresses little details, like when to use *that* or *which* and when to use commas or semicolons. It also addresses broader questions, such as how to conquer writer's block, how to revise your work or a colleague's, and how to draft various documents. This book, combined with your citation reference, should provide you with all the information you need to answer your writing questions clearly and quickly. This book is yours to use as a reference, a tutorial text, or an efficient helper. Tailor its use to your writing style, process, and personality.

Finding the Information You Need

To find an answer to any writing question, simply look up your topic, using the term that seems logical to you. You should find either the information you want under that topic or find a cross reference to the entry that does contain the information. For example, if you were facing the task of writing a contract for the first time, you could look up CONTRACTS, DRAFTING and find an overview of the writing tasks most important in contract drafting. If you were puzzling over ways to use a source, you could look under READING, CASE BRIEFS, and NOTES to find ways of analyzing and recording uses for that source. You could also look under REASONING and LEGAL ANALYSIS to think about ways that source might fit into your analysis. If you were not sure whether you needed to use commas or semicolons to punctuate a list, you could look under LISTS, SEMICOLONS, or COMMAS. If you looked under LISTS, you would find an entry entitled LISTS, STRUCTURE OF that gives you all the details you need, and you could then find a subsection in that entry covers your specific question. If you looked under COMMAS, you would find general information and cross references to the LISTS, STRUCTURE OF entry. And if you looked under SEMICOLONS, you would find the answer you need and, if you needed more detail, a cross reference to LISTS, STRUCTURE OF. For ideas on how to design and structure issues, you can look under ISSUE STATEMENTS or BRIEFS.

If you do not find the answers you need under the term you check first, think of an idea related to the entry and look there, or check the list of entries. If you do not find the needed information under that topic, you can scan the alphabetical list of entries that follows this section to find the information you need. To help you further, consult the topical list of entries.

To avoid a clutter of quotation marks, examples within the text are set off in italics. Longer examples are indented, with good examples in bold type. In longer entries, subsections are numbered for easier and more precise reference. Citations used in examples are fictitious, but conform in format to *The Bluebook*. Controversial grammatical points have been resolved in favor of the clearer choice for legal writing. When applicable, we have resolved these points according to the Bluebook and the *U.S. Government Printing Office Style Manual* (2001) because these sources are the recognized authorities in legal writing.

Using This Book To Find Quick Answers

Your favorite way to use this book may be as a quick reference, a place to find answers in a minute and get back to the task at hand. Having the book on your desk frees you from having to remember details. For example, you may be writing a brief and be unsure about whether to use *affect* or *effect*. Rather than guessing which to use, you can look it up quickly, fix it, and move on. Or you might be puzzling too long over the point headings in your argument. To accelerate the process, you can look up POINT HEADINGS, apply the techniques you find there, and move to the next task. Or, if you are having trouble getting started on a tough letter to a client, you can turn to the entries on BAD NEWS, GIVING IT or BAD NEWS, SOFTENING IT and imitate the form to get started, refining it to fit with your own style and your particular situation.

Using This Book to Improve Your Knowledge About Writing

You can also use the book as your personal writing guide, using it to build up your knowledge of writing in the areas of greatest interest to you. Scan the topical list of entries and note those of particular interest to you. Read the complete group of entries under a topic if you like, or read them in smaller spurts, checking off the entries you have read. Mark up the book, fold down page corners, attach sticky notes, and comment in the margins. Make it your own personal legal writing guide.

You may use this book to satisfy your curiosity about all sorts of writing questions, large and small. You can learn more about any topic easily by referring to the other entries or outside sources cross-referenced within the entry. For example, if you are examining memo writing, you might want to read all the entries under MEMOS in the topical index. Inherent in analysis is an approach to ORGANIZATION, so you might want also to assign entries listed under that topic. In addition, you might want to cover those entries under LEGAL ANALYSIS. Typical mistakes occur in memo writing, such as overuse of FLOWERY LANGUAGE and misuse of MODIFIERS, so you might want to add those entries as well.

Using This Book To Improve Your Writing Ability

You may want to develop your own plan for improvement with a little less structure than a course, but a more systematic approach than just looking up questions as they arise. One way to do this is to start recording entries you consult as you are writing. Over time, note the entries that you look up the most. You might keep a separate file, or mark this book with your own code of tabs to remind yourself periodically of those trouble areas. You might keep a list.

<u>Date</u>   <u>Reader</u>   <u>Main Problems</u>   <u>Entries</u>

After you have identified these areas, you can begin collecting further feedback. For example, specifically request feedback about those areas from your colleagues or supervisor. You can also read cross-referenced entries, especially those that discuss the related, broader topics. Gradually, after you categorize these areas, read supplemental entries when you are beginning the writing process or when you get to those areas of concern. Consciously build techniques to combat the problems. This way, you may gradually remove weaknesses and develop strengths.

Another way to encourage and guide your own improvement is to set goals for yourself as a writer and work toward those goals over time. Rather than starting with your problem, begin with your interest and read entries that are related to that interest. You can move through the book gradually, in order of importance for you. To help you find related entries of interest to you, consult the topical list of entries following this section.

*

Index to Entries

A

F

I

O

P

Q

T

U

*

Topical List of Entries

WRITING PROCESS
General Concepts

Making Preliminary Decisions

Memo Writing

Brief Writing

PERSUASION IN GENERAL

CITATIONS

VARIOUS LEGAL DOCUMENTS

CHECKLISTS

GRAMMAR CONCEPTS

Generally

Nouns

Verbs

Modifiers

ORGANIZATION

Processes of Organization

USAGE

Legal Writing: Getting It Right and Getting It Written

Fourth Edition

*

ABBREVIATIONS IN TEXT

Use abbreviations only in the following situations.

1. Abbreviate the name of a party if the initials are widely recognized, such as *NLRB* or *NBC*.

2. Abbreviate words commonly used and abbreviated in company titles, such as *Co., Corp., Inc., Ltd.,* &, and *No.*

3. Abbreviate conventional personal titles, such as *Mr.* and *Ms.*

4. In CITATIONS, abbreviate according to the form your AUDIENCE uses.

For related information, see INITIALS.

ABHORRENCE OF OR *ABHORRENCE FOR?*

Use *abhorrence of; abhorrence for* is incorrect.

ABOVE

Above is equivalent to *supra*. Although you can use *above* to refer the reader to previous text, avoid sending the reader back farther than a few paragraphs. Legal readers like to keep moving.

When using *above* as a preposition, use it to indicate spatial relationships.

The defendant then placed the insecticide in the cabinet above the refrigerator.

Use *over*, rather than *above*, to indicate higher quantities.

The driver was over 21.

rather than

The driver was above the age of 21.

For related information, see LEGALESE.

ABSTRACT NOUNS

Abstract nouns describe ideas or general concepts, in contrast to concrete nouns, which describe tangible items. For example, *justice* and *transportation* are abstract; *courtroom* and *bicycle* are concrete. In general, choose concrete nouns because they are more readable and more memorable. Use abstract nouns when you need them to describe ideas accurately or to de-emphasize an unfavorable fact, such as the details of an auto accident caused by your client. In that situation, you might use the abstract noun *accident* rather than the concrete phrase *when the truck hit the car.* For problems related to abstract nouns, see PRECISION, subsection 2; ACCURACY, subsection 1(b); and AMBIGUITY,

WAYS TO AVOID, subsection 4. For uses of abstract nouns, see PER-SUASIVE WRITING, subsection 3(b), and NOUNS.

ACCURACY

In legal writing, your final documents must always be accurate. Even when you are revising for READABILITY and eloquence, do not sacrifice accuracy. The following rules should help you maintain accuracy while revising. For related writing concerns, see PRECISION.

1. Accuracy in WORD CHOICE.

(a) Use only one term to identify each key person, thing, or idea.

Even though the defendant <u>admitted</u> while in custody that he had been using drugs, this <u>admission</u> of impropriety is not relevant to the present case.

The following version, in contrast, leaves the reader guessing about the relationship between *commented* and *admission of impropriety*.

Even though the defendant <u>commented</u> while in custody that he had been using drugs, this <u>admission</u> of impropriety is not relevant to the present case.

Using synonyms is particularly risky with legal readers because they will wonder if you intended to change the meaning, even though you may have only been trying to add variety. For more examples and discussion of this point, see REPETITION, subsections 1 and 3; and AMBIGUITY, WAYS TO AVOID, subsection 4.

(b) Use the most specific word you can. Often inaccuracies occur because the writer chose an unnecessarily general term and as a result inadvertently broadened the term's reference. For example, do not say *vehicle* when you mean to refer only to *school bus*. For more on this, see PRECISION, subsection 2.

(c) Make the meaning of your words clear in context so you avoid unintended innuendo or humor. In the following examples, the first version is not as concise or as interesting as the second, but it is more accurate.

She released him from employment as soon as she was no longer bedridden.

rather than

She let him go as soon as she could get out of bed.

Although you always need to be accurate in legal writing, you may sometimes need to be less specific, even somewhat vague. For discussions of times you may avoid specificity, see EMPHASIS, subsection 2; and PRECISION, subsection 2.

(d) Make sure each pronoun is unambiguous. For example, if only one woman is mentioned in your text, you need not worry about *she* causing inaccuracy. If, however, two or more appear, then *she* is likely to be ambiguous. In this situation, check each *she*.

> **Ms. Jones did not ask Ms. Wilson to double-check the amount, because Ms. Wilson** [not she] **routinely checked all the amounts listed.**

For more on this, see AMBIGUITY, WAYS TO AVOID, subsection 2. For general information, see PRONOUNS.

(e) Make sure each *this* is unambiguous. *This* is the pronoun most likely to cause inaccuracies. *This* can refer to an idea or a thing, one word or a whole sentence; as a result, you must make sure that the reader always knows what *this* means. If there is any question, add the appropriate noun after *this*.

> **The court reasoned that the difference in the age of the fetuses was not the factor determining this issue. This reasoning**. . . .

For more examples, see AMBIGUITY, WAYS TO AVOID, subsection 2. For related information, see VARIETY, paragraph 2.

2. Accuracy in sentence structure.

Whenever possible, place all modifiers and modifying phrases immediately next to the word modified.

> **Our client has arranged with <u>other subcontractors</u> to fill the ditches.**

rather than

> Our client has arranged to fill the ditches <u>with other subcontractors</u>.

> **Only Ms. Sparks suggested filing a suit for adverse possession.**

rather than

> Ms. Sparks only suggested filing a suit for adverse possession.

For related general information, see MODIFIERS and SENTENCE STRUCTURE, subsections 1 and 7. For related information, see MODIFIERS, DANGLING.

3. Accuracy in citations.

(a) Make sure all the volume and page numbers are correct. Incorrect citations irritate readers because the reader finds the volume and page, only to find some case having nothing to do with the point.

(b) Use a pinpoint cite to refer to a particular rule, holding, quotation, or proposition in a source. PINPOINT CITATIONS pinpoint the exact page. These specific references are greatly appreciated by any reader whose job it is to evaluate the merits of the point being made. Using pinpoint cites routinely also discourages you from using unneeded string cites.

(c) Use correct citation form. Especially watch the spacing, a frequent source of error. Judges in particular find citation errors distracting, so use letter-perfect citations to enhance your credibility.

For details on proper citation form, see CITATIONS; CITATIONS, BASIC FORMATS; CITATIONS, PARALLEL; and CITATIONS, STRING.

Accuracy comes into play before, during, and after you revise your text. For general accuracy concerns in the earlier stages of the writing process, see ORGANIZATION, LARGE–SCALE and ORGANIZATION, SMALL–SCALE. For accuracy concerns in some specific legal situations, see CONTRACTS, DRAFTING; GENERAL CORRESPONDENCE LETTERS; and BAD NEWS, SOFTENING IT. For related writing concerns, see PRECISION.

ACTIVE VERBS

See ACTIVE VOICE.

ACTIVE VOICE

Active voice is the term for the grammatical structure indicating that the subject of the sentence performs or causes the action expressed by the verb.

1. How active voice works.

Because the subject does the acting and the verb describes that action, active voice moves the action with the reader's eye from the left to right.

The boy hit the ball.

Defendant argued that the court should suppress the evidence.

The court decided that freedom of association was not an issue.

This use of active voice prevents the legal reader from having to double back to understand the point.

The ball was hit by the boy.

It was argued by the defendant that the evidence should be suppressed by the court.

It was decided that freedom of association was not an issue.

The passive voice can also create a sentence that is less precise, as in the last example, which makes the reader wonder who decided. Active voice also makes the sentence shorter in most cases.

The <u>court held</u> that the <u>plaintiff could not collect</u> punitive damages.

rather than

<u>It was held</u> by the court that punitive <u>damages could not be collected</u> by the plaintiff.

Therefore, if wordiness is a problem in your writing, read through the draft once when revising just for passive voice. Check each subject and verb and translate from passive to active whenever active is appropriate. For an example of how this step fits in the writing process, see REVISING PROCESS CHECKLIST. For related information, see CONCISENESS, subsection 6.

2. How to determine whether voice is active or passive.

If your computer has a grammar checker, you can use that to scan your documents for passive voice. Otherwise, the quickest way to determine whether you are using passive or active voice is to locate the verb in a sentence or clause and to ask yourself, "Who or what did this action?" If the answer to your question is not the same word as the subject of that verb, then you have used passive voice. If you use that answer as your subject, then you convert the sentence to active voice.

The <u>ball was *hit*</u> by the boy.

Who did the hitting? The boy, so this is passive voice. The same content in active voice would read as follows.

The boy hit the ball.

<u>It was argued</u> by the defendant that <u>the evidence should be suppressed</u> by the court.

Who did the arguing? The defendant. Who did the suppressing? The court. So the active voice would be as follows.

The defendant argued that the court should suppress the evidence.

Sometimes the actor is unclear, as in the following example.

<u>It was decided</u> that freedom of association was not an issue.

Who did the deciding? We do not know as it is now worded. To change this sentence to active voice, you would need to identify the decider.

3. When to use active voice.

Use active voice unless the writing requires the passive for effect. For examples of times when passive is useful, see PASSIVE VOICE, sections 1 through 4.

The government's actions violated the plaintiff's right to privacy.

rather than

The Plaintiff's right to privacy was violated.

When using active voice, avoid canceling its advantages by using vague verbs, such as *consists of, seems, feels, concerns,* or *involves.*

The court has presented two inconsistent standards of review in jury misconduct cases.

rather than

The court seems unsure about the standard of review in these kinds of cases.

4. Active voice and linking verbs.

Using active voice rather than passive is not a matter of avoiding any form of the verb *to be. To be* is necessary and useful in legal writing because it is a linking verb that functions as a verbal equals sign. For information about using *to be,* see VERBS, LINKING.

ACTUALLY

Actually means *in fact.* It is an ADVERB used to communicate that the action stated did indeed happen and the writer is communicating literally, not figuratively.

The defendant actually hid the knife by sliding it under the cake.

Because legal writers rarely use figurative speech, they also rarely use *actually.* Therefore, for ACCURACY, avoid using it. For related information, see LITERAL MEANING and FIGURATIVE MEANING.

AD HOC

This Latin phrase means *for a particular, specific purpose.* Usually it applies either to committees that have been created to fulfill a certain function or to situations that are unusual and need particular attention.

The ad hoc committee on Zoning Enforcement will meet each Thursday for four weeks.

or

The ad hoc solution is to pay the directors less and the workers more.

In legal writing, ad hoc is neither capitalized nor italicized. As with all LATIN PHRASES, use it sparingly; substitute English where possible. For related information, see READABILITY, subsection 3, and JARGON.

ADJECTIVES

Adjectives modify nouns or pronouns. Use adjectives only when they are needed or, as Twain said, "As to the adjective: when in doubt, strike it out." If you find yourself writing several adjectives to modify one noun, stop and find the noun that more precisely states your meaning.

Mr. Barnes has frequently testified as an expert witness on bone disease.

rather than

Mr. Barnes is a known, respected, and often-used authority on bone diseases.

Proper adjectives are adjectives derived from proper names. Capitalize most proper adjectives: *American banking system, the Atlantic seaboard, Vietnamese refugees*. Do not capitalize an adjective derived from a proper name when it has been used frequently and for a long time in the general language: *cesarean operation, india ink, italic type, murphy bed*, or *venetian blinds*. For an extensive list of adjectives derived from proper names, see the U.S. Government Printing Office Style Manual (2001).

Predicate adjectives are adjectives that follow linking verbs, such as *is* or *seems*, and describe the subject of those verbs.

The case is relevant.

For related examples and explanation, see MODIFIERS and ADJECTIVES AFTER A LINKING VERB.

ADJECTIVES AFTER A LINKING VERB

Adjectives after the verb, or predicate adjectives, do not require hyphens.

The youth was fear stricken and guilt ridden.

rather than

The youth was fear-stricken and guilt-ridden.

In contrast, adjectives placed before the subject may need HYPHENS.

The fear-stricken, guilt-ridden youth could not move from the street.

For the relevant general rules, see HYPHENS, subsection 2.

ADVERBS

Adverbs modify verbs, adjectives, or other adverbs.

Mr. Smith cannot justly be penalized for acting very carefully.

Avoid overusing them; too many adverbs can bog down a sentence while adding a minimum of information. Three adverbs you can omit readily are *clearly, merely,* and *obviously.* Another adverb you can view with suspicion is *very*, because it usually weakens the point rather than strengthening it, as in the example above. For related information, see CONCISENESS, subsection 7, and MODIFIERS.

AFFECT OR *EFFECT*?

In legal writing you usually want *effect* when using the noun and *affect* when using the verb.

This law had a sweeping effect.

but

This law affected police procedures.

This is because *effect* as a noun means *something that was the result of another action*, while *affect* as a noun means a *feeling*. *Affect* as a verb, however, means *to influence*. Occasionally you will need *effect* as a verb if you mean *to cause to come into being*.

Through persistent lobbying, the group effected a change in the inheritance laws.

AFORESAID

When writing to clients, substitute *mentioned earlier, named earlier,* or some other more explanatory phrase. One of the most virulent complaints coming from the general public is that lawyers use LEGALESE, and *aforesaid* is viewed as legalese.

In a legal document written to be read by other lawyers, such as a pleading, you may use *aforesaid*, but you must use it precisely because lawyers will interpret the term literally. Never toss it in carelessly, thinking that it will in itself add a patina of authenticity to the document. *Aforesaid* means you are referring to something mentioned earlier rather than something mentioned afterward. For example, you would say the *aforesaid defendant* only if another defendant is mentioned later and you mean to exclude that other defendant. Do not use *aforesaid defendant* if you have only one defendant or if you mean to include all defendants.

If you observe this rule, you will find that you have few occasions to use *aforesaid*.

AFRICAN AMERICAN OR *AFRICAN–AMERICAN*?

Write it without the hyphen, just as you would write *Swedish American* or *Chinese American*. *African American* is capitalized because it derives from the names of geographic areas. Some people prefer *African American* over *black*; be sensitive to the preferences of your AUDIENCE.

AGES

Spell out ages zero to ninety-nine in text, zero to nine in footnotes, just as you do with other numbers.

Sixty-five-year-olds are eligible for Social Security.

Use HYPHENS when the age is expressed as a modifier before a noun.

She is a six-year-old child.

But do not use hyphens when it comes after a linking verb.

She was six years old.

Newspaper style books differ on this point, using numerals for ages, unless the age is the first word in a sentence.

The document is 75 years old.

AGREEMENT, SUBJECTS AND VERBS

Agreement here means using plural verbs with plural subjects and singular verbs with singular subjects. Problems with agreement most frequently occur when the subject and verb are separated by a long phrase and the writer loses track of the subject along the way. As a result, the verb may agree with some noun in the long phrase rather than with the subject. You can usually avoid this problem by keeping the subject and verb close together. This will also improve the readability of your text.

Since 1979, section 4 of the Export Administration Act has created much controversy. That section gives the President authority to impose foreign policy and national security controls on exports.

rather than

Since 1979, the section of the Export Administration Act giving the President authority to impose foreign policy and national security controls on exports have created much controversy.

For a general discussion of related concerns, see READABILITY, subsection 5, and SENTENCE STRUCTURE.

AGREEMENTS, WRITTEN

See CONTRACTS, DRAFTING.

AGREE TO OR *AGREE WITH?*

The choice between *agree to* and *agree with* is based on IDIOM, which means there is a right or wrong choice in most cases. For example, you would always say, *I agree to help you*, but *I agree with your idea*.

In general, use *agree to* when the subject is concurring with something and will act accordingly. For example, *agree to* is frequently used in contracts.

We agree to represent you in this matter.

or

My client agrees to settle out of court with the following provisions.

Use *agree with* when the subject is voicing agreement but not making any actual legal commitments.

I agree with you that large settlements are increasing insurance premiums.

or

The State agrees with the court's concern for the preservation of fifth amendment rights, but . . . .

ALL AROUND OR *ALL ROUND?*

Use *all round*, because you mean *well rounded*, not *circling around*.

ALLITERATION

Alliteration is the repetition of similar consonant sounds, as the *f*'s in *fast and furious fighting*. Alliteration can occasionally be useful in legal writing because it can help the reader remember a phrase or can add drama, but it must be used sparingly and with care.

Having been terrified twice by the defendant's previous assaults, the plaintiff hesitated before she fled.

but not

Two times terrified, Theresa tarried before taking off down the alley.

When using alliteration, first be sure that the content of the phrase is indeed worth remembering. If it is not, the alliteration will be a distraction, no matter how graceful it sounds. Second, make sure that the repeated sound creates an appropriate feeling. For example, a repeated *t* sound can sound harsh, while a repeated *s* can sound soothing.

The attorney was known for the smoothness and simplicity of his writing style.

Finally, read the passage aloud to make sure it works, because *tongue twisters torture tired readers*. For a discussion of related techniques, see ASSONANCE and REPETITION, subsection 4.

ALL READY OR *ALREADY?*

All ready means a group is *prepared for some sort of action*. *Already* means *by this or a specified time* or *previously*.

ALL RIGHT OR *ALRIGHT?*

In legal writing, use the space. *Alright* is the informal, less accepted equivalent.

10

ALL ROUND **OR** *ALL AROUND?*

See *ALL AROUND* OR *ALL ROUND?*

ALL, **SINGULAR OR PLURAL?**

All is singular when it means *the only thing*.

All that the new law can do is force the courts to resolve the conflict.

All is plural, however, when it means the *whole group*.

All the changes in the contract were made in writing.

ALL TOGETHER **OR** *ALTOGETHER?*

All together means that a group of people, things, or events are together. *Altogether* refers to an entity or group. *Altogether* means *entirely and with all included*, or *on the whole, with everything considered*.

The plaintiffs were all together as they left the courtroom.

but

Altogether, the medical costs for these victims exceeded $3 million.

ALREADY **OR** *ALL READY?*

See *ALL READY* OR *ALREADY?*

ALRIGHT **OR** *ALL RIGHT?*

See *ALL RIGHT* OR *ALRIGHT?*

ALTERNATIVE

Use *alternative* only when referring to two choices, not more. Commonly *alternative* is used when more than two choices exist; however, readers who enjoy the proper use of language will appreciate your precise use of *alternative*. When discussing more than two choices, use *options, choices,* or another similar term.

ALTHOUGH **OR** *THOUGH?*

In many situations you can use either word. *Although* is more elegant and therefore more appropriate for briefs, law review articles, and all but informal legal writings.

Use *though* in only two situations.

1. Use *though* in such phrases as *even though* or *as though*.
2. Use *though* at the end of a sentence or at the end of a phrase.

She promised, though.

or

She promised, though, to come to the hearing.

Though at the end of a sentence is correct but rather informal for legal writing, so try substituting the following.

Nevertheless, she promised.

or

She promised, however, to come to the hearing.

ALTOGETHER OR *ALL TOGETHER?*

See *ALL TOGETHER* OR *ALTOGETHER?*

ALWD CITATION MANUAL

The *ALWD Citation Manual,* sponsored by the Association of Legal Writing Directors, offers simplified citation forms as an alternative to the BLUEBOOK, whose entries are sometimes more complex or detailed than many legal writers need. Before you start TAKING EFFECTIVE NOTES, check with your AUDIENCE and your jurisdiction to see which version to use. Then you can record your initial citations in the form you will use for the document's final version. For more information on ALWD citation form, see CITATION TABLE.

A.M.

It is written *a.m.* Use the phrase only after an hour.

We will meet at 9:00 a.m.

When *a.m.* appears at the end of a sentence, as in the previous example, use only one period.

AMBIGUITY, WAYS TO AVOID

In legal writing, a word or phrase is ambiguous if, in context, it permits more than one meaning. "Given a choice between a word that can carry the proper meaning and one that must carry it, choose the latter." William Rivers, *Writing: Craft and Art* 34 (Prentice–Hall 1975). The following four rules should help you avoid ambiguity.

1. Avoid misplaced MODIFIERS.

Sometimes a phrase, because of its position, could modify any of several words in a sentence.

The defendant refused to service the car belonging to the man who insulted him <u>with good reason</u>.

Here *with good reason* should modify *refused* instead of *insulted*. To avoid ambiguity, place the modifying phrase next to the word modified.

The defendant, <u>with good reason</u>, refused to service the car belonging to the man who had insulted him.

For other problems associated with modifiers, see MODIFIERS, DANGLING and MODIFIERS, SQUINTING.

2. Avoid ambiguous PRONOUNS.

Sometimes pronouns cause ambiguity because they can logically refer to either of several nouns. The pronoun most likely to cause ambiguity is *this*, because *this* can refer to any idea or object.

You must ultimately make a judgment about the weight of the evidence. This will help you decide what the verdict should be.

Does *this* refer to *judgment* or *evidence*? To avoid the problem, add the appropriate noun after *this*.

You must ultimately make a judgment about the weight of the evidence. This judgment will help you decide what the verdict should be.

The pronoun second most likely to cause ambiguity is *it*, again because *it* can refer to any object or idea. Usually *it* becomes ambiguous when some other noun comes between *it* and the antecedent, which is the noun to which *it* refers.

The first will is less ambiguous than the second will because *it* omits the deceased's spouse.

To solve this problem, you may replace *it* with the noun.

The first will is less ambiguous than the second because the first will omits the decedent's spouse.

Or you may rephrase the sentence, so that no other noun comes between *it* and its antecedent.

The second will created some confusion by referring to the decedent's spouse; as a result, the first will is less ambiguous because *it* omits the decedent's spouse.

Although *this* and *it* are the most likely offenders, all pronouns should be watched for potential ambiguity. In general, check *he* or *she* whenever the content of your writing involves two people of the same sex. Check *they* to make sure there is no question about who is included in the group.

We is a special problem in legal writing because you may, by using *we*, inadvertently speak for your whole law firm or organization. Never use *we* when you really mean *I*; use we only when you are speaking officially for the organization of which you are a part, as one judge may do when drafting an opinion for the whole bench. For related information, see PRONOUNS and ANTECEDENTS.

3. Avoid unnecessarily vague word choice.

    (a) Use only one term to identify each key person, thing, or idea.

> **Even though the defendant <u>admitted</u> while in custody that he had been using drugs, this <u>admission</u> of impropriety is not relevant to the present case**.

rather than

> Even though the defendant <u>commented</u> while in custody that he had been using drugs, this <u>admission</u> of impropriety is not relevant to the present case.

The latter version leaves the reader guessing but not knowing the exact relationship between *commented* and *admission of impropriety*. Using synonyms is particularly risky with legal readers because they will wonder if you intended to change your meaning, even though you may have only been trying to add variety. For more examples and discussion of this point, see REPETITION, subsections 1 and 3, and PRECISION, subsection 3.

(b) Use the most specific word you can. Often inaccuracies occur because the writer chose an unnecessarily general term and as a result inadvertently broadened the term's reference. For example, do not say *vehicle* when you mean to refer only to *school bus*. For more on this, see PRECISION, subsection 2.

(c) Make the meaning of your words clear in context.

> **She released him from employment as soon as she was no longer bedridden**.

rather than

> She let him go as soon as she could get out of bed.

The first version is not as concise or as interesting, but it is accurate.

> Although you usually need to be specific in legal writing, you may need to be vague on some occasions. For a discussion of these exceptions, see EMPHASIS, subsection 2.

4. Avoid unnecessary abstraction.

Whenever possible, use concrete nouns and specific verbs rather than ABSTRACT NOUNS and general verbs. This will help focus the reader on your main points.

> **The defendant moves to dismiss the case under Fed. R. Civ. P. 12(b)(6)**.

rather than

> This concerns the defendant's motion to dismiss.

For related information, see PERSUASIVE WRITING, subsection 3.

AMENDMENT CAPITALIZED?

Capitalize *Amendment* when you are using it in text to refer to a particular amendment to the U.S. Constitution, but do not capitalize it in citations.

The Fourth *Amendment* to the United States Constitution prevents warrantless searches except in extraordinary conditions.

but

U.S. Const. *amend.* IV, § 1.

When using the word generally to refer to amendments in other documents, do not capitalize it.

The state legislature ratified four amendments to the environmental impact statute.

AMONG OR *BETWEEN*?

Use *between* when discussing two options and *among* when discussing more than two.

Conferences were held between the plaintiff's and the defendant's attorneys, the plaintiff's attorney and estate's trustees, and the defendant's attorney and the estate's trustees.

rather than

Conferences were held between the plaintiff's attorney, the defendant's attorney, and the estate's trustees.

Although the former version is less concise, it leaves no question about who met with whom.

Use *among* to indicate that more than two parties are meeting.

The issue has been discussed among the plaintiff's attorney, the defendant's attorney, and the estate's trustee.

ANALOGOUS CASES

An analogous case is one that is similar in some way to the situation being analyzed. In traditional U.S. legal reasoning, use analogous cases to support the stare decisis rationale that similar situations should be treated similarly. A case may be analogous because of the reasoning, policy, holding, facts, or any other aspect of the case relevant to your client's situation. Be sure to select it for the aspects that compare most strongly to your situation.

When writing about the analogous case in a memo or brief, communicate the strengths of those analogies in a way that shows the reader how and why the case fits into your overall analysis. Describe the essential details of the analogous case. Which details are essential depends on the point you are making, and may include the rule, rationale, holding, legally significant facts, or dicta of that case. If the case's rationale is similar and sound, use the same rationale in your analysis. If the case's policy principles provide a good foundation for your analysis, use those principles. If the facts are similar, use those.

Make sure to include enough information about the analogous case to allow the reader to compare or distinguish this case from your situation while avoiding unnecessary detail. Above all, focus on explaining your thinking and the support for that reasoning, rather than mechanically filing parts of a case into a paragraph. This should help you avoid a wooden or superficial presentation of your reasoning. For related information, see ARGUMENT SECTION, DISCUSSION SECTION, RULES, HOLDINGS, and PARALLEL STRUCTURE, subsection 2.

ANALYSIS

See LEGAL ANALYSIS.

AND

There are three points to remember about this conjunction. First, although it is not wrong to start a sentence with *and*, doing so draws attention to the word. Therefore, before starting a sentence with *and*, ask yourself if that word is really what you want to emphasize. Often it is not.

Second, use *and* to join sentences only when the sentence logically should be joined with the verbal equivalent of a plus sign.

Finally, avoid overusing *and* to join sentences, because it can lead to long, lackluster sentences. For related general information, see CONJUNCTIONS.

AND/OR

Avoid this construction because it creates ambiguity.

Either the Company or its agents, or both, may....

rather than

The Company and/or its agents may....

Instead of using *and/or*, decide whether the logical connection between the two phrases, words, or clauses is disjunctive, which requires *or*, or conjunctive, which requires *and*. If the items can be disjunctive, conjunctive, or both, then state that explicitly.

The court may, in its discretion, meet with the child or parents <u>or both</u> to determine <u>all of</u> the following factors affecting the best interests of the child: (1) the child's own preferences, (2) the parents' ability <u>and</u> willingness to provide consistent, adequate care, <u>and</u> (3) the parents' willingness to cooperate with each other if joint custody is awarded.

rather than

> The court may, in its discretion meet with the child and/or parents to determine factors affecting the best interests of the child, such as (1) the child's own preferences and/or desires, (2) the parents' ability and/or willingness to provide consistent and/or adequate care, and/or (3) the parents' willingness to cooperate with each other if joint custody is awarded.

For related information, see OR, AND, and CONJUNCTIONS.

ANIMAL—*HE, SHE,* OR *IT*?

> Use *it*.

ANSWERS TO COMPLAINTS

When drafting an answer, you have three tasks: (1) to tell the court and the opposition how your client is responding to each paragraph in the complaint, (2) to begin or preserve any counter actions your client may want to pursue, and (3) to establish your theory of defense. Also you need to observe the practices and forms accepted by the court and required by professional responsibility.

1. Responding to each paragraph.

> In some jurisdictions, a client making a general denial may state that in one paragraph.

> **Defendant denies each allegation in Plaintiff's complaint**.

In other jurisdictions, however, the preferred form is to respond to each paragraph separately. In that situation, list all the paragraph numbers separately and write out the appropriate answer after each number.

Usually your client will deny some, but not all, of the allegations. For example, the client may admit paragraphs that correctly identify your client, but may have insufficient knowledge to determine if paragraphs identifying other parties are correct. Thus often you must tell the court which paragraphs your client denies, admits, or can neither deny nor admit. Additionally, your client may admit that some of the facts stated in the complaint are true, although he or she will usually deny the legal conclusions based on those facts.

1. **Defendant admits the allegation**.
2. **Defendant has insufficient information to admit or deny the allegation**.
3. **Defendant admits in part, denies in part the allegation**.
4. **Defendant denies the allegation**.

Some jurisdictions may allow you to group the references to the complaint's paragraphs as follows.

1. **Defendant admits the allegations in paragraphs 1, 5, 7, and 8.**

2. **Defendant denies the allegations in paragraphs 4, 9, 10, 11, and 12.**

3. **Defendant does not have sufficient information to admit or deny allegations in paragraphs 2, 3, and 6.**

Consider, however, whether this is the most convenient form for the reader. It may be more courteous to the court to respond to the paragraphs separately.

2.   Beginning or preserving any counter actions.

Think carefully about the decisions you make when answering, for your client's responses begin to shape the course of the litigation. Good legal writing at this point usually requires research and a quick review of all possible substantive and procedural options, including standard of review. By providing such thorough treatment early in the case, you are sure you do not overlook any claims and thus inadvertently waive any of your client's rights. Answering a complaint requires careful and thorough thought about strategies and issues, which goes beyond the scope of this text.

3.   Establishing your theory of the case.

When you answer a complaint, you are framing your theory of the case. What you choose to say or omit initiates your strategy of the case. You may choose to deny everything, suggesting a motion to dismiss. Or, knowing the standard of review is *gross abuse of discretion*, you may answer in such a way as to get the case to trial because you are confident you will win there. Make sure you consider all reasonable possibilities before you respond. As with all documents for a court, learn and follow all rules and forms in your jurisdiction. For related information, see PLEADINGS and COMPLAINTS.

ANTECEDENTS

An antecedent is the noun to which a pronoun refers.

Ms. Williams' <u>aunt</u> willed her estate to charity.

Here *aunt* is the antecedent of *her*. For problems related to this, see AMBIGUITY, WAYS TO AVOID, subsection 2. For related information, see NOUNS and PRONOUNS.

ANTE– OR ANTI–?

Ante- means in *front of* or *before*, as in *antebellum*.

Anti- means *against*, or *opposite*, as in *anti-intellectual* and *antibody*.

ANYBODY, SINGULAR OR PLURAL?

Anybody uses singular verbs.

Anybody who believes in justice believes in a fair trial.

Anybody is rather informal, so use *anyone* in formal legal writing, such as briefs or articles.

ANYONE, SINGULAR OR PLURAL?

Anyone uses singular verbs.

Anyone is entitled to a fair trial.

A OR AN?

Use *an* before all nouns beginning with a vowel or vowel sound; this includes nouns that begin with *h* where the *h* is not voiced, such as *an hour*. Use *a* before all nouns beginning with a voiced consonant, such as *a hearing*. For related information, see ARTICLES, GRAMMAR.

APOSTROPHES

Apostrophes, like decimal points, belong in specific places and have specific uses:

(1) to create the possessives of nouns,

(2) to express the plurals of numerals in some situations,

(3) to create a contraction,

1. Creating the possessives of nouns.

Use an apostrophe to create the possessive form of a noun.

plaintiff's = belonging to one plaintiff.

plaintiffs' = belonging to more than one plaintiff.

Pettuses' = belonging to the Pettuses.

Do not, however, use an apostrophe to form the plural of a name ending in *s*. Instead use *es*: the Joneses. See the examples listed below. For related information, see PLURALS OF NAMES.

Also do not use an apostrophe to form possessives of PRONOUNS.

its = belonging to it.

yours = belonging to you.

theirs = belonging to them.

whose = belonging to whom.

ours = belonging to us.

hers = belonging to her.

For more explanation, see POSSESSIVES.

2. Expressing the plurals of numbers in some situations.

Whether you use an apostrophe expressing figures depends on your AUDIENCE. General style manuals have shifted to forming the plural of a letter, figure, or symbol by adding s without an apostrophe. But the <u>U.S. Government Printing Office Style Manual</u> (2001) still requires the apostrophe.

general style manuals	Government manual
7s	**7's**
Cs	**C's**

But in either style, use an apostrophe when it is needed to keep the text readable.

a's, ha's

rather than

as, has

3. Creating a contraction.

Use an apostrophe as a substitution for a letter or letters.

it's = it is

you're = you are

don't = do not

In most legal writing, however, do not use contractions. For more explanation, see CONTRACTIONS.

APPEAL

Use *appeal* as a term of art only, referring to the appeal of a case. Avoid using *appeal* informally in legal writing.

The appeal will be decided next week.

rather than

The defendant's counsel appealed to the court to deny the motion.

For related information, see TERMS OF ART.

APPELLATE BRIEFS

Appellate briefs need to be accurate, focused, perfectly formatted, and timely. Each of these goals is addressed in a following subsection.

1. Identifying the standard of review.

Your first step is to research the grounds for appellate review. In doing so, you may frame your argument accordingly, narrowing it if the standard is strict or broadening it if the standard is more flexible. Determine when a standard of review or conflicting standards present possible arguments for your client. You must organize around those arguments, which may differ greatly from the arguments made at trial.

This focus on the relevant appellate criteria is often lost, even by experienced legal writers, when faced with the reality of the client's plight. But to win on appeal, the writer must stay focused on the questions the appellate court will ask, not the desires of a disappointed client. Therefore, use the standard of review to establish your theory of the case.

2. Focusing the issues.

Unlike trial courts of general jurisdiction, appellate courts have more focused job descriptions. Courts of appeal are error-correcting courts. In each jurisdiction, courts of appeal review claims made by a party (usually the loser) in a previously tried case. State and federal supreme courts have a broader range of issues that they review; nevertheless, they grant petitioners the right to a hearing only for specific reasons. The justice system reviews cases for specific kinds of claims only. Your first job in an appellate brief is to convince the court that your case falls into one of those categories. For example, you may claim that some decision of the trial judge was an *abuse of discretion*. You may also be required to show that this error was substantial, or affected the outcome of the case, in order to get the appellate court to take corrective action. You cannot ask an appellate court to review a case and set aside its result without meeting one of the allowable, very specific criteria.

3. Organizing the argument.

Once you establish your theory of the case and focus your issues on appeal, organize your argument to match this theory. Gather all relevant components: standard of review, issue, facts, law, policy, equity, impact on future cases, and remedy desired. Then review your document's purposes, audiences and scope. Experiment with different ways to emphasize your points and different arrangements of the components. Many combinations will be technically correct, but only a few will fuse all the components together to communicate with greatest effect.

Your theory will help you select those few. Organize your points to prove your theory of the case. For example, if your theory is that police should not be allowed to get away with this behavior and the standard of review is *de novo*, then you may organize inductively, from the specific incidents to the general points, to demonstrate each police infraction. If your theory is that the trial court did everything well and your standard of review is abuse of discretion, you may organize deductively by first defining the general standard of abuse of discretion and then showing how this specific trial court's decision does not rise to that level.

When you find the best arrangement of the components, you may feel a sudden sense of clarity like the click of a combination lock reaching the final number that opens the lock. You can see the difference, the clarity of the thought, in the version that best fuses theory and all parts.

4. Formatting.

Appellate courts have specific rules about the format of appellate briefs. Read your local rules carefully, because most appellate courts will reject briefs that do not conform to their rules. For example, most courts require certain colors for covers; certain typesets, margins, and page lengths; and certain organization and content. Be aware of these rules before you begin writing your appellate brief, so that you know the confines within which you must work.

Appellate courts also have rules about the parts needed in their briefs. Generally, an appellate brief contains

- a table of contents that includes the point headings,
- a TABLE OF AUTHORITIES that includes references to specific pages where each authority is used,
- a STATEMENT OF THE CASE with specific references to the record,
- ISSUE STATEMENTS,
- an ARGUMENT SECTION with POINT HEADINGS and sub-headings, and
- a conclusion (see CONCLUSIONS).

Use PERSUASIVE WRITING when preparing your appellate brief. For more information on format, also see BRIEFS.

5. Timeliness.

All may be lost if you miss a deadline in the appellate process, so you must plan scrupulously. Check the number of days you have for writing the brief and know how your jurisdiction counts those days. Pay particular attention to how your jurisdiction counts weekends and holidays. Then mark the deadline on that calendar and count backwards to schedule your WRITING PROCESS. And stay on schedule.

In your schedule, make sure you allow a lot of time at the end for refining the format. The table of contents and table of authorities take time to assemble. Allow enough time so you will be sure to meet your deadline. Do not count on everything going smoothly, because it seldom does. For related information, see DEADLINES, MEETING THEM.

APPENDIX

Appendices can be used in any kind of legal writing to assist the reader, but not to replace important material that should be included in the text. Legal readers prefer appendices to refer to statutes, cases, excerpts from the record, and similar documents that are not needed in their entirety in the text but are helpful for reference. Therefore, use appendices

- in MEMOS to include applicable statutes;

- in PRETRIAL BRIEFS to include affidavits, any pretrial documents referenced in your brief, and applicable statutes;
- in TRIAL BRIEFS to include any referenced portions of the record and applicable statutes unless your court prefers them inserted in a section of the brief; and
- in APPELLATE BRIEFS to include referenced portions of the pretrial record, trial record, JURY INSTRUCTIONS, and applicable statutes.

Label each appendix as Appendix A, B, C, and so forth. Refer to each appendix separately in text by surrounding this phrase with PARENTHESES. *(See Appendix A)*. In briefs, check your local rules for any specific requirements for appendices.

APPLICATION

What most people mean when they say *application* is the reasoning that appears between the discussion of the laws, policies, and philosophies invoked by the legal issues and your conclusion. In an opinion, for example, the application may be a matter of analogizing cases, weaving ideas together, stating policies, using hypotheticals, arguing with the dissent, or supporting arguments and countering opposing arguments.

Your application process actually begins in your research. When you read, you analyze the materials and application methods used by courts, opposing counsel, or associates to reach a conclusion. When you write, you then choose from those the materials and methods that apply to your situation.

This process requires you to select the parts of the precedent and the current situation that are relevant to that analysis and to demonstrate to the reader why these parts are relevant. This often requires selecting language that reveals that relevance in a different way. For example, an airplane may be described as a *motorized vehicle, a means of transportation, a source of pollution*, or *a war instrument*. How you characterize that airplane becomes an important part of your application. Rather than tallying up how similar the facts are in two cases, you must explain the relevance of particular similarities, which may be something other than factual similarities. Thus a fact-to-fact comparison, without attention to the reasoning behind that comparison, is likely to go astray.

If you are arguing that a statute regulating the safety of all motorized vehicles is applicable to airplanes, then you will describe the airplane as a *motorized vehicle* in your application, and you will explain why these aspects of the airplane are relevant here. If, however, you are arguing for the creating of a new, broadly applicable environmental law, then you will use *source of pollution* as the relevant characterization. In any situation, you must present the relevant support in words that demonstrate that relevance, rather than words that supported the outcome independently of such considerations. In this way, the reader can better follow your application.

Some legal writers use the word *application* to refer to most of the analytical process rather than this one part of that process. For guidance on this larger process, see LEGAL ANALYSIS.

APPOSITIVE

An appositive is a noun or phrase that comes right after a noun and describes that noun.

The defendant, <u>Great West Power</u>, settled before the trial began.

It is useful for inserting extra information into a sentence. Keep the appositive short, however, for readability. For related problems, see READABILITY, section 5, and AGREEMENT, SUBJECTS AND VERBS. For a discussion of other uses of appositives, see UNOBTRUSIVE DEFINITIONS, section 1.

ARGUING IN THE ALTERNATIVE

Sometimes when planning your argument you will want to argue alternative theories because you believe you could win under either theory. You can do this, for example, by dividing your Argument into two sections, each with its own major point heading and subheadings. In your Introduction or Conclusion, you can connect the first and to second arguments by wording your transitions appropriately.

The evidence should be suppressed <u>not only</u> because the search was unreasonable but <u>also</u> because the evidence was discovered in an area outside the scope of the warrant.

Arguing in the alternative can become more cumbersome to structure, however, when one argument becomes relevant only if you lose your previous argument. When presenting an alternative you do not want to concede, as in the following example, use the SUBJUNCTIVE MOOD to indicate that you are not conceding. Therefore, you would write the first sentence rather than the second.

Even if the Defendant <u>had fired</u> the shot that killed Ms. Jaeger, her action <u>would have been</u> an act of justifiable self defense, not manslaughter.

rather than

Even if the Defendant <u>did fire</u> the shot that killed Ms. Jaeger, her action <u>was</u> an act of justifiable self defense, not manslaughter.

The subjunctive mood is used specifically to communicate something that is not in fact true, and so it keeps that belief in front of the reader, even as you make the alternative argument.

ARGUMENT HEADINGS

See POINT HEADINGS.

ARGUMENT SECTION

The Argument is a section in a pretrial, trial, or appellate brief. This section presents the law and its application from the client's point of view. Specifically, the Argument's goal is to persuade the court by explaining how the law supports the decision you advocate. It provides the court with the reasoning it will need when writing an opinion in your client's favor. Another goal of the Argument is to remind the court why it would be just to apply the law in this way. Yet another is to assist the court in fitting this argument in with past and future situations. Done well, the Argument convinces the court to use your reasoning by persuading the heart as well as the mind.

To achieve these goals, you first select a theory of the case and the reasoning you will develop under that theory. You then shape that reasoning to support your client's position. As you shape, you decide how to use the raw materials you have gathered during your research. These materials may include, for example, the standard of review you must follow, the legally significant facts, the relevant law, any policies that might affect the outcome, any ethical questions, any emotionally significant facts or holdings, and any appeal to fairness.

1. Selecting the theory to use.

Any case has several possible theories. For example, if you are defending a client accused of theft, you can select a theory that police did not properly follow procedure and ask for dismissal. Or you can select a theory that police arrested the wrong person or that proof is only circumstantial. You choice depends on how your client's situation fits into the law, including procedure and the standards of review that will be used for the case. You will find that within your office, different lawyers will feel strongly about one or the other theory. If you are working collaboratively, make sure you agree on the theory, because your selection of arguments and organization will follow from the theory.

2. Selecting the major arguments.

From the various theories and arguments you read when you research and from your own synthesis of the material, select a theory that you think will win. For example, if you were representing an indigent immigrant, you might want to select a theory that the law must become more tolerant of those in need. If you were representing a client accused of insider trading, you might want to select a theory that the law requires specific, incontrovertible proof. After you select your theory, build your Argument accordingly. For the immigrant, you might show the history and context for immigration law; for the corporate client, you might give detailed examples of how specific the proof must be.

3. Shaping the law.

When explaining the applicable rules, include all that you will use to make your point. Support your assertion that these rules are relevant by explaining enough about the sources so the court will agree with you. Whether you win or lose the case often depends on whether the court applies the rules you want.

The court may be persuaded that you have chosen the correct statutory rules because

- the plain meaning of the law fits the situation, or

- the legislative purpose behind the law fits the situation.

The court may be persuaded that you have chosen the correct rules from common law because:

- they are mandatory authority of the jurisdiction,

- they were established in cases that solved similar legal problems,

- they were established in cases with similar facts or outcomes, or

- they were established in cases with similar policies.

You must consider which reasons are strongest in the court's eyes and, after choosing your reasoning, explain the progression of that reasoning step by step. You usually will not include all of the possible arguments because they will dilute the overall effect. Instead, eliminate those that are unhelpful, weak, or minor, and group together the remaining arguments in select, strong point headings.

4. Deciding how to use the raw material.

When you have convinced the court that you have chosen the correct law, you need to explain how that law works in this case. This may seem obvious to you, after all the research you have done. But it needs to be explained coherently and convincingly, so the court will not be left thinking *So what?*

To be coherent, you need to select the components in your client's situation that are most relevant to the theory and the reasoning you want the court to adopt. Coherence is more than a fact-by-fact comparison of your case and the precedent case; in traditional reasoning, it involves convincing the court that the similarity or difference that you have chosen is indeed relevant to the legal reasoning you explained earlier. To do this, highlight relevant aspects of precedent and minimize ones that do not support your position. For ways to do this, see POSITIONS OF EMPHASIS and PERSUASIVE WRITING, section 3.

Beyond the letter of the law lies its spirit. Any court wants to do justice in each case, and policy arguments show the court how justice is served by applying the law in favor of your client. Often you can weave the policy argument into your presentation of precedent cases by adding a sentence that explains the policy behind the court's decision in the precedent case. For example, assume you are arguing that a disabled adult child should be allowed a wrongful death action for the loss of a parent when precedent exists for minor children having an action, but not adult children. You must think about how your client is like the parties who have been allowed a cause of action, and you must then use policy to begin weaving the relevance of that similarity into your presentation of the rule. Thus if your rule of law was

A minor child can have a cause of action for wrongful death of a parent.

you might add the following sentence to explain the policy behind that rule.

Since a minor child is economically and emotionally dependent on a parent, allowing the action fulfills the purpose of the wrongful death statute.

Then, when you later argue that a wrongful death action should be allowed for a bedridden adult child, you can argue more easily that the precedent is appropriate.

Like a minor child, Johanna Flynn was economically and emotionally dependent on her mother.

You are then in a position to argue that your client logically fits in the category this law addresses.

5.   Deciding on the sequence of points.

For more help, see ORGANIZATION, LARGE–SCALE and ORGANIZATION, SMALL–SCALE. For further help, see BRIEFS.

6.   Presenting the argument to conform to convention.

To make your structure apparent, include point headings and subheadings, which outline the arguments and give the reasons behind those arguments. For examples, see POINT HEADINGS. Make sure your brief conforms with your local rules on filing briefs.

ARTICLES, GRAMMAR

Articles is the grammatical term for *a, an,* and *the.* For a discussion of their use, see *A* OR *AN?* and THE.

ARTICLES, PUBLISHED

Articles differ from other forms of legal writing because their AUDIENCE is scholarly as well as practical and because they reflect the writer's opinion more openly than do other forms. These two differences make writing articles different from other forms of legal writing. Consider the following in writing an article.

1.   State your theme or message at the beginning.

Tell the reader your point at the beginning of the article rather than building up to it at the end. Most legal readers like to know what they are reading about and then see the explanation because they can then follow and evaluate the writer's reasoning that leads to that point. Even if the readers are likely to question your position, you are more likely to convince them if they read your article with questions in mind other than *Where is this article going?* You may state your point at the end of your introduction or in the very first sentence of the article. For related information, see ORGANIZATION; ORGANIZATION, LARGE–SCALE; and PARAGRAPHS.

2.   Construct your article to convey the message.

Make sure that your format reflects the substance of your piece. As in a brief, any headings or subheadings should be helpful signals, not merely a parroting of traditional format. Try using sentences or phrases that communicate your argument, rather than just depending on words like *Introduction,* or *Historical Background.* For example, you might want to convey that international law does not adequately address human rights in newly formed countries. To convey that message, you might structure your presentation by explaining which international law may apply, demonstrating how that law works in some other countries, explaining its weaknesses, and finally demonstrating how those weaknesses keep it from being effective in newly formed countries. Alternatively, you might select a structure that begins with a scenario from a particular country, giving details of human rights violations. You could then invoke the international law that might apply and demonstrate how it is inadequate. Construct creatively but carefully. Make sure the structure is congruent with your content, so that readers understand your message not just from the words but also from the structure. For help on using the headings to convey this structure, see HEADINGS.

3.   Use footnotes to acknowledge, educate, and substantiate.

Use footnotes to acknowledge the sources of your points. This attribution, and the manner in which you present it, is key to the value given your scholarship. Also use footnotes to educate readers about valuable historical or background information and about sources a future researcher would need for reference. Specifically, you may want to think of footnotes for scholarly writing as falling into three categories: citing directly to authority, giving attribution to the ideas of others, and adding text to elaborate on a particular point. Avoid using footnotes just for appearances; instead, make sure they are sensible and useful to the reader. For additional information, see Elizabeth Fajans & Mary R. Falk, Scholarly Writing for Law Students (2d ed. 2000).

4.   Be original and expressive.

Allow yourself more latitude in using figurative meaning, emotional language, and your own persuasive style than you would in briefs or memos. Because the article is your commentary on a given subject, also allow your style and tone wider range. Do not, however, range so far that you lessen your credibility. For an explanation of these terms, see FIGURATIVE MEANING and EMOTIONAL LANGUAGE. For relevant techniques, see TONE.

5. Create a concise presentation.

In articles, honor the same fundamental of legal writing that you do in briefs; make every word count. It is tempting to say more than is necessary in articles, but giving into that temptation can lose readers. For related information, see SCHOLARLY WRITING, SCHOLARLY WRITING CHECKLIST, SCHOLARLY WRITING PROCESS, CONCISENESS, and READABILITY.

AS

To avoid ambiguity, avoid using *as* in place of *because*.

The trial was delayed because the plaintiff fell ill.

rather than

The trial was delayed as the plaintiff fell ill.

For related information, see TRANSITIONS and PRECISION.

AS A MATTER OF FACT

You probably do not need this phrase. Try marking it out and revising what is left into a more concise, forceful statement.

It was within her power to do so. She was the supervisor on duty.

rather than

It was within her power to do so. She was, as a matter of fact, the supervisor on duty.

For related information, see CONCISENESS, section 9.

AS IF OR *AS THOUGH?*

Either one means *in the same way that it would be if*. They can be *used interchangeably*.

AS OR *LIKE?*

In a comparison, use *as* to connect CLAUSES.

She argues as a good lawyer should argue.

rather than

She argues like a good lawyer should.

Use *like* only to introduce a noun phrase.

She argues like Justice Cardozo.

AS PER

Substitute *under, according to,* or another appropriate term.

Under the terms of this contract, ...

rather than

As per the terms of this contract, ...

Or use

This number is inaccurate according to the most recent data.

rather than

This number is inaccurate as per the most recent data.

The number of words that substitute for *as per* indicate that the phrase is vague, as well as an example of JARGON.

ASSONANCE

Assonance is repeating vowel sounds within a series of words to create a specific effect. Because it requires a broader discretion in word choice, it is a more useful tool for poets than for legal writers. But it may occasionally be useful in a persuasive Statements of Facts. Use it sparingly, or you may engender humor. Also avoid sacrificing CLARITY for effect. For example, to create a staccato effect, you might repeat the short "i" sound.

The plaintiff's insistent clicking of his stick against the defendant's chair irritated the situation and provoked the assault.

But repeating an *oo* sound that much would invite readers to giggle, because the repetition is more obvious.

The moonlight soothed the plaintiff's mood, so she was moved to sign the new contract.

For related information, see ALLITERATION and REPETITION.

ASSURE, ENSURE, OR *INSURE*

Assure, ensure, and insure can all mean to make certain of something. However, only *insure* means to guarantee against loss, and only *assure* has the sense of setting a person's mind at rest. To avoid ambiguity, use the words as follows.

Use *assure* for removing doubt.

The judge assured us that she would give the maximum penalty if the defendant was found guilty.

Use *ensure* for making certain of something.

Taking that approach ensures that our client will be vindicated.

Use *insure* for guaranteeing against loss.

Our client, State Farm Mutual, insured the plaintiff against hurricane damage.

ASTERISKS

Asterisks are sometimes used for acknowledgements in law review articles or for a single footnote. In typeset print, asterisks are also sometimes used interchangeably with ELLIPSES. In typewritten, formal legal writing, asterisks are distracting, so use ellipses. In informal writing, asterisks are used to mark a single footnote; in legal writing, this is only likely to happen when adding a small point to an informal memo to a coworker.

For related information, see QUOTATIONS, HOW TO PUNCTUATE.

AS THOUGH OR *AS IF*?

See *AS IF* OR *AS THOUGH*?

AS TO

As to can be used as a preposition, in which case it takes an object.

As to the adjective: when in doubt strike it out.—Mark Twain

As to jury trials, defendants can waive their rights if they so choose.

Use *as to* rarely and with care to avoid two problems. First, do not use *as to* if it is stuffy in context. For example, in a letter to a client, write the following.

Regarding your request for. . . .

rather than

As to your request for. . . .

Second, avoid overusing *as to*. If you use it once a page, you are probably overusing it. To find a different but equally accurate connecting phrase, see TRANSITIONS.

AT THE TIME THAT

Use *when* instead. See CONCISENESS.

AT THIS POINT IN TIME

Use *now* or *currently* for CLARITY and CONCISENESS.

ATTORNEY OR *LAWYER*?

Generally, *attorney* is used to refer to the specific person representing a party to a suit, although *lawyer* is also appropriate.

Attorney Schwartz moved for a new trial.

or

The attorney for the defense objected to the question.

The term *lawyer* often refers to the general category of people qualified to practice law, although *attorneys* is also appropriate.

Several hundred lawyers attended last year's ABA convention.

AUDIENCE

To maximize the effectiveness of your writing, understand your audience, or readers, before your begin to write. This will help you communicate more effectively. The concept of audience is one of the three guiding stars that you must keep in sight throughout the WRITING PROCESS. (The others are PURPOSE and PROFESSIONAL POSTURE.)

Consider your audience throughout PREWRITING, WRITING, REWRITING, REVISING, and POLISHING.

1. When prewriting.

When you begin a project, first identify the potential readers of your document.

The Primary Reader

The primary reader is the reader to whom you must direct your message. Find out as much as you can about that reader's preferences.

- Is your primary audience a nonlawyer, a lawyer, or a judge? Adjust your content, wording, topic sentences, and tone for that reader. For further information, see TOPIC SENTENCES and READABILITY, subsections 3 and 5.

- What are the reader's objectives and concerns regarding this subject matter? Frame issues that address those objectives and include counterarguments that address those concerns. For further information, see ISSUE STATEMENTS and COUNTERARGUMENTS, HOW TO HANDLE.

- How much detailed support does this reader want? This knowledge can help you gain credibility by providing enough, but not too much, supporting explanation. For further information, see LEGAL ANALYSIS and APPLICATION.

- Is the reader is hostile or open to your position? This will help you know how to structure your argument effectively. For further information, see PERSUASIVE WRITING, subsections 1 and 2.

The Secondary Readers

Secondary readers are those who read the document for other purposes. Most legal writing is read by more than one person, and those readers each have different levels of expertise, experience, and patience. For example, BRIEFS will be reviewed by judges, the judge's clerks, opposing counsel, clients, and sometimes the press or the public; OPINION LETTERS AND EMAIL may be used in negotiations with other entities or reviewed by supervising attorneys before being sent to clients. You must try to communicate to each of these potential readers, all of whom should be able to understand the document in the first reading. Yet you must not lose focus on the primary reader. This is a challenge for any writer.

To adjust the document for secondary readers, consider the readers' levels of expertise. If all of the document's readers will be lawyers, you may use TERMS OF ART and briefer references to generally held legal assumptions. But if you have some readers who have very little legal experience, avoid unfamiliar words. When terms of art are needed, consider adding definitions or explanations. For help here, see UNOBTRUSIVE DEFINITIONS. Similarly, you may need to include appendices or summaries. See APPENDIX. If you do not know your readers' level of expertise, it is safest to include the explanatory information needed for the non-legal reader.

The Purpose

After you have identified your audience, consider the document's purpose. You might want to write out that purpose, such as *to inform the client of her tax liability* or *to suggest that the client settle the case*. As you research and write, let this purpose guide your decisions about what information to include. For more information, see PURPOSE.

When you have clarified your audience and purpose, organize the document so each reader will understand the purpose and message. Depending on your personal WRITING PROCESS, you may do this before or after writing your initial draft. This fine-tuning may require sketching several possible organizational schemes for the document, especially when addressing hostile audiences or varied purposes.

Ask yourself what ORGANIZATION will best track the primary audience's reasoning processes. It may help to ask yourself what questions the reader will have in mind when reading a particular passage of text. Then write to answer those questions. For example, when explaining your point to a client who is a nonlawyer,

- begin your explanation with the effect of the law on the reader, rather than with the legal language itself;
- omit unneeded legal terms; and
- define any remaining terms.

For example, the following paragraph from an opinion letter begins with the effect of the law before moving to an explanation of the law itself.

> **To transfer ownership of this land to your son, you will need to**.... **According to Illinois property law, all transfers of ownership must**.... **The reason the law requires you to do this is because some land has not been transferred according to the parent's wishes when**....

rather than

> Parkinson v. Palmer outlined Illinois precedent for the proper transfer of property in fee simple absolute.... Accordingly, current property law requires all deed transfers to be.... Thus, deeding this property properly to your issue would require....

This fine-tuning may require sketching several possible organizational schemes for the document during PREWRITING, especially when addressing hostile audiences or varied purposes.

2. When writing.

When you need to choose between several possible organizations, choose the version that will suit the greatest number of readers, giving the primary reader highest priority. When you have determined your structure, communicate it clearly by using HEADINGS, TOPIC SENTENCES, and graphics to illustrate that structure. These will help your reader know at a glance where you are going and how you are getting there. For additional information, see GRAPHICS, HOW TO USE.

3. When rewriting.

Even though you have chosen and organized your content with the reader in mind, you still need to write to ensure immediate comprehension by the reader. To do this, consider the following questions.

- Are the PURPOSE and message clear to any reader? Usually the reader wants to know the reason for reading the document, as well as its thesis. Present both immediately: in an Introduction or in the QUESTION PRESENTED and BRIEF ANSWER of a MEMO; in the introductory paragraph of an OPINION LETTER; or in the opening of a BRIEF. Then, throughout the document, make sure each of the primary and secondary readers can continue to understand the questions, the answers, and the reasons for reaching the answers.

- What content may cause problems for either primary or secondary audiences? Review your audience to make sure that your analysis includes all essential authority and steps. Make sure you have responded to all requests, including those for practical information, remedies, actions, or advice.

- Omit tangents; delete redundant and unneeded support. Strike out unnecessary detail. Omit unnecessarily long explanations.

- Reorganize, if necessary, to serve your audiences' needs. Check largescale organization for coherence. If your audience is friendly, you may be able to use a more straightforward organization of the law. If they are hostile, you may need to organize for persuasiveness, to offer more definitions and detail, and to use more distinct markers for your arguments. See PERSUASIVE WRITING, and COUNTERARGUMENTS, HOW TO HANDLE.

4. When revising.

At this stage, look for smaller scale concerns that will affect your readers' understanding of your message. For example, consider the following.

- Will any words cause problems? Omit jargon and flowery language. Resist any urge to impress the reader by driving him or her to the dictionary; you would annoy, not impress. Make sure that terms of art are used accurately and definitions are included wherever needed. See JARGON, TERMS OF ART, and READABILITY, subsection 3.

- Be concise, especially when WRITING TO OTHER ATTORNEYS. See CONCISENESS.

- Keep the tone businesslike, rather than particularly formal or informal. Avoid extremes. Get to the point, but then support it adequately. Be professional but not pretentious, advocating yet not biased, and caring yet not illogical. For how-to information, see TONE.

5. When polishing.

Are your readers particular about format or style? If so, conform to their wishes. Even if you disagree with these requirements, it is wiser to follow them. Your job as a writer is to communicate your point, not to change the readers' preferences. If no common ground exists among your readers, choose the primary reader's preference. If you do not know what they prefer, use a conventional format familiar to all legal readers. When in doubt about whether to include a component, err on the side of including components that will answer, not raise, questions.

AUXILIARY VERB

See VERBS, AUXILIARY.

BACKGROUND FACTS

These facts fill in the gaps between legally significant facts. Although they are not essential to the issues, they are essential to the reader's understanding of the general situation. Thus the statement of facts contains enough background to complete the context. Background facts should be minimized, however, to avoid making the Statement of Facts too long. For related information, see LEGALLY SIGNIFICANT FACTS, EMOTIONAL FACTS, and STATEMENT OF FACTS.

BAD NEWS, GIVING IT

For any lawyer, being the bearer of bad news is as unavoidable as it is distasteful. Unlike a fortune teller, who can base predictions solely on the client's desires, the lawyer must base his or her prediction on sound analysis of law and fact.

A lawyer can, however, use an understanding of readers and of writing to make that bad news more palatable. The following techniques can be helpful for presenting bad news

(1) in a letter,

(2) in an email,

(3) in a memo, or

(4) in a brief.

For related information, see TONE.

1. In a letter.

When you must write a bad news letter, try organizing the letter into three parts that do the following: (a) set the tone, (b) deliver the bad news, and (c) re-establish the tone. Think of this as a sandwich organization; place your meat between two slices of bread to make it more palatable.

(a) The first slice of bread: set the tone. In the first paragraph, establish the tone you want to take with the reader. For example, you might want to be kind.

> **Mr. Alexander has asked us to help straighten out some apparent confusion regarding your bill to him for equipment repairs made in June 2005. As I understand it,** . . . .

Or you might want to be tough.

> **You stated in your letter of March 14 that our client, Mr. Alexander, owes you $480 for equipment repairs you made in June 2005. This is incorrect. As Mr. Alexander has explained previously,** . . . .

You might choose to be warm and personal.

> **Thank you for inviting me to speak at the Society's annual awards banquet. Regrettably,** . . . .

You might choose to be distant.

> **This letter concerns a bill for $480 from Efficient Equipment Repair Service to Alexander Associates, which**

states that the charges are for equipment repairs completed in June 2005....

If answering a request, you may want to open by restating that request, so that the reader knows you paid attention before saying no.

> **In your letter to Mr. Alexander dated March 14, you asked him to pay $480 for "equipment repairs made to three computers in June 2005." You stated that this payment was long overdue and you threatened to bring suit if you did not receive payment by May 1, 2005.**

(b) The meat: deliver the bad news. At the beginning of the second paragraph, state the bad news plainly so that the reader cannot misinterpret what you are saying.

> **In your letter to Mr. Alexander dated March 14, you asked Mr. Alexander to pay $480 for "equipment repairs made to three computers in June 2005." You stated that this payment was long overdue and you threatened to bring suit if you did not receive payment by May 1, 2005.**
>
> **Mr. Alexander, however, does not believe he owes you this money**....

Follow this statement with your explanations, as appropriate. This paragraph will be unemotional and matter-of-fact, regardless of the tone of the other paragraphs.

> **Mr. Alexander, however, does not believe he owes you this money because he has no record of these repairs being made. Instead, his records show only that Efficient Equipment Repair Service repaired one computer on June 12, 2005. Alexander Associates received a statement charging $140 for this work from the repairman before he left. On July 1, 2005, Alexander Associates mailed a check for $140 to Efficient Equipment Repair Service**....

This section may also extend for several paragraphs if needed.

(c) The other piece of bread: re-establish the tone. In the final paragraph, re-establish your tone while you state some closing technicalities. It is crucial to echo the same tone used in the first paragraph for credibility and effectiveness. For example, you may suggest that the reader call if he or she has questions.

> **If you have any further questions concerning this matter, you may call me at (505) 555-1234.**

If you are being kind, you may wish the reader some sort of relevant good fortune.

I enjoyed our conversation at the convention and look forward to reading your article on . . . .

If you are being tough, you may close with a final declarative statement.

I trust that this explains the matter to your satisfaction.

For related information see BAD NEWS, SOFTENING IT; GENERAL CORRESPONDENCE LETTERS; and TONE IN LETTERS.

2. In an email.

When presenting bad news in an email, you have only one or two sentences to set the tone before you present your bad news. You need to present the bad news so that it will appear in the initial screenful of information, or you risk having the reader miss your message. Unlike a letter, in which your reader sees a whole page at once, email presents only a screenful of information at a time. Because of this fact, and because readers do not always scroll all the way down to the bottom of a message, you cannot delay the bad news very long.

You can, however, avoid stating the bad news in the subject line or in the first line of the email. To do this, use the subject line to announce the topic of the email but not the outcome. For example, the following subject lines are informative but not as blunt as the alternatives.

3. In a memo.

Sometimes you must tell a senior partner that a client does not have a case. When this happens, state your conclusion in specific, matter-of-fact language.

Mr. Allen will probably not be able to convince a jury to award damages under the theory of strict liability because he cannot show that . . . .

Then lay out your reasoning thoroughly. Answer all possible questions your reader will likely ask, one by one.

If possible, offer viable alternatives. Maybe some other theory is possible. Maybe some other approach, such as negotiation, is desirable. These options greatly reduce the sting of a negative answer. Do not, however, commit large amounts of the client's money by researching these issues at length without the client's or your senior partner's permission. For related information, see MEMOS; and ORGANIZATION, LARGE–SCALE.

4. In a brief.

Sometimes you must deal with precedent, policy, or facts that go against your client's position. For help here, see COUNTERARGUMENTS, HOW TO HANDLE.

BAD NEWS, SOFTENING IT

Soften bad news when you want to keep the reader from reacting to the news in some undesirable way. Be careful about softening bad news so much, however, that the reader misses the point altogether. For example, if in an opinion letter you needed to tell your client that he or she would lose a suit, you might state the following.

Although you may bring suit, your chance of recovering your investment is slim. The company at fault has declared bankruptcy, and thus . . . .

rather than

Although the results might not be exactly what you desire, you may nevertheless choose to bring suit.

With that caveat in mind, use the following techniques to soften the blow. For related information, see BAD NEWS, GIVING IT; GENERAL CORRESPONDENCE LETTERS; TONE; and TONE IN LETTERS.

1. Use a dependent clause.

You can put the bad news in a dependent clause (see SENTENCE, PARTS OF) and then put that clause in a sentence based on a more favorable fact.

Although he was driving 63 miles per hour, Mr. Jones was driving no faster than other cars on that road at that time. Indeed he was passed by several cars just a few minutes before the accident.

This technique is particularly useful in PERSUASIVE WRITING. To determine what word to use at the beginning of your dependent clause, see TRANSITIONS. For a general discussion of the technique, see SENTENCE STRUCTURE, subsection 3.

2. Use more abstract terms.

A second way to soften bad news is to state it more generally, rather than in specific and concrete terms. This technique is most likely to be useful when you have an unfavorable fact that cannot be logically set in a more favorable context. Thus if your client hit a parked car, you might refer to the event this way.

Both cars were damaged in the collision.

If, however, the other party hit your client's parked car, you might refer to the same event this way.

When the defendant's car smashed into the rear left fender of the plaintiff's car, the impact crumpled the fender and shoved it into the back seat, so that the folded metal came within three inches of the driver's seat.

The limitations of this method are obvious in this example; even if you offer the court your abstract version, your adversary will probably offer the concrete one. It may be, however, that your adversary will overdo it, or underdo it, and you can take advantage of that mistake.

3. Put the bad news in a less emphatic part of the sentence.

You can use sentence structure to de-emphasize one point at the same time you are using it to emphasize another, more favorable point.

Although the defendant violated his parole on one occasion three months ago, he has shown exemplary behavior ever since.

4. Use a less interesting sentence structure.

You can use passive voice, for example, to make a fact stand out a little less. Thus a defendant's statement of facts might include the following sentence.

Damages caused by the accident included crumpled fenders, broken lights, and other damage to the rear of the plaintiff's car.

Since less interesting structures are usually harder to read and reduce the appeal of the overall text, use this option sparingly.

BAD OR *BADLY*?

Use *bad* when modifying a noun and *badly* when modifying a verb. The main problem writers have here is exemplified in the following sentence.

I feel bad about....

rather than

I feel badly about....

Use *bad* because you are describing your emotions, not your ability to physically feel things. Grammatically, *feel* is a LINKING VERB, so the ADJECTIVE is used. When the verb modified is an action, then the ADVERB *badly* is used.

He performed badly in the game following the incident.

You will probably find few occasions to use this phrase in legal writing because *bad* is a personal judgment rather than a provable fact.

BAR GRAPHS

See GRAPHICS, WHICH FORMS TO USE, subsection 2.

BASED ON

Watch this phrase at the beginning of a sentence, because it can create a dangling modifier.

Based on the plain meaning of this word, this interpretation of the clause is valid.

rather than

Based on the plain meaning of this word, my client should not have to honor this contract.

The interpretation, not the client, is based on the plain meaning. For related general information, see AMBIGUITY, WAYS TO AVOID, subsection 1, and MODIFIERS, DANGLING.

BASICALLY

This word often has no specific meaning in a sentence; if it does not, omit it. Use *basically* if you are in fact contrasting the basis of something to some other aspect of that same thing.

Basically, this is a good theory, but in practice....

It would be better to state your point more precisely.

This theory is based on precedent, but its application of that precedent is flawed in three ways.

BECAUSE OR *SINCE*?

Use *because* if you mean *because*. *Because* is a precise term with only one meaning; it means that one event or thing is the cause of something else.

The restraining order was issued because the defendant had repeatedly approached the plaintiff, stopping him on the street and even coming to his home.

Use *since* if you mean to show a relationship in time.

Since the restraining order was issued, the defendant has approached the plaintiff four times.

If you are worried about overusing *because*, you can do three things. First, check to see how frequently *because* appears. As a general rule, you need not worry about overusing *because* until it appears once in every paragraph and more than once in many paragraphs. Second, even if you are using *because* frequently, consider whether that use is needed to make your text clear. For example, you may decide that using *because* more frequently is appropriate because you are explaining the reasoning for a particular conclusion. Finally, if you decide you must omit some *because's*, restructure the sentence to use *as a result, therefore,* or some other accurate transition. For help here, see TRANSITIONS and CONNECTIONS, MAKING THEM.

BEGINNING

For help beginning the writing process, see GETTING STARTED. For help with specific kind of documents, see entries for those documents. For ways to use the beginning of a section of writing for emphasis, see EMPHASIS, subsection 1.

BEING THAT

Avoid this term, especially at the beginning of a sentence. It sounds informal and invites the creation of sentence fragments.

BENCH MEMOS

Bench memos are memos written by clerks for use by a judge as that judge prepares to decide a case. Bench memos provide an objective review of both sides of the controversy and evaluate the merits of the arguments made in both briefs. To write an effective bench memo, remember the following principles.

(1) Organize with your reader in mind.

(2) Depend on your own legal reasoning, not just the advocates.

(3) Adjust your writing style to meet your reader's needs.

1. Organize with your reader in mind.

When organizing a bench memo, keep your reader's needs uppermost in your mind. Often, clerks fail to do this. Instead, they organize bench briefs in a way that reflects their own thought processes: they summarize one side's argument, summarize the other, and then evaluate the case. But this organization is not always the most efficient one for the court. For an alternative and more efficient organization, think about the questions in the judge's mind, and ask the judge specifically what he or she prefers. There are many different approaches to bench memos, so be flexible in adapting to the judges' preferences.

An effective structure often includes the following components.

- **Procedural Posture: explain how the case arrived in this court and whether there are any procedural issues.**

- **A Statement of Facts: organize the facts as one unified summary of the relevant information, noting any points where the two parties differ on the facts.**

- **A Summary of the Issues: frame the issues so that the court understands exactly what needs to be decided, and in what order.**

- **A Discussion: organize your analysis by explaining the law the court should use to decide the issue and the relevant STANDARD OF REVIEW or its logical equivalent.**

  - **If there is an issue about what law the court should use, overview the alternatives, discuss each alternative, and then evaluate the choices.**

  - **If the issue is not about what law applies but how that law applies, then lay out the law and discuss its application, presenting alternative applications where they arise and evaluating the merits of each application.**

- **A Conclusion or Recommendation: advise the court what to decide and why.**

2. Depend on your own legal reasoning, not just the advocates'.

When writing a bench brief, you need to focus on the best interests of justice and of your reader. Your reader, the judge, wants to do what is fair under the law. Your reader also does not want his or her opinion to be reversed or even criticized by the appellate court. You therefore need to determine how the law should be applied to serve the purpose of that law and to conform with precedent, especially with any appellate or supreme court decisions on that issue.

In light of this focus, writers of bench briefs often find themselves disagreeing with both of the party's arguments rather than choosing one argument over another. This is normal, because you are reading the law from the wider view of justice and consistency with policy, precedent, or judicial preferences. The attorneys who wrote the briefs were writing in their client's best interests, and often that includes stretching the law to cover new territory.

To determine your own reasoning, you will need to check the sources cited in both briefs to determine whether the attorneys interpreted those sources correctly. Never trust the attorney's word alone. Always check their reasoning and measure it against your own objective view as well as against the arguments of the opposing attorney.

3. Adjust your writing style to meet your reader's needs.

Judges hire clerks to ease the workload, so make sure that your bench brief meets this objective. As a judge's clerk, you have the luxury of writing for one particular reader, and a reader that you have come to know well. Use this knowledge to organize and write bench briefs that are perfectly suited to your reader. For example, you may like to add a touch of elegance to your writing, but your judge may prefer a straightforward, abrupt style. If this is your situation, then save your elegant touches for other documents. Instead, state the paragraph's point in the first sentence, keep your sentences short and simple, and omit any unneeded information. Or you may have a judge who is particular about specific details, such as citation form or placement of commas. In this situation, proofread your bench memos for these details before you give them to your judge.

If you do not yet know your reader's preferences, you may be able to discover them by studying some of the judge's opinions. For help in making this evaluation, see GHOST WRITING. Often you will learn your reader's preferences through trial and error. Keep a list of those preferences as you discover them, and review the list as part of your normal revision process on every bench memo. This should minimize your errors and help you impress the judge with your writing and your ability to learn.

BENDING THE RULES

This can be done with law, with grammar, or with general writing principles. With the law, bend as far as POLICY, EQUITY, canons of construction, and custom will dictate.

With grammar, bend less. Bending grammatical rules often results in ambiguity, which is costly in legal writing. (See AMBIGUITY, WAYS TO AVOID.) Further, many legal readers pride themselves on their knowledge of grammatical rules and are easily distracted by any bending. Your goal in legal writing is to have your reader understand your content, not to push the grammatical envelope.

> **Undaunted, Attorney Jones proceeded with the cross-examination, ignoring the defense's objections.**

rather than

> Attorney Jones proceeded undauntedly with the cross-examination, irregardless of the defense's objections.

With general writing principles, bend only with good reason. Although concrete rules are useful to help any writer make decisions quickly, at some time or another some rules just do not make sense. For example, you may need to split an infinitive to make your point clear.

> **The mayor and council agreed to only suggest the alternative, not to formally recommend it.**

rather than

> The mayor and council agreed only to suggest the alternative.

Here, leaving the infinitive unsplit creates a SQUINTING MODIFIER.

The safer route, however, is to avoid bending the rule by REVISING.

> **The mayor and council agreed that they would only suggest the alternative.**

If you cannot revise to avoid the problem, ask yourself, "What will be clear to my reader?" "What most accurately states my point?" Then, using the answers to these questions and your own common sense, bend the rules if need be. For more detail on this point, see COMMON SENSE. For some related concerns, see ACCURACY; PRECISION; READABILITY; and AMBIGUITY, WAYS TO AVOID.

BETWEEN OR *AMONG?*

See *AMONG* OR *BETWEEN?*

BETWEEN YOU AND ME OR *BETWEEN YOU AND I?*

Use *between you and me*, always; *me*, the objective case, is the object of the preposition *between*.

BILLS, WRITING THEM

See LEGISLATION or REQUESTS FOR PAYMENT.

BLACK

This term is not capitalized.

For blacks, the Act was particularly significant.

Also see AFRICAN AMERICAN.

BLUEBOOK

This term refers to The Bluebook: A Uniform System of Citation (Columbia Law Review Ass'n et al. eds., 18th ed. 2005), a recognized authority for citations across the country. If your colleagues follow The Bluebook, become familiar with each section, especially with the inside front and back covers, where forms appear for footnotes and for court documents and memos respectively. Another helpful section is Table T.1, which includes standard citations for U.S. jurisdictions.

Bluebook rules currently govern citation form for law review articles. Most jurisdictions have some additions or changes, however, so always check citation rules relevant to your situation. For details on citation forms derived from The Bluebook, see the following: CITATION TABLE; CITATIONS; CITATIONS, BASIC FORMAT; CITATIONS, PARALLEL; CITATIONS, STRING; and FOOTNOTES.

BLUEBOOK TABLE

See CITATION TABLE.

BOLDFACE TYPE

Boldface has become a popular substitute for underlining to create emphasis. But when used too much within a paragraph, boldface text can affect the reader like a sudden increase in the volume of a television: it draws attention, but to the medium rather than the message. For alternative ways to stress a point, see EMPHASIS.

A better use of boldface is for headings or other words that stand apart from the body of the text. But the words in bold will stand out on the page, so the reader may scan those words before reading the rest of the text. Therefore, make sure that each boldfaced phrase makes sense. For example, you might use bold for the following.

Do not answer any questions until you have talked to me.

As with any graphic device, avoid overusing the technique. For more on the effective use of graphic aids, see GRAPHICS, HOW TO USE, subsection 3.

BOTH

Use *both* when you are joining two people or things logically in a sentence.

Both courts used this reasoning.

but

The cases are similar.

rather than

Both cases are similar.

In the latter example, the writer is not saying that both cases are similar to something else and therefore the writer should not join the two logically in the sentence.

BOTH ... AND

Use *both* ... *and* to emphasize an upcoming pair of entities or concepts.

Both the mayor and the city council approved this action.

rather than

The mayor as well as the city council approved this action.

Using *both* ... *and* adds clarity when each of the two concepts listed requires many words to explain. For related information, see CONJUNCTIONS and TRANSITIONS.

BRACKETS

In general, brackets indicate changes made in a quote. Use brackets around *sic* to indicate any significant mistakes occurring in an original quote.

"The court hold [sic] the evidence admissible."

Also use brackets to change a letter from upper case to lower case or vice versa and to substitute words or letters or other material into the text.

"[E]xcellence in [administrative] procedures is indispensable to carrying out the statute's intent."

Brackets have a few other specialized uses, such as marking shortened forms of case names within footnote citations.

For more specific information on how to use brackets in quotes, see QUOTATIONS, HOW TO PUNCTUATE, subsections 7 and 9. For related information, see SIC.

BREAKING THE RULES

See BENDING THE RULES.

BRIEF ANSWERS

In some memo formats, a Brief Answer serves as a substantive executive summary. In this context, the purpose of the Brief Answer is to inform the reader at a glance of the answer to the legal issue and the reasons. This may be the first section the reader reads in a memo, so it should give the answer to the QUESTION PRESENTED as definitively as possible, such as *Yes, No,* or *Probably yes,* and then give the specific reason for that answer. This should be done in one concise sentence, if possible. In any case, it should be brief. Avoid simply restating the Question Presented in sentence form or answering in vague terms.

Additionally, a Brief Answer can foreshadow the organization of the coming discussion section through its organization and wording. For example, a Brief Answer can consist of two sentences when two major points need to be made to explain the answer. A Brief Answer including a list can be followed by a discussion that uses those listed items as its organizing framework.

Together with the Question Presented, the Brief Answer provides a concise thesis of your memo. For example, if the Question Presented is

Under Fed. R. Civ. P. 4(d)(1), Summons: Personal Service, was notice effective when it was delivered to the defendant's wife at her home?

then the Brief Answer could be as follows.

Yes; notice was effective because the home of the defendant's wife is his "usual place of abode," that is, the defendant had lived there within the last year, he had moved back there one week after the summons was delivered, and he had received other mail there.

After finishing your discussion section, review your questions presented and brief answers to make sure all parts remain logically and verbally congruent. For more examples, see CONCLUSIONS.

BRIEFS

Briefs are persuasive documents filed with a court to support a client's case. Briefs use persuasive writing to predispose the reader to the client's point of view by informing the reader of the applicable law and persuading the reader to decide the issue in favor of the writer's client. They may take the form of PRETRIAL BRIEFS (sometimes called *Memorandum in Support of a Motion* or *in Opposition to a Motion* or MEMORANDUM OF POINTS AND AUTHORITIES), TRIAL BRIEFS, post-trial briefs, or APPELLATE BRIEFS. For general advice, see PERSUASIVE WRITING. These briefs should not be confused with case briefs, which are a writer's personal research documents. For information on those, see CASE BRIEFS.

The format of briefs varies with jurisdiction, so check your local rules for any variation from the following standard format.

[CAPTION]

Check your jurisdiction for the formalities of the caption. The caption usually includes (1) the name of the court in which the memorandum is filed; (2) the names of the parties; (3) their status, such as *plaintiff* or *defendant*; (4) the case file number; and (5) the title of the memorandum of points and authorities and a description of the motion the memo supports or opposes. For samples and related information, see CAPTIONS.

INTRODUCTION

This section usually includes the theory of the case and the remedy, a short synopsis or summary of the argument that sets the tone, focuses the reader, and prepares for the right disposition of the case. It is sometimes just an introductory paragraph, rather than a formal introduction.

STATEMENT OF THE CASE

The Statement of the Case should contain the Procedural History and the Statement of Facts. These may be two formal sections or may be combined into one statement. Include those points of procedural history that explain how the case arrived in this particular court. Omit any extraneous details; include enough to locate the reader in procedure unless your theory is a procedural one. If the theory is procedural, then you may construct the entire Statement of the Case around procedure. The Statement of Facts should include the legally significant facts, the background facts, and the significant emotional facts. The facts should be organized logically: by topic, by chronology, or by a combination of both. Facts should be cited to the record or to the pretrial documents as they exist at the time of filing the brief. For related information, see CHRONOLOGICAL ORGANIZATION, TOPICAL ORGANIZATION, PARENTHETICALS and PERSUASIVE WRITING. For more discussion of the content, see LEGALLY SIGNIFICANT FACTS, BACKGROUND FACTS, EMOTIONAL FACTS and STATEMENT OF THE CASE.

ISSUE[S]

Issue statements present the legal questions that, when answered, will determine the outcome of the case. In persuasive writing, Issues also suggest why your client should win. An Issue should include the rule of law applicable in this case, the legal question, and the legally significant facts. While terminology varies among users, Issues in briefs differ from the Question Presented in memos by point of view; the Issue is persuasive. It should be worded so that the subject and verb focus the judge on the precise question he or she should answer, and so the Issue suggests an outcome. For examples of this method, see ISSUE STATEMENTS. Many courts like to have the Issue presented first, although some prefer this section to follow the Statement of the Case. Check your jurisdiction's rules early in the writing process, because the placement of the issue in the document can create a need for changes in its wording. For related information, see QUESTION PRESENTED.

ARGUMENT

The Argument explains how the law justifies your client's position and why the opposition's arguments should not prevail. Thus, unlike a memo's Discussion, which explores the opposition's arguments and evaluates them, an argument seeks to shape the law and, by doing so, to preempt the opposition's points. You organize around your theory of the case. Although you explain why the opposition's points should not prevail, it is done as you argue your point, rather than dictating your large-scale organization. For more on this, see COUNTERARGUMENTS, HOW TO HANDLE.

Although it has a different point of view, the Argument's content is similar to that of a memo. Like the Discussion of a memo, the Argument presents the general rules of law, any exceptions, and examples of previous applications of that law. The Argument applies that law to this case, often using a form that fuses all raw materials into a coherent whole. The general organization uses point headings and subheadings to outline salient legal points and reasoning. Thus the Argument, like a Discussion, can take organizational cues from the law, but presents the law from the perspective most favorable to the client. For more help here, see SYLLOGISMS; ORGANIZATION, LARGE–SCALE; and ORGANIZATION, SMALL–SCALE. For more suggestions on how to build reasoning, see Pierre Schlag and David Skover, Tactics of Legal Reasoning (1986); and Jill J. Ramsfield, The Law as Architecture: Building Legal Documents (2000).

CONCLUSION

The Conclusion should summarize briefly the reasoning presented in the argument, focusing it into a cohesive and eloquent whole. It should also request specific relief. The court should know at a glance what result the writer asks for and why. Avoid the traditional *For the foregoing reasons*. This empty form forces the reader to either reread the entire Argument Section or skip the point. Instead, use this last opportunity for a focused summary that delivers the final punch. For related information, see CONCLUSION.

BULLET POINTS

A bullet point, a large, centered dot placed before a line of text, can be useful to mark the division of points when their order and significance are interchangeable.

This new will includes the three changes you requested, as we discussed at our last meeting.

- **Provision for minor grandchildren's college education**
- **Designation of alternate personal representatives**
- **Special bequest to Middleton College**

As with any graphic tool, however, avoid using this solely because it is in fashion; use it instead to clarify your meaning without distracting from it. If the sequence of points is significant, use ENUMERATION. If the order moves from most to least important, consider saying so in your introductory sentence. Also avoid overusing this or any particular graphic device. For more on the effective use of graphic aids, see GRAPHICS, HOW TO USE, subsection 3. For related information, see LISTS, STRUCTURE OF, subsection 3.

BUSINESS EMAIL

See EMAIL.

BUSINESS LETTERS

See GENERAL CORRESPONDENCE LETTERS.

BUT

But is a powerful conjunction that can mean any of the following: (1) *on the contrary,* (2) *however,* (3) *except that,* or (4) *other than.* Use it in legal writing to make a strong distinction between ideas. Because *but* is strong, be careful not to overuse it.

> **He has a case for an appeal, but he failed to file the notice of appeal on time.**

> **They should have objected, but neither they nor the court noticed the objectionable grounds in time.**

But can also be effective to begin a sentence if you want to emphasize the logical connection between two sentences.

> **No moral right as such exists in America. No state has passed a moral right law. But Congress has made several attempts to add the moral right to Title 17.**

For related general information, see CONJUNCTIONS; TRANSITIONS; and CONNECTIONS, MAKING THEM. For the use of *but* to begin a sentence, see POSITIONS OF EMPHASIS.

CAN

Use *can* as an auxiliary word when you want to suggest capacity.

> **The plaintiff can anticipate such misuses of their product; ample cases of misuse of similar cutting tools exist.**

For more information, see CAN OR MAY? and VERBS, AUXILIARY, subsection 4.

CAN HARDLY OR *CAN'T HARDLY*?

Can hardly is correct. *Can't hardly* is not. In legal writing, it is often better to replace *can hardly* with some other phrase, like *can scarcely* or *can barely*. *Can hardly* is used loosely and frequently in speech, and as a result sounds rather informal.

CANNOT OR *CAN NOT*?

Cannot is the correct form in almost all cases.

I cannot represent you in this case.

Can not appears only when *not* is part of another phrase.

He can *not only* request a new hearing but also require a change of venue.

CANONS OF CONSTRUCTION

Canons of construction are customs developed in the common law for interpreting statutes. Not literally required, these canons form a backdrop for understanding the reasoning courts may use in construing statutes. The canons are also available to lawyers for suggesting ways to interpret statutes, but no jurisdiction has formally required them. The canons may be most helpful in reading or in prewriting as ways to understand how a statute can work. For example, a common canon suggests that statutes should be construed according to the plain meaning of their texts. Another suggests that the same terms should be construed in the same way throughout the statute. And another suggests that grammar and punctuation should be construed according to strict rules. But courts will commonly disregard these canons, stating that such interpretations should be ignored when they reach absurd results or open the statute to several interpretations. Thus, like *STARE DECISIS*, canons of construction describe ways to interpret the law, but they do not substitute for LEGAL ANALYSIS.

CAN OR *COULD*?

See VERBS, AUXILIARY, subsections 4 and 6.

CAN OR *MAY*?

Use *can* when you mean that the subject is able to do something.

The plaintiff can still lift packages weighing up to thirty pounds.

Use *may* when you mean that the subject has the permission to do something.

The police may search the glove compartment without first obtaining a search warrant if . . . .

For more information, see MAY and VERBS, AUXILIARY subsections 4 and 6.

CAPITALIZATION

Legal writers have trouble with capitalization in five places: (1) with proper adjectives; (2) with titles of officials, courts, and organizations; (3) with the first word after a colon; (4) with common nouns used to refer to specific people or groups; and (5) with subheadings.

1. Proper adjectives.

Capitalize most proper adjectives, which are adjectives formed from proper nouns, such as *American banking system, the Atlantic seaboard,* or *Vietnamese refugees.* Do not capitalize an adjective when it has been used frequently and for a long time in the general language, such as *cesarean operation, india ink, italic type, murphy bed,* or *venetian blinds.* For an extensive list of adjectives derived from proper names, see the <u>U.S. Government Printing Office Style Manual</u> (2001).

2. Titles of officials, courts, and organizations.

Capitalize a title, such as *judge* or *justice,* only when it precedes the judge's or justice's name or when it replaces the name.

Justice Brennan wrote the concurring opinion.

Thank you, Judge, for your advice.

but

The judge signed the search warrant at 3:00 a.m.

You can also capitalize *court* when you are referring to the judge reading the document or to the U.S. Supreme Court, to show respect. Do not capitalize *court* when you are referring to a different court that decided another case. Different jurisdictions vary, however, so always check for local practice.

This Court has upheld this principle three times.

but

There, the trial court ruled in favor of the defendant.

For related information, see JUDGES, HOW TO ADDRESS.

3. The first word after a colon.

In general, do not capitalize the first word after the colon, because doing so usually makes the sentence self-consciously ornate, like a person wearing a tiara to a picnic. Capitalize the first word after the colon only to emphasize that word or phrase.

Plaintiff asks the court to invoke the most severe penalty: Child abuse must be stopped.

For an explanation of when to use colons, see COLONS.

4.   Common nouns used to refer to specific people or groups.

Capitalize *Elk* in *He was an Elk*, because the word refers to a specific person and organization, rather than to generic elk grazing on the ranges of Montana. Similarly, write *The Representative spoke at length to us,* because the term *Representative* replaces the person's name, and thus refers to a specific person.

Capitalize *Plaintiff* and *Defendant* when they are used in a litigation document in place of the name of the party. In this use, the words are used without *the*.

Plaintiff objected to Defendant's request for tax records.

But do not capitalize these terms when referring to a plaintiff or defendant in any other case.

A court denied the defendant's request for tax records when the information they contained was irrelevant. Hasbro v. Connoly, 599 N.W.2d 444 (2007). In Hasbro, the plaintiff objected to defendant's request for tax records from 1983–1986 because the alleged fraud occurred well after that time period. Id. at 448.

Capitalize *Constitution* only when naming any constitution in full, as in *Constitution of the State of Iowa*, or when referring to the *United States Constitution*. Also capitalize parts of the U.S. Constitution when referring to them in text.

Fourth Amendment Article I, Section 8 Preamble

But do not capitalize these terms in CITATIONS.

5.   Subheadings.

In subheadings, capitalize the initial word and all other substantive words; do not, however, capitalize CONJUNCTIONS or PREPOSITIONS of four or fewer letters. Also do not capitalize *a, an,* or *the*. One common exception to this is in POINT HEADINGS, where often a specific court will require you to capitalize every word, even conjunctions, prepositions, and articles. See *AMENDMENT* CAPITALIZED?

CAPTIONS

Captions appear at the beginning of interoffice memos and all legal documents filed with the court. Captions identify the parties to the dispute, the type of document, and the purpose of the document. Although this may seem to be a troublesome formality, it is a detail that is important to the court record system. Each document has its own specific format and requirements for the caption.

1.   Interoffice memos.

In interoffice memos, captions should identify to whom the memo is addressed, who wrote the memo, what the subject matter of the memo is, and what the date is. Check the specific requirements of your office for captions. A typical memo caption follows.

MEMO

To: **Fred P. Jones**
From: **Emily Barnett**
Re: **Krugman, file no. 48–6709; possible motion to suppress identification evidence**
Date: **March 27, 1996**

2. Pretrial and trial documents.

The caption for a pretrial or trial document filed with a court usually identifies the court; the parties; the status of the parties, such as *plaintiffs, defendants, respondents,* or *appellants*; the file number of the case, which will remain the same for every document; and the title of the brief. Always check your jurisdiction for its conventions in doing a pretrial brief caption. Many courts will not accept a document for filing if its caption does not conform to that court's rules. A typical caption follows.

IN THE SUPERIOR COURT OF THE STATE
OF WASHINGTON FOR KING COUNTY

STATE OF WASHINGTON,	)	
ABRAM AND SARAH GOLD,	)	NO. 93–3–11658–6
Plaintiffs,	)	BRIEF IN SUPPORT OF MO-
vs.	)	TION TO SUPPRESS IDENTIFICA-
SIDNEY KRUGMAN,	)	TION EVIDENCE
Defendant.	)	

3. Appellate briefs.

Check your jurisdiction for your specific requirements for the caption of an appellate brief. A typical one follows.

NO. 93–1–01248–5

COURT OF APPEALS, DIVISION II OF
THE STATE OF WASHINGTON

STATE OF WASHINGTON,

Appellant,

v.

MITCHELL WAYNE JOHNSON,

Respondent.

APPEAL FROM THE SUPERIOR COURT
FOR PIERCE COUNTY

The Honorable Robert H. Peterson, Judge

BRIEF OF APPELLANT STATE OF WASHINGTON

Marilyn F. Corning
Attorney for Respondent
123 Broadway Avenue
Suite 500
Albuquerque, NM 87106

(505) 555–2222

CASE

To avoid confusion, use *case* only as a term of art when literally referring to a case. For example, instead of *in case of,* use *if*; instead of *in many cases,* use *often*; instead of *that is not the case,* use *that is not the situation.* For related, general information, see TERMS OF ART.

CASE BRIEFS

When briefing cases, consider first the reason for which you are briefing, whether it is for class, for research, or for some other purpose. Then tailor your format to that purpose. A number of possibilities exist, ranging from full, formal briefs that find a place for every detail of the case to book briefing, where comments are made in the margins of your casebook. Whatever your system, make sure it works for you.

From the following list and other sources, collect the suggestions that you like to create your own system. Using someone else's system, no matter how comprehensive, will not work unless it makes sense to you.

1. Case briefing for class.

Brief for classes by focusing on the topic outlined by your professor or referred to in your casebook's table of contents. Then make sure that the issue and HOLDINGS that you articulate in your brief focus on that topic. For example, if the topic is intentional torts, make sure that you frame the issue around some aspect of an intentional tort. Also make sure the holding responds to that issue. If you know that your professor always asks particular questions about the cases in class, add notes for responding to those questions. For related information, see QUESTION PRESENTED.

As you progress through a course and through law school, allow your briefing process to evolve. You will probably see a good deal of change as you gain understanding and build efficiency.

2.   Case briefing for research.

Tailor your case brief in research to the project's issues, outlined in Step 3 of the RESEARCH STRATEGY CHART. Then brief the case for its purpose in that context and omit information irrelevant to that purpose. For example, if you are researching the question of mistake in formation of the contract, brief the case for what it says about mistake; do not go into the details of any irrelevant procedural questions.

There is one exception to this. You may include some other details, such as reversal based on a procedural issue, when the result of the case being briefed differs from the result you want in your factual situation but you still want to use the case to support your client's position.

3.   Format.

Whatever your format, make sure it fulfills your purpose. Consider the following checklist of possible components of your brief, selecting from it to create a briefing format that works for you.

CASE BRIEF

(a) Citation.

Make sure you put down the complete citation of the case in proper form here; this will save you time later.

(b) Parties.

Include all parties to the suit and their status, such as *plaintiff-respondent-victim* or *defendant-appellant-tortfeasor.*

(c) Prior Proceedings.

Include any relevant procedural history here, such as *trial court found for the defendant; defendant appealed, court of appeals reversed the trial court's decision; and now this appeal is before the supreme court.*

(d) Objectives.

Consider here the objectives of the parties and write them in your own words, such as *getting specific performance—he wants the goods themselves* or *getting damages—all $55,000 or getting acquitted.*

(e) Theories of the Parties.

Include here the doctrine under which the plaintiff or appellant is bringing the case, such as *false imprisonment* or *breach of contract*, and any defenses the defendant might be raising, such as *consent* or *lack of consideration*. Try to translate those into a sentence that represent the respective theories of the case, which are the thesis statements that combine the doctrine with the party's reason for winning: *defendant claims plaintiff was not falsely imprisoned because she consented to ride in the vehicle* or *plaintiff claims defendant breached the contract because of the lack of consideration when defendant failed to pay for the goods.*

(f) Facts.

List here all LEGALLY SIGNIFICANT FACTS and any BACKGROUND FACTS necessary to your own understanding of the case.

(g) Issue.

State the issue in terms of your purpose in reading the brief. Be as specific as you can with respect to that issue. See QUESTION PRESENTED and ISSUE STATEMENTS.

Did defendant Curtis falsely imprison plaintiff Butterworth when he drove around in the car for seven hours without stopping to let her out?

(h) Holding.

Answer the issue and give a reason here. See HOLDINGS.

Yes; Curtis falsely imprisoned Butterworth because he used words or acts intended to confine Butterworth, he actually confined her in the car, and Butterworth was aware that she was confined without her consent.

(i) Reasoning.

This is probably the most important part of the case brief because it exposes the court's reasons for reaching the holding. By deciphering the reasoning, you can determine how strong or weak the case is, what can be compared to or distinguished from your case, how outdated or forward-looking the decision is, where it fits in history, and so on. This section includes relevant RULES, the APPLICATION of those rules, and the conclusion the court reached. To expose the reasoning, you may want to try stating it in terms of a syllogism: the rule is the major premise, the application is the minor premise, and the conclusion is the conclusion. For example, you might first state the entire rule of false imprisonment in your jurisdiction. Then you might show how the court applied that rule to the specific facts of this case; take it step by step so that any holes in the reasoning become clear. Finally, show how the court reached its conclusion. For related information, see SYLLOGISMS.

(j) Dicta.

In an opinion, *dicta*, which means *words*, is anything a court says that does not have a direct effect on the outcome of the case. Dicta differs from a holding in that dicta is not binding on courts in subsequent opinions. Dicta can be significant, however, in your use of a case in research or in class. Use dicta to predict a trend in the law, to illuminate the reasoning in this case, or to understand future cases.

(k) Comments.

Write here any reaction you have to the case. This may become important when you continue your research or when you are asked in class to give your opinion of the case. Include your gut reaction and any other response you have that synthesizes this case with other cases in the chapter, with other cases in your research project, or with your own understanding of the trend of the law in this particular area. When briefing for class, ask yourself, "Why did the textbook author choose this case? Why is it here?" Answer those questions here.

For a detailed approach to case briefing, see William P. Statsky & R. John Wernet, *Case Analysis and Fundamentals of Legal Writing* (West 1989).

CASE NAMES

Check first with your audience to learn their preferences in presenting case names, and then conform to those preferences when deciding what typeface or underlining is required. If nothing is specified, underline the case names. The Bluebook and ALWD state that only italics are used in law review footnotes, but either italics or underlining may be used in court documents or legal memoranda. When using italics or underlining, include the *v.* and any procedural phrases, such as *In re* and *Ex parte*, and include the spaces between the underlined words but not the comma that follows the case name.

Spann v. Goldberg et al., 999 U.S. 101 (2007).

Spann v. Goldberg et al., 999 U.S. 101 (2007).

Avoid using case names as the subject of a sentence or as an adjective. Also avoid using full case citations in a sentence. When using just the case name in a sentence, use a preposition and identify the case by using the same script you are using for the full citations, either italics or underlining.

The court in Spann v. Goldberg hesitated to go further ....

While the judge in _Spann v. Goldberg_ hesitated to go further
....

rather than

The *Spann* court hesitated to go further . . . .

For related information, see CITATIONS, ITALICS, and FOOTNOTES.

CASUAL LANGUAGE

See COLLOQUIALISMS.

CERTAIN

Use *certain* only if your point is literally certain. Because few points you make in legal writing are indeed certain, beware frequent use of the word. For a discussion of related concerns, see MODIFIERS and LITERAL MEANING.

CERTAINLY

See CERTAIN.

CHARTS

Charts can be useful to summarize a mass of detailed data or to communicate its significance. But the points a chart supports should also be stated explicitly in the text; this helps you insure that your point is communicated to everyone in your AUDIENCE, whether they study graphics or skip them. For more information, see GRAPHICS, WHICH FORM TO USE.

CHOICES IN LEGAL WRITING

You have them. What makes your analysis and writing effective is your exercise of intelligent choices among many options as you move through the writing process. In prewriting, you can select among many relevant sources, forms, theories, arguments, and analytical patterns. In writing, you can select among several ways to convey your theme, structure, and tone. In rewriting, you can rearrange your presentation, add or subtract components from your document, and connect the themes and subthemes. In revising, you can alter sentence structure, word choice, sentence rhythm, and other components of style and tone.

Develop your awareness and use of these choices over your career. At first, you may think that there are only a few standard ways you can present a document. But do not be distracted by format, which is just the overall cosmetic plan for the document. Instead, note the different ways in which writers present what is within each part of the format. Like sonnet writing, legal writing requires you to make creative choices within certain structures. Over time, develop your repertoire of choices; avoid limiting yourself to any prescribed formulas.

CHRONOLOGICAL ORGANIZATION

Chronological organization means organizing events in the order in which they happened. Use chronological organization in a statement of facts or Statement of the Case when the order of occurrence is legally significant.

Avoid using this scheme when topical organization would be more beneficial to the analysis. Sometimes combining both works best; for example you may separate the facts into substantive and procedural categories and then give the chronological order of events under each category. Shape your presentation according to the document's purpose. For example, if you are trying to persuade a court, you may want to use an organization of the facts that best suits your desired remedy or theory. Chronological organization may be too bland, long, or unrelated. For related information, see ORGANIZATION; ORGANIZATION, LARGE–SCALE; TOPICAL ORGANIZATION; STATEMENT OF FACTS; and STATEMENT OF THE CASE.

CIRCUMLOCUTION

See CONCISENESS, subsection 2.

CITATIONS

The traditional text for citations is *The Bluebook: A Uniform System of Citation* (18th ed. 2005). Recently, however, some jurisdictions have adopted the *ALWD Citation Manual* (2d ed. 2003). Most jurisdictions make some adjustments to these standard citation rules. See *The Bluebook's* Bluepages table BT.2 for a list of jurisdiction-specific citation rules and style guides. If your jurisdiction has its own style manual or has otherwise established exceptions to the Bluebook or ALWD rules, follow those exceptions in all documents filed to courts in that jurisdiction.

1. When to use citations.

Citations serve two functions: (a) to provide the reader with a specific authority within the text and (b) to replace long explanations of how that authority is used, for example as a quotation, as a rule, as a related authority, or as an authority that states the contrary of the proposition. Correct use of citations both establishes your credibility as a careful analyst and streamlines your legal writing style. To make citations work for you in these capacities, consider the following guidelines.

Use citations and signals to make the reader aware of your precise use of authority. For example, using no signal automatically indicates that the cited authority clearly states the proposition, identifies the source of a quotation, or identifies an authority referred to in the text. For further reference, see SIGNALS and your specific citation manual.

2. How to use citations.

Use citations as separate sentences following a proposition; avoid using a citation at the beginning of a sentence.

A contract can provide some protection for an artist's moral rights. Young v. Taylor, 999 F.3d 999 (9th Cir. 2007).

rather than

Young v. Taylor, 999 F.3d 999 (9th Cir. 2007) states that a contract can provide some protection for an artist's moral rights.

A citation stops the reader's eye before the substance of the statement is clear. If it is necessary to cite support for the first proposition in a sentence, you may use a citation as a clause mid-sentence.

While a contract can provide some protection for an artist's moral rights, Young v. Taylor, 999 F.3d 999 (9th Cir. 2007), no single contract can cover the entire scope of those rights.

This use does not stop the reader as much as a cite before the proposition being cited, but it is still less than ideal. For this reason, use this structure only when it would be inaccurate to place the citation at the end. For related information, see INTRUSIVE PHRASES.

Eliminate text that repeats information given in the citation, such as *The court stated that* . . . or *The court went on to say that* . . . or *Another case stated the opposing view* . . . .

Use short citation forms when citing to immediately preceding authority. If the previous citation is a page or two back, use the full citation, so the reader does not have to back track too far.

Give pinpoint cites when referring to any rules, holdings, quotations, specific propositions, or particulars of a case. See CITATIONS, PINPOINT.

Reason v. Pearson, 999 U.S. 977, 979 (2007).

Put spaces after abbreviations that include more than a capital letter.

33 Wis. 2d 987.

or

222 Wash. 2d 346.

Do not insert spaces when the abbreviation is only a capital letter.

345 N.W.2d 31.

or

486 P.2d 692.

Check your citation manual and your jurisdiction rules for its variations on these formats. For related information, see BLUEBOOK TABLE; CITATIONS, BASIC FORMAT; CITATIONS, PARALLEL; CITATIONS, PINPOINT; and CITATIONS, STRING.

CITATIONS, BASIC FORMAT

Case citations generally include (1) the name of the case; (2) the volume, standard abbreviation for the book, and page number of the case; (3) the parallel citation, where appropriate; and (4) the year in which the decision was made. The reader should also be able to determine from the citation what court made the decision. Thus if the name of the court is not evident from the abbreviation of the book, as in *Wash. 2d* which indicates the Washington Supreme Court, then indicate (5) who the court is by putting its abbreviation before the date inside the parentheses.

Leraas v. Martin, 894 U.S. 723 (2002).

but

Johnson v. Strus, 499 P.2d 387 (Alaska 2005).

Here, for example, because the Alaska Supreme Court does not have an official reporter, the official reporter for that state's decisions is the Pacific Reporter. But the reader would not know what court had made the decision unless *Alaska* was put in the parentheses with the date. Similarly, for federal district court decisions and federal circuit court decisions, the court must be indicated in the parentheses with the date.

Knight v. Skover, 999 F. Supp. 287 (S.D. Iowa 2007).

CITATIONS, PARALLEL

All United States Supreme Court cases, most state cases, and some federal cases appear in more than one book. Thus a case may have more than one citation, and those are called parallel citations.

The United States Supreme Court and most other courts have one official reporter, which is that jurisdiction's authoritative text. For example, the United States Supreme Court's official reporter is labeled *U.S.* Your citation manual may require you to cite to that official text but not the parallel citations in the unofficial reporters. For state cases, your manual or local rules may require parallel citations to unofficial reporters in certain circumstances. Or you may want to include parallel citations as a courtesy to your reader. When including parallel citations, list the official reporter first.

Fischer v. Doerr, 437 U.S. 893 (2001).

but

Lamb v. Laffon, 145 Ariz. 212, 700 P.2d 1312 (2003).

Check your citation manual for specific directions regarding which reporters to cite in parallel citations for each state. When using pinpoint cites, include the specific page number for the parallel cite as well. See CITATIONS, PINPOINT.

CITATIONS, PINPOINT

Pinpoint citations are those that include the exact page on which the quote, proposition holding, or rule is found. Use them to show your reader the exact source of important points. Pinpoint citations are used more frequently than general citations because most citations refer to quotes, propositions, holdings or rules. If required to use parallel pinpoint cites, indicate a specific page for both the official reporter and the unofficial reporter or reporters.

> **In custody disputes, the appellate court will reverse the trial court only where there is an abuse of discretion. In re Marriage of Smith, 94 Wash. 2d 369, 371, 333 P.2d 43, 44 (2005).**

> **Where there are no exigent circumstances, police must obtain a search warrant before searching the premises. Id. at 486, 483 P.2d at 58.**

CITATIONS, STRING

String citations include citations to two or more cases for the same point. Semicolons separate the individual cites in a string cite, and cases are cited in order of strength, jurisdiction, or year, depending on the context.

> **Arkansas has uniformly applied the rule of awarding children to the parent who can serve their best interests. Lorey v. Jacobi, 99 Ark. 111, 222 S.W.2d 22 (2004) (holding that mother should be awarded custody of eight-year-old son when father cannot support the son); Zuckerman v. Kidwell, 100 Ark. 841, 224 S.W.2d 444 (2003) (holding that mother should be awarded custody of ten-year-old daughter and three-year-old son when father has been absent for over two years); Arthur v. Christopoulos, 101 Ark. 502, 226 S.W.2d 321 (2001) (holding that father should be awarded custody of six-year-old twins when mother showed continuous abusive behavior).**

String citations can be used to convey the message to the reader that not just one authority stands for a point, but two, three, or four do. If that message is essential to your analysis, then use the string cite. Do not, however, use a string cite just to show that you found more than one case. If one case is sufficient to make the point, omit the other citations. Remember that the doubting legal reader will check most authorities and will be annoyed if each is not pertinent. For format and order of string cites, see your citation manual.

CITATION TABLE

The following table can help you find the correct citation form quickly for many common citations. Refer to your citation manual for specific directions; what follows are the most generally used Bluebook and ALWD citation forms.

BLUEBOOK CITATION TABLE

RULE	CATEGORY	SCHOLARLY WRITING	PRACTITIONER WRITING
10	Supreme Court	Erie R.R. v. Tompkins, 304 U.S. 64 (1938).	Erie R.R. v. Tompkins, 304 U.S. 64 (1938).
10	Circuit Court of Appeals	Weyerhaeuser Co. v. Costle, 590 F.2d 1011 (D.C. Cir. 1978).	Weyerhaeuser Co. v. Costle, 590 F.2d 1011 (D.C. Cir. 1978).
10.1	District Court	ACLU v. Florida Bar, 744 F. Supp. 1094 (N.D. Fla. 1990).	ACLU v. Florida Bar, 744 F. Supp. 1094 (N.D. Fla. 1990).
	Federal Rules Decisions	Georgine v. Amchem Prods., Inc., 157 F.R.D. 246 (1994).	Georgine v. Amchem Prods., Inc., 157 F.R.D. 246 (1994).
Table T.1	Bankruptcy Court	In re A.H. Robins Co., 63 B.R. 986 (Bankr. E.D. Va. 1986).	In re A.H. Robins Co., 63 B.R. 986 (Bankr. E.D. Va. 1986).
10.3.1	Decision available on electronic databases	Yates v. State, No. A-5244, 1996 WL 543305 (Alaska Ct. App. Sept. 25, 1996).	Yates v. State, No. A-5244, 1996 WL 543305 (Alaska Ct. App. Sept. 25, 1996).
		Earth Island Inst. v. Christopher, No. 95-208, 1995 Ct. Int'l Trade LEXIS 266, slip op. (Ct. Int'l Trade Dec. 29, 1995).	Earth Island Inst. v. Christopher, No. 95-208, 1995 Ct. Int'l Trade LEXIS 266, slip op. (Ct. Int'l Trade Dec. 29, 1995).
		Parker v. Independent Sch. Dist. No. 1-003, No. 95-7081, 1996 U.S. App. LEXIS 9991, at *12 (10th Cir. Apr. 30, 1996).	Parker v. Independent Sch. Dist. No. 1-003, No. 95-7081, 1996 U.S. App. LEXIS 9991, at *12 (10th Cir. Apr. 30, 1996).
		Shore Drive Apartments, Inc. v. United States, No. FL 75-542-Civ.-CA, 1976 WL 1181, at *1 (M.D. Fla. July 16, 1976).	Shore Drive Apartments, Inc. v. United States, No. FL 75-542-Civ.-CA, 1976 WL 1181, at *1 (M.D. Fla. July 16, 1976).
10.8.3	Brief, Record or Appendix	Respondents Brief in Opposition to Petition for a Writ of Certiorari, Park Place, Inc. v. City of Cleveland, 103 S. Ct. 144 (1982) (No. 82-255).	Respondents Brief in Opposition to Petition for a Writ of Certiorari, Park Place, Inc. v. City of Cleveland, 103 S. Ct. 144 (1982) (No. 82-255).

RULE	CATEGORY	SCHOLARLY WRITING	PRACTITIONER WRITING
10.9	Short forms for cases	United States v. Fleet Factors Corp., 901 F.2d 1550 (11th Cir. 1990), cert. denied, 111 S. Ct. 752 (1991). Fleet Factors, 901 F.2d at 1554. 901 F.2d at 1556. Id.	United States v. Fleet Factors Corp., 901 F.2d 1550 (11th Cir. 1990), cert. denied, 111 S. Ct. 752 (1991). Fleet Factors, 901 F.2d at 1554. 901 F.2d at 1556. Id.
11	Constitution	U.S. CONST. art. I, § 8, cl. 3.	U.S. Const. art. I, § 8, cl. 3.
12.1	Federal statutes	Freedom of Information Act, 5 U.S.C. § 552 (1996). 11 U.S.C. § 362(d)(1) (1996). 45 U.S.C.A. § 541 (West 1987) (authorizing the creation of the National Railroad Passenger Corporation, or Amtrak).	Freedom of Information Act, 5 U.S.C. § 552 (1996). 11 U.S.C. § 362(d)(1) (1996). 45 U.S.C.A. § 541 (West 1987) (authorizing the creation of the National Railroad Passenger Corporation, or Amtrak).
12.4	Session laws	Tax Reform Act of 1976, Pub. L. No. 94-455, 90 Stat. 1520 (codified as amended in scattered sections of 26 U.S.C.). Banking (Glass-Steagall) Act of 1933, ch. 89, 48 Stat. 162 (1933) (codified as amended in scattered sections of 12 U.S.C.). Financial Institutions Reform, Recovery, and Enforcement Act of 1989, Pub. L. No. 101-73, 103 Stat. 183. Private Securities Litigation Reform Act of 1995, Pub. L. No. 104-67, 109 Stat. 737.	Tax Reform Act of 1976, Pub. L. No. 94-455, 90 Stat. 1520 (codified as amended in scattered sections of 26 U.S.C.). Banking (Glass-Steagall) Act of 1933, ch. 89, 48 Stat. 162 (1933) (codified as amended in scattered sections of 12 U.S.C.). Financial Institutions Reform, Recovery, and Enforcement Act of 1989, Pub. L. No. 101-73, 103 Stat. 183. Private Securities Litigation Reform Act of 1995, Pub. L. No. 104-67, 109 Stat. 737.
12.9	Short forms for statutes	Financial Institutions Reform, Recovery, and Enforcement Act of 1989 § 907. 28 U.S.C. § 1927.	Financial Institutions Reform, Recovery, and Enforcement Act of 1989 § 907. 28 U.S.C. § 1927.
13.2(a)	Unenacted bill	H.R. 14476, 94th Cong. (1976).	H.R. 14476, 94th Cong. (1976).

CITATION TABLE

RULE	CATEGORY	SCHOLARLY WRITING	PRACTITIONER WRITING
13.3	Hearing	*Independent Counsel Reauthorization Act of 1992: Hearings on S.24 Reauthorization of the Independent Counsel Law Before the Senate Comm. on Governmental Affairs*, 103d Cong. (1993).	Independent Counsel Reauthorization Act of 1992: Hearings on S.24 Reauthorization of the Independent Counsel Law Before the Senate Comm. on Governmental Affairs, 103d Cong. (1993).
13.4	Report	S. REP. NO. 104-98 (1995). H. R. REP. NO. 102-474 (1992), *reprinted in* 1992 U.S.C.C.A.N. 1954. H. R. CONF. REP. NO. 102-1018 (1992), *reprinted in* 1992 U.S.C.C.A.N. 2472.	S. Rep. No. 104-98 (1995). H.R. Rep. No. 102-474 (1992), reprinted in 1992 U.S.C.C.A.N. 1954. H.R. Conf. Rep. No. 102-1018 (1992), reprinted in 1992 U.S.C.C.A.N. 2472.
13.4	Committee Print	STAFF OF HOUSE COMM. ON BANKING, FINANCE AND URBAN AFFAIRS, 102D CONG., REPORT ON THE BANK OF NEW ENGLAND FAILURE AND RESOLUTION (Comm. Print 1991).	Staff of House Comm. on Banking, Finance and Urban Affairs, 102d Cong., Report on the Bank of New England Failure and Resolution (Comm. Print 1991).
13.5	Congressional Record	137 CONG. REC. S503 (1991) (statement of Sen. Dole).	137 Cong. Rec. S503 (1991) (statement of Sen. Dole).
14.2	Federal Regulations	Federal Food, Drug, and Cosmetic Act, 21 C.F.R. § 101.30(c)(1) (1996). 50 C.F.R. § 227.72(3)(ii) (1996).	Federal Food, Drug, and Cosmetic Act, 21 C.F.R. § 101.30(e)(1) (1996). 50 C.F.R. § 227.72(3)(ii) (1996).
14.2	Federal Register	58 Fed. Reg. 9,015 (1993).	58 Fed. Reg. 9,015 (1993).
14.4	Opinion of the Attorney General	43 Op. Att'y Gen. 75 (1977).	43 Op. Att'y Gen. 75 (1977).
15	Books	MARY B. RAY & JILL J. RAMSFIELD, LEGAL WRITING: GETTING IT RIGHT AND GETTING IT WRITTEN (1993). HOMER, ODYSSEY (Robert Fitzgerald trans., Vintage Classics 1990). LAURENCE H. TRIBE, AMERICAN CONSTITUTIONAL LAW (1978).	Mary B. Ray & Jill J. Ramsfield, Legal Writing: Getting It Right and Getting It Written (1993). Homer, Odyssey (Robert Fitzgerald trans., Vintage Classics 1990). Laurence H. Tribe, American Constitutional Law (1978).

RULE	CATEGORY	SCHOLARLY WRITING	PRACTITIONER WRITING
	Short forms for books	RAY & RAMSFIELD, *supra* note 1, at 47-53.	Ray & Ramsfield, *supra* note 1, at 47-53.
		Id. at 50.	*Id.* at 50.
15.8	Legal Encyclopedias	35 C.J.S. *Extradition* § 11 (1960 & Supp. 1996).	35 C.J.S. Extradition § 11 (1960 & Supp. 1996).
		73 AM. JUR. 2D *Subrogation* §§ 106-128 (1974).	73 Am. Jur. 2d Subrogation §§ 106-128 (1974).
15.8	Black's Law Dictionary	BLACK'S LAW DICTIONARY 754 (6th ed. 1990).	Black's Law Dictionary 754 (6th ed. 1990).
15.8	The Federalist	THE FEDERALIST No. 70 (Alexander Hamilton).	The Federalist No. 70 (Alexander Hamilton).
16	Law Reviews	David H. Souter, *A Tribute to Justice Harry A. Blackmun*, 104 YALE L. J. 5 (1994).	David H. Souter, A Tribute to Justice Harry A. Blackmun, 104 Yale L.J. 5 (1994).
16.7	Short forms for law reviews	Richard A. Posner, *Goodbye to the Bluebook*, 53 U. CHI. L. REV. 1343 (1986).	Richard A. Posner, Goodbye to the Bluebook, 53 U. Chi. L. Rev. 1343 (1986).
		Posner, *supra* note 1, at 1346.	Posner, supra note 1, at 1346.
		Id. at 1349.	Id. at 1349.
16.4	Nonconsecutively Paginated Journals or Magazines	Elizabeth Gleick, *O. J. Feels the Heat*, TIME, Dec. 2, 1996, at 60.	Elizabeth Gleick, O. J. Feels the Heat, Time, Dec. 2, 1996, at 60.
16.5	Newspapers	Ann Devroy & John E. Yang, *Clinton-GOP Budget Negotiations Break Down*, WASH. POST, Jan. 10, 1996, at A1.	Ann Devroy & John E. Yang, Clinton-GOP Budget Negotiations Break Down, Wash. Post, Jan. 10, 1996, at A1.
16.6.6	American Law Reports Annotations	Jane M. Draper, Annotation, *Workers' Compensation: Tips or Gratuities as Factor in Determining Amount of Compensation*, 16 A.L.R. 5th 191 (1993).	Jane M. Draper, Annotation, Workers' Compensation: Tips or Gratuities as Factor in Determining Amount of Compensation, 16 A.L.R. 5th 191 (1993).
17.1.3	Letters	Letter from Jill J. Ramsfield, Professor, Georgetown University Law Center, to Dylan Cors, Editor-in-Chief, Duke Law Journal 1 (Nov. 25, 1996) (on file with author).	(Letter from Ramsfield to Cors of 11/25/96 at 1.)

RULE	CATEGORY	SCHOLARLY WRITING	PRACTITIONER WRITING
17.1.4	Interviews	Interview with Jill J. Ramsfield, Professor, Georgetown University, in Washington, D.C. (Dec. 15, 1996).	Interview with Jill J. Ramsfield, Professor, Georgetown University, in Washington, D.C. (Dec. 15, 1996).
17.1.5	Speeches and Addresses	Roscoe Pound, Address to the American Bar Association (Aug. 29, 1906), *in* 35 F.R.D. 273 (1964).	Roscoe Pound, Address to the American Bar Association (Aug. 29, 1906), *in* 35 F.R.D. 273 (1964).
18.1	Electronic Sources and Databases	T.R. Fehrenbach, *TV's Alamo Tale Fairly Accurate*, SAN ANTONIO EXPRESS-NEWS, Mar. 17, 1996, at A1, *available at* 1996 WL 2824823.	T.R. Fehrenbach, *TV's Alamo Tale Fairly Accurate*, San Antonio Express-News, Mar. 17, 1996, at A1, *available at* 1996 WL 2824823.
		Justice Minister Calls for Solving Int'l Legal Conflicts, JAPAN ECON. NEWSWIRE PLUS, Apr. 22, 1991, at 1, *available at* DIALOG, File No. 612.	*Justice Minister Calls for Solving Int'l Legal Conflicts*, Japan Econ. Newswire Plus, Apr. 22, 1991, at 1, *available at* DIALOG, File No. 612.
18.2	Internet Sources	*Georgetown University Men's Basketball Home Page* http://www.guhoyas.com/sports/m-baskbl/gu-m-baskbl-body.html (last visited Oct. 20, 2004).	Georgetown University Men's Basketball Home Page http://www.guhoyas.com/sports/m-baskbl/gu-m-baskbl-body.html (last visited Oct. 20, 2004).
		Sterling Wentworth Corporation http://www.sterwent.com (last modified Nov. 26, 1996).	Sterling Wentworth Corporation http://www.sterwent.com (last modified Nov. 26, 1996).
19.1	Looseleaf Services	Defenders of Wildlife, Inc. v. Watt, [1982] 12 Envtl. L. Rep. (Envtl. Law Inst.) 20,210 (D.D.C. May 28, 1981).	Defenders of Wildlife, Inc. v. Watt, [1982] 12 Envtl. L. Rep. (Envtl. Law Inst.) 20,210 (D.D.C. May 28, 1981).
10.1	State Supreme Court	Sawada v. Endo, 561 P.2d 1291 (Haw. 1977).	Sawada v. Endo, 561 P.2d 1291 (Haw. 1977).
10.1	State Appellate Court	Blue Bell, Inc. v. Peat, Marwick, Mitchell & Co., 715 S.W.2d 408 (Tex. Ct. App. 1986).	Blue Bell, Inc. v. Peat, Marwick, Mitchell & Co., 715 S.W.2d 408 (Tex. Ct. App. 1986).
10.1	State Trial-level Court	People v. Gotti, 146 Misc. 2d 793, 552 N.Y.S.2d 485 (N.Y. Sup. Ct. 1990).	People v. Gotti, 146 Misc. 2d 793, 552 N.Y.S.2d 485 (N.Y. Sup. Ct. 1990).
	State court decisions contained in documents submitted to a state court	Ploof v. Putnam, 71 A. 188 (Vt. 1908).	Ploof v. Putnam, 81 Vt. 471, 71 A. 188 (1908).

RULE	CATEGORY	SCHOLARLY WRITING	PRACTITIONER WRITING
Table T.1	California state court decisions submitted to California courts	Bily v. Arthur Young & Co., 834 P.2d 745 (Cal. 1992) (en banc).	Bily v. Arthur Young & Co., 3 Cal. 4th 370, 834 P.2d 745, 11 Cal. Rptr. 2d 51 (1992) (en banc).
Table T.1	New York state court decisions submitted to New York courts	Turcotte v. Fell, 502 N.E.2d 964 (N.Y. 1986).	Turcotte v. Fell, 68 N.Y.2d 432, 502 N.E.2d 964, 510 N.Y.S.2d 49 (1986).
11	State Constitution	MD. CONST. art. III, § 1.	Md. Const. art. III, § 1.
Table T.1	State Statutes	DEL. CODE ANN. tit. 8, § 145 (1991 & Supp. 1996).	Del. Code Ann. tit. 8, § 145 (1991 & Supp. 1996).
		MINN. STAT. § 302A.251(5) (Supp. 1995).	Minn. Stat. § 302A.251(5) (Supp. 1995).
		IND. CODE ANN. § 23-1-35-1 (Michie 1995).	Ind. Code Ann. § 23-1-35-1 (Michie 1995).
Table T.1	State Subject Matter Codes	CAL. FISH & GAME CODE § 2537 (West 1996).	Cal. Fish & Game Code § 2537 (West 1996).
		MD. CODE ANN., HEALTH OCC. § 16-103 (1996).	Md. Code Ann., Health Occ. § 16-103 (1996).
		N.Y. PARTNERSHIP LAW § 26(c) (McKinney 1996).	N.Y. Partnership Law § 26(c) (McKinney 1996).
		TEX. AGRIC. CODE ANN. § 74.004 (West 1996) (authorizing the state to destroy any cotton plants containing the boll weevil).	Tex. Agric. Code Ann. § 74.004 (West 1996) (authorizing the state to destroy any cotton plants containing the boll weevil).
12.4	State Session Law	Act of Apr. 30, 1996, ch. 91, 1996 Md. Laws 576 (to be codified at scattered sections of MD. CODE ANN., COM. LAW).	Act of Apr. 30, 1996, ch. 91, 1996 Md. Laws 576 (to be codified at scattered sections of Md. Code Ann., Com. Law).
18.1.1	Statutes available on electronic databases	CAL. BUS. & PROF. CODE 1670 (West, Westlaw through 1995 portion of 1995-96 Sess.).	Cal. Bus. & Prof. Code 1670 (West, Westlaw through 1995 portion of 1995-96 Sess.).
		WASH. REV. CODE 13.64.060 (VersusLaw through 1999 legislation).	Wash. Rev. Code 13.64.060 (VersusLaw through 1999 legislation).
		WIS. STAT. 19.43 (LEXIS through 1994 legislation).	Wis. Stat. 19.43 (LEXIS through 1994 legislation).

RULE	CATEGORY	SCHOLARLY WRITING	PRACTITIONER WRITING
12.8.2	Local Ordinance	HOUSTON, TEX., CODE OF ORDINANCES § 42-85(b)(5) (1985).	Houston, Tex., Code of Ordinances § 42-85(b)(5) (1985).
		D.C. MUN. REGS. Tit. 14, § 2903.2 (1996).	D.C. Mun. Regs., tit. 14, § 2903.2 (1996).
12.8.5	Restatements	RESTATEMENT (SECOND) OF TORTS § 552 (1977).	Restatement (Second) of Torts § 552 (1977).
12.8.6	Model Codes	MODEL PENAL CODE §§ 6.01-6.13 (1962).	Model Penal Code §§ 6.01-6.13 (1962).
		REVISED MODEL BUS. CORP. ACT. § 8.08(a) (1994).	Revised Model Bus. Corp. Act. § 8.08(a) (1994).
		MODEL CODE OF PROF'L RESPONSIBILITY DR 4-101 (1969).	Model Code of Prof'l Responsibility DR 4-101 (1969).
		MODEL RULES OF PROF'L CONDUCT Rule 1.6 (1983).	Model Rules of Prof'l Conduct Rule 1.6 (1983).
21.4	Treaties, three or fewer parties	Treaty of Friendship, Commerce and Navigation, U.S.-Japan, art. X, Apr. 2, 1953, 4 U.S.T. 2063.	Treaty of Friendship, Commerce and Navigation, U.S.-Japan, art. X, Apr. 2, 1953, 4 U.S.T. 2063.
		Agreement Concerning Payments for Certain Losses Suffered During World War II, U.S.-Fr., Jan. 18, 2001, Temp. State Dep't No. 01-36, 2001 WL 416465.	Agreement Concerning Payments for Certain Losses Suffered During World War II, U.S.-Fr., Jan. 18, 2001, Temp. State Dep't No. 01-36, 2001 WL 416465.
21.4	Treaties, more than three parties	Geneva Convention Relative to the Treatment of Prisoners of War art. 3, Aug. 12, 1949, 6 U.S.T. 3316, 75 U.N.T.S. 135.	Geneva Convention Relative to the Treatment of Prisoners of War art. 3, Aug. 12, 1949, 6 U.S.T. 3316, 75 U.N.T.S. 135.
		Police Convention, Feb. 29, 1920, 127 L.N.T.S. 433.	Police Convention, Feb. 29, 1920, 127 L.N.T.S. 433.
21.5.1	International Court of Justice and Permanent Court of International Justice	Military and Paramilitary Activities (Nicar. v. U.S.), 1986 I.C.J. 14 (June 27) (separate opinion of Judge Ago). Reservations to Convention on Prevention and Punishment of the Crime of Genocide, Advisory Opinion, 1951 I.C.J. 15 (May 28).	Military and Paramilitary Activities (Nicar. v. U.S.), 1986 I.C.J. 14 (June 27) (separate opinion of Judge Ago). Reservations to Convention on Prevention and Punishment of the Crime of Genocide, Advisory Opinion, 1951 I.C.J. 15 (May 28).
21.5.2	Court of Justice of the European Communities	Case C-392/93, The Queen v. H. M. Treasury, ex parte British Telecomm. plc, 1996 E.C.R. I-1631.	Case C-392/93, The Queen v. H. M. Treasury, ex parte British Telecomm. plc, 1996 E.C.R. I-1631.
		Case T-488/93, Hanseatische Industrie-Beteiligungen GmbH v. Commission, 1995 E.C.R. II-469 (Ct. First Instance).	Case T-488/93, Hanseatische Industrie-Beteiligungen GmbH v. Commission, 1995 E.C.R. II-469 (Ct. First Instance).

RULE	CATEGORY	SCHOLARLY WRITING	PRACTITIONER WRITING
21.5.3	European Court and European Commission of Human Rights	Papon v. France (No. 2), 2001-XII Eur. Ct. H.R. 235. Kampanis v. Greece, 318 Eur. Ct. H.R. 29, 35 (1995).	Papon v. France (No. 2), 2001-XII Eur. Ct. H.R. 235. Kampanis v. Greece, 318 Eur. Ct. H.R. 29, 35 (1995).
21.5.4	Inter-American Commission on Human Rights	Tortrino v. Argentina, Case 11.597, Inter-Am. C.H.R., Report No. 7/98, OEA/Ser.L./V/II.98, doc. 7 rev. ¶ 15 (1997). Calderón v. Colombia, Case 10.454, Inter-Am. C.H.R., Report No. 32/92, OEA/Ser.L./V/II.83, doc. 14, corr. 1 (1992–93).	Tortrino v. Argentina, Case 11.597, Inter-Am. C.H.R., Report No. 7/98, OEA/Ser.L./V/II.98, doc. 7 rev. ¶ 15 (1997). Calderón v. Colombia, Case 10.454, Inter-Am. C.H.R., Report No. 32/92, OEA/Ser.L./V/II.83, doc. 14, corr. 1 (1992–93).
21.7	United Nations Charter	U.N. Charter art. 51.	U.N. Charter art. 51.
21.7.2(a)	United Nations General Assembly	G.A. Res. 832, ¶ 19, U.N. GAOR, 9th Sess., Supp. No. 21, U.N. Doc. A/2890 (Oct. 21, 1954).	G.A. Res. 832, ¶ 19, U.N. GAOR, 9th Sess., Supp. No. 21, U.N. Doc. A/2890 (Oct. 21, 1954).
21.7.2(b)	United Nations Security Council	S.C. Res. 508, ¶ 9, U.N. Doc. S/RES/508 (June 5, 1982).	S.C. Res. 508, ¶ 9, U.N. Doc. S/RES/508 (June 5, 1982).
201.7.3(a)	United Nations Economic and Social Council	U.N. Econ. & Soc. Council [ECOSOC], Sub-Comm. on Prevention of Discrimination & Prot. of Minorities, Working Group on Minorities, Working Paper: Universal and Regional Mechanisms for Minority Protection, ¶ 17, U.N. Doc. E/CN.4/Sub.2/AC.5/1999/WP.6 (May 5, 1999) (prepared by Vladimir Kartashkin).	U.N. Econ. & Soc. Council [ECOSOC], Sub-Comm. on Prevention of Discrimination & Prot. of Minorities, Working Group on Minorities, Working Paper: Universal and Regional Mechanisms for Minority Protection, 17, U.N. Doc. E/CN.4/Sub.2/AC.5/1999/WP.6 (May 5, 1999) (prepared by Vladimir Kartashkin).
21.8.4(d)	World Trade Organization/ GATT founding documents	Final Act Embodying the Results of the Uruguay Round of Multilateral Trade Negotiations, Apr. 15, 1994, 33 I.L.M. 1125 (1994).	Final Act Embodying the Results of the Uruguay Round of Multilateral Trade Negotiations, Apr. 15, 1994, 33 I.L.M. 1125 (1994).
21.8.4(d)	GATT founding agreement	General Agreement on Tariffs and Trade, Oct. 30, 1947, 61 Stat. A-11, 55 U.N.T.S. 194.	General Agreement on Tariffs and Trade, Oct. 30, 1947, 61 Stat. A-11, 55 U.N.T.S. 194.
21.8.4(b)	GATT dispute resolution panel reports	Report of the Panel, Japan—Restrictions on Imports of Certain Agricultural Products, ¶ 5.2.2, L/6253, (Feb. 2, 1988), GATT B.I.S.D. (35th Supp.) at 163, 229 (1989).	Report of the Panel, Japan—Restrictions on Imports of Certain Agricultural Products, 5.2.2, L/6253, (Feb. 2, 1988), GATT B.I.S.D. (35th Supp.) at 163, 229 (1989).

ALWD CITATION TABLE

RULE	CATEGORY	ALWD
12.0	Supreme Court	Erie R.R. v. Tompkins, 304 U.S. 64 (1938).
12.0	Circuit Court of Appeals	Weyerhaeuser Co. v. Costle, 590 F.2d 1011 (D.C. Cir. 1978).
12.0	District Court	ACLU v. Fla. B., 744 F. Supp. 1094 (N.D. Fla. 1990).
12.0	Federal Rules Decisions	Georgine v. Amchem Prods., Inc., 157 F.R.D. 246 (1994).
12.0	Bankruptcy Court	In re A.H. Robins Co., Inc., 63 B.R. 986 (Bankr. E.D. Va. 1986).
12.12	Decision available on electronic databases	Yates v. State, 1996 WL 543305 (Alaska App. Sept. 25, 1996).
		Earth Island Inst. v. Christopher, 1995 Ct. Intl. Trade LEXIS 266 (Ct. Intl. Trade Dec. 29, 1995).
		Parker v. Indep. Sch. Dist. No. I-003 of Okmulgee County, 1996 U.S. App. LEXIS 9991, at *12 (10th Cir. Apr. 30, 1996).
		Shore Drive Apts., Inc. v. U.S., 1976 WL 1181, at *1 (M.D. Fla. July 16, 1976).
12.20	Brief, Record or Appendix	Respt. Br. in Opposition to Pet. for Writ of Cert., Park Place, Inc. v. City of Cleveland, 103 S. Ct. 144 (1982).
12.21	Short forms for cases	U.S. v. Fleet Factors Corp., 901 F.2d 1550 (11th Cir. 1990), cert. denied, 111 S. Ct. 752 (1991). Fleet Factors, 901 F.2d at 1554. 901 F.2d at 1556. Id.
13.0	Constitution	U.S. Const. art. I, § 8, cl. 3.
14.2(g)	Federal statutes	Freedom of Information Act, 5 U.S.C. § 552 (1996).
14.0		11 U.S.C. § 362(d)(1) (1996).
14.2(b)(2), 14.2(e)(2)		45 U.S.C.A. § 541 (West 1987) (authorizing the creation of the National Railroad Passenger Corporation, or Amtrak).
14.2(b)(2), 14.2(e)(2)		10 U.S.C.S. § 142(c) (LEXIS 1985) (providing that while holding office, the Chairman of the Joint Chiefs of Staff outranks all other military officers, but may not exercise military command over the armed forces).
14.7	Session laws	Tax Reform Act of 1976, Pub. L. No. 94-455, 90 Stat. 1520 (1976) (codified as amended in scattered sections of 26 U.S.C.). Banking (Glass-Steagall) Act of 1933, ch. 89, 48 Stat. 162 (1933) (codified as amended in scattered sections of 12 U.S.C.). Financial Institutions Reform, Recovery, and Enforcement Act of 1989, Pub. L. No. 101-73, 103 Stat. 183 (1989). Private Securities Litigation Reform Act of 1995, Pub. L. No. 104-67, 109 Stat. 737.

RULE	CATEGORY	ALWD
14.6	Short forms for statutes	Financial Institutions Reform, Recovery, and Enforcement Act of 1989 § 907. 28 U.S.C. § 1927. § 1927. Id. at § 1929.
15.0	Unenacted bill	H.R. 14476, 94th Cong. (June 21, 1976).
15.7	Hearing	S. Comm. on Govtl. Affairs, Independent Counsel Reauthorization Act of 1993: Hearings on S. 24 Reauthorization of the Independent Counsel Law, 103d Cong. (May 14, 1993).
15.9	Report	S. Rep. No. 104-98 (June 19, 1995). H.R. Rep. No. 102-474 (Mar. 30, 1992) (reprinted in 1992 U.S.C.C.A.N. 1954). H.R. Conf. Rep. No. 102-1018 (Oct. 5, 1992) (reprinted in 1992 U.S.C.C.A.N. 2472).
15.11	Committee Print	Staff of House Comm. on Banking, Finance and Urban Affairs, 102d Cong., Report on the Bank of New England Failure and Resolution (Comm. Print 1991).
15.12	Congressional Record	137 Cong. Rec. S503 (daily ed., Jan. 14, 1991) (statement of Sen. Dole).
19.0	Federal Regulations	Federal Food, Drug, and Cosmetic Act, 21 C.F.R. § 101.30(e)(1) (1996). 50 C.F.R. § 227.72(3)(ii) (1996).
19.3	Federal Register	58 Fed. Reg. 9015 (Feb. 18, 1993).
19.7	Opinion of the Attorney General	43 Op. Atty. Gen. 75 (1977).
22.0	Books	Mary B. Ray & Jill J. Ramsfield, Legal Writing: Getting It Right and Getting It Written (West Publg. Co. 1993). Homer, The Odyssey (Robert Fitzgerald trans., Knopf Publg. Group 1990). Laurence H. Tribe, American Constitutional Law (Found. Press 1978).
22.2	Short forms for books	Ray & Ramsfield, supra n. 1, at 47–53. Id. at 50.

CITATION TABLE

RULE	CATEGORY	ALWD
26.0	Legal Encyclopedias	35 C.J.S. Extradition § 11 (1960 & Supp. 1996). 73 Am. Jur. 2d Subrogation §§ 106–128 (1974).
25.0	Black's Law Dictionary	Black's Law Dictionary 754 (6th ed. 1990).
	The Federalist	Alexander Hamilton, The Executive Department Further Considered in The Federalist No. 70.
23.1	Law Reviews	David H. Souter, A Tribute to Justice Harry A. Blackmun, 104 Yale L.J. 5 (1994).
23.2	Short forms for law reviews	Richard A. Posner, Goodbye to the Bluebook, 53 U. Chi. L. Rev. 1343 (1986). Posner, supra n. 1, at 1346. Id. at 1349.
23.1(f)(3)	Nonconsecutively Paginated Journals or Magazines	Elizabeth Gleick, O. J. Feels the Heat, Time 60 (Dec. 2, 1996).
23.1	Newspapers	Ann Devroy & John E. Yang, Clinton-GOP Budget Negotiations Break Down, Wash. Post A1 (Jan. 10, 1996).
24.0	American Law Reports Annotations	Jane M. Draper, Workers' Compensation: Tips or Gratuities as Factor in Determining Amount of Compensation, 16 A.L.R.5th 191 (1993).
32.0	Letters	Ltr. from Jill J. Ramsfield, Prof., Georgetown Univ. L. Ctr., to Dylan Cors, Editor in Chief, Duke Law Journal, *Author Review of Article* 1 (Nov. 25, 1996) (on file with Author).
31.0	Interviews	Interview with Jill J. Ramsfield, Prof., Georgetown Univ. L. Ctr., in Washington, D.C. (Dec. 15, 1996).
30.0	Speeches and Addresses	Roscoe Pound, Address to the ABA, *The Causes of Popular Dissatisfaction with the Administration of Justice* (St. Paul, Minn., Aug. 29, 1906) (available at 35 F.R.D. 273 (1964)).
39.0	Electronic Sources and Databases	Larry Zoglin, Practice Serves Long Term Business Objectives: Stable Cross-Holdings of Shares Likely to Withstand Pressures, Japan Econ. J. 7 (June 21, 1986) (available LEXIS, Asiapc Library, Allasi File).
40.0	Internet Sources	Georgetown University, Men's Basketball, http://www.guhoyas.com/sports/m-baskbl/gu-m-baskbl-body.html (accessed Oct. 20, 2004). Sterling Wentworth Corporation, http://sterwent.com (last updated Nov. 26, 1996).
28.0	Looseleaf Services	SEC v. Melchior, [1992–1993 Transfer Binder] Fed. Sec. L. Rep. (CCH) ¶ 97,356 (D. Utah 1993). Ind. Mich. Power Co., [July–Sept. 1995] Fed. Energy Reg. Commn. Rep. (CCH) ¶ 61,153 (Aug. 3, 1995).

RULE	CATEGORY	ALWD
12.0	State Supreme Court	Sawada v. Endo, 561 P.2d 1291 (Haw. 1977).
12.0	State Appellate Court	Blue Bell, Inc. v. Peat, Marwick, Mitchell & Co., 715 S.W.2d 408 (Tex. App. 5th Dist. 1986).
	State Trial-level Court	People v. Gotti, 552 N.Y.S.2d 485 (N.Y. Sup. 1990).
Depends on local rules for that particular state– see Appendix 2	State court decisions contained in documents submitted to a state court	Ploof v. Putnam, 81 Vt. 471, 71 A. 188 (1908).
	California state court decisions submitted to California courts	Bily v. Arthur Young & Co., 3 Cal. 4th 370 (1992) (en banc).
	New York state court decisions submitted to New York courts	Turcotte v. Fell, 68 N.Y.2d 432 (1986).
13.0	State Constitution	Md. Const. art. III, § 1.
14.4, Appendix 1	State Statutes	Del. Code Ann. tit. 8, § 145 (1991 & Supp. 1996).
		Minn. Stat. § 302A.251(5) (Supp. 1995).
		Ind. Code Ann. § 23-1-35-1 (West 1995).
Appendix 1	State Subject Matter Codes	Cal. Fish & Game Code § 2537 (West 1996).
		Health Occ. Md. Code Ann. § 16-103 (1996).
		N.Y. Partnership Law § 26(c) (McKinney 1996).
		Tex. Agric. Code Ann. § 74.004 (1996) (authorizing the state to destroy any cotton plants containing the boll weevil).
14.9, Appendix 1	State Session Law	1996 Md. Laws 576 (to be codified at scattered sections of Md. Code Ann., Com. Law).
14.5	Statutes available on electronic databases	Alaska Stat. § 16.05.407 (Westlaw current through end of 1996 1st Spec. Sess.).
		Cal. Fam. Code § 65 (Westlaw current through end of 1995-96 Reg. Sess. and 1st–4th Extra Sess.).
		Iowa Code § 523.H7 (LEXIS current through all 1996 legis.).
		La. Rev. Stat. Ann. § 14-313 (LEXIS current through 1995 Sess.) (prohibiting the wearing of masks or hoods in public places except on Halloween and during Mardi Gras).

RULE	CATEGORY	ALWD
18.0	Local Ordinance	Houston Code Ordinances (Tex.) § 42-85(b)(5) (1985).
		Mun. Regs. (D.C.) tit. 14, § 2903.2 (1996).
27.1	Restatements	Restatement (Second) of Torts § 552 (1977).
27.3	Model Codes	Model Penal Code §§ 6.01-6.13 (1962).
		Rev. Model Bus. Corp. Act. § 8.08(a) (1994).
		Model Code Prof. Resp. DR 4-101 (1969).
		Model R. Prof. Conduct 1.6 (1983).
21.0	Treaties, bilateral, U.S. a party	Treaty on Limitation of Anti-Ballistic Missile Systems between United States and U.S.S.R. (May 26, 1972), 23 U.S.T. 3435 [hereinafter the SALT I Agreement].
		North American Free Trade Agreement between United States, Mexico and Canada (Dec. 17, 1992), 32 I.L.M. 296.

CLARITY

Clarity means writing so the reader can follow the writing step by step, without wondering what a phrase means or what the point of the paper is. When the writing is clear, the reader can forget about the writing itself and focus instead on the merit of the content. The main tools of clarity are (1) matching the document's organizational plan to its message and (2) matching the document's syntactical usage to its substance. For example, a Brief Answer can by its syntax suggest an order for explaining the analysis and the discussion can in turn use that same order. The order springs from the fusion of law and your client's situation. A paragraph's structure, rather than following a set formula, can reveal its purpose, such as providing a transition or developing an analogy. Similarly, sentences can be written to use syntactical devices that match the substantive message; for example, parallel structure can be used for parallel ideas and dependent clauses for dependent ideas. For related information, see ORGANIZATION, LARGE–SCALE; ORGANIZATION, SMALL–SCALE; PRECISION; and READABILITY.

CLAUSES

A clause is a group of words that includes a subject and a predicate. Several clauses may be combined to form a compound or complex sentence.

dependent clause   independent clause

> *Even if the court remands the case*, **the Plaintiff will not appreciably increase his reward.**

An independent clause can stand alone as a logical sentence.

> **The plaintiff will not appreciably increase his reward.**

A dependent clause cannot stand alone because it begins with a word or phrase that makes the clause depend logically on another point.

> *Even if the court remands the case*

Not knowing the difference between dependent and independent clauses can lead a writer to misuse commas. This occurs most often with the word *however*.

> **The court remanded the case; however, the plaintiff did not receive an appreciably higher reward.**

rather than

> The court remanded the case, however, the plaintiff did not receive an appreciably higher reward.

Because *however* joins two independent clauses, those clauses must be separated with a semicolon. For a discussion of clauses in the context of sentences, see SENTENCE STRUCTURE, subsections 3 and 7. For relevant punctuation rules, see COMMAS, subsections 1–3.

CLEARLY

Is the point really clear? If not, omit *clearly*. Similarly, whenever you read the word clearly in a text, look for a hole in the writer's logic. In most situations, *clearly* will remind you of the orator who pounds on the podium in the hope that his ardor will obscure his argument's weakness. For a discussion of related concerns, see MODIFIERS; LITERAL MEANING; and CONCISENESS, subsection 7.

CLEAR WRITING

See READABILITY and CLARITY.

CLIENT CORRESPONDENCE

In client letters and email, both content and tone are important. Client letters may be formal or informal OPINION LETTERS or GENERAL CORRESPONDENCE LETTERS AND EMAIL. See those entries and also TONE IN LETTERS AND EMAIL. If appropriate, also see BAD NEWS, GIVING IT or BAD NEWS, SOFTENING IT.

CLOSINGS FOR LETTERS AND EMAIL

Choose the standard closing that suits your writing style and the tone of your letter or email. In email, closings are sometimes eliminated because the reader knows the sender from the heading. But you may want to create either a friendlier or more formal tone by being less abrupt and including a closing to your email. If the tone of your letter or email is businesslike yet friendly, try

Sincerely,

or

Sincerely yours.

If your tone is more formal, try

Yours truly,

or

Very truly yours.

Do not worry about seeming insincere; these closings are not taken literally.

Using innovative alternatives only creates undesirable responses, rather than underscoring your sincerity. If you were to use something more accurate, like *Don't bother me anymore*, you would only seem unprofessional or petulant. If you omit the closing in a letter, you create an abrupt, impersonal tone that is usually not appropriate, even in a tough collection letter. For more detail on related issues, see TONE IN LETTERS and GENERAL CORRESPONDENCE LETTERS.

COHERENCE

Coherence in writing means writing so that any reader can see how all the content fits together. Your tools for achieving coherence are

- organization
- consistent and unambiguous wording, and
- clear and adequate transitions.

For detail on how to accomplish this, see ORGANIZATION, SMALL–SCALE; PARAGRAPHS; PRECISION; REPETITION; AMBIGUITY, WAYS TO AVOID; CONNECTIONS, MAKING THEM; and TRANSITIONS.

COLLABORATION

Collaborative writing is wonderful, when it works. It improves the product when it builds on individual strengths and compensates for individual weaknesses. It improves the process when it reduces the pressure to be perfect, provides more perspective as the process wears on, and provides someone with whom you can commiserate and celebrate. Collaboration is not just choosing a co-author for an independent project. Collaboration occurs within law offices when supervising attorneys assign projects to others. Seen as a collaboration, such a project can yield superior results. Without collaboration, it can foster divisiveness and poor results.

Successful collaboration requires clear-headed planning; the collaborators need to have congruent expectations regarding the project, the process, and each other. The following process is one way to achieve this congruency.

1. Set parameters for the project.

Meet to decide on the project's purpose and scope. A little time spent determining the goals and limits of the document can help you find common ground and identify any areas where compromise is needed. Then discuss all possible issues, theories, and strategy, and decide which you will pursue. Even at this early stage, begin to develop a sense of your communal voice to the extent you can. For help here, see PURPOSE, VOICE, and PREWRITING.

Determine concrete constraints such as page length, scope of research, and use of citations. Discuss such factors as the client's priorities, the audience, and the balance you seek between thoroughness and conciseness. Include other important areas, such as professional posture, time commitments, and other personal goals regarding this piece of writing. Determine priorities together, identifying what qualities are not just desirable, but essential. This will help you allocate time most effectively and avoid long debates over minor wording or style points as the deadline nears. For help here, see AUDIENCE and PROFESSIONAL POSTURE.

2. Establish your procedural structure.

Note the final deadline and set interim deadlines. You will be dependent on each other to finish this document, so be clear on who gets what to the others, and when. When using word processors, check such details as whether you are using compatible SOFTWARE AND COMPUTER systems and whether you will be exchanging text on disks, on paper, or directly from computer to computer. If sending files as email attachments, learn about the limitations of your colleague's server, so you do not crash the system with a large file. For related information, see COMPUTERS, USE OF. If you are not in the same location, determine whether you will trade text by mail, electronic mail, or *FAX*. Resolving these questions can avoid costly delays as you near the project's deadline. For related information, see time management. For further help, see TIME MANAGEMENT and DEADLINES, MEETING THEM.

3. Establish your technical roles.

Whenever possible, determine who is in charge of each technical area of writing. For example, choose one person to resolve grammar questions, another to plan persuasive strategy, another to monitor the document's tone, and another to resolve questions of citation location and form. Although these questions may not arise until much later, establish your roles early. This division of responsibilities will enable you to avoid time-consuming debates over small points; you can instead refer the question to one collaborator. Additionally, this structure will shift the focus of this part of the collaborative writing process from personal ego to personal responsibility.

4. Clarify tasks throughout the writing process.

Before the end of each meeting, decide together what each collaborator will accomplish before the next meeting. Preferably, put these lists in writing, so each collaborator has a copy. These lists encourage helpful communication and reduce the chance for duplication of effort or failure to complete some necessary task.

5. Keep in touch.

Since the main benefits of collaboration flow from an interchange of questions and suggestions, do whatever you can to make it easy for those exchanges to occur. Confer while writing. These conversations need not be long; you may just ask a collaborator a question or share a new idea you plan to bring up at the next meeting. As soon as you finish them, share drafts of essential guiding points, such as issue statements and point headings, or section headings and subheadings. Do not wait for several revisions before you share drafts. Long periods of separate work invite writers to become personally invested in their own wording and approaches; that makes it harder to listen to suggestions or questions from collaborators. Effective collaboration requires sharing the whole process, not just the credit for authorship.

Frequent interchange during writing will also help you develop a consensus of thought that will allow you to fuse the parts into a seamless whole. Without this consensus, no amount of editing can create a cohesive presentation of each message.

6. Focus on the questions that are most important to your stage in the writing process.

During prewriting or writing, whenever you have organization roughed out, meet to combine your work and review the overall logic of the organization you have chosen; consider variations on the organization, so you can make sure your choice is the best one. Check your scope to make sure it still fits your purpose and adequately supports your reasoning. Also begin to discuss tone. Although you will revise for tone later, begin to think about the appropriate tone at this early stage in the process, especially in light of your audience. If you wait until revision to address this aspect, you will find it harder to establish a unified tone.

During rewriting, ask yourselves if the overall purpose has been sustained, if the theme is consistent, if the law is accurate and complete, and if the organization is coherent. See REWRITING, RHETORIC, and ORGANIZATION.

When revising, put all collaborators' work together, if you have not done so earlier in the process. Have each collaborator edit the text as a whole, so that individual voices begin to blend into one unified melody. For qualities to check at this stage, see REVISING CHECKLIST.

When polishing, divide the responsibilities between collaborators, so you can be sure to check each item that needs checking. For example, you might check the complete text for consistent use of terms, accurate citation, conciseness, correct spelling, correct use of commas, and so on. For further information on what should be checked, see POLISHING CHECKLIST. Refer questionable passages to the appropriate collaborator whenever possible.

Discuss any remaining debatable points as a group. Move through these questions carefully, but quickly. Avoid the tendency to dwell with great emotion on the placement of a comma or a phrase. You want to get it right, but you must get it written.

7. Celebrate completion.

Congratulate yourselves when you are done. You have all worked hard, and you deserve the euphoria you will likely feel. For related information, see EDITING and MANAGING WRITERS.

COLLECTIVE NOUNS

A collective noun represents a collection of persons or things regarded as a unit. A collective noun takes a singular verb when it refers to the collection as a whole.

The EPA is determined to press its [not their] **claim.**

The American Bar Association meets at least once a year.

A collective noun takes a plural verb, however, when it refers to the collection as separate persons or things.

The Student Bar Association have all gone home.

Make sure you do not treat a collective noun as both singular and plural in the same construction. For a general discussion, see NOUNS.

COLLOQUIALISMS

Colloquialism refers to informal or regional phrases, or words or phrases used in conversation but not in formal writing, such as *ripped off* or *got into*. Rarely will you use colloquialisms in legal writing, not only because they are informal but also because they are usually not precise enough for legal writing. Colloquialisms may appear, however, as a part of a quote. Never resort to colloquialisms only because you cannot think of another word for the idea. Do not enclose a colloquialism in quotation marks to excuse its use. There is always another word or phrase, so using the colloquialism would be admitting that your vocabulary is inadequate. For related information, see LITERAL MEANING and QUOTATION MARKS.

COLONS

The most common use of a colon in legal writing is to introduce a list.

> **In justifying the exclusion of expert psychiatric evidence, the court listed three concerns: maintaining the integrity of the bifurcated trial procedure, avoiding allowing the guilty to go free, and preserving the defendant's right against self-incrimination.**

or

> **The Company's liability does not include any of the following:**
>
> **(1) any damage occurring in connection with the use of the equipment in any nuclear facility;**
>
> **(2) any consequential or incidental damages, including but not limited to loss of profit, damage to associated equipment, cost of capital, and cost of substitute products;**
>
> **(3) any costs beyond the price of the product and service that gives rise to the claim; or**
>
> **(4) any claims arising from advice or assistance given by the Company without separate compensation for that advice.**

Do not, however, use a colon if each item listed is punctuated as a complete sentence. In that situation, write the introduction to the list as a complete sentence and end it with a period, not a colon.

> **During the period of this maintenance agreement, if the Company determines that it cannot maintain the equipment in good working order, then the Company must replace the equipment with another unit in good working order. This requirement is subject to the following provisions.**
>
> **1. If the Company replaces the equipment within two years of the warranty expiration date, then the replacement unit must be one that is newly manufactured, remanufactured, or reconditioned.**
>
> **2. If the Company replaces the equipment more than two years after the warranty expiration date, then the replacement unit will be one that is refurbished in accordance with the process used to refurbish rental units.**
>
> **3. If the Company cannot replace the equipment with another unit of the same model, then the replacement unit will be substantially similar or will have greater capabilities.**
>
> **4.** . . . .

You may use a colon instead of a period between two sentences if one sentence sets up an expectation in the reader's mind that the next sentence fulfills.

The intent was clear: he pointed the gun directly at the victim's chest.

You may also use a colon, for emphasis, to introduce a phrase that is not a complete sentence.

The plaintiff has only one motive: recovery for his loss.

Avoid overusing the colon; it creates a dramatic sentence structure that will become too noticeable if overused. For related information, see EMPHASIS.

In general, do not capitalize the first word after the colon, because doing so usually makes the sentence self-consciously ornate. If you want, however, you may capitalize the first word after the colon to emphasize that word.

Plaintiff asks the court to invoke the most severe penalty: Child abuse must be stopped.

COMBINING WORDS

There is no easy rule for when to combine words, use a hyphen, or use two separate words. Instead, consult a dictionary under the particular word or see the specific word entry in this book. For other general information, see HYPHENS.

COMMAS

One important use of commas is to show how extra information has been inserted into a sentence. The heart of every sentence is composed of the subject, verb, and sometimes object. Those parts make the sentence complete and grammatical. Usually, however, you want to include more information than that. Commas show the reader how you have added that information.

That extra information may be added

(1) before the subject,

(2) between other parts of the sentence,

(3) after the main sentence, or

(4) after the whole sentence when another sentence has been joined to it.

Commas are also used conventionally to

(5) coordinate dates,

(6) set off quotes, and

(7) separate items in a list.

Do not use a comma to

    (8) separate a subject from its verb or

    (9) join two sentences without a conjunction.

1.   Comma setting off an introductory phrase.

If you have added extra information before the subject, use a comma to set off that introductory phrase.

> **In negligence actions, the theory is that the person being sued had a duty to act and failed to fulfill that duty.**

> **If the consumer disagrees with the information in the report, the agency must investigate again.**

> **First, it assumes that creditors have a definite criteria for creditworthiness.**

> **In contrast, a father who once attempted to retain physical possession of his son by the use of a gun was later determined by the supreme court to be a fit parent for custody. In <u>Edwards v. Edwards</u>, the father obtained a divorce from his wife**. . . .

If the introductory phrase is very short, you may omit the comma.

> **Thus the outcome is clear.**

2.   Comma setting off an interrupting phrase.

A pair of commas, placed before and after the extra information, shows that information that has been inserted between the subject and verb or between the verb and object.

> **The case is, however, a sample from that system.**

> **The plaintiff, despite warnings from his friends, jumped off the embankment.**

> **Willard Evans, Louise's father, testified at the hearing on the post-conviction motion.**

A pair of commas also marks an insertion within a subordinate clause.

> **Most economists agree that, in terms of equity, this income should be taxed.**

Do not, however, put commas around a restrictive phrase, which comes after the subject but is necessary to describe the subject accurately.

> **The defendant's belief <u>that the man was reaching for a gun</u> supports instructions about both self-defense and manslaughter.**

> **The standards <u>adopted by the court</u> reflect a prudent lawyer's conduct with his or her client.**

For more explanation of restrictive phrases, see *THAT* OR *WHICH?*

3.   Comma indicating that more information follows.

A comma can be added after the verb or object to show that extra information has been added at the end of the sentence.

The holding was poorly reasoned, filled with vague terms and illogical statements.

Privileges fall into the category of exceptions to a general rule, the rule of disclosure.

This court announced its decision in <u>Sherman v. Freedman</u>, which abolished the locality rule.

4.   Comma before a conjunction introducing a new subject and verb.

Use a comma before a conjunction that joins two independent clauses.

The defendant expressed a desire to change his plea, but his attorney advised him not to do this.

Some proposals advocate continued use of the family as the basic unit of taxation, but others urge a return to the individual as the taxable unit.

If a conjunction joins two short phrases, you may omit the comma.

The attorney recommended this action [ ] and the client did not object.

For related explanations, see CLAUSES.

5.   Commas coordinating dates.

Use a comma between a specific date and the year (*July 4, 2005*) but not between a month and the year (*July 2005*). Also do not use a comma when the date is written before the name of the month (*4 July 2005*).

6.   Commas setting off quotes.

When the phrase introduces a quote, use a comma immediately after a phrase preceding the quote.

She said, "I killed him."

Do not use a comma when the quotation is short and is an integral part of the sentence.

He said "killed" not "stabbed."

Place the comma inside the quotation marks. One exception to this is legislation in some jurisdictions, where the comma goes inside the quotation marks only when it is part of the quote. Another exception is British English, which also puts commas and periods outside the quotation marks when they are not part of the quote. For related information, see QUOTATIONS, HOW TO PUNCTUATE, subsection 3 and 4, and LEGISLATION.

7.   Commas separating items in a list.

In legal writing, place a comma at the end of each item listed, including the item listed immediately before the *and*.

My estate is to be divided equally among my nephew, my son, my daughter, and my son-in-law.

Adding the comma before *and* avoids any possible confusion about how many items are listed. For more detail, see LISTS, STRUCTURE OF, subsection 2.

Also use a comma to separate two modifiers listed before a noun. This comma is the grammatical equivalent of *and* in this situation.

The <u>urgent, persistent</u> messages were ignored by the defendant.

In contrast, if two words work together to state one modifying idea, do not use a comma. In this situation, one of the modifiers is an ADVERB.

The defendant ignored these <u>exceedingly</u> clear messages.

Sometimes, you may need a hyphen instead.

Age-old traditions do not necessarily create legal precedent.

For related information, see HYPHENS.

8.   Do not use a comma to separate a subject from its verb.

If two verbs share a common subject, do not put a comma before the conjunction between the verbs.

The driver lost control of his car while moving to the passing lane [ ] and slammed into the rear left fender of the defendant's truck.

Both the defendant and the plaintiff agree that the defendant had the obligation to post appropriate warnings [ ] and was within his rights when he posted the "no trespassing" signs.

The defendant had a duty to act [ ] and failed to fulfill that duty.

Do not use a comma between two subjects that share one verb.

Both custodial spouses seeking back payments of child support [ ] and divorcing parents seeking an order for child support will benefit from this rule.

Do not use a comma to separate a long subject from its verb. Instead, reword the sentence so the subject is not so long.

A bystander does not have a duty to stop and render assistance solely because he or she passed by soon after an accident occurred.

rather than

Any bystander who sees an automobile accident but is in no way responsible for that accident, injured by the accident, or in any other way directly involved other than coming by soon after the accident occurred, does not have a duty to stop and render assistance.

You may add a comma, however, if omitting causes a misreading of a sentence.

The defendant did see that an ambulance was called, and notified the proper authorities.

You may also add a comma if the second verb presents a sharp contrast with the first and functions, in effect, as an INTRUSIVE PHRASE.

The plaintiff was able to reach, but not grasp, the release lever.

COMMON NOUN

See NOUNS.

COMMON SENSE

You must use common sense in legal writing because few rules are absolute. But proceed cautiously when common sense hints at breaking a rule; do so only if the answer to all of the following questions is yes.

1. Can I break the rule without sacrificing one shred of ACCURACY?

2. Can I break the rule without sacrificing CLARITY?

3. Can I break the rule without sounding cute, trendy, or overly dramatic?

4. Am I breaking this rule only to meet the requirements of some higher rule? For example, you might choose a less concise phrase because it is more accurate or more readable. You might break a grammar rule because you must quote the court directly, because the court broke the rule, and because you do not want to call attention to the error with *[sic]*. Usually, you can avoid this situation; for ways to do this, see SIC. For related information, see BENDING THE RULES.

COMPARE AND CONTRAST

When presenting legal arguments, you will often use comparison and contrast, or analogizing and distinguishing, as part of your reasoning. Often, for example, you will argue that the reasoning used on one case should also be applied to your case because the two cases are similar. And when you contrast facts in two situations, you also need to convince the reader that the difference you have established is indeed relevant to the decision made in the case. As you do this, remember that one comparison does not an analysis make. Only one step in your logical argument is established by convincing a reader that two cases, two lines of reasoning, or any other pair of components are similar. To complete your argument that the reasoning should be applied, you need many more components, such as other cases that compare and contrast. And, fundamentally, you also need to convince your reader that analogical reasoning is relevant to the legal decision being made. For help in presenting all the steps of your reasoning when comparing and contrasting, see ANALOGICAL REASONING, LEGAL ANALYSIS, REASONING, and *STARE DECISIS*.

COMPARE TO OR *COMPARE WITH*?

Use *compare to* when you are introducing a similarity.

This harm, losing the ability to continue running competitively, can be compared to losing the ability to continue working.

Use *compare with* when you are introducing two items you will subsequently compare or contrast.

This situation can be compared with the defendant's situation in <u>Wheeler v. Bailey</u>....

COMPARISON

Three techniques can be used to clarify comparisons: parallel structure, clear transitions, and effective subjects and verbs. Before structuring any comparison, however, make sure that the items are indeed comparable.

1. Use PARALLEL STRUCTURE.

One of the best ways to write a graceful, effective comparison is to place the items compared in parallel structures. The framework of the parallel structure highlights the similarity or difference in the substance.

In <u>Sampson</u>, the landlord had been asked by at least seven tenants to replace burnt-out light bulbs in a stairwell, but had refused to do so. In <u>Smith</u>, the landlord had been asked by a half dozen tenants to repair the security system. And in <u>Ortez</u>, the landlord had been asked by the tenants' organization to schedule roof repairs. In all three cases, the landlord had been asked by tenants to make basic repairs, had failed to act, and was found liable. Similarly, Mr. Tyler has been asked by at least seven tenants to repair the intercom system, but he has refused to do so.

2. Use clear transitions.

Additionally, you can use TRANSITIONS to let the reader know that a comparison or contrast is coming.

In 1919, when the doctrine of the best interest of the child became the controlling consideration in custody disputes, the results of those disputes changed. **Until then,** custody usually was awarded to fathers. **After 1919, however,** custody usually was awarded to mothers.

3. Use effective subjects and verbs.

Another way to make a comparison shine is to make sure that you have placed the items compared in the main parts of the sentence: the subject and verb. For example, the following passage emphasizes the point that both fetuses were viable. The main parts of the sentences are *the court found that the unborn infant was viable* and *Dr. Bernhardt found that the Jones infant was viable*. Making these points the main parts of the sentences emphasizes the similarity, while the difference (*eighth month of gestation* instead of *seventh month*) is stated but downplayed in prepositional phrases.

In *Kwaterski*, the court found that the unborn infant, in its eighth month of gestation, was viable before the car accident causing its death. Similarly, Dr. Bernhardt found that the Jones infant, in its seventh month of gestation, was viable before the accident causing its death.

For a general discussion of this technique, see SENTENCE STRUCTURE. For related information, see PREPOSITIONAL PHRASES.

COMPLAINT

Generally, a complaint is the document that starts a lawsuit. Its primary audience is the court and the defendant's attorneys. Its purposes are to inform the defendant of the nature of the action and to withstand any motions to dismiss. Beyond these purposes, a complaint can be worded strategically to encourage settlement or to delay informing the defense of your strategy.

A complaint usually has six parts:

- the caption,
- the commencement,
- the body,
- the demand for judgment,
- the signature, and
- the verification.

Although your writing concerns will differ for various parts, your overall priorities will be identifying the content needed and ordering that content effectively.

1. General writing principles for different parts of the complaint.

When drafting the caption, signature, and verification, focus on observing all pertinent court rules and avoiding unnecessary legalese. You may find it helpful to look at samples of other complaints before writing your first one; see FORM BOOKS, USE OF for ways to do this effectively. For related information, see POLISHING and CAPTIONS.

When writing the body and demand for judgment, focus on identifying all the needed content while omitting extraneous information. The complaint must be precise enough to provide adequate notice to your opponent and to survive a motion to dismiss, yet flexible enough to allow you to include information you may want to introduce at trial. For samples and discussion of strategies and concerns involved in writing complaints, see Mary B. Ray and Barbara J. Cox, Beyond the Basics: A Text for Advanced Legal Writing, Chapter 11 (2d ed. 2003).

2. Process for identifying the content.

To identify your content effectively, you need to research thoroughly so you can develop your theory and practical goals for the case, including avoiding any appeals. To make certain that you do not miss any needed points, try working backwards.

- Identify the relief you want, including alternatives the trial court might provide.
- Identify results you would want from an appeal court, if that were needed.
- Identify the causes of action that support the request and the relevant law.
- Identify the elements of each cause of action and choose the facts that show those elements are met.

This should provide the content you need for your complaint.

3. Organizing the content.

You may find it most effective to organize the complaint inductively, alleging the specific facts going to this particular element, then the element those facts show, and finally the legal conclusion supported by the facts and elements alleged. Also observe your jurisdiction's format; many jurisdictions divide the content into numbered paragraphs.

Usually, the first paragraphs identify the parties. The next paragraphs lay out the evidence establishing that the first element of the first charge is met. After this evidence is stated, the following paragraph asserts that the evidence shows the ultimate fact, or the logical conclusion stating that an element of the cause of action has been met.

For example, a complaint might be organized as follows.

1. **[identity of plaintiff]**
2. **[identity of defendant]**
3. **[identity of additional defendant]**

4–5. [evidence of standard sanitization practice used at hospital]

6–7. [evidence of actual practice used on a particular day when injury occurred]

8. [ultimate fact that hospital staff failed to exercise due care]

9–20. [other evidence, followed by ultimate facts establishing other elements of negligence]

21. [assertion that defendant's actions constituted negligence]

22. [allegation of damages plaintiff suffered as a result of the negligence]

WHEREFORE [demand for judgment]

COMPLETELY

If it is not literally complete, do not use *completely*. Also see MODIFIERS and LITERAL MEANING.

COMPLEX SENTENCES

A complex sentence has two or more CLAUSES, or groups of words that each has its own subject and verb; however, unlike in a compound sentence, a complex sentence contains a dependent clause, as in the following example.

Although John was in the room while his father was reading and discussing the will with the attorneys, John sat on the opposite side of the room and did not participate in the discussion.

A dependent clause cannot stand on its own as a sentence because it is attached to the other clause with a subordinating conjunction.

although John was in the room

while his father was reading and discussing the will with the attorneys

Complex sentences are useful for downplaying information because the reader views the independent clause as more important than the dependent clause. But use this structure with discretion; if complex sentences are overused, the text becomes hard to read.

If you wanted to read about complicated sentences, rather than about the grammatical category of complex sentences, see READABILITY, subsections 1 and 5, or SENTENCE STRUCTURE, subsection 7.

COMPOUND SENTENCES

A compound sentence has two or more independent clauses that are joined by a conjunction. Independent clauses are clauses that have a subject and verb and could stand on their own as complete sentences. Although compound sentences are not as frequently useful in legal writing as complex sentences, they can be helpful for combining two points that are both logically and structurally parallel.

independent clause

Other doctors in similar situations do disclose some risks to

Conjunction   independent clause

their patients, and thus you may argue that Dr. Walker did not meet the standard of disclosure set by his profession for cases such as yours.

Occasionally compound sentences can also be helpful for avoiding undue emphasis of a minor point. Short sentences are emphatic, so putting a minor point in a short sentence confuses the reader by overemphasizing that point.

The supervisor told Mr. Sykes to remove the cartons from the loading dock before the end of the day, and Mr. Sykes did so.

rather than

The supervisor told Mr. Sykes to remove the cartons from the loading dock before the end of the day. Mr. Sykes did so.

For related information and definitions, see SENTENCE STRUCTURE, subsection 2, CLAUSES, CONJUNCTIONS, and COMPLEX SENTENCES.

COMPUTERS FOR RESEARCH

Using computers for research is fast and effective, but can be expensive in money and time if not used wisely. Make computers part of a larger research strategy rather than relying on one computer source to begin and complete your research. When you decide to use a computer, go through the first six steps of the following Ten–Step Guide before going to the terminal. Additionally, know the vocabulary of the computer system you are using, because the systems do have differences. However you use the computer, remember that it is not a panacea; it cannot solve all research problems. Finally, remember that the computer is not error-proof. It is literal, so formulate your process, especially your query, carefully.

TEN-STEP GUIDE TO COMPUTER RESEARCH

At your desk.

92

1. Collect the facts by listing *who*, *what*, *where*, *when*, *why*, and *how*.

2. Analyze the facts according to your preferred system.

   For Westlaw, it is *parties, places, objects, basis, defense, relief.*; for Lexis, it is *things, acts, persons, places*. Brainstorm at this stage; avoid editing. Give each category a page or a column, and then think of every possible synonym and antonym in order to get accurate search words.

3. Formulate the question presented.

   Brainstorm again, thinking of all the possible questions. If you are not familiar with this area of the law, do some background reading in a secondary source, such as a hornbook or treatise. Research the precise vocabulary that addresses the topic you are researching. Look particularly at TERMS OF ART and verbs to determine how scholars and decision makers address the topic and state results. Write out those questions following this three-step formula.

   > ***Under*** **[the governing legal source, such as *Nebraska's motor vehicle statute*,]**

   > ***did*** **[the legal question, such as *did a driver take due care*]**

   > ***when*** **[the LEGALLY SIGNIFICANT FACTS, such as *when she swerved out of the lane while talking on her cell phone*]?**

   Then organize the issues logically, putting threshold issues first, such as *standing*, and substantive issues later such as *whether X assaulted Y*. For related information, see QUESTIONS PRESENTED, LEGALLY SIGNIFICANT FACTS, and ISSUE STATEMENTS.

4. Formulate your query.

   (a) Choose terms from the list you made in Step 2 and identify the search words most important to your issue, concentrating on terms a court might have used, such as *consideration*, rather than more general terms, such as *payment*.

   (b) Formulate the query according to your specific computer language system, using root expanders, natural language, or other tools helpful for that system.

   (c) Carefully limit your query. Consider first the scope of the topic. If it is wide, use more restrictive connectors or specific terms. If the scope is narrow, use broader connectors or more general terms.

5. Choose a database specific to your jurisdiction, topic, and desired result.

   Each computer system has a list of databases, such as Northwest (*NW*), which corresponds to the *North Western Reporter*, or New York (*NY–CS*), which includes the *New York Reporter*. Make sure you know which jurisdiction's law will apply and therefore which database you wish to search. For related information, see SCOPE.

6. Map out your research strategy, depending on what sources you already have and what data bases you would like to search.

At the computer terminal.

7. Before beginning, be certain you know the features and options of the system.

For example, make sure you know how to save your research for a later time, how to move between the researching function and your word processing system, and how to print excerpts and exceptions.

8. Enter your query according to the directions.

Use the proper connectors or the natural language search, and see how many sources you find. If it is a usable amount, continue your search; if not, edit your query.

9. Print out only the material essential to your work; take notes on the rest.

If you do not have unlimited access to the database, be especially aware of your time, so that you can minimize the time charged to your client or office. One useful shortcut is to print a list of cases, sign off, and then locate the cases in the reporters.

10. Update the law, using whatever updating service you prefer.

For related information, see SHEPARD'S, RESEARCH STRATEGY CHART, WRITING PROCESS, and GETTING STARTED.

COMPUTERS FOR WRITING

Computers can make your life as a writer much easier with their capacities for processing text, generating graphics, and managing files. But beware of their liabilities: computers can either devour your time and energy or save it, depending on how you use them. You may spend more time staring at one screen than you would if you talked through the assignment with a colleague or supervising attorney who took notes as you spoke. Or you may spend more time fussing over technicalities than you would if you drafted the steps in the analysis by hand. For some tasks, like notes for an oral argument, handwriting may be faster.

Computers can also change qualities in your writing. For example, your writing may become wordier, more complex, or less personal. You may lose voice or a sense of communication with your reader. Your headings may become inconsistent because you have viewed the document screen by screen. Your document, like the leaning Tower of Pisa, may look fine layer by layer but may in fact be tilting precariously.

Assess whether or not you are making use of the computer's strengths or if it is actually generating more writing weaknesses. To maximize the usefulness of computers to you as a writer, remember these general principles.

1. Focus on completing the writing task.

   Use the computer whenever it helps, but consider whether it is more efficient to use simpler technologies such as the phone, the sticky note, or the pencil. For example, computers are wonderful for generating rough drafts for some writers, particularly those who touch-type. Yet they are not necessarily efficient for a writer who feels more comfortable and focused with a yellow pad or a dictation microphone.

2. Use the computer when it helps.

   Computers are very helpful for generating Tables of Contents, and Tables of Authorities. They also help you conform to format requirements. Computers distract when they lead you to focus on those areas at the expense of focusing on analysis. Computers help you see how the writing will look on the page, but often lure you into thinking the writing is solid because it looks polished. A neat appearance does not compensate for unreadable sentences and poor logic. Develop a wariness about how the computer may veil the weaknesses. Learn when it is best for you to move away from the screen and work on paper.

3. Decide whether or not you need to learn to use a new computer program.

   Mastery of a computer or piece of software takes time; you must determine when that investment of time is worthwhile. For example, if you need a complex table or other graphic, it may be more efficient to delegate the job. Learning the program may be worthwhile only if you will be using graphics more in the near future. In contrast, learning to use a basic word processing program is more likely to be useful because you can rewrite your own drafts on the computer and see results immediately.

4. When you decide to learn a new computer program, allocate time for that learning.

   Do not plan to learn about the computer while you are working on an important project. Rather, choose a simpler project and allocate additional time to both learning the program and using it while completing the project. Or schedule a separate training time, which you can use as a break from other projects.

5. Consider the computer as one of your tools, not the only one.

   Remember that your writing process should be the main focus. The computer should serve the writing process; the writing process should not serve the computer.

CONCISENESS

Conciseness is highly valued in legal writing. Achieve it whenever possible, although never at the expense of accuracy, thoroughness, or readability. Attaining conciseness is best approached as a revision task, after you have determined what content is needed and how that content is most effectively organized. For an explanation of the larger process, see WRITING PROCESS and REWRITING.

Once you have cut and reshaped your document's overall structure, revise for conciseness by doing the following.

1. Eliminate facts or law that does not bear on this particular analysis.

Concentrate on the scope of this problem, so the reader can concentrate on that too. For example, if the only legal issue being discussed in a memorandum is *whether or not there has been an intentional tort*, do not include facts in the analysis that do not bear on intentional tort. For related information, see STATEMENT OF FACTS or STATEMENT OF THE CASE.

2. Make sure that each paragraph advances one of the points in your reasoning.

This should help you avoid circumlocution, or discussing again a point already established. Similarly, present only one main point in a paragraph. This will help you make sure you support and explain that point adequately, which will lessen the chance that you will repeat the point later to bring in further support. For related information, see PARAGRAPHS and ORGANIZATION, SMALL–SCALE.

3. Move important material to the beginning of paragraphs and sections.

Moving this information to the beginning will eliminate long explanations that reach a result. Instead, give the result and explain it. For more detail and related information, see POSITIONS OF EMPHASIS.

4. Use the key words in a sentence for your subjects and verbs.

Exigent circumstances justify the police's failure to obtain a warrant.

rather than

The crucial fact here is that exigent circumstances existed, justifying the police's failure to obtain a warrant.

5. Make citations speak for themselves.

Begin the sentence with your content, rather than using *the court held* or *the court went on to say*.

The doctrine of moral right is not expressly recognized in New York. Hesler v. Alley Book Division, 952 N.Y.S.2d 552, 555, 761 Misc. 2d 104, 105 (1999).

rather than

The New York Court in Hesler v. Alley Book Division, 952 N.Y.S.2d 552, 555, 761 Misc. 2d 104, 105 (1999), has stated that the doctrine of moral right is not expressly recognized in New York.

For more information, see CITATIONS.

6.   Use active voice.

Whenever possible, use active voice, rather than passive, because passive voice often requires more words.

The defendant argued that the court should suppress the evidence.

rather than

It was argued by the defendant that the evidence should be suppressed by the court.

For more information, see ACTIVE VOICE.

7.   Omit unneeded adjectives and adverbs.

Let the facts speak for themselves, rather than adding your opinion about those facts.

The court in Thomas does not establish a standard for viability that is any more specific than the fetus' ability to exist separately from its mother.

rather than

Obviously, the court in Thomas appears to fail to definitively establish an unambiguous and undebatable determining standard for when a fetus reaches the medical state of viability that seems to be any more clearly specific than ascertaining medically the fetus' ability to exist separately and apart from its biological mother.

8.   Omit duplicate terms.

For example, use the following

The donation's purpose was to provide assistance to the community's AIDS victims, not to expand the program's administration.

rather than

The donation's thrust and purpose was to provide aid and assistance to the community's AIDS sufferers or victims, not to augment or expand the program's administration and overhead.

9.   Delete unneeded prepositional phrases.

For example, substitute *legally* for *on a legal basis* or *defendant's* for *of the defendant*.

The defendant's obligation may have existed morally, but not legally.

rather than

The obligation of the defendant may have existed in a moral sense but not on a legal basis.

10.   When possible delete *that* constructions.

These constructions usually make sentences longer and more complicated. Examples of these constructions are *there are ... that, there is ... that*, and *it is ... that*. When possible, revise the sentence so the construction is unneeded.

You must go through this process to identify any opinion's key facts.

rather than

This is the process that you must go through to identify any opinion's key facts.

11.   Delete empty phrases.

These phrases are groups of words that may sound good when rolling off the tongue but actually add no meaning. If sentences were twenty mule teams, these phrases would be weak mules dragging down the rest of the team. For example, remove *it is clear that*, and just state your point. Remove *it is important to state at the outset that* and just say *first*.

CONCLUSIONS

The conclusion brings together the analysis in an answer that demonstrates the culmination of reasoning. Rather than repeat what has gone before, the conclusion has a "therefore" quality that synthesizes your findings. Situated at the end of the document, the conclusion is the second most important position of emphasis, so avoid skipping the conclusion or using *For the foregoing reasons*. These methods force the reader to reread the Discussion or Argument or skip the culminating moment completely. Instead, use the conclusion to deliver a final punch, soften the bad news blow, or carry the reader into helpful, practical advice.

In its simplest form, a conclusion is the final section of a syllogism, the part that shows that the middle term is shared by the major premise and the minor premise. In the following example, *derivative work* is the middle term.

Major Premise: **All *derivative works* are copyrightable only for their original aspects.**

Minor premise: **"Four Meryls" is a *derivative work*.**

Conclusion: **Therefore, "Four Meryls" is copyrightable only for its original aspects.**

rather than

Major Premise: All *derivative works* are copyrightable only for their original aspects.

minor premise: "Four Meryls" is a *derivative work*.

Conclusion: Derivative works are copyrightable in part and "Four Meryls" is one of them.

Use the conclusion to finalize your proof, whether in the final paragraphs of an opinion letter, the formal conclusion of a memo or a brief, or the less formal oral presentation. Distinguish it from the answer, which often precedes the analysis itself. The Answer gives the ultimate good news or bad news, the remedy, or the desired result. The Answer usually appears at the beginning of the document, the analytical conclusion at the end. While they have features in common, the conclusion should have the quality of unifying the analysis, not summarizing it. Your Answer in a memo may be,

Probably yes. "Four Meryls" is largely reminiscent of Warhol's "Four Marilyns" because both are paintings, both have quadrants, and both show the identical faces of a famous actress. While "Four Meryls" uses more natural colors and shows a profile of the actress, those elements are not enough to make it an original work. Laffon can copyright only those two original aspects of his work.

The conclusion in the same memo might be,

"Four Meryls" is a derivative work because it is so distinctly reminiscent of the Warhol piece. The name, the quadrants, the identical profiles, and the movie star all recall Warhol's work. Such similarities make the work derivative, not original. To be original, the work would have had to be substantially different, such as using a different medium as in *Scallon*, posing the subject in different postures, as in *Laurel*, or creating a different effect on the audience, as in *White*. We should advise Mr. Laffon that his work is derivative and that only the colors and profiles are copyrightable as original.

The conclusion encapsulates the memo's reasoning, but accounts for more details than the Answer and heads in the direction of advice or recommendation. In a memo or opinion letter, the conclusion synthesizes the reasoning in the Discussion, encapsulating the reasoning that led to the shorter Brief Answer. It may also add a recommendation based on that analytical conclusion. In a brief, the conclusion brings the reasoning to a head and often ties that legal reasoning to the desired remedy.

In your writing process, write your conclusion when it is most helpful to do so. For example, if you are having trouble seeing how all your points fit together, you may find it helpful to write the conclusion before finishing the rest of your draft. Conversely, you may find it more helpful to write the conclusion only after you have written the rest of your draft and your reasoning is clarified.

CONCLUSORY

This term refers to a presentation of legal analysis that jumps from the general principle or rule to the conclusion. A conclusory presentation omits the reasons for reaching the conclusion as well as the logical connections between the steps in the reasoning. In a syllogism, conclusory analysis jumps from the major premise to the conclusion, omitting the minor premise.

Major premise: All dogs have four legs.

Conclusory conclusion: Clearly, then, Spot has four legs.

Make sure your analysis is complete so no reader will apply the term conclusory to your writing. For more related information, see SYLLOGISMS. For how-to information, see LEGAL ANALYSIS.

CONCRETE NOUNS

See ABSTRACT NOUNS.

CONFORM TO, CONFORM WITH, OR CONFORM IN?

Conform to.

CONJUNCTIONS

Conjunctions join phrases, words, or sentences.

1. Classifying conjunctions.

Conjunctions can be coordinating, such as *and, but, for,* or *or.* They are correlating when they include two words working together, such as *both . . . and* or *either . . . or.* Finally, they are subordinating when they introduce dependent clauses, such as *although, because, unless, despite, until.*

2. Using conjunctions effectively.

Conjunctions serve as clear and effective transitions only when used accurately, so choose the conjunction that most accurately communicates the logical connection between the two sentences.

Although the project was not finished by the date scheduled for completion, the contract was not breached because the delay was due to a hailstorm.

rather than

The project was not finished by the date scheduled for completion and the contract was not breached because the delay was due to a hailstorm.

For help in finding the most accurate conjunction, see TRANSITIONS. For related information, see CONNECTIONS, MAKING THEM.

3. Avoiding problems with conjunctions.

Two problems to watch for when using conjunctions are (1) overusing one conjunction, such as *and*, and (2) using a conjunction to join two things not logically and grammatically parallel. For a discussion of the latter, see PARALLEL STRUCTURE. For advice on the use of specific conjunctions, see AND, AND/OR, BOTH ... AND, BUT, OR, NOT SO MUCH ... AS, and NOT ONLY ... BUT ALSO. For related information, see HOWEVER and SENTENCE STRUCTURE, subsection 2.

CONNECTING WORDS

See TRANSITIONS.

CONNECTIONS, MAKING THEM

Making the connection clear between phrases or sentences is like using your car's turn signals correctly when leading a convoy. By letting your readers know where you are going, you increase the chance that those readers will be able to follow your logical route. Consider the following techniques in constructing strong connections.

1. Use parallel structure.

This structure can immediately underscore both the similarities and differences. For example, you can compare two items like this.

> **In <u>Sampson</u>, the landlord had been asked by at least seven tenants to replace burnt-out light bulbs in a stairwell, but had refused to do so. In <u>Smith</u>, the landlord had been asked by a half dozen tenants to repair the security system. And in <u>Ortez</u>, the landlord had been asked by the tenants' organization to schedule roof repairs. In all three cases, the landlord had been asked by tenants to make basic repairs, had failed to act, and was found liable. Similarly, Mr. Tyler has been asked by at least seven tenants to repair the intercom system, but he has refused to do so.**

For more on this technique, see PARALLEL STRUCTURE, subsection 2.

2. Repeat key terms.

Use repetition when it is needed for accuracy. For example, if you mean this *contract*, do not shift to this *document* or this *agreement*. Changing terms confuses legal readers, who will think that you must mean something else if you changed terms. For more on this technique, see REPETITION, subsection 3. For related information, see ACCURACY, subsection 1.

3. Use a transition.

A transition, such as *furthermore, because, although,* or *even if* can add clarity quickly. Keep in mind, however, that this connection is only as good as the accuracy of the transition word.

101

The Act did not successfully treat the broader problem of marital status discrimination. Instead, it shifted inequitable tax burdens between taxpaying groups.

rather than

The Act did not successfully treat the broader problem of marital status discrimination; however, it shifted inequitable tax burdens between taxpaying groups.

Because using an inaccurate transition is more confusing than using none, never throw in a transition carelessly. For help with this choice, see TRANSITIONS.

CONNECTORS

See TRANSITIONS and CONNECTIONS, MAKING THEM.

CONNOTATION

Connotation refers to the meaning implied by a word beyond that word's literal meaning. For example, a person holding the same position could be described as *stalwart, resolute, determined, unwavering, headstrong, stubborn, mulish,* or *pigheaded.* These words do not differ so much in literal meaning as they do in connotation.

As you can see from these examples, words do not just have a positive or negative connotation, but fall on a continuum stretching from extremely positive to extremely negative. The extremes of the continuum are effective only if the reader or listener already agrees with you. In legal writing, because you are not addressing such an audience, avoid the extremes on either end of the continuum. For a discussion of this and related concerns, see AUDIENCE, WORD CHOICE, and PERSUASIVE WRITING, subsection 3. For related explanations, see LITERAL MEANING.

CONTACT

Contact is rather vague; before you use the word, make sure you want to be that vague. For example, contact is not as specific as *telephone, write,* or *meet with.* For related concerns, see PRECISION.

CONTEND

Courts do not *contend,* only counsel does. Generally avoid using *contend* in arguments, because it creates a defensive tone and adds unnecessary words. For alternatives to this wording, see COUNTERARGUMENTS, HOW TO HANDLE. For related general techniques, see SUBJECT–VERB COMBINATIONS.

CONTEXT, CLARIFYING

To keep your readers engaged, remind them often of the context in which you are explaining, comparing, arguing, or illustrating. Avoid the pitfall that engulfs many legal writers, who lose their readers by racing into an idea without connecting it logically to the previous section or paragraph. Remind your reader of your topic, answer, analysis, or direction in the following ways.

1. In memos.

Create clear Questions Presented that focus the reader on the precise question being resolved. Give the Brief Answers as soon as possible, using details that orient the reader and a structure that foreshadows the structure of the discussion section. For related information, see MEMOS.

2. In briefs.

Explain in the introduction specifically why the case is before the court. Use the point headings to remind the reader of the context throughout the document. For more details, see BRIEFS.

3. In both.

Use headings, in sentence form, to explain your message and to guide the reader through the document. To make sure that they present a complete and unified synopsis of your message, read your headings in order without the intervening text. For examples, see POINT HEADINGS.

Use topic sentences as first sentences of paragraphs. These sentences can sometimes relate to the previous paragraph or to the overall message, as well as introduce the idea of this paragraph. In opinion letters, the topic sentences often relate how the content applies to the reader's situation. To check the logical flow of your presentation, read through all your topic sentences, without the supporting text. To clarify the logical flow, use techniques explained in subsection 7.

Four other techniques can add substantial clarity. You can use sentence structure that reflects the logical structure of the content. For how-to information, see SENTENCE STRUCTURE, subsection 7 and PARALLEL STRUCTURE. You can also use repetition of key words to show how central concepts recur throughout the text. For how-to information, see REPETITION, subsections 3 and 4. You can also chain ideas together from sentence to sentence. For example, the idea at the end of one sentence often reappears early in the next.

The judge omitted the jury instruction on strict liability. Because of this omission, ...

For more on this, see CONNECTIONS, MAKING THEM. Finally, finish your reasoning. Follow it step by step until you reach the answer to the reader's question. Do not leave the reader wondering *So what is the answer to my question?*

CONTEXT–INDEPENDENT WRITING

Most legal writing should be self-sufficient; that is, it should include all the information needed to understand the full meaning. Many legal documents have long lives and many readers, so include enough information or cross-references to enable a new reader to understand the document in one sitting. Making the document context independent will build your credibility, ease the reader's burden, and keep the document resilient through its potentially many uses. For related information, see CREDIBILITY.

In a memo, for example, include all the legally significant facts and any other facts needed to understand the memo without having to go to the pleadings, correspondence, or previous memos. This inclusion is needed because a memo written to a supervising attorney in June may be used in December by a new lawyer assigned to the case. Include enough about the cases for the reader to understand your reasoning without having to read the cases themselves. Similarly, cite to the record in a brief and include essential excerpts in an APPENDIX. These additions will avoid requiring the judge to leave the brief and search the record to understand the argument.

CONTINUAL OR *CONTINUOUS*?

Continual means *intermittent* or *repeated at intervals,* such as *continual requests for advice. Repeated* may be a clearer alternative. *Continuous* means *uninterrupted* or *unbroken,* such as *continuous vigil* or *continuous preoccupation with the law.*

CONTRACTIONS

Do not use contractions, such as *don't* or *isn't,* in legal writing. They are too informal for almost all legal situations. The only exceptions would be in a letter or memo where you want to sound casual.

CONTRACTS, DRAFTING

When writing contracts, your dominant concerns must be thoroughness, accuracy, and consistency. To achieve this, keep the following ideas general in mind throughout the drafting process.

1. When prewriting.

Before writing, make sure you are clear about what parts the contract must include and what situations the contract must cover. Know what the parties in fact want and what they can afford. Precisely because this is an obvious point, it is often overlooked. Try outlining the contract to make sure that all the needed pieces are included and are organized logically. Avoid, however, worrying so much about covering every contingency that you allow the contract to grow beyond a workable size or expense. You need to find a balance. Remember your client's pocket book, including what the client most needs without creating an overwhelmingly detailed contract. For ways to accomplish this, see OUTLINES and ORGANIZATION FOR THOSE WHO CAN'T OUTLINE.

Also make sure you are clear about local practices and conditions. Contract drafting can be more traditional than other legal writing, and you may be bound to follow what has preceded you. Be very careful about copying mindlessly, though. Make sure you understand each sentence in any contract you are transcribing. For related information, see FORMS, USE OF and FORM CONTRACTS, USE OF.

2. When writing.

Reconcile yourself to writing many drafts of the contract to get it right. If you try to get all the details right in the first draft, you are likely to miss some important larger points. For help in organizing your drafts, see WRITING PROCESS.

3. When rewriting.

Make each clause do one thing, not more. OUTLINES can help you here by breaking down the whole contract into a series of small points.

4. When revising.

Use clear, simple, businesslike language. Much progress has been made in this area, particularly in the areas of insurance and finance. Be on guard, however, for slipping back into the mire of LEGALESE. Use only the technical terms you need and define them if necessary. If technical terms are used from the business the contract addresses, be sure to use them in their common meaning within that field. If many definitions are needed throughout the contract, you may include a definition section to define all your key terms. For ways to do this, see UNOBTRUSIVE DEFINITIONS.

Check for ambiguities.

- Check to make sure that you have used only one term for one item or person. Referring to the same person, item, or concept by two different terms creates an ambiguity that invites misunderstandings later. For related information, see KEY TERMS and AMBIGUITY, WAYS TO AVOID.

- Check to make sure that you have not used one term for several different items or persons. This can create unwanted ambiguities. For discussion of related ideas, see AMBIGUITY, WAYS TO AVOID; LISTS, STRUCTURE OF; and PUNCTUATING LISTS.

- Check each list to make sure it is logically and grammatically parallel. Avoid overlapping concepts as well as avoiding omissions.

Somewhere along the line, consult with others. No one person can imagine all the pitfalls that the parties to any contract are hoping to avoid. No one person can imagine all the ways some reader can miscon-strue a point.

5.   When polishing.

Proofread each clause in the contract and then reread the document as a whole, looking for larger contradictions between parts of the contract, rather than wording problems within one clause. In your concern for the details, you may have overlooked some larger ambiguities.

CONTRAST

The writing techniques useful in presenting a contrast are the same as those needed for a comparison. For specific information, see COMPARISON.

CORPORATIONS, *THEY* OR *IT*?

The corporation is *it* because it functions as a single entity. For related information, see COLLECTIVE NOUNS.

CORRELATING CONJUNCTIONS

See CONJUNCTIONS and READABILITY, subsection 7.

CORRESPOND TO OR *CORRESPOND WITH*?

Use *correspond with* if you mean that you and another party are writing to each other. Use *correspond to* if you mean that one point is analogous to another.

COULD

Use *could* to suggest a capacity that has not been used.

The defendant could have prevented the misunderstanding simply by answering the plaintiff's question about the back-hoe's maintenance requirements.

Thus *could* is useful to add a negative shading to an action by suggesting that it was possible for something else to have happened. For related general information, see VERBS, AUXILIARY.

COULD CARE LESS OR *COULDN'T CARE LESS*?

Use neither in formal legal writing.

COULD OR *CAN*?

Could implies a capability that was not used. *Can* implies a capability that will be used. For examples and more detail, see CAN OR MAY? and VERBS, AUXILIARY.

COUNSEL

Counsel is used to refer to the attorney representing a particular person or organization.

Mr. Yang has retained counsel to represent him in these negotiations.

Do not confuse *counsel* with *council*, which refers to an organized group that works on particular issues.

Mr. Yang presented the plan to the City Council.

COUNTERARGUMENTS, HOW TO HANDLE

When defending against a counterargument, do so without losing the focus of your own argument. To do this, use the POSITIONS OF EMPHASIS to advance your position. Begin your PARAGRAPHS, PARAGRAPH BLOCKS, and sections with your affirmative position.

The proper standard here is the strict level of scrutiny; the category of persons suffering the discrimination is clearly defined.

Then, after you have established your reasoning in the reader's mind, address the alternative position, usually later in the paragraph. As you do this, you may refer to the opponent's reasoning, but do so briefly, as an introduction to your counterargument. Rather than spending a sentence referring to the opposing position, merely imply that position as you state your own. As in the following example, relegate the opponent's position to a dependent clause, such as *when this court has allowed a lower standard;* keep your SUBJECT–VERB COMBINATIONS focused on your own assertions, such as *the category of persons being discriminated against was not clearly defined.*

When this court has allowed a lower standard, the category of persons being discriminated against was not clearly defined. In contrast, here the category is unquestionably women in their fifties and sixties.

or

Although the defendant quoted reasoning from several cases that applied a lower standard of scrutiny, those cases did not address the precise issue of the age of the persons who were discriminated against. They dealt with factors such as personality traits and personal behavior. But the category in this case is women of a certain age. Thus . . . .

rather than

The defense argues that a lower standard of scrutiny should be applied to this case because the plaintiff is not part of a clearly defined group, as would be the case if discrimination were claimed to be based on race or gender. The defendant cites many cases to support this proposition. These cases include arguments of discrimination based on personality traits not directly related to the person's job or on the plaintiff's behavior in his or her personal life. Those cases did not address the precise issue of this case, which is the combination of the gender and age of the plaintiff.

By putting your argument first and subordinating your opponent's position, you clarify the surrounding reasons for your discussion while still maintaining your own position. It helps you avoid allocating too much space in your brief to your opponent's arguments and prevents the opponent's brief from dictating your organization.

When phrasing your counterargument, avoid wording that focuses on the opposition, such as *the opponent contends*. Similarly, avoid inserting personal attacks, such as *opposing counsel's claims are unreasonable and unwarranted* or *opposing counsel did not do her research;* these phrases detract from your CREDIBILITY and add no substance to your argument.

For ways to word alternative arguments, see VERBS, MOODS, subsection 2.

COURTS, HOW TO ADDRESS

See JUDGES, HOW TO ADDRESS.

COURTS, *THEY* OR *IT*?

Even though several judges together make up the court, refer to the court as *it* when discussing the legal entity.

The court made its reasoning clear when it stated that it would not grant a new trial.

Use *they* only in the rare situation when you are referring to the individual judges serving within one court.

When preparing to hear oral arguments, the appellate court may ask their individual clerks to prepare bench briefs. They may also specifically ask their clerks to review the record when the briefs present disparate accounts of the facts.

In this situation, however, it would probably be clearer to use *judges* or *justices* instead of *court*.

CREDIBILITY

Your credibility as an attorney and a person can be affected by your writing. To make sure that the effect is positive, do the following.

1. Be accurate.

Misstating facts, citing incorrect sources, and misrepresenting the situation would be remembered not only through this legal situation, but also in future dealings with this reader. For more how-to information, see ACCURACY.

2. Keep to the point.

Make sure your documents do not stray from the problem you are trying to solve. A clear focus will save your reader time and will help you earn a reputation as an incisive and clear-headed writer who takes time to understand thoroughly the problem he or she is addressing. For related information, see ORGANIZATION, LARGE–SCALE and COUNTERARGUMENTS, HOW TO HANDLE.

3. Check your citations.

Make sure that each is impeccably presented, both in content and form. These are the proof that you have carefully researched the subject and that you are both familiar with the law and certain about its precise use for this case. Check statute numbers, case names, pinpoint cites, and SIGNALS. For related information, see CITATIONS.

4. Proofread.

See that all documents leaving your office are proofread for correct spelling of names, correct dates and times, and correct spelling, punctuation, and grammar.

5. Meet your deadlines.

This alone shows that you are in command of the case. If you know that you cannot meet the deadline, such as when it conflicts with other court dates, identify the problem at the outset and seek an extension immediately. Asking for extensions at the last minute would impair your credibility. See DEADLINES, MEETING THEM.

6. Hold your temper.

No matter how irate you are, avoid resorting to name calling. For alternatives, see TOUGH, SOUNDING THAT WAY.

CUTTING CORNERS

See TIME MANAGEMENT, TRIAGE, and DEADLINES, MEETING THEM, subsection g.

DANGLING MODIFIERS

See MODIFIERS, DANGLING.

DASHES

The dash, the gigolo of the punctuation world, has its uses and its dangers. It intrigues the writer with its drama and its convenient ambiguity. Like a gigolo, however, its effectiveness is determined by the user's *savoir faire* and restraint. If you overuse the dash in legal writing, you run the risk of looking desperate.

1. Danger of the dash.

Beware the ambiguity of the dash. It can replace a colon, a pair of commas or parentheses, or a transition, so you might use it without thinking too much. As a result, the reader has to do the extra work of determining how the dash is functioning in this particular context. The reader may not appreciate doing this, may decide not to bother, or may come to the wrong conclusion.

Ms. Willard had decided not to pursue the action further because litigation would be too expensive.

rather than

Ms. Willard has decided not to pursue the action further—litigation would be too expensive.

Printing terms related to the dash can be confusing. The dash, also known as the–em dash, is the equivalent of two hyphens. A *3–em dash,* the equivalent of three hyphens, is used in bibliographies to indicate repetition. The *en-dash* is the equivalent of the HYPHEN on the computer, and has equivalent uses.

2. Uses of the dash.

Dashes have three uses. First, a dash will make a phrase stand out on the page. If you use dashes for drama, make sure the content within the dashes is indeed dramatic.

The defendant's action in this case—both understandable and humane—cannot be rightly condemned.

There are no spaces before or after the dash. COMMAS would be more formal here, but not as dramatic. Second, a dash can show a sudden turn of thought with an undercurrent of humor. This is a pleasing and deft touch, but one for which legal writing provides few opportunities.

Mrs. Smith thought the intruder might be a burglar—or her husband.

Again, you must be very sure that the content can sustain the drama and wry humor the dash promises. Finally, a dash can set off a mid-sentence phrase when commas would confuse the reader and parentheses would trivialize the content of the interruption.

Julia was on a large and complex daily regimen of drugs. Daily she took three kinds of barbiturates—Tuinal, Fiornal, and Fiornal with Codeine—one of which included an opium derivative.

Here you are using it out of rude necessity, and you may prefer to revise the sentence.

Julia was also on a large and complex daily regimen of drugs. Daily she took three kinds of barbiturates, one of

which included an opium derivative. These barbiturates included Tuinal, Fiornal, and Fiornal with Codeine.

For alternative punctuation marks, see COMMAS, subsection 2; COLONS, and PARENTHESES. For related information and techniques, see EMPHASIS.

DATA

Data means *information* and is now commonly used in both the singular and the plural, as in *these data are fascinating* or *this data is inconclusive.* When your AUDIENCE includes scientists or mathematicians, always treat *data* as plural.

DEADLINES, MEETING THEM

Meeting deadlines is a skill you must develop to succeed as a legal writer, because failure to meet them can be a source of malpractice suits. The secret to meeting deadlines successfully is becoming familiar with your overall writing process and adjusting it, so that you do not get behind at any stage in the process. For more on this, see WRITING PROCESS. Once you have developed your own process, break that process into subsections and set interim deadlines for each subsection. Mark those deadlines on your calendar, moving backwards from the deadline date and making a special effort to meet each of those interim deadlines.

1.   Common problems and possible solutions.

If you have trouble getting started, you may need some more external motivation. Sometimes it helps to tie the deadline to a person, such as to your secretary or a person who will do a read-through of the ideas. The potential embarrassment at missing the interim deadline may motivate you to meet it. For more help, see GETTING STARTED.

If you find yourself falling behind, examine your list of tasks to be done and determine which tasks are critical to that stage of the process. For example, you may not have updated your cases and instead you are spending time reading law review articles. Or you are spending too much time revising and leaving no time for POLISHING or for absorbing unforeseen disasters. Force yourself to shift to completing the critical tasks before you spend time on nice-but-nonessential tasks.

If you feel uncomfortable or bogged down somewhere in the writing process; pinpoint which part of the process is uncomfortable. Overcoming this discomfort can help you meet deadlines. For example, you may feel uncomfortable in

- PREWRITING, when you are doing research, collecting facts, taking NOTES, reading the law, outlining and organizing;
- WRITING, when you are actually translating ideas to paper by dictating or typing or writing the first draft;

- REWRITING, when you are checking large-scale organization and ideas, making sure that all parts of your analysis are present and in a logical order (see ORGANIZATION, LARGE–SCALE);

- REVISING, when you are checking small-scale organization, PARAGRAPHS, SENTENCE STRUCTURE, WORD CHOICE, TRANSITIONS, POINT HEADINGS, and HEADINGS;

- POLISHING, when you are checking CITATIONS, spelling, punctuation, and typos; or

- scheduling, when you are allocating time for each stage of the writing process.

One way to overcome this discomfort is to decide which stage is most uncomfortable for you, divide it into subparts, and attack those subparts directly. Look under specific entries for each subpart for more information in this area, or see WRITING BLOCKS.

2.   Meeting deadlines throughout the writing process.

Meeting deadlines is part of the writing process. Sometimes writers have trouble with deadlines because they delay starting or stopping any of the parts of the writing process. The following suggestions should help you avoid this pitfall. By focusing on specific goals at each stage of the writing process and by meeting your interim deadlines for each of these stages, you can successfully meet your final deadline. For related concerns, see WHEN TO STOP.

(a) In prewriting.

If you are uncomfortable in PREWRITING, give yourself a time limit by which to have your prewriting done. Then divide your prewriting tasks by doing background research, briefing, and outlining separately. This can help you focus on each task so you do it more efficiently. Set a time to translate that prewriting to writing and force yourself to meet that deadline. Forcing yourself to meet these interim deadlines will help you avoid unnecessary procrastination and will allow you adequate time to fix any problems you find throughout the subsequent stages of writing.

Sometimes in prewriting you can let PROCRASTINATION work for you by putting down one project and picking up another. A short detour to another project may refresh your mind. But beware of your tendencies to miss deadlines; do not let your procrastination slide into avoidance. As you delay writing, however, let the ideas flow by keeping a notebook handy for any new ideas that can occur any time, any place. Develop a system of taking NOTES that allows you to incubate on your ideas, even if you are not actually at your desk or in the library. Thus procrastination becomes creative incubation. For related concerns, see GETTING STARTED.

(b) In writing.

If you are uncomfortable about WRITING the first draft, clear your calendar and set aside a time just for that. Remember that the goal here is not to get it right, but to get it written. Do not revise as you write. It takes too much time, is too painful, and distracts you from your main task at this stage, which is to get all your ideas down on paper. Let the creative voice work here; let the ideas flow, no matter how strange they seem. Just get your ideas into words somehow and finish the draft within the time period you set. Then do something else. Let the draft sit. For related concerns, see WRITING BLOCK.

(c) In rewriting.

REWRITING is often ignored or subsumed within other writing stages, and this causes problems with meeting deadlines. Give rewriting its own time, again by clearing the calendar and setting aside one large block of time or several small blocks only for that. At this stage, do any major shifting of large sections. Check large-scale organization and make sure all the ideas you wish to include have been stated and are placed in a logical order. See also ORGANIZA-TION, LARGE–SCALE.

(d) In revising.

After rewriting, shift to the REVISING stage. Check small-scale organization, TOPIC SENTENCES, TRANSITIONS, SENTENCE STRUCTURE, and WORD CHOICE. Give particular attention to your ISSUE STATEMENTS or QUESTIONS PRESENTED and to the specific details of the Conclusion. See also CONCLUSIONS.

(e) In polishing.

Allow at least one day to proofread large documents. Check cites, punctuation, spelling, grammar, typos, and any problems peculiar to your writing. See POLISHING.

(f) Scheduling.

Be concrete and realistic in planning your schedule. Do not plan the timing assuming everything will go well. Laying out a schedule early in the writing process will help you focus and divide the task into manageable pieces. The following example shows one way you might organize your writing process and interim deadlines for an appellate brief.

Notice of appeal filed	April 16
Read Record For Error	April 18
Preliminary Issues	April 22
Research Strategy for Each	April 22
Research	April 22–May 2
Select Arguments	May 5

Complete research

OUTLINING   May 6
    Draft POINT HEADINGS

Fill in holes by doing more research

WRITING (Dictating) First Draft   May 8–9
    Issue I to sec'y   May 12
    Issue II to sec'y   May 13
    Issue III to sec'y & Conclusion   May 14

REWRITING
    Issue I   May 19
    Issue II   May 20
    Issue III   May 21
    Pull Table of Cases, Contents   May 21

REVISING
    Issue I   May 22
    Issue II   May 23
    Issue III   May 26

POLISHING   May 28
    Point Headings
    Cites
    Text
    Tables
    Conclusion

Brief Due   June 2

(g) When time is short.

If time is so short that you need an emergency plan, see TRIAGE.

DEEM

Deem is LEGALESE for *is* or *hold*. The court may deem something to be a conclusion, but this word is an imprecise assessment of the court's action.

The court held that a 22–week-old fetus is a minor child for the purposes of a wrongful death action.

rather than

The court deemed the 22–week-old fetus to be a minor child for the purposes of a wrongful death action.

Identify the action as a HOLDING or as DICTA, but avoid *deem*, which is ambiguous and archaic.

114

DEFINITELY

Definitely means *for certain* or *assuredly*, and therefore should be avoided in legal writing unless the point is literally definite. For related information, see LITERAL MEANING.

DEFINITIONS, WHEN TO INCLUDE

Add a definition when you are using any technical term, legal or otherwise, that may be unfamiliar to your reader and that is central to your point. If you are worried about insulting the reader by defining a term, see UNOBTRUSIVE DEFINITIONS.

DEMAND FOR PAYMENT

See REQUESTS FOR PAYMENT.

DEPENDENT CLAUSES

A clause is a PHRASE that includes a subject and a verb; a dependent clause is a clause that is inserted into another sentence and cannot stand alone as a sentence. A dependent clause begins with a subordinating conjunction, such as *when*. For example, in the following sentence, *when it refused to submit a jury instruction on manslaughter* is a dependent clause.

The court abused its discretion when it refused to submit a jury instruction on manslaughter.

For more on how these dependent clauses work in sentences, see SENTENCES, PARTS OF, subsection 8 and SENTENCE STRUCTURE, subsection 3. For related definitions, see CLAUSES.

DESIGN

Another way to think about what you do as you write is that you are designing a document. Just as an architect designs a building, so you can design the document. You can consider what kind of document it is, how long it is supposed to last, how big it is, how many sections will be needed, what the relationships are among those sections, and where the document is generally situated, such as in a public or private setting.

You are not building your dream house. Rather, as a designer, you are creating a document to be used by others, such as to accomplish something or prevent a particular result. In doing so, you are asking questions and making decisions about your design. As you gain more experience in particular practice area, you develop complex bases for those decisions as you specialize. You can begin by asking general questions about how the document is situated.

- What are the document's *purposes*? Which purpose is most important and why?

- Who are the document's *audiences*? Who is most important and why?

- What is the document's *scope*? How big will it be?

- What is the document's *stance* or point of view? From what angle do you want others to view it?

You will return to these questions throughout the design process, reviewing your choices and priorities. In a sense, they are at the center of a circle that represents both your personal writing process and the product itself. That product can be thought of as involving questions about design elements, such as these.

- What is your document's message or *theme*? Can you summarize it in one sentence?

- What *materials* are you using and why? What are essential building materials and what do you leave out? What arguments, policies, facts, laws, and so on must be included?

- What structure or *form* are you designing? What goes first and why? What goes second, third, and so on? How are the parts related to each other? How do you demonstrate the interrelationships? How does the form flow from the document's purposes? How does it address the document's audiences? How many "entrances" does it have, that is, does the reader have to move from the beginning to the end, or can she enter the document at various, well-marked places? Is the overall form dictated primarily by a doctrinal structure (such as elements of a statute), your arguments (such as strongest to weakest), your facts (such as unfavorable ones buried), or a complex combination of all of them?

- What *proportions* does each section take in relation to the others? Are more important sections longer? Are unimportant ones shorter? Do the proportions reflect the relative weight of each section to the theme?

- What does the *interior design* look like? Are sentences, word choice, transitions, and syntactical structures traditional or modern? Are long sentences and elaborate words intertwined with modifiers to suggest a stuffed nineteenth century interior? Or are they short, minimalist?

- What is the document's *finish* like? Sharp, shiny, with a sheen to it? Or rough and scratchy? Or smooth, but friendly? Is every detail accounted for? Is the overall effect more like a glass office building or a log cabin?

These questions require revisiting throughout the writing process. Keep returning to your drafting board to make adjustments as you answer the questions.

116

Also be willing to try several different designs before settling on your final choice. Quite often, your first design choice is writer-based, that is, it makes sense to you but not to your audiences. Live with it a bit longer so that you create a design suited to your purposes and audiences. There are always several possible designs that work; the key is selecting the one that best fits with your answers to the questions above. For related information on structure, see OUTLINES, ORGANIZATION, ORGANIZATION FOR THOSE WHO CAN'T OUTLINE. For more on designing documents, see Jill J. Ramsfield, The Law As Architecture: Building Legal Documents (2000).

DESPERATION

See HELP.

DICTA

In an opinion, *dicta*, which means *words*, includes anything a court says that does not have a significant effect on the outcome of the case. Dicta differs from a holding, which is the case's outcome, and a rule, which is a more general statement of the legal foundation for the holding, both of which are binding on courts in that jurisdiction in subsequent opinions. Dicta is not binding on courts in subsequent opinions. Dicta can be significant, however, in your use of a case in research or in class. Use dicta to predict a trend in the law, to illuminate the reasoning in this case, to develop a new theory, or to understand future cases. For contrast and context, see HOLDINGS and CASE BRIEFS.

DICTATION

Dictation complements your writing by bringing speech into your repertoire. Speaking has its own strengths, including fluidity, spontaneity, and energy. Writing by hand or on a computer may sometimes become too formal or stuffy, especially if you are inclined to ponder each sentence for several minutes. Many lawyers who dictate also do so because it saves time and because it makes them better speakers in the courtroom

You have two choices now for dictation: dictating to your computer or to a tape that is then transcribed by someone else. Dictation software allows you to speak while your computer types. This frees you to use the medium and, if you prefer, to see the words unfold on screen, because your product appears as you speak. When you dictate the first time, allow a few hours to dictate the sentences required by the program, which memorizes your voice. Then allow enough time to get used to the quirks of the program you are using. Once you get past the set-up, you can follow the instructions below.

Your second choice is to dictate to a tape machine. When using this alternative, speak to the transcriber before you dictate anything. Ask about particular preferences in format, pronunciation, punctuation, and paragraphing. The more specific you are about the details of dictation, the fewer questions you will have to resolve later.

If you have never dictated, begin with small texts, such as a letter or NOTICE OF MOTION. Before dictating,

- make some notes for your reference;
- have your large-scale organization written out and dictate accordingly;
- use numbers and parallel structure to help keep your dictated text organized; and
- make rewriting corrections on the first draft you get back from the secretary.

If you are really uncomfortable about dictating, you may write out what you are going to dictate and then just read it into the recorder to get used to the medium. Then, with each task, write less and talk more.

When you get the draft back from the transcriber, delete any passages that are too conversational or otherwise inappropriate. In particular, check for wordiness, a common problem in dictated texts. For help here, see CONCISENESS. Also check for clear, coherent ORGANIZATION. For help here, see TRANSITIONS; ORGANIZATION, LARGE–SCALE; and ORGANIZATION, SMALL–SCALE. As you discover what your dictation habits are, you can work gradually to eliminate the bad habits, so that less rewriting will be necessary.

Eventually, with concentration, you can use dictation to close the gap between speaking, which can be too colloquial and wordy, and writing. As you revise works you have dictated, work to bring a readable quality to the text; note the changes and try to integrate them into your dictation so that you develop a versatile and eloquent dictating voice.

DICTION

Diction is your choice of words and vocabulary in speaking and writing. To keep your written diction clear, consider the following guidelines.

1. Avoid jargon and legalese; use plain English instead.

For how-to information, see READABILITY, subsections 3 and 4.

2. Use one sentence per legal point, and in that sentence use words that frame your meaning precisely.

For help here, see SUBJECT–VERB COMBINATIONS.

3. Avoid unnecessary modifiers, which may muddle, rather than clarify, your meaning.

Modifiers may also raise questions of subjectivity. Your reader may doubt your assessments and be unnecessarily lured away from your precise meaning. For how-to information, see MODIFIERS.

4. When polishing, take time to check for the grammar problems that you know are most likely to occur in your writing.

Especially check subject and verb agreement in complex sentences. For how-to information, see POLISHING.

DIFFERENT FROM OR *DIFFERENT THAN*?

Different from is always correct. *Different than* is allowable sometimes, according to some sources, but the rule is unsettled here, so to be safe use *different from*.

DIGRESSION

Digression, or straying from the main point, usually occurs when you are not sure of the main line of the analysis. If you feel yourself digressing, stop and reread your QUESTION PRESENTED or ISSUE STATEMENTS and the rules you are applying. Think about them. Then reanalyze your ORGANIZATION and decide whether or not the point is essential to the analysis. For help, see RULES and LEGAL ANALYSIS.

If you are still uncertain, leave the point and move to your Brief Answer or Conclusion. Try to see the larger picture and the result, both of which may illuminate the point's relevance. Alternatively, move to another part of the analysis and then come back. If you can sense that a point is digressing, fight the temptation to elaborate on it, or you will have to eliminate a great deal of your text when REVISING.

For related writing problems, see CONCISENESS. See also BRIEF ANSWERS, CONCLUSIONS, and SUBJECT–VERB COMBINATIONS.

DIRECT OBJECTS

See SENTENCE, PARTS OF, subsection 4.

DISCUSSION SECTION

The Discussion is the section in a memo that presents and analyzes the law. As such, it explains to the reader how the law applies to the facts under analysis and predicts the possible outcome of the problem. The Discussion should use an objective style and should consider the specific requests of the audience. For help here, see OBJECTIVE WRITING. For related information, see AUDIENCE.

A traditional Discussion should incorporate the following elements into a logical, unified whole:

(1) the rules relevant to the analysis;

(2) holdings from cases that define the rule;

119

(3) descriptions of cases that are analogous to the facts, issues, and reasoning being analyzed;

(4) an application of this law to the current situation, which includes both sides' arguments about how the law applies to the facts being analyzed;

(5) policy and equity arguments, which are woven into both sides' arguments

(6) a balancing of those arguments and an analysis of who wins and why; and

(7) a balancing of both sides' arguments that justifies a prediction of an outcome.

For help with these components, see RULES, ANALOGOUS CASES, APPLICATION, POLICY, and EQUITY.

Let the logical organization of the law and its legal setting dictate your organization, rather than the history or sources of that law. For example, if discussing a tort with three elements, you might organize by discussing the elements in the order presented in a statute or in the order that most favors your client. Do not, however, organize by grouping the cases according to chronology or whether the plaintiff won or lost, regardless of the reasons.

Move from the rule to be applied through the application to the specific outcome. Avoid writing as if the law, application, and outcome are discrete subsections. For example, if you have a simple rule you might state the rule, give an example of it, apply it to your facts, and then reach a conclusion. If, however, you have a complicated rule with several subparts, you might state the point of law for each subpart and apply it to your facts before explaining the next subpart. For broader context, see MEMOS.

DISINTERESTED OR *UNINTERESTED?*

Use *disinterested* if you mean that the person is neutral on the point. Use *uninterested* if you mean that the person does not care about the point.

DO

As an auxiliary verb, *do* adds emphasis, especially when answering a question affirmatively when the reader is expecting a negative answer.

Our client does expect to have the building ready for occupancy by the agreed-upon date.

For related information, see VERBS, AUXILIARY, subsection 9.

DOVETAILING

See CONNECTIONS, MAKING THEM.

120

DRAFTING

See the entry for the specific kind of drafting you are doing, such as CONTRACTS, DRAFTING; COMPLAINTS; LEGISLATION; NOTICE OF MOTION; MOTIONS; or WILLS, DRAFTING. For general writing concerns particularly important in drafting, see ACCURACY; ORGANIZATION, LARGE–SCALE; LISTS, STRUCTURE OF; and PRECISION. For general relevant topics, see WORD PROCESS and ORGANIZATION.

DRAFTS

Always try to write more than one draft of any given legal piece. Let the first draft be creative, thorough, and imperfect. Include everything you think necessary to the piece and all things that you think might be useful. Your goal at this point may be to get it written, rather than getting it right.

Then use second, third, fourth, and other drafts for getting it right. For help here, see REWRITING, REVISING, and POLISHING. For related information, see WRITING, and PERFECTIONISM.

DUE TO

Use *due to* only after a linking verb, such as *is* or *seemed*, and only where the phrase following *due to* modifies the subject of the sentence.

This omission was due to negligence, not unforeseeable circumstances.

Here *due to* modifies *omission* and *was* is a linking verb. See VERBS, LINKING.

In all other situations, use *because of*.

This omission occurred because of negligence, not unforeseeable circumstances.

Here *because of* modifies *occurred*, and *occurred* is a transitive verb. Using *due to* to modify a verb may become acceptable someday, but is not generally accepted yet. For related information, see TRANSITIONS.

DUNNING LETTERS

See REQUESTS FOR PAYMENT.

DURING THE TIME THAT

Try substituting *while*.

EACH

Each means *one of two or more persons, objects, or things considered individually*. As such, *each* takes a singular verb when used as a pronoun.

Each lawyer has his or her own manner of presenting an opening argument.

Fourteen exhibits were presented at the trial; each is important to the outcome of the case.

EDITING

Whether you are editing your own writing or someone else's, you will find that editing involves adopting a role that is distinct from that of the writer. If your job is to be an editor, then make whatever adjustments to the text are necessarily for its readers. If your job is to supervise this writer, you don't want to take an editing approach. See MANAGING WRITERS.

To adjust quickly and comfortably to this editing role, consider the following general principles, specific techniques, and overall process.

1. General principles.

   (a) Focus on the task.

   Edit the document to fulfill its purpose and communicate to its audience. Editing a document does not involve questions of personal style, nor does it involve evaluating the writing or the writer. Unlike teaching, editing focuses on how the document itself affects the reader. For related information, see PURPOSE and AUDIENCE.

   (b) Focus on particular aspects of writing.

   As you edit, focus on only a few aspects at once. Avoid reading from beginning to end and looking for everything at once. Most texts need attention on several levels, from the overall structure to the polished details. Therefore looking for everything at once creates fatigue and inefficiency. Instead, create a triage for checking important points first, such as THEME, accuracy of the law, structure, HEADINGS, TRANSITIONS between sections and paragraphs, and citations. For some ideas on what to check for, see REWRITING CHECKLIST, REVISING CHECKLIST, and POLISHING CHECKLIST.

   (c) Review the document in different ways.

   Adjust your editing plan so that each part of the document receives a careful edit. Editing is hard work, and attention tends to lag after a few hours. If you always begin your editing at the same place, such as the beginning of the document, you are likely to have a document that is flawless at the beginning, adequate in the middle, and weak at the end. To avoid this problem, look at different aspects of the document on different reviews. For example, read the headings separately to check for a unified them and consistent format. Review the thesis sentences separately to see if the logic flows smoothly through the document. Review citations separately for form and accuracy. When you reread the whole text, begin at different points in the document as you edit for particular aspects of writing. For example, review for a unified theme. This approach increases the likelihood that you will catch any errors you missed on your previous editing pass.

2. Specific techniques.

(a) Avoid personal references in comments.

When making comments to the writer, speak in terms of the reader and the document, not the writer and editor.

Reader may need a definition or paraphrase to follow this point.

rather than

You didn't define this.

This helps reduce the sting of having one's work criticized. It also creates a broader sense of audience expectation, which the writer can apply to the next project.

(b) Avoid absolute judgments.

Instead of stating judgments about the overall writing quality, describe the problem or revision within this specific context.

The logical link between these two paragraphs could be clearer—add a transition phrase? Repeat a key word?

rather than

Unclear logic

Although this focused editing may require more words, it will save you time in the long run, because the clearer comment helps the writer revise successfully and willingly not only in this draft but also in the next draft; you will avoid volleying comments and building tension.

(c) Comment on strengths as well as weaknesses.

Add a few comments on strong passages as well as weak ones. This will help the writer see your goals more clearly, besides avoiding the purely negative context most writers have come to expect and dread. The temptation to omit compliments is great when you are pressed for time, but resist the urge. The energy and goodwill that comes from those compliments will save you time in the long run.

3. Overall process.

Even when time is limited, try the following three-step approach to editing. This approach helps you avoid the frustration of writing detailed comments that become moot later in the process.

(a) Scan the document.

Read through the document quickly from the AUDIENCE'S point of view. Ask yourself, *What does this reader want to know from this document? How will he or she use the document?* Flag any places where you were confused or had unanswered questions, but do not stop to determine the cause of the problem.

When you have finished this first reading, pause to consider whether REWRITING is needed. Note any of the following problems:

(1) content problems such as

- missing topic statements
- missing support
- missing logical links
- inaccurate statements
- inaccurate or incomplete CITATIONS
- counterarguments unaddressed
- unnecessary content
- distracting or unhelpful tangents

(2) organization problems such as

- missing logical steps
- two steps blurred together
- one step split unnecessarily
- steps out of logical order.

These changes often fundamentally change the document. When this happens, note the changes needed and return it to the writer. At this stage, avoid commenting on smaller points such as phrasing or punctuation. You want the writer to focus on large-scale concerns first, and you want to avoid editing text that will ultimately be deleted or totally reworked.

If your suggestions for REWRITING are minor, move on to REVISING concerns. But resolve any major organization or content problems before moving to step two.

(b) Review for readability.

Check the document for READABILITY and lack of AMBIGUITY. Reread the text and mark any passages that force you to slow down or backtrack. Specifically, check the text for the following problems.

- words unfamiliar to the reader
- inconsistent terms
- vague phrases
- double entendres

- poorly worded transitions
- inaccurate or inadequate signals of structure
- long introductory phrases
- long sentences
- choppy sentences
- confusing lists

If the document needs substantial work, divide this review into multiple passes, scanning for just one or two problems at each pass. Dividing the tasks is also helpful when you are fatigued, because you are more likely to be reliable when checking for only a few variables at one time.

When improvements occur to you readily, note them. When you see a problem but a solution does not readily come to mind, describe the problem in your role as reader. Also read HEADINGS and TOPIC SENTENCES without the intervening text. If these two parts of the document outline the main points and organization, the chances are much greater that the message will be communicated to the AUDIENCE.

If the changes here are so significant that you cannot see how the text will look after they are made, return the document to the writer. If not, proceed with step three.

(c) Review for smoothness and professional polish.

As you begin this set of passes over the document, focus on POLISHING. Check for the following.

- inconsistent TONE
- awkward WORD CHOICE
- distracting REPETITION
- unneeded PASSIVE VOICE
- inappropriate or inconsistent level of formality
- incorrect format
- PUNCTUATION
- GRAMMAR
- typographical errors
- anomalies caused by previous changes

If you see repeated PATTERNS of problems, note this objectively, so the writer can begin to check future documents for these problems before they reach your desk.

EDITING QUOTES

Although some editing of quotes is desirable for effective focus and for READABILITY, too much can make the reader suspicious, as in the following example.

> The court stated its reasoning explicitly when it said, "[w]e cannot ignore the plaintiff's complaint.... [because] [i]n this case, the issue of mutuality ... requires ... examin[ing] ... the parol evidence.... "

When faced with this situation, paraphrase or summarize the quote rather than overediting. Be sure to add pinpoint cites after the paraphrase. For specific ways to handle quotes, see PARAPHRASE and QUOTATIONS, HOW TO PUNCTUATE, subsections 7–9.

EFFECT OR *AFFECT*?

See *AFFECT* OR *EFFECT*?

E.G.

See SIGNALS.

ELEGANT VARIATION

Elegant variation means using different words for the same idea, solely for variety. Do not use this technique in legal writing, especially when using terms of art or key legal terms.

This contract supersedes all previous contracts.

rather than

This document supersedes all previous contracts.

In the latter version, the reader cannot determine whether the *document* is a contract or something else. For more examples and discussions of related general points, see REPETITION, subsections 1 and 2. For related general information, see WORD CHOICE.

ELLIPSES

An ellipsis is a series of four spaces alternated with three periods (...) used to show omissions in quotes. For details of its use, see QUOTATIONS, HOW TO PUNCTUATE, subsection 8.

E–MAIL OR *EMAIL*?

Check with your audience. Formal sources list *e-mail* as the first variation, but in practice *email* is more commonly used, at least in electronic sources. *E-mail* is perhaps a little easier to read, but *email* is becoming acceptable because it is used so frequently. If your audience does not have an opinion on this, you may choose *e-mail* to be more formal, *email* to be informal.

126

EMAIL

Email often replaces both phone calls and formal correspondence. Therefore, it requires a range of presentation, content, and tone. As you decide how to compose an email, consider its audience and purpose. Your audience may be a colleague, a law partner, or a client. Sometimes your purpose will be to give substantive advice as in an OPINION LETTER, sometimes it will be to offer casual comment or information. Most email is simply the spontaneous creation of a writer under pressure. Be careful. Email is as easy to save and forward as it is to create. Words you craft in a moment can haunt you for years. As you compose your email, keep in mind that email is official legal correspondence, discoverable when not protected by the attorney-client privilege. Even when protected, email can reveal thought processes, attitudes, or opinions that can damage client relationships.

To be safe, treat all email at work as formal correspondence, using a writing process that includes safety and quality checks. Email affects credibility and professional stance just as much as any other legal writing. Treat email as carefully as you do any other legal writing; you can still enjoy its speed and facility. By using the following guidelines, you can ensure that your email is received as you intend it to be.

1. Determine the audience.

You may think that you are writing a quick note to a supervising attorney, but she may be forwarding it as an opinion to a nervous client. Think of all possible audiences for the email and make sure that the content and tone are appropriate. Decide to whom you will address it, and who might receive courtesy copies.

2. Determine the purpose.

If you are providing a quick answer to a simple question, you can keep the email short and direct. If you are rendering a complex opinion or reporting on difficult research, you may need to save the email as a draft and return to it later to review it once more before sending it. In legal practice, email usually fall into one of five categories:

(a) answering quick questions,

(b) making requests,

(c) giving formal legal opinions,

(d) negotiating, and

(e) keeping a record.

Whatever your purpose, you will want to communicate your key information early in the email, within the first screen the reader will see. The amount of misreading of email is enormous. In particular, readers often do not scroll all the way to the bottom of the message. Important information placed late in the message may thus be missed.

(a) Answering quick questions.

Decide how much of an electronic trail you want to create. If you think you will be using this correspondence in the future, you may want to include the sender's message with the reply. You can keep the seed question alive by continuing to reply to the current email and keeping the trail of correspondence within each email. This approach also facilitates record keeping because you have the whole conversation saved in one email. Often in practice, discussions you thought finished will later revive. So you may want to keep files of any email that address a particular case, useful source, or common issue. For assistance on how to compose a good email, see GENERAL CORRESPONDENCE LETTERS AND EMAIL.

(b) Making requests.

When you are making a request to someone you converse with frequently, you may be able to simply state the request in a sentence or two. If you do not know the person as well, you may want to begin with a sentence explaining the context in which you are making the request. Do not, however, explain at such length that the request appears later than the end of the first paragraph. Remember that email readers do not always scroll to the bottom of a message.

If you have multiple requests, make that clear to the reader, whether by enumeration, separate paragraphs or some other means. Some readers like to respond within the message, and dividing the request clearly facilitates that kind of response. As with any request, your goal is to communicate that the request is in the reader's interest and then make it as easy as possible for the reader to respond.

(c) Giving formal legal opinions.

You may choose to put the opinion in the body of the email or to append a formal letter. In either situation, treat the analysis as formally and thoroughly as you would in a written letter. If you append the letter, be aware of the potential limitations of the reader's email system for opening attachments. Be sure to mention the attachment in the email itself, and ask the reader to contact you if he or she is unable to open the file. For assistance on how to do this, see OPINION LETTERS, GENERAL CORRESPONDENCE LETTERS AND EMAILS, and GRAPHICS IN EMAIL.

(d) Negotiating.

Reconsider using email to negotiate substantive points. These discussions might be better done in person or even over the phone. Email can be too cold or one-way for careful discussion of sensitive issues, whether with a client, another attorney, or a colleague. Additionally, they are more easily misread than other forms of communication. Finally, they can also elicit quick "no" responses, easier to send over the wire than to say in person. Get up and go see the recipient when your physical presence will have a greater effect than your electronic one.

(e) Keeping a record.

Email records take up the least space in your files, and many time managers say that the best use of computers is for storage. Write your email in a manner that will make your records easy to find and refer to. The subject line is a crucial component in this process. Craft subject lines that refer to the substance of the email. Avoid using the subject line to record the date, since that is displayed automatically elsewhere in your email file. For help with this, see subsection 5 below and SUBJECT LINES.

Within the body of the email, write context independent texts. Include pertinent information in the email rather than assume your reader knows and remembers the context for the email. Your readers may get hundreds of pieces of email a day. Even if some of those are about this client, so many interruptions makes it hard for readers to remember a document's setting. Just a phrase or two to orient the reader is helpful, such as, *As you recall, we need to call Dr. Windmere as an expert on product safety. He will be deposed on January 22, 2006 at 11:10 a.m. in our conference room 10A.*

Create a system for subject line, client, and general topic so that your readers can use the email appropriately. If you are attaching a file like others being submitted to the reader, put your name on the file, e.g., *Smith comments on Russell brief*. If you are suggesting a direction a case might take, label your suggestion, e.g, *Russell brief– economics theory on issue #2*. You may also want to label the priority of your email or color code it if your system allows you to do so.

3. Determine the scope.

Most readers are impatient with any email that goes beyond a screen in length. If your purpose is to communicate something long and complex, you may want to consider putting it in a readable attachment that your reader can easily download. You also can help limit the length of the email by focusing each email on one point only. Avoid collecting a variety of topics and including them all in one email. It may seem handy at the time, but it makes filing and storage much more difficult, and it increases the chance that some information may get forwarded inappropriately.

4. Determine the stance.

Your immediate response to an incoming email may be abrupt and impatient, and some readers may be offended by this tone. Such a stance will outlast the message, so decide what stance is appropriate for the email's audience and purpose. For related information, see TONE IN LETTERS AND EMAILS.

5. Determine the subject line.

Readers use the subject line to determine how to treat and file the email, so write a precise, descriptive subject line. This is easier to do if you address only one topic in an email. If you need to put the case number in the line, do so. Or put the client's name and the subject of the email, such as **Russell case—deposition with Dr. Windmere**. If you anticipate creating a series of email on the same subject, you can even number them: **Russell #1—deposition information**, **Russell #8— confirmation of pretrial hearing date.** Be as specific as you can.

Re: Canceled meeting on Russell defense

rather than

Meeting canceled

6. Use the first paragraph as an executive summary.

If you cannot summarize the content in the subject line, state your theme and a summary of the content immediately. This allows the reader to prepare for anything more detailed. Be careful not to be too abrupt, but avoid stalling on the major points. Get your message across in one screen.

7. Number subpoints within the text.

If you have several points or questions, numbering them will help your reader to respond easily if that is your purpose.

8. Check for accuracy.

Reread the email to make sure the content is correct. Too often, email remains writer-based, clear to the writer but not the immediate reader nor anyone to whom the email will be forwarded. Make sure that the subject line, executive summary, and points are all accurate. Set up the spell checker to check each email when it is queued.

9. Assume the email will be forwarded.

Email can be forwarded easily and even accidentally, so compose the email as though anyone might read it. This means that content, tone, and style should be appropriate to the message and conform to standards accepted by the public. Avoid personal references, opinions you do not want public, or any random or casual thoughts. See the email published in the paper, and write accordingly.

EMAIL, HOW TO READ

Reading your email may make or ruin your day, depending on how you do it. If you always read all your email first, no matter how much you have, you may find the job expanding to take your whole morning. If you read every email whenever it comes in, you may find it difficult to focus on any other tasks. In contrast, if you read it at designated times throughout your day, and you can preserve time for your other work tasks, such as researching, writing, and meeting with people. The following techniques can help you keep email under control.

1. Set aside specific times to read your email.

You may want to do this on the hour, as a break from composing, or at a given time morning and afternoon. Make an appointment with yourself to read the email, and concentrate completely on that task. Otherwise, turn off the email signal and the screen pop-ups and allow yourself to be free of interruptions as you do your other work.

When time is short and email is numerous, you may need to perform TRIAGE. To do this, scan the names of people sending you email and read essential ones first, such as messages from clients or your supervisor. Then scan the subject lines of the remaining email and read those that may need immediate attention, such as queries about current projects or meetings scheduled for the same day. Save other topics, such as ongoing discussions on listserves, to read at a later time when you are not so rushed.

2. Touch each email once.

If possible, dispose of each email once you read it. Delete, respond, or file. Avoid keeping email alive like a pile of paper on your desk, waiting for you to respond. Instead, respond as you read by giving each email an electronic home.

3. Time how long it takes you to read.

Look at the clock when you begin and note the number of email to be read. Look at the clock when you finish and note how many minutes you average per email. Do this a dozen times to determine your average; this will help you determine how much time you need to set aside for reading and responding.

4. Create an electronic filing system.

(a) Create folders to house groups of email.

Move your email on the same case or topic to one folder on your hard drive. Use subfolders to file them according to particular subcategories of the case, just as you would organize paper folders. Create a system that allows not only you to retrieve the documents quickly but also anyone working with you on the case.

(b) Back up your hard drive.

Especially when electronic files replace the hard copies, make sure that you have a separate back up system. Do this regularly and keep it in a separate place, perhaps at home, to be safe. For current files, you may want to carry the electronic folder with you on a separate CD or flash drive that you could use on another machine.

(c) Print essential documents.

Decide what selected documents to print. You may need these to read while you are traveling, while you are in court, or while you are negotiating a deal. Do not, however, assume that you need paper copies of everything you have done electronically. Develop a system that balances paper and electronic needs.

EMOTIONAL FACTS

As used in persuasive writing, these facts are carefully chosen and included in a statement of the case to subtly persuade the reader. They have no bearing on the legal reasoning, unlike LEGALLY SIGNIFICANT FACTS. Nor are they the chronological or informational facts necessary to complete a legal analysis, unlike background facts. Rather, they play on the reader's emotions. For example, if Malcolm assaulted Alice one Saturday night with an unloaded gun, the writer may tell the reader that they had a sexual relationship in the past. This is an emotionally significant fact that has no bearing on the legal definition of assault. Because these facts are not legally significant, avoid inserting them carelessly or too often or too obviously. Too much use of emotional facts can impair your credibility. For related information, see PERSUASIVE WRITING.

EMOTIONAL LANGUAGE

Emotional language is appropriate only in persuasive writing, and then only if used sparingly. Use emotional language to describe significant emotional facts, emotional arguments, or possibly POLICY arguments. Use emotional language only if it is necessary to convey the point and if it does not impair your tone.

Emotional language can impair credibility if used inappropriately, personally, or excessively.

Admitting this evidence would rob the defendant of his due process rights.

rather than

The plaintiff's counsel foolishly suggests the court admit the evidence; such a move would be silly, unjust, and just plain wrong.

For related problems, see CONNOTATION. For related information, see EMOTIONAL FACTS, STATEMENT OF THE CASE, and PERSUASIVE WRITING, subsection 3.

EMPHASIS

When emphasizing a point, you want to emphasize the content, not the writing itself. For this reason, avoid heavy-handed use of any emphasizing techniques. With that caveat in mind, try using one or more of the following techniques to emphasize your point.

(1) Put the point in a position of emphasis.

(2) State the point in concrete, specific terms.

(3) Put the point in a short sentence.

(4) Put the point in a one-sentence paragraph.

(5) Use strong subject–verb combinations.

(6) Put the point to be emphasized in an inverted sentence structure.

1. Put the point to be emphasized at a position of emphasis.

To emphasize a point, place it in the beginning or end of a sentence or a paragraph. Conversely, bury phrases you want to de-emphasize in the middle, because the middle of sentences, paragraphs, and even whole sections gets less attention than the beginnings or ends.

One way you can do this is to use citations at the ends of sentences, not as introductions to a sentence.

Only under exigent circumstances may police enter a person's home without a warrant or consent. <u>Dayton v. New York</u>, 945 U.S. 573, 590 (2005).

rather than

<u>Dayton v. New York</u>, 945 U.S. 573, 590 (2005) states that only under exigent circumstances may police enter a person's home without a warrant or consent.

In legal writing, the beginning gets more attention than the end because the legal reader does not always finish reading. Therefore, get your main points in early. This technique is particularly useful for introducing key terms and terms of art that will reappear throughout the text, because the terms can both gain emphasis and serve as transitions. See POSITIONS OF EMPHASIS, TERMS OF ART, and PARAGRAPHS.

2. State the point in concrete or specific terms.

This increased specificity adds emphasis to a point. Conversely, use abstract or more general terms to de-emphasize a point. When a point is stated in concrete or specific terms, the reader creates a mental picture of the point; this picture makes the point easier to remember. In contrast, something stated abstractly or generally does not leave a picture in the reader's mind and is less easy to remember.

When asked where he had been at 10:00 p.m. on the night of the assault, the alleged assailant looked away and mumbled, "Nowhere."

rather than

When asked where he had been, he seemed uneasy.

When stating the point more generally, avoid becoming CONCLUSORY. For related information, see ABSTRACT NOUNS.

3.   Put the point to be emphasized in a short sentence.

Because short sentences are relatively rare in legal writing, they are particularly effective for emphasis. A short sentence will make a stronger statement and will also be easier to read; both work together to make the point easier to remember.

The defendant then fired three shots.

Watch out, however, for using several short sentences in a row, because this can create an impatient, slightly angry tone. For occasions when you want to create this tone, see TOUGH, SOUNDING THAT WAY. For related information, see SENTENCE STRUCTURE, subsection 1.

4.   Put the point to be emphasized in a one-sentence paragraph.

Use this technique only when you have a sentence that can stand on its own logically. When you can use a one-sentence paragraph, however, it can make the point stand out from other paragraphs, just as a short sentence stands out from other longer sentences. For more information, see ONE–SENTENCE PARAGRAPHS.

5.   Use strong subjects and verbs.

The reader of English must identify the subject and verb in every sentence to understand and process the content of that sentence. Therefore, strong, clear words used as subjects and verbs will emphasize the terms central to your point. These subjects and verbs may often include terms of art or other words you want to emphasize.

The Family Car Doctrine holds parents liable for their children's accidents.

rather than

Under the Family Car Doctrine, liability exists for parents whose children have accidents.

Or use the following when representing the plaintiff.

Panicking, the defendant accelerated and struck the plaintiff's stalled vehicle at 40 miles per hour.

rather than

Seeing the plaintiff's stalled vehicle in the road, the defendant panicked, stepping on the wrong pedal and accelerating to 40 miles per hour.

Conversely, de-emphasize points by putting them in dependent clauses. For example, the following sentence de-emphasizes *the defendant had not come to a full stop* by placing it after *although*.

> **Although the defendant had not come to a full stop at the official stop sign, he had slowed to less than five miles per hour and was not accelerating at the time of the accident.**

For related information, see SUBJECT–VERB COMBINATIONS, KEY TERMS, and TERMS OF ART.

6. Put the point to be emphasized in an inverted sentence structure.

In general, something unusual gets more attention just because it is unusual.

> **Imprudent it was, but not illegal.**

But beware of overusing this technique. Inverted sentence structure draws attention to the writing itself as much as to the content; if you use it frequently, the reader will start to think about your writing style and may be distracted from your content. For more of this, see SENTENCE STRUCTURE, subsection 4.

EMPHASIS ADDED

See QUOTATIONS, HOW TO PUNCTUATE, subsection 6.

END RESULT

Result is adequate unless you are discussing complicated math formulas with both interim results and end results.

ENGLISH AS A SECOND LANGUAGE

If English is your second language, consider cultural and linguistic differences throughout the writing process, beginning in prewriting. For example, ask yourself the following questions.

1. In prewriting.

Ask yourself, *What are the expectations of this audience?* The U.S. legal audience often expects detailed analysis that reveals every step in the reasoning process. Because the U.S. system is based on *stare decisis*, your briefs and memos need to include more information about cases than would be expected in a civil code context. Although this may seem unnecessary to non-U.S. readers, it is a necessary component because U.S. readers use this information to determine how the law should be applied in subsequent cases. For more on how to do this, see SUPPORT, STARE DECISIS, and AUDIENCE. You might want to begin a project by studying several examples of the type of writing you are doing, such as briefs, memos, letters, or pleadings. For help with these documents, see entries under the document names.

2. In prewriting and rewriting.

As you work through these stages of the writing process, ask yourself, *Does the organization reflect the logic of the content?* Develop and refine your organization as you plan to write, and check it after you have drafted. Organization may be the place where contrasts are strongest between your legal culture and ours. The hybrid system of statutory and common law yields dozens of organizational approaches, many of which may work, one of which is best for your document. You can derive examples from the cases you read for class and for research. You will see that no single pattern appears; rather, U.S. legal writers choose a combination of approaches that best suits the doctrine and the document. As you decide how to organize your document, keep in mind some basic principles of traditional U.S. legal reasoning.

Traditional U.S. legal reasoning often moves from the general to the specific, using a deductive structure. For example, you may choose to state a statute and then apply it to reach a conclusion, which is a deductive approach. Or with a common law doctrine, you may choose to state the common law rule, which is a synthesis of the holdings that have developed that common law, then apply that rule to reach a conclusion. That overall approach may seem very similar to what you do in your legal culture.

Within that overall deductive structure, however, U.S. lawyers use cases as illustrations and analogies, inductive structures that move from specific to general. You can use cases inductively in at least two ways: to define the statute's terms and to give examples of how that statute has been applied previously. In the first, use case holdings to define the statute's terms. You can include the holdings after you state the general statute or as you introduce each statutory term. These illustrations are inductive because they use specific examples to illustrate what the statutory terms mean. In the second, use cases to give parameters of what courts have held. For example, you can group together case holdings that show particular outcomes as examples of when courts have applied the statute to reach certain results. You can group together other holdings that show opposite results. These groups are inductive because they demonstrate several examples of the range of results under the statute.

As you proceed through a traditional U.S. analysis, you are expected to analogize your situation to previous ones to show how your situation fits or does not fit with precedent. The many components you can compare offer several different variations and combinations, from which you must select one. For example, you may compare holdings, rules, policies, facts, dicta, or equities. When making your choice, select that combination that best suits your audience and choose one that favors the result you want in a persuasive document. After you have developed your analogy, you can explain the reasoning that leads to your conclusion.

3. In revising.

Ask yourself, *What writing conventions are appropriate for U.S. legal writing?* Generally, U.S. legal readers expect the writer to state the point directly and to guide the reader through every step in the analysis. To meet this expectation, state the main point at the outset of the document, and use the first sentence of each paragraph to introduce the main idea in that paragraph. Again, this may seem rude, but is simply considered straightforward by U.S. legal readers. Then use transitions to explain how each part of your analysis is related to the next part. Generally confine each sentence to one legal point, each paragraph to one idea. Concentrate on specific subjects, verbs, and objects; omit unnecessary modifiers and vague terms. Also omit lengthy introductions to the main point, such as *it is my considered opinion that.* Finally, whenever possible, use the ACTIVE VOICE rather than passive voice. For how-to information, see TOPIC SENTENCES; CONNECTIONS, MAKING THEM; CLARITY, and CONCISENESS.

4. In polishing

Ask yourself, *Do the language and citations conform to legal conventions and U.S. English usage?* Because U.S. legal decisions are influenced directly by written documents and are themselves issued in writing, U.S. lawyers rely on precise, correct expression. To bring your written English closer to that standard and to sound more idiomatic, evaluate the patterns in your writing. For example, you may discover that you omit articles or use several clauses in one sentence. Or you may have a problem with comma usage. Short form citations may give you trouble. Whatever pattern you find, check exclusively for it. Then check for the next pattern, and so on.

When crossing over to English from another language, you may bring writing patterns that are closer either to your language or to British English. With the help of a native speaker, identify successful and unsuccessful patterns in format, content, and style. After you have identified any patterns that are not used in U.S. English, read through your paper, checking exclusively for these non-native patterns. For example, if your native language uses complex sentence structure separated by commas, adjust throughout for the shorter and more direct English structure; separate the thoughts into complete sentences. If your language does not use articles, read your final product specifically for those and insert them. Check also for proper use of prepositions. For help here, see WRITING PROCESS CHECKLIST and specific entries for the grammar areas that concern you.

ENSURE, INSURE, OR *ASSURE?*

See *ASSURE, ENSURE,* OR *INSURE?*

ENUMERATION

Enumeration, or inserting numbers into a list, can add clarity to a potentially overwhelming amount of information. Generally, enumeration is an option when each item in the list is more than a few words long or if the list includes more than four items. Alternatively, you may want to choose bullets for some lists and reserve enumeration for the lists that imply an actual sequence. For more detail on how and when enumeration is useful, see LISTS, STRUCTURE OF.

If enumeration is used too much in a document, however, it becomes distracting rather than helpful. Scan the pages of your documents to see if the frequency of enumeration draws the eye from the content. For related information, see BULLET POINTS; GRAPHICS, WHEN TO USE; and LISTS, PUNCTUATION OF.

EQUITY

Equity refers to justice and fairness. If, for example, legal procedures and existing laws give inadequate or no redress for a grievance, then *equity* would require creating some redress. It is a TERM OF ART, so use it in legal writing only within that legal meaning.

Equity has several shades of meaning, which are beyond the scope of this book, but be sure to consider equity in making a complete analysis in your discussion section, argument section, or explanation in an opinion letter. For related information, see POLICY.

ETC.

Use *etc.* only in informal writing, because it looks rather informal and can be vague in some circumstances. Instead, use *and so forth, and others,* or another appropriate phrase. Better yet, complete the phrase with specific terms.

EVERYBODY

Everybody takes a singular verb.

Everybody has the right to his or her own fair trial.

Everybody is rather informal; consider substituting *everyone*.

EVERYONE

Everyone takes a singular verb.

Everyone is writing an outline for the course.

Do not confuse *everyone* with *every one*; *every one* refers to each person or thing of a specific group, and is usually followed by *of.*

Every one of the defendants is at fault.

EVERYONE OR *EVERY ONE*?

See EVERYONE.

EVIDENCE

Evidence takes a singular verb.

The evidence points to this conclusion.

This is true even if there are many bits of evidence, because *evidence* is a collective noun. If you want to use a plural verb, you will need to make some other word the subject.

All the pieces of evidence point to this conclusion.

For related information, see COLLECTIVE NOUNS.

EX–

As a prefix, use *ex* with a hyphen.

ex-wife, ex-Governor Smith

As a part of a Latin phrase, write it as a separate word.

ex post facto

EXACTNESS

See WORD CHOICE.

EXCLAMATION

Exclamations are used in legal writing only as part of a quote. For related information, see INTERJECTIONS.

EXCLAMATION POINT

An exclamation point is rather like shouting and thus is not used in legal writing, except as part of a quote. Let someone else do the shouting. For better ways to emphasize a point, see EMPHASIS and POSITIONS OF EMPHASIS.

EXPLANATIONS, WHEN AND HOW MUCH?

Explanations, like good motor oil, can reduce friction and increase efficiency. But also like oil, too much can create a sticky situation.

Explain a point when it is your professional responsibility to do so. For example, explain why you recommend a specific way of structuring a bequest in a client's will, even if the client is inclined to trust you and does not seem to require the explanation. Similarly, explain your reasoning in an opinion letter so the client has enough information to determine whether or not to follow your advice.

Explain the reason for an action or a request whenever your reader would want an explanation. Different readers require different levels of explanation. Also explain when it is the reader's right or business to know the explanation. So, for example, explain to a client why you are requesting a piece of information whenever that reason is not readily apparent.

In persuasive writing, explain the reason for a request or action when you think that the explanation will increase the likelihood of a favorable response. Thus you might explain to an opposing attorney why you think a negotiation meeting between your two clients would be beneficial.

In contrast, do not explain reflexively, solely out of habit. Sometimes silence is wiser. It might be inappropriate or unwise to explain the motivations behind your client's request for a negotiation meeting. It would also be ineffective to explain to your superior why the memo you are submitting is longer than expected; in that situation, the context needs to communicate your reason. For related information, see CONTEXT–INDEPENDENT WRITING, PERSUASIVE WRITING, and UNOBTRUSIVE DEFINITIONS.

EXPLANATORY PHRASES

If you want to explain a term that some readers may not understand, you may choose to add a short phrase within the sentence stating your point.

The gaffer, or stage electrician, was responsible for setting up the band's equipment.

For ways to include these gracefully, see UNOBTRUSIVE DEFINITIONS.

EXPOSITORY WRITING

Much legal writing is expository writing. Traditionally, the primary function of expository writing is to inform a reader, rather than to narrate or convince. Expository writing explains factual information, supports a subject, or presents an idea. You often do one or all three when writing a memo, opinion letter, substantive email, or scholarly article: you describe the legal foundation of the analysis, support your reasoning, or present a new theory of law. As a reference, you can use the seven traditional devices for expository writing listed here.

1. Enumeration.

Enumeration explains a topic by identifying its divisions. For example, a memo might be structured by listing a statute's elements, the subissues that might be raised when considering a larger issue, or a series of provisions in a contract.

2. Definition.

Definition explains a topic by setting the limits of the topic or locating the topic within a larger structure or explanation. For example, an article might define a legal issue by placing it within a larger legal context, or by classifying the issue and then distinguishing it from other issues within that class. This technique is useful for isolating and distinguishing an issue from related issues or for defining subissues.

3. Process.

Process explains a topic by listing the steps that lead to the completion of an action. This expository device is often used to address a topic, event, or idea that involves some sort of change or development; the device identifies the steps in that change and their order. You might use process to identify the steps in filing a suit, in completing a settlement negotiation, or in gathering information for a will.

4. Analysis.

In the expository sense, analysis explains a topic by dividing it into its separate component parts by division, classification, or a combination of the two. Analysis by division is used when a subject is analyzed as a singular item, and its component parts are used to explain it. In contrast to enumeration, which simply lists the parts in the whole, division analyzes how the parts together create the whole. For example, several causes of action may make up an entire case, several errors by the trial court may comprise an abuse of discretion, and legal secretaries, paralegals, associates, and partners may make up a law firm.

Analysis by classification is used when a subject is analyzed as a plural; that is, the subject is viewed as a set of items bearing common characteristics. This method focuses on the whole more than the part; the whole is then analyzed in relation to a larger subject, rather than the parts of the topic in relation to itself, as in division. In a memo, for example, the law applicable to your client's case may be divided into statutes, cases, and regulations; all of these are then applied to your client's factual situation. Or, in a scholarly article, several cases may have developed a trend in a legal doctrine; that doctrine is then used to create a new legal theory.

5. Cause and effect.

This device explains why an event occurred. This technique is used to develop reasoning, to create proof, or to establish an explanation. For example, if a defendant watched a violent movie and then subsequently committed a similar crime, the defendant's attorney might argue that the crime was caused by the first event.

To determine a cause-and-effect relationship, first sift through facts, law, practical circumstances, and your own point of view; then determine the premise, the causal relationship, and the conclusion. Beware of several traps, including hasty generalization, *non sequitur*, and the *post hoc* fallacy. In a hasty generalization, only one reason is used to create a cause-and-effect generalization, when in fact many other reasons could contribute. In the *non sequitur*, there is no connection between the first and the second events, so there can be no cause and effect. In the *post hoc* fallacy, there is a false assumption that where there is a time relationship between two events, there is also a cause-and-effect relationship between them.

6. Comparison and contrast.

This device explains the subject by measuring it against something else. This is often used in traditional legal writing when analogizing and distinguishing cases. To predict an outcome in a MEMO, for example, you may analyze your client's case by noting the similarities and differences between it and previous cases.

7. Illustration.

This device explains a topic by using an example or analogy to give concrete meaning to abstract ideas, to clarify or refine definitions, or to provide precise instances and meanings for generalizations. An example illustrates a point by giving a concrete illustration; an analogy compares the situation to something that is more familiar to the reader.

In legal writing, you are concerned with effectiveness rather than pure literary form. So, if it is effective to do so, you may combine expository writing with narration or persuasion. For example, in a BRIEF's Argument, you may want to narrate the facts of a case that is dramatically similar to yours and then use the expository device of comparison to show the court it must rule in your favor because of the similarity. Or you may want to enumerate several constitutional violations at the outset of an Argument to persuade the court that so many violations require reversal. Whatever your choices, make them carefully and deliberately so that the document's structure fulfills its purpose.

For more detailed information on expository writing, see Louis A. Arena, Linguistics and Composition: A Method to Improve Expository Writing Skills at 94–120 (1975); Thomas S. Kane, The New Oxford Guide to Writing (1994).

EXTENDED QUOTES

Resist the urge, please, to use quotes that extend for whole pages. No matter how good the quote is, many readers will skip over it, so use quotes of more than a few sentences only when neither paraphrasing nor editing quotes is a viable alternative. If you must quote an extended passage, such as the full text of a statute, do so, but make sure the explanation surrounding it is adequate to make the reader see that essential use. If possible, append the full text and then refer to that appendix, unless referring frequently to the appendix will distract the reader. See also APPENDIX; PARAPHRASE; QUOTATIONS, HOW TO PUNCTUATE, subsections 8 and 9; and ACCURACY, subsection 3.

FACT OF THE MATTER, THE

This phrase can almost always be omitted with no loss of meaning.

The plaintiff did not raise this claim until she learned of the defendant's affluence.

rather than

142

The fact of the matter is that the plaintiff did not raise this claim until she learned of the defendant's affluence.

For further discussion and examples, see SUBJECT–VERB COMBINATIONS.

FACTS

There are four types of facts in legal writing: LEGALLY SIGNIFICANT FACTS, or those facts that, if changed, would change the outcome of the analysis or case; BACKGROUND FACTS, or those contextual facts that readers need to make sense out of the legally significant facts; and EMOTIONAL FACTS, or those facts that are not legally significant but may evoke an appropriate reader response to a difficult or unusual situation; and extraneous facts that are true but not relevant to the legal subject you are addressing.

FACT THAT, THE

Avoid this phrase. Usually it adds extra words without adding extra meaning.

This failure was caused by the machine's inadequate design.

rather than

This failure was caused by the fact that the machine was inadequately designed.

For related information, see CONCISENESS, subsection 4.

FALLACIES

See LOGICAL FALLACIES.

FARTHER OR *FURTHER*?

Farther refers to literal distance.

She moved farther away from me than I had wanted.

Further refers to all other senses, such as additional degree, time, or quantity.

The attorney stretched the argument further than anyone could have imagined.

Further also denotes figurative distance.

That line of reasoning is further from the truth than would be acceptable.

FAXING

Fax machines make it easy to send documents back and forth quickly, even when those documents need signatures or are not stored in electronic files. But, as with email and instant messaging, the very speed that a fax machine allows creates potential pitfalls for legal practice. Whenever possible, allow an important document or legal decision to breathe. Set a document aside for a few hours or overnight and review it again before faxing it; the mental distance afforded by this breath can often prevent expensive errors.

FEEL

Use this word when you mean to talk about emotions, rather than thoughts or beliefs. Often in legal writing *think* or *believe* is the more accurate choice.

The defendant felt remorseful about his actions.

but not

The defendant felt that he did the wrong thing.

FEWER OR *LESS?*

Fewer refers to things that are being viewed as individual units, and would be counted as such. It takes a plural verb.

Fewer students are enrolling than the university had projected.

Less refers to things that cannot be counted.

Plaintiffs believed there was less likelihood of success if they waited too long to file.

We need less talk, more action.

Less also refers to things that could be counted, but are being referred to as a group rather than as individual units. Examples of this include periods of time, sums of money, measures of distance, and weights.

Plaintiff must file in less than sixty days.

The prayer for relief asked for less than one million dollars.

The engine lasted for less than 45,000 miles.

While the plaintiff weighed almost 200 pounds, the defendant weighed less than 130 pounds.

FIGURATIVE MEANING

In legal writing do not use a word figuratively, rather than literally, if there is any chance that the legal reader could take you literally.

When he tried to drive his car out of the marsh, he instead drove it farther into the mud.

rather than

When he tried to drive his car out of the marsh, he foundered in a swamp he himself created.

144

You may use a word figuratively when (1) the word cannot be misunderstood as literal and (2) the figurative term is commonly used by the reader.

The plaintiff's own word bars his suit.

In this example, nothing is *barred* in the sense of *barred from entering the room,* but any legal reader will know what you mean.

You may also use figurative meaning, with restraint, for EMPHASIS in persuasive or scholarly writing. For examples, see IMAGERY. For related concerns, see AMBIGUITY, WAYS TO AVOID; LITERAL MEANING; and JARGON.

FIND

In legal writing, use this term of art precisely. Courts *find*; counsel does not. See also *FIND, HOLD,* OR *REASON?*

FIND, HOLD, OR REASON?

Technically, *hold* refers to a specific legal outcome in a given case.

The court held that the defendant's actions were willful because he consciously chose between two alternatives.

Find refers to an outcome, usually a more general one.

The court found the defendant guilty.

It also may be used in the phrase *fact finding* or *finding of fact,* as distinguished from the determination of the answer to a legal question.

Reason refers to the more complicated series of analytical steps that the court used to reach its decision. For that reason, avoid using it as a verb when it incorporates too many legal steps. Instead, explain your reasoning fully. Avoid depending on "reason" as a verb to communicate your reasoning.

The court compared defendant's decision to turn the respirator off to a truck driver's decision to take a back road, a housewife's choice to bake chicken instead of ham, and an athlete's decision to turn and run up field, all of which were willful actions.

rather than

The court reasoned that the defendant's actions were willful.

FLOWERY LANGUAGE

Avoid flowery language, or the use of unnecessarily ornate words in legal writing. Usually the ideas in legal writing are so complicated that flowery language will only serve to make them more complicated. The only time that flowery language might be appropriate would be if

145

requested by an audience, such as a client requesting it in a will. Clients probably want flowery language much less than lawyers think they do.

In law review articles you may bend this rule a little; a few arcane words are allowable if they do not hide crucial meaning. Do not, however, *surfeit your reader with a multifarious array of sententious phrases*. Too quickly that becomes obnoxious and loses the reader. See also JARGON, LEGALESE, and ELEGANT VARIATION.

FOCUS

Focusing on the essentials in both writing process and product helps you avoid wasting your energy on unnecessary chores. More important, it avoids wasting the reader's time on unnecessary tangents. For example, when writing a brief, focus on the precise questions the court must answer to resolve each issue; this focus will help you resolve such varied questions about the final product as what research to include, what argumentation to use, and what tone to create.

Similarly, when writing a memo, focus on the questions the supervising attorney wants answered. When writing to a client, focus on what information the client needs to make a decision or take action, and let that focus dictate what points you emphasize.

In your writing process, focus on what parts of the process are most difficult or uncomfortable for you, and let that knowledge of your weaknesses help you choose what parts of your process to change or to give more time.

Your focus on the audience, purpose, and scope, together with your understanding of the process will keep your product useful and your process efficient. For related information, see AUDIENCE, PURPOSE, WRITING PROCESS CHECKLIST, TIME MANAGEMENT, and COLLABORATION.

FOOTNOTES

Use footnotes in articles and treatises, but avoid them in LETTERS, MEMOS, pretrial documents, OPINIONS, or BRIEFS. In scholarly writing, footnotes are appropriate for attribution and for general discussion on related points. You can also use them in scholarly writing to expand a point beyond the information essential to the presentation. For example, a footnote in an article might give the text of a statute or case that is better read on that page than appended to the main text. Also use footnotes to substantiate points and to provide valuable historical or background information. Finally, use them to include sources a future researcher would need for reference. Avoid using footnotes just for appearance; instead make sure they are sensible and useful to the reader.

In documents other than scholarly writing, citations appear in text and are used to establish credibility. This audience is impatient with footnotes, so they can detract from your overall purpose of informing or persuading. Footnotes require readers have to stop reading the text to find the footnote. Readers then must create their own coherence, and you may lose them. If the footnote would include the full text of a statute, put it in a separate section, an appendix, or a well-stated paragraph. If the point seems tangential, make the difficult decision to include or exclude it. If you think a point should be included, rewrite the paragraph or section so that its inclusion is easily understood by the reader, such as putting at the middle or end of the paragraph, breaking it up into smaller points, or condensing the information into a series within a sentence. As you do this, avoid cluttering the text with too many PARENTHETICALS, which can also reduce readability and impact.

Thus footnotes in law review articles and treatises are helpful to document authority, but footnotes in a memo or brief generally distract the reader. Specifically, you may want to think of footnotes for scholarly writing as falling into three categories: citing directly to authority, giving attribution to the ideas of others, and adding text to elaborate on a particular point. For additional information, see SCHOLARLY WRITING CHECKLIST, subsection 3(f) and Elizabeth Fajans & Mary R. Falk, Scholarly Writing For Law Students (2d ed. 2000).

FOR

Sometimes *for* is used as a subordinating conjunction.

She had no patience with imprecise language, for she had a background in legal drafting.

Although this use of *for* is not grammatically wrong, it suggests a rather fuzzy logical relationship. *For* is not as precise as *because*. If you mean to show a causal connection, use *because*.

The operator cannot be considered negligent because he was not told that it was his job to check the hoses before starting the motor.

If you mean something less precise, try to revise to state exactly what you mean. For related information, see TRANSITIONS and CONJUNCTIONS.

FORCEFUL WRITING

See EMPHASIS and POSITIONS OF EMPHASIS.

FORMAT

Legal readers are particular about format because they want the structure to be transparent enough to make the substance visible. For example, know and follow the requirements of the format peculiar to your jurisdiction when writing briefs. Similarly, know and follow also the demands of your employer for format in email, memos, and opinion letters. For specific formats, see MEMOS, BRIEFS, COMPLAINTS, and OPINION LETTERS.

FORM BOOKS, USE OF

Referring to forms can save time and avoid the problem of missing a needed element in a routine task. Using forms, however, can also cause problems, such as including contradictory clauses in a contract or nonsensical phrases in a letter. Therefore, do not use forms as a substitute for your own thinking about the writing task you face.

With this caveat in mind, when you do refer to forms, you can make good use of them if you remember to do the following three things.

1. Compare.

Compare different forms before you settle on one to follow. Comparing different forms, whether from form books or from samples you have collected, helps you see which content and formats are common and which are unique to certain forms. This comparison in turn helps you get a clearer sense of the options you have and of the standard content and format used for this kind of legal document.

2. Prepare.

Prepare by identifying all the elements needed to complete your document, omitting any unneeded elements found in the forms but inappropriate to your document, and checking for logical inconsistencies between these elements. Check carefully for those logical inconsistencies, so that your document is not the next in the line of cases that outlines the problems of ambiguous and inconsistent clauses. Resist the temptation to include even one word you do not understand.

3. Repair.

Finally, repair the elements you have chosen from various forms. Draft original sections as needed to cover all aspects of your situation. Then organize all sections and check for completeness and consistency. When all content is in place, edit the whole document. Most of the forms have unneeded LEGALESE, FLOWERY LANGUAGE, obtuse SENTENCE STRUCTURE, and unnecessary words. You have used the forms to get a sense of content, structure, and format; you can retain those elements and still revise to gain increased READABILITY. For help in omitting unnecessary words, see CONCISENESS. For related information, see CONTRACTS, DRAFTING; WILLS, DRAFTING; NOTICE OF MOTION, and ORDERS.

FORM CONTRACTS, USE OF

Form contracts can be useful as long as they are used as a resource rather than a substitute for your own thinking about the agreement. To use forms effectively, follow the three steps listed under FORM BOOKS, USE OF. For a checklist for drafting contracts, see CONTRACTS, DRAFTING.

FORMER

Former refers to the first of two things mentioned; *latter* refers to the second. This elegant pairing can be effective in fixing two thoughts in the reader's mind. If the reference of *former* is more than a few words back, however, repeat the word to which you are referring rather than using *former*. To understand what *former* means, the reader must remember the items listed, remember which was first, and then insert that information into the sentence. As a result, *former* can inconvenience the reader, which should not happen just for the writer's convenience.

Also remember that *former* and *latter* can be ambiguous when they refer to a list of more than two items.

FOR THE PERIOD OF

For CONCISENESS, use *for*.

FURTHER OR *FARTHER*?

See *FARTHER* OR *FURTHER*?

FUTURE PERFECT TENSE

See VERBS, TENSES, subsection 9.

FUTURE PROGRESSIVE TENSE

See VERBS, TENSES, subsection 8.

FUTURE TENSES

See VERBS, TENSES, subsection 7.

GENDER–FREE PROSE

See SEXIST LANGUAGE, WAYS TO AVOID.

GENERAL CORRESPONDENCE LETTERS AND EMAIL

One common problem legal writers have with letters and electronic correspondence with clients is time; correspondence takes too long to write. Often this happens because writers spend a long time deciding how to begin and how to organize each type of correspondence.

Only four kinds of general correspondence are commonly written by lawyers:

(1) answering or making requests,

(2) delivering information (for-your-information, or FYI letters),

(3) delivering bad news, and

(4) persuading the reader.

All correspondence is affected by your choices regarding

(5) tone, and

(6) openings and closings.

You can use a standard organization for each of these kinds of correspondence, after you decide is what kind of document you are writing. Then you need only choose the appropriate tone for your correspondence and the appropriate salutation and closing.

To decide what kind of correspondence you are writing, first jot down in one sentence the main point. Be blunt; this is for your private use, not necessarily for inclusion. For example, your point might be

(1) *Here is your revised will;*

(2) *You may need to change your method of keeping tax records;*

(3) *After meeting you, I know that there is no way I would hire you;* or

(4) *I want to get you to pay even though I can't sue you because suit would cost more than it is worth.*

Then decide which of the four kinds of correspondence this point requires.

1.   Answering or making requests.

If the document is delivering requested information (as in the first example: *Here is your revised will.*), refer to the request and then respond to that request.

At our conference on January 23, you asked me to help you make several changes in your will. I have subsequently drafted a new will incorporating these changes and am including a copy of this draft with this letter.

Elaborate or explain as needed in the second paragraph.

Please review this draft carefully. Specifically, consider the following questions:

(1) . . .

Then close politely in the last paragraph.

If you have any questions or wish to make any further changes in the will, do not hesitate to call. I will have the final will prepared and you may come to the office to execute it on February 12, as we have scheduled.

When making a routine request, one which the reader will not think twice about answering, determine whether the context of the request needs to be explained. If not, simply begin with a polite request.

Please send me . . .

If some context is needed, summarize that briefly with the request.

A few technical points need to be clarified to enable us to begin your lawsuit. Please provide answers to the following technical questions.

If there is any chance the reader will feel uncomfortable about fulfilling your request, or if the reader will hesitate at all, follow the approach for a persuasive letter, outlined in subsection 4.

2. Delivering information (for-your-information, or FYI correspondence).

If it is an FYI message (as in *You may need to change your methods of keeping tax records.*), start with a statement of the point.

As your attorney, I want to notify you of some recent changes in the tax law that may require a change in your record-keeping practices.

If needed, include this opening in a brief description of who you are or an explanation of why you are writing. In subsequent paragraphs, elaborate as needed.

Specifically, the new law requires you to keep a log of your use of the computer, so that you can document the percentage of time. . . . **Additionally, the law requires**. . . .

In the final paragraph, close politely.

Please feel free to call to set up an appointment if you have any questions about this or other tax matters.

3. Delivering bad news.

If the correspondence is delivering bad news (as in *After meeting you, I know that there is no way I would hire you to work in our company.*), try organizing it in three parts that do the following: (1) set the tone; (2) deliver the bad news; and (3) re-establish the tone. Think of this as the sandwich organization, because in effect you place your meat between two slices of bread to make it more palatable.

(a) The first slice of bread: set the tone.

In the first paragraph, establish the tone you want to take with the reader. For example, you might want to be kind.

It was a pleasure to have the opportunity to interview you last week. . . .

Or you may be tough.

Mr. William Marshfield has asked me as his attorney to answer your demands that he pay for computer software he neither ordered nor received. . . .

You may choose to be warm and personal.

Thank you for inviting me to speak at the Society's annual awards banquet. Regrettably,. . . .

You may prefer to be distant.

Your request for a reduction in your child support payments has been received by. . . .

If answering a request, you may want to restate that request, so that the reader knows you paid attention to the request before saying no.

In your letter dated March 3, 2005, you requested a restructuring of your payment schedule for the land contract on . . . . **Your reasons were that** . . . .

(b) The meat: deliver the bad news.

At the beginning of the second paragraph, state the bad news plainly so that the reader cannot misinterpret what you are saying. Follow this statement with your reasons, if appropriate. This paragraph will be unemotional and matter of fact, no matter what the tone of the other paragraphs. This section may also extend for several paragraphs if needed.

In your letter to Mr. Alexander dated March 14, you asked Mr. Alexander to pay $480 for "equipment repairs made to three typewriters in June 1985." You stated that this payment was long overdue and you threatened to bring suit if you did not receive payment by May 1, 1986.

Mr. Alexander, however, does not believe he owes you this money because he has no record of these repairs being made. Instead, his records show only that Efficient Equipment Repair Service repaired one typewriter on June 12, 1985. Alexander Associates received a statement charging $40 for this work from the repairman before he left. On July 1, 1985, Alexander Associates mailed a check for $40 to Efficient Equipment Repair Service. . . .

(c) The second piece of bread: re-establish the tone.

In the final paragraph, re-establish your tone while you state closing technicalities. For example, you may suggest that the reader call if he or she has questions.

If you have any further questions concerning this matter, you may call me at (505) 555–1234.

If you are being kind, you may wish the reader some sort of relevant good fortune.

> **I enjoyed our conversation at the convention, and look forward to reading your article on** . . . .

If you are being tough, you may close with a declarative statement.

> **I trust that this settles the matter.**

For related information, see TONE; BAD NEWS, SOFTENING IT; REQUESTS FOR PAYMENT; and TOUGH, SOUNDING THAT WAY.

4.   Persuading the reader.

If the letter is being written to persuade the reader (as in the third example: *I want to get you to pay even though I can't sue you because suit would cost more than it's worth.*), you may use the same organization used for bad news correspondence.

Start with a paragraph that sets the tone of the letter, such as a kind tone.

> **Throughout the years, Everly Auto Parts has valued Morgan Auto as a customer. Because Everly hopes to maintain this solid working relationship, Bob Everly has asked me to write to you concerning the rather large outstanding balance in your account.**

You may set a tough tone.

> **Despite receiving three statements from my client, Everly Auto Parts, your company has not yet paid the balance of $2,015 owed for parts purchased four months ago.**

Or you may choose something in between.

> **My client, Everly Auto Parts, has asked me to write to you concerning the outstanding balance on your company's account.**

Do not go on too long, however, because a lengthy introduction can make the writer look rather timid or can make the reader impatient.

At the end of the first paragraph or the beginning of the second, state your point. Write this sentence with care; it must be unambiguous and yet inoffensive.

> **Everly will not be able to extend further credit to your company until this balance has been paid.**

Then launch into your reasons, which may go on for several paragraphs. Make one point at a time, rather than rambling back and forth between several points.

> **Everly Auto Parts, as a general policy, limits credit to any company to** . . . . **Additionally,** . . . .

In the last paragraph close politely, or at least civilly.

Everly Auto Parts will appreciate your prompt payment of this outstanding balance and looks forward to your continued patronage.

In general, persuasive correspondence will take more time and care than the other three kinds because you must tailor your argument and tone to suit the individual circumstances.

Choose not what persuades you, but what will persuade your reader. If you are trying to persuade a party to settle out of court, for example, do not use threats if you think the party would view that threat as a challenge and submission as a weakness. In that situation, you might instead explain that the suit is not worth the expense of trial. For related suggestions, see SETTLEMENT LETTERS; REQUESTS FOR PAYMENT; and TOUGH, SOUNDING THAT WAY.

Similarly, if you think the reader is someone motivated by certain values, try to explain how the action you recommend is consistent with those values. For example, you might argue that paying a bill is essentially the same as keeping a promise. In short, try to explain how the action you recommend is consistent with some goal the reader has. Try to help the reader feel good, or at least not defeated, about taking the action you recommend.

In general, use an unemotional, polite tone. In most legal writing situations, the emotions you would arouse would work against you rather than for you. There are some exceptions to this, such as fund-raising correspondence to sympathetic constituents or correspondence advising clients to do what they want to do already. Even here, however, you will usually want to present yourself as a logical, reasonable person who, although impassioned about a cause, is still capable of making a coherent and logical argument. For a discussion of related points, see PERSUASIVE WRITING.

5.   Setting the tone.

Tone is especially important in correspondence. As the tone of your voice creates an impression in the mind of the listener, so the tone of your letter creates an impression in the mind of the reader. Thus, although your tone in various correspondence may range from friendly to tough, it should always be within the limits of temperate, businesslike communication. A chatty tone will seem slightly unprofessional in all but purely personal correspondence. A tirade will also seem unprofessional, even in the toughest collection letter. Email crafted too quickly can create an abrupt tone and, over time, a series of such email can impair your credibility or persuasive ability. Within these limits, however, you must make your own choices, based on what is appropriate to the situation and what suits your personal communication style.

Using tone effectively in correspondence involves three tasks:

(a) choosing the appropriate tone,

(b) creating that tone through word choice and sentence structure, and

(c) keeping the tone consistent.

(a) Choosing the appropriate tone.

Before you begin writing the letter, consider your relationship to the reader. For example, if your reader is a judge or your supervisor at work, you will probably want to use a tone that is both businesslike and respectful. This means that you will state your points as concisely as possible but will not omit appropriate opening and closing sentences, such as the following closing to a letter requesting a favor.

> **Thank you for your help in this matter.**

If your reader is a client or colleague, you may choose to be polite and businesslike or, if appropriate, you may choose a friendly tone.

> **Please call if you have any further questions.**

Or even

> **I am looking forward to our next tennis match.**

If your reader is your client's opponent or a client who has not paid you for three months, you may sometimes choose a tough, businesslike tone.

> **Please pay this bill promptly.**

or

> **I trust this settles the matter.**

(b) Creating the appropriate tone through word choice and sentence structure.

Choosing your words carefully is one effective way to establish your tone. For example, if you want to create an informal and friendly tone, use less formal words, such as *talk* and *meeting*. If you want to create a more formal tone, use more formal words, such as *confer* and *discussion*.

Avoid, however, using formal words to the point that your letter becomes hard to read or stuffy.

> **Regarding this question, I have conferred with Ms. Jamison's attorney, who explained that** . . . .

rather than

> In pursuit of this query, I have held consultations with counsel for Ms. Jamison, who elucidated the point by stating that . . . .

Another way to avoid a stuffy tone is to avoid inappropriately using the third person, such as *this attorney*, when the first person, *I*, is accurate. In general, correspondence is addressed from one person to another, and so the use of *I* is appropriate, or *we* if you are speaking officially for a group of people, such as a whole law firm.

You may also establish your tone by using appropriate sentence structure. For example, if you want to create a friendly, informal tone, use longer sentences rather than terse ones.

> **Thank you for your kind invitation to speak at your annual banquet honoring outstanding alumni from the law school.**

rather than

> Thank you for the invitation to speak at the law school alumni banquet.

Conversely, if you want to create a tough, no-nonsense tone, use short, rather choppy sentences.

> **My client, Ms. Ambrose, does not intend to pay this bill. She has no reason to pay you. She did not receive any software from your company. She did not order any software from your company. Until receiving your bill, she did not know your company existed.**

rather than

> My client, Ms. Ambrose, does not intend to pay this bill because she has no reason to do so. She did not receive or order any software from your company, and in fact did not know your company existed until receiving your bill.

(c) Keeping the tone consistent.

Inconsistent tone occurs most often when a letter or email includes words that are noticeably more formal or informal than the rest. So avoid using a formal phrase, such as *please be advised that*, in an otherwise informal email, and using a colloquialism, such as *ripped off*, in an otherwise businesslike letter.

Uneven tone also sometimes occurs when sentence structure changes markedly. For example, a reader might be taken aback by a series of three SHORT SENTENCES near the end of an otherwise friendly letter. Similarly, a reader might be put off by a long, complex sentence in an otherwise informal letter. Therefore revise your correspondence for consistent tone.

For more help in choosing the appropriate tone, see the following more specific entries: GENERAL CORRESPONDENCE LETTERS; REQUESTS FOR PAYMENT; or TOUGH, SOUNDING THAT WAY. For related information, see WORD CHOICE and SENTENCE STRUCTURE.

6. Opening and closing.

(a) Including or omitting salutations.

In general letter writing, include a salutation. Some writers omit the salutation in business letters, substituting instead a subject line, and this is not technically wrong. Omitting the line, however, makes the letter seem rather abrupt and impersonal, which is not usually the tone you want in a letter. In email, use the salutation to create a friendlier and more courteous opening.

(b) Writing non-sexist openings.

Use the title your reader prefers. If you do not know that preference and do not even know the sex of the person to whom you are writing, substitute the name without a title.

Dear D.A. Young:

Dear Terry Holmes:

If you do not know a name, use the person's title, or some appropriate generic term.

Dear Administrator:

Dear Client:

If you cannot come up with even a generic term, you may use the following.

Dear Sir or Madam:

Use *Dear Sir* only when you are sure the reader is male.

(c) Choosing commas or colons for salutations.

Use colons in business writing. If you are writing something that is a social courtesy, such as a thank you note or an expression of congratulations, you may use a comma. A colon would also be appropriate, except in a note that is much more personal than businesslike in tone. Use commas in email.

(d) Choosing an appropriate closing.

Choose the standard closing that suits your writing STYLE and the tone of your letter. If the tone of your letter or email is businesslike and yet friendly, use *Sincerely* or *Sincerely yours*. If your tone is more formal, use *Yours truly* or *Very truly yours*. Use these or other comfortable closings in email to create a courteous ending. Do not worry about seeming insincere; these closings are not taken literally.

Using innovative alternatives, rather than underscoring your sincerity, would only create undesirable responses. If you used something more accurate, like *Don't bother me anymore*, you would seem unprofessional or petulant. If you omitted the closing, you would create a distant, impersonal tone, even in email, which is not usually what you want.

GENERALLY

Generally is an adverb that means *for the most part* or *usually*. Be careful to use it in its exact meaning, rather than as a meaningless introduction.

Generally, states do not consider a non-viable fetus a "minor child."

but not

Generally, the defendant is requesting a pardon.

GERUNDS

Gerunds are NOUNS formed from the *-ing* form of a verb.

Seeing is believing.

Using gerunds can often make a sentence more concise.

Imagining alone does not constitute intent.

rather than

The act of imagination alone does not constitute intent.

Gerunds, however, sometimes create subjects that are too long. Remember to keep the subject and verb within seven words of each other, for readability.

Any attorney finds it difficult to master both persuasive and objective writing.

rather than

Becoming a writer equally skilled in both persuasive and objective legal writing is difficult for any attorney.

GETTING ORGANIZED

For help here, choose the entry most closely related to your concern: GETTING STARTED, OUTLINES, ORGANIZATION FOR THOSE WHO CAN'T OUTLINE, WRITING BLOCKS, or WRITING PROCESS.

GETTING STARTED

You may have trouble getting started for any of several reasons. You may dread the job because it is boring, difficult, or crucial to your career. You may not know where to start. Or you may be stuck in the first step. Do not despair; all of these problems are fixable. But to solve these problems you may have to change your approach to the problem. For related information, see WRITING BLOCKS and HABITS, WRITING.

1. When you dread the job.

Try listing what needs to be done and then dividing the tasks on the list into subtasks. Keep dividing them until you get down to tasks that are small enough to feel manageable. Even if the list seems very long, just start completing the tasks one by one. If time is short, do first those tasks essential to the job, such as clear organization, and then those tasks desirable but not necessary, such as emphatic sentence structure. For help determining these tasks, see TRIAGE. For more ideas, see DEADLINES, MEETING THEM.

Sometimes you may dread the job because it is important to you, and you fear failure. If this is the case, do not hesitate to begin the job. You will not feel any better if you procrastinate, and your chance of success will be lessened. Instead, proceed quickly to divide the writing into subtasks, as described in the previous paragraph. Additionally, divide your goal of sufficient quality into subtasks. For example, focus first on getting some ideas on paper. As a second step, focus on getting all the supporting sources listed. Later focus on explaining each point clearly, and then, separately, explaining how those points fit together, like a syllogism, to make your point. Save concerns about conciseness, clarity, grammar, and other qualities for the revision process. When the job is important, you especially need to divide and conquer, and you need to do it early in the writing process.

2.   When you do not know where to start.

Start anywhere. Many people think that they have to start with an outline, but in reality you can start in any of several places. For example, you might start drafting one subpoint of the Discussion of a memo because you understand that particular point best. Or you might start by trying to get your QUESTIONS PRESENTED exactly right. In a law review article, you might start with one sentence that sums up the point of your whole article, not worrying about whether that sentence will appear in the final draft. Then you could list the points needed to back up that statement and develop that list into an OUTLINE. For more ideas, see PREWRITING.

3.   When you are stuck.

Sometimes shifting your writing medium may help. For example, leave the computer screen and walk to a colleague's office to talk about the topic. After a few minutes, you may be able to return to the computer with a clearer idea of what you want to say. Or you might shift to writing on a notebook or dictating. Often just looking away from the text you have written and talking to yourself helps you find the words you need.

Alternatively, try starting at a different point in the document. For example, if you cannot get the Question Presented right, try writing the Discussion or the Argument. If the Discussion or Argument is rambling, try writing your Conclusion; that may help you see how to organize the Discussion. You may discover that starting with any one of these always helps you get the job done more efficiently. The best starting place for one person is not the best for another, so experiment to discover what works for you. Remember, good writing does not depend on whether you start in the right place; it depends on whether you do all you need to before you stop.

GHOST WRITING

As a legal writer, you may be called upon to become a ghost writer, to write documents for another author in that author's style. You may be asked to write a letter or email from a supervising attorney, signed by her, not you, that speaks in her voice. To do this well, you can study the attorney's writing characteristics. Some authors use short sentences and words to create blunt, businesslike effect. Others eschew formality, using contractions, informal language, and short paragraphs. Yet others are consistently formal, never splitting infinitives and employing the subjunctive mood.

You may consider the writing "good," "bad," or otherwise; ghost writing requires you to set aside that judgment and to imitate for the sake of perpetuating the author's work. Such imitation yields two advantages: you learn more about writing by reverse engineering another's work, and you earn accolades for being someone whose writing resembles the author's.

This book's entries offer categories for studying an author's writing characteristics, such as ORGANIZATION, OUTLINES, TOPIC SENTENCES, HEADINGS, SENTENCE LENGTH, SENTENCE STRUCTURE, TONE, WORD CHOICE, JARGON, FLOWERY LANGUAGE, and VOICE. As you reverse engineer another author's writing, consider the following, in addition to the entries listed above.

1. Ask about the author's preferences.

Ask your author about particular writing characteristics that he or she values. Some authors will give specific directions on being *terse, elegant,* or *no nonsense.* Translate these qualities into the appropriate writing choices, as described below.

2. Consider other variables.

Note the document's setting and audience. If it is a letter to a familiar client, you may be imitating an informal, friendly approach; if it is the third pretrial brief in tiresome litigation, you may be imitating an impatient, curt approach.

3. Collect and review samples.

Ask your author to provide some samples, or research to find samples of the author's work. Try to get at least three samples of the kind of writing you are imitating, such as a letter, formal email, brief, contract, or opinion. As you review samples of the author's other writing, note the author's writing patterns in this particular kind of document.

(a) Consider how the author presents the subject of the document. For example, the author may use any of the following.

- An sentence toward the beginning or the document
- Formal issue statements
- A paragraph at the end of the introductory section
- A preamble
- A separate section later in the document

(b) Consider the document's structure. For example, the author may use any of the following structural devises.

- Headings
- Strong topic sentences
- A paragraph describing the document's structure
- An outline format
- Bullet points

Also consider the logical flow that your author prefers. For example, the author may develop points in any of the following ways

- From general point to specific support, or deductive
- From specific example to general point, or inductive
- From illustrative example to general point to specific support
- From familiar to new information
- From the reader's preferences to contrary views
- In the order traditionally used when discussing these points
- By the major policies behind the points

(c) Consider how your author tends to group information. Some authors work with larger groups of information, others prefer smaller groups. For example, you may notice any of the following in your author's writing.

- Frequent paragraphs running one-half a page
- Frequent short or one-sentence paragraphs
- Frequent sentences running more than four lines
- Frequent sentences running one line or less
- Frequent use of several long sentences followed by a short one that acts as a punch line
- Headings or subheadings appearing on every page
- Headings or subheadings appearing on every fourth page
- Relatively long and detailed headings
- Relatively short and spare headings

(d) Consider the writer's word choice. Just as some attorneys choose to dress more formally than others, some writers choose different levels of formality and register in their words and sentence structures. For example, your writer may frequently use any of the following.

- Formal or scholarly words
- Down-to-earth or familiar words
- Strong subject-verb combinations
- Intransitive subject-verb combinations, such as *there are* or *it is.*
- Short words
- Multi-syllabic words
- Nominalizations
- Intrusive phrases
- Long introductory phrases
- Lists
- Specific and detailed descriptions
- General, broader descriptions
- Rhetorical questions

(e) Consider how strictly the author honors conventions. For example, determine which of the following conventions are important to this author.

- Bluebook conventions
- ALWD citation conventions
- Comma usage
- Editing of quotations
- Use of italics
- Use of quotation marks
- Use of parenthesis
- Use of underlining or boldface for emphasis

4. Try to hear the author speaking.

Look for patterns in tone and voice. You may even want to tape record the author, with permission, so that you can translate the voice accurately to the page.

By being a good ghost writer, you create a document ready-made for the author. By analyzing her writing, you add to your own repertoire of writing techniques. Even if you would not choose to use the same patterns, your awareness of her patterns makes you more selective of your own. When you have this imitative writing opportunity, enjoy it as a way of building your writing repertoire.

GIVEN THAT

See BEING THAT.

GOOD OR *WELL?*

Use *good* to modify a noun.

She had good reason to doubt his word.

Use *well* to modify a verb or an adjective.

She could hear well enough to understand the general topic of the defendants' conversation.

Use *good* after *feel*, because *good* here modifies the subject, not the verb.

I feel good about this decision.

Well would be correct only if you were talking about your ability to feel physically, which almost never comes up in writing. For related information, see BAD OR BADLY?

GRAMMAR

Grammar refers to the rules for constructing communications in a language. In contrast, *usage* refers to how words are used by native speakers and *style* is a more amorphous concept that usually implies a set of additional conventions adopted by a particular set of writers, such as journalists, scientists, or scholars. Differing from the reader's expectations in any of these areas may make the meaning awkward, ambiguous, or hard to understand, but grammar errors make it incorrect.

As in other kinds of professional writing, grammar counts in legal writing. An error in grammar usually makes the communication inaccurate or unclear. Grammatical mistakes are potholes in the superhighway of a presentation. Therefore, use grammar carefully to convey your legal ideas clearly, and revise specifically for its proper use. For help in this area, see POLISHING.

For specific grammar information, see PARTS OF SPEECH; SENTENCE STRUCTURE; VERBS, TENSES; MODIFIERS; PARALLEL STRUCTURE; SUBJECT–VERB AGREEMENT and PUNCTUATION.

GRAPHICS, HOW TO USE

Graphics aids may be as elaborate as flow charts and three-dimensional graphs, or as simple as subheadings and tabulation. But in all situations, the graphics should support and clarify the information in the document's text. They should also be understandable even when the text of your document is not read. To make sure your graphic aid is effective, first make sure it is needed (for more on this, see GRAPHICS, WHEN

TO USE). Then, when preparing the graphic, observe the following guidelines.

- Keep graphic aids as simple as possible.
- Make sure that the graphic aid and the text both communicate the message.
- Avoid overusing graphic aids in a document.
- Make each graphic an accurate visual representation of the content.

The technology and the audience's acceptance have reached the point where graphics will be more widely used. As these innovations move into the legal world, be prepared to use new tools, such as color, boxes, and lines. No matter what tool you are using, follow these guidelines.

1. Keep graphic aids as simple as possible.

The reader sees a graphic presentation as a whole first; then the eye scans around the graphic for details. To make the most of that first impression, omit any information that distracts from the main point. For example, if you wanted to communicate that the chance of a drowning occurring increases as the depth of a pool approaches 15 feet, and that this correlation is more significant than other factors, you would first present a graph establishing the correlation with depth.

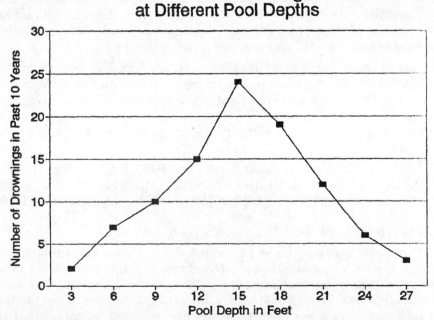

Then you would explain that this correlation was stronger than other factors, perhaps representing each other factor in a separate graph, like the one below, that could be compared with the first.

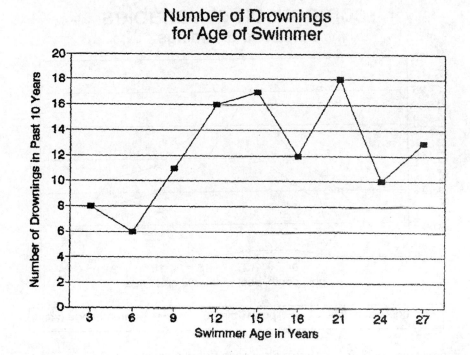

Number of Drownings
for Age of Swimmer

Avoid trying to present all the information in one graph; so much information together is likely to confuse the point rather than underscore it.

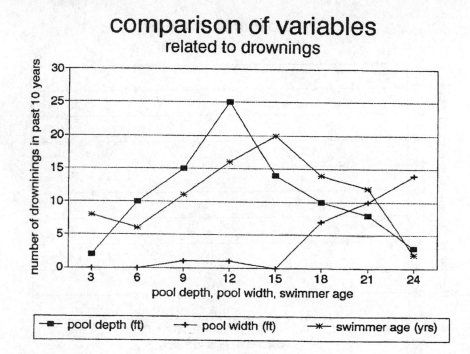

Separating the information makes each point clearer.

2. Make sure that the graphic aid and the text both communicate the message

Some readers will skip the text and go directly to the graphics. For that reason, word your titles and legends to communicate the same message as your text. Other readers will skip the graphics, so summarize in the text any message illustrated in the graphics.

Map of Intersection

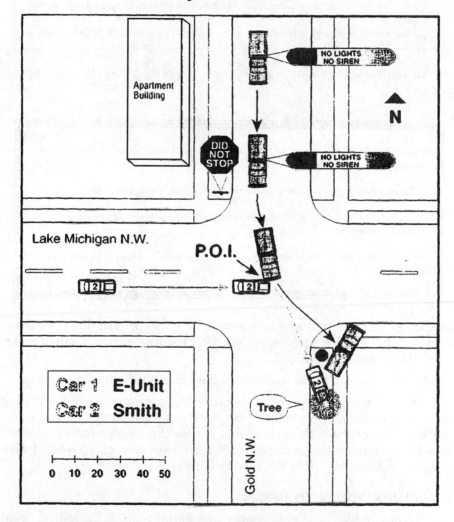

Visual Evidence Center, Inc. Reprinted with permission.

Checking the correlation of graphics and text will also help you as a writer. Because graphics are generated separately from the text, they can become isolated from the text in the writer's mind. To keep this from happening, compare the text and graphics when REVISING, looking specifically for any differences that could confuse the reader.

3. Avoid overusing graphic aids in a document

    For example, the following text is visually clear and appealing.

When using boldface, check each page by reading the boldface words only. Check for the following qualities.

- The meaning of the words in boldface is clear without reading other text.
- The number of phrases in boldface is enough that the point of using bold is intuitively clear.
- The number of phrases in boldface is not so great that the effect of emphasis is lost.

In contrast, the following version is too busy to be clear or appealing.

When using boldface, *check each page* by reading the boldface words only. *Check for* <u>the following qualities</u>.

*The *meaning* of the words in boldface **is clear without reading** other text.

The *number* of phrases in boldface **is enough that the point of using bold **is** intuitively **clear.**

***The *number* of phrases in boldface **is not so great that the effect** of emphasis **is lost.**

Similarly, avoid using too many graphs or tables within one document. Just as with writing techniques for EMPHASIS, graphics can distract more than clarify if overused.

4. Make each graphic an accurate visual representation of the content

    The format of a graphic presentation communicates something about the content, even before the reader sees the numbers and other specific data involved. Because of this, choose the graphic form that most clearly communicates your point. For an overview of possible forms graphs can take, see GRAPHICS, WHICH FORM TO USE.

GRAPHICS, WHEN TO USE

Graphs, tables, and other such illustrations can be useful in legal writing. They can, for example, help illustrate the location of vehicles in an accident, show the significance of complex statistics on damage awards, summarize a company's financial situation, and explain complicated technological processes.

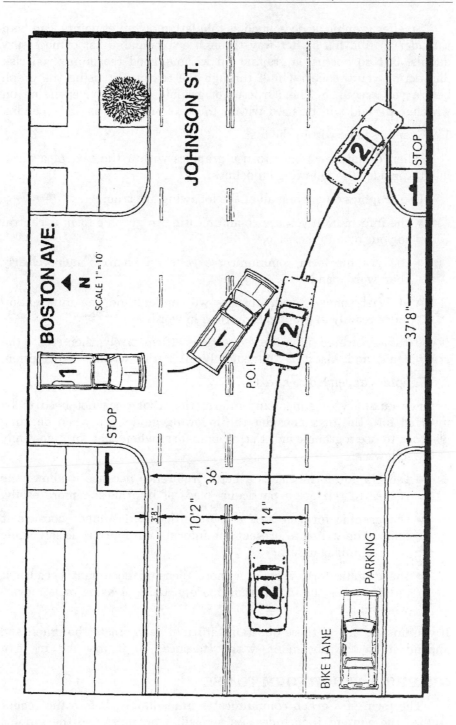

Visual Evidence Center, Inc.

Smaller graphic devices, such as tabulation or bullet points, can help a reader to find his or her way through a formidable list of necessary details. But do not use a graphic aid without good reason, or you risk distracting your reader. Think through the reason for using the graph before you create it. The purposes of graphic aids vary depending on whether the aid will be used within the text or added as an appendix.

1. Graphics used within the text.

When deciding whether to use graphics within the text of a document, consider the following guidelines.

Use graphics only when all of the following are true:

- the information you are communicating in graphic form is central to your overall message,

- the graphic form communicates your information more clearly than words, and

- at least some of your readers will understand the information more readily in graphic form than in words.

If you have answered all of these questions affirmatively, then create the graphic aid and insert it immediately after the written explanation.

2. Graphics appended to a text.

For auxiliary or supporting information that does not need to be inserted into the text, consider the following guidelines when deciding whether to use a graphic aid. Use graphic form when that form does any of the following:

- the graphic form makes a better reference because it allows the reader to retrieve a particular piece of information more easily,

- the graphic form creates a more efficient document because it allows the writer to present the information more concisely while maintaining clarity, or

- the graphic form creates a more pleasing document because it either makes the information more visually pleasing or less overwhelming.

If you answer any of these questions affirmatively, create the graph and append it to the document, with references to it inserted in text.

GRAPHICS, WHICH FORM TO USE

The form of a graph communicates immediately, before the reader studies the content it includes. As a result, you must use the graphic form that accurately conveys your meaning. Some common graphics and their uses are outlined below.

170

1. Pie charts.

Pie charts usually show how a whole unit is apportioned between subcategories. For example, they can show how much of your work day is devoted to various legal tasks or what portions of a company's income come from different sources.

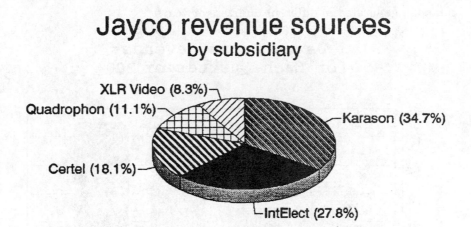

Jayco revenue sources
by subsidiary

Pie charts are the natural choice for showing how a whole is divided, especially because most audiences are familiar with this use. But avoid using them for other purposes, because most would be confused by that non-standard use.

2.   Bar graphs.

These graphs usually show how the quantity of something changes across the items compared. They suggest a pile of something, such as money, and so are particularly useful for this kind of information. For example, they can show how many complaints a company received over time regarding an item it continued to produce or how much income a company generated in different quarters or years.

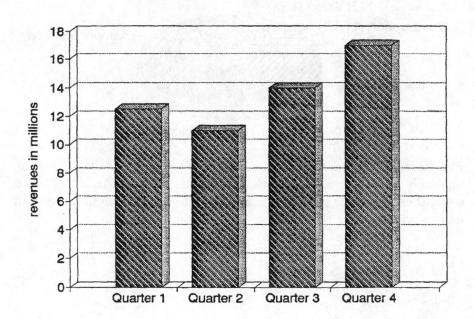

Jayco Gross Revenues
for Each Quarter of 2004

Watch the arrangement of bar graphs to make sure that you do not communicate an upward or downward trend if you do not intend to do so. For example, the following graph suggests bad news where none was intended, solely because of the order in which the categories are placed.

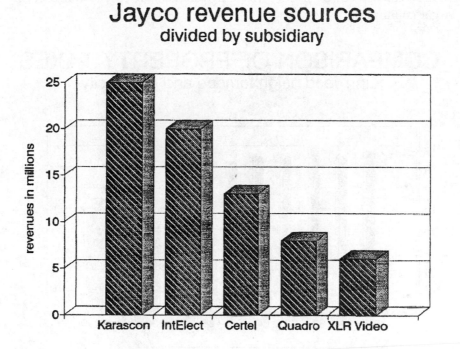

3. Stacked bar graphs or side-by-side bar graphs.

These formats enable bar graphs to compare two quantities to each other while also showing how both change across the items compared. For example, a side-by-side bar graph could show how one neighborhood's real estate taxes have risen in comparison to the taxes of the larger community.

COMPARISON OF PROPERTY TAXES
Linnwood neighborhood and rest of city

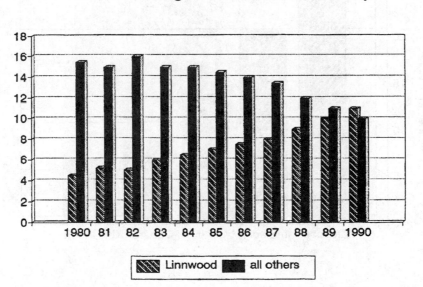

A stacked bar graph could show how the neighborhood's taxes have risen even while the overall community's tax rate remained relatively unchanged.

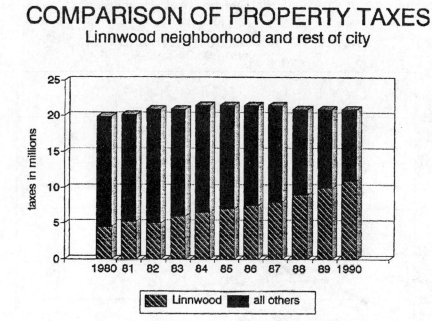

COMPARISON OF PROPERTY TAXES
Linnwood neighborhood and rest of city

4.   Line graphs.

Line graphs often show change across time or compare two variables that interact. These graphs suggest numbers and change, more than the discrete quantities that bar graphs suggest. For example, line graphs can illustrate the variability in a fire station's response time, or the rise in accident rates at a particular intersection over several years.

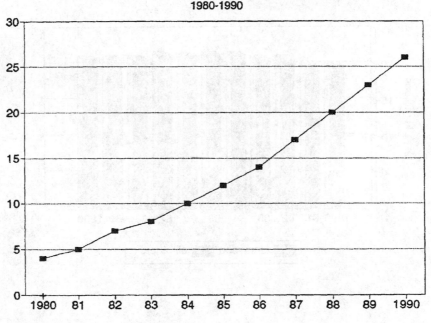

NUMBER OF ACCIDENTS AT 12TH AND VINE
1980-1990

5.   Tables.

These divide data into discrete categories and coordinate those categories so any reader in your audience can find a particular category quickly. A table also organizes and unifies data, so the detail does not overwhelm any reader. For example, a table could chart how many clients came to a firm with each particular legal problem a firm handles, how many problems were subsequently settled out of court, and how many went to trial. (See next page.)

To design useful tables, you need to determine

• what information your audience needs and

• what kind of category is most likely to be meaningful to that audience.

Then divide the information about those categories into groups that answer questions the audience will have. This step is important, because often the categories that are meaningful to the audience differ from those that occur first to the writer. For example, when categorizing patients denied health coverage, you might first think of grouping them by the reason coverage was denied. Your reader, however, might be more concerned about the nature of the coverage denied, the effect of different state regulations on denial, or the cost that providing that coverage would have entailed. As always, be governed by what will be convenient and effective for the reader, rather than for the writer.

Summary of 2004 Cases by Problem and Settlement Level

Cases		Level at Which Settled					
Client	Problem	Prelim. Corres.	Pre-Trial	Trial	Pre-Appeal	Post-Appeal	Total
Family	Custody	2	3	2	40	23	70
	Child Support	3	3	21	45	9	81
	Maintenance	5	9	12	23	9	54
	Other	15	20	4	3	0	42
Business	Contract Litig.	2	7	2	0	1	12
	Debtor	36	35	15	5	0	91
	Other	8	8	14	0	0	30
Injury	Worker's Comp.	0	2	13	0	2	17
	Tort	10	36	34	4	2	86
	Other	3	15	7	2	0	27
Total		**84**	**138**	**124**	**122**	**46**	**510**

For related information, see GRAPHICS, WHEN TO USE and GRAPHICS, HOW TO USE.

GRAPHICS AND SYMBOLS IN EMAIL

See SYMBOLS IN EMAIL.

HABITS, WRITING

Habits form in writing just as they do everywhere else. Good writing habits can make work more effective, efficient, and pleasant. Because legal writing often requires high efficiency in short periods of time, keeping bad writing habits can cost both you and your client. Old habits die hard; you must consciously kill them. Therefore, in moving from the prewriting stage through writing, rewriting, revising, and polishing, consider which habits work for you and which habits do not. Then start with the most troublesome habit and eradicate it by replacing it with a better habit. For example, if you habitually try to revise each sentence as you write, you will probably find that the writing process has become very time-consuming and agonizing. Instead, try giving yourself a time limit and forcing yourself to write without any revision until you finish your first draft. Then go back and rewrite. Similarly, if you spend too much time doing research, you may not have enough time for the actual writing. Instead, pause periodically in your research and reevaluate your document's purpose and scope. Streamline your research strategies accordingly. Determine how much time you need to write and allocate time accordingly.

For suggestions for breaking habits in each stage of the WRITING PROCESS, see PREWRITING, WRITING, REWRITING, REVISING, and POLISHING. For help in facing the writing process itself, see

GETTING STARTED, RESEARCH STRATEGY CHART, PROCRASTI-NATION, and WRITING BLOCKS.

HANGED OR *HUNG?*

If you are talking about a person being *hanged by the neck until dead*, use *hanged*. If you are talking about *hung* in any other sense, such as a thing *hung on the wall*, use *hung*. Informally, you may refer to a *hung jury*.

HARDLY

Hardly is more informal than its synonyms *scarcely* or *nearly*, so avoid it in formal writing, such as MEMOS and BRIEFS. See also *CAN HARDLY* OR *CAN'T HARDLY?*

HEADINGS

In most legal writing, headings identify the subsections of a memo, email, brief, letter, or article. Headings should ease the eye and the mind of the reader, so that the legal analysis is easier to follow. In briefs, headings take the specific form of point headings, subheadings, and sub-subheadings, which outline the specific legal points of the argument and the reasoning behind those points. These headings should be sufficient to communicate the basic legal argument even when read without the text. In memos, headings distinguish each part of the memo, such as Questions Presented, Brief Answers, Discussion, and Conclusion. Subheadings may be used to divide the Discussion Section, so that the reader can see at a glance which legal issues are being discussed where. Usually these subheadings take the form of a label, such as

False Imprisonment

or

Jurisdiction

although a sentence can be even more helpful.

This District Court Has Jurisdiction.

In long opinion letters, subheadings similarly subdivide the explanation. The same is true with articles.

In your headings and subheadings, try to convey a definite message to the reader. Use complete sentences rather than single words or abstract phrases. When appropriate, use parallel structure to convey your theme from one heading to the next. Include law, facts, and other information specific to your analysis, so the reader can understand the overall logic and content just by reading the headings. For related information, see ARTICLES, PUBLISHED and POINT HEADINGS.

HEADNOTES

Headnotes are numbered paragraphs in legal reporters that summarize the legal points of a court's opinion. These summaries are written by the editors of the reporter in which the case appears, and they appear before the actual text of the case begins.

Headnotes are designed as research tools to aid the reader in using the case. For example, if you are researching intentional torts and a case contains, among others, a procedural headnote on jurisdiction and a substantive headnote on intentional torts, then you can use the headnote number to find the section of the case discussing intentional torts where that number reappears. Using that headnote, you can update just that section of the case on intentional torts. See UPDATING THE LAW.

Because headnotes are research tools and are not written by judges, never cite to a headnote. Also, never depend on the headnote to supply your understanding of the case. Read the text and check whether you believe the case indeed covers this point.

HELP

If you have turned to this, you are probably in the midst of your writing process and under pressure. Consult the most relevant of the following entries: GETTING STARTED; OUTLINES; ORGANIZATION FOR THOSE WHO CAN'T OUTLINE; WRITING BLOCKS; WRITING PROCESS; WHEN TO STOP; or DEADLINES, MEETING THEM. Also look for an entry under the particular kind of writing that concerns you, such as ARTICLES, PUBLISHED; BRIEFS; CASE BRIEFS; CONTRACTS, DRAFTING; GENERAL CORRESPONDENCE LETTERS; MEMOS; and so forth. If none of these entries seems right, consult the master list of entries in the front of the book. You can get the job done one step at a time. Divide the tasks and conquer.

HELPING VERBS

See VERBS, TENSES and VERBS, AUXILIARY.

HE OR SHE?

When the sex of the person referred to is unknown, *he or she* is preferable to *s/he* or *he*. For a general discussion of this question, see SEXIST LANGUAGE, WAYS TO AVOID.

HEREBY

Avoid using this term unless absolutely needed. See LEGALESE.

HE/SHE, WHEN TO USE?

Use this construction only in a form document when the signer is meant to strike out the inappropriate form. Otherwise, use *he or she,* or *she or he.* The slash version saves the writer's energy at the cost of the reader's. Do not ask the reader to make a decision you should have made. For related information, see S/HE or SEXIST LANGUAGE, WAYS TO AVOID.

HOLD

Courts *hold*; counsel does not.

For related information, see *FIND, HOLD*, OR *REASONED*? and TERMS OF ART.

HOLDING

The holding is the decision a court reaches in a case. A holding thus disposes of an issue raised in the case, whether procedural or substantive. As such, it theoretically binds that court and those under it to follow that decision in making subsequent holdings in similar legal situations. Therefore, holdings often provide the focal point for research constructing arguments, and measuring the strength of a client's case. Consider the following in using case holdings.

1. In CASE BRIEFS.

    Use the holding to state the answer to the Issue and give a reason for that answer.

    > **Yes; Curtis falsely imprisoned Butterworth because he used words or acts that intended to confine Butterworth, he actually confined her in the car, and Butterworth was aware that she was confined.**

    For related information, see ISSUES, DICTA, and CASE BRIEFS.

2. In a MEMO.

    Use holdings to explain rules.

    > **Hospitalization for alcohol abuse does not preclude being awarded custody of a child. Nagle v. Nagle, 941 P.2d 1, 3 (Utah 2005). But long-term institutionalization because of drug dependency does preclude an award of custody. James v. James, 944 P.3d 433 (Utah 2004).**

    Use holdings to describe analogous cases.

    > **In Nagle, the mother was awarded custody of the daughter despite her previous hospitalization for alcohol abuse. Nagle, at 3. And in Carter, the mother was awarded custody when she showed successful completion of an Alcholics Anonymous program. Carter, at 767.**

    For related information, see RULES and ANALOGOUS CASES.

3. In BRIEFS.

    Use a holding to argue.

180

> Even a mother who has been hospitalized for alcohol abuse can win custody of her daughter. <u>Nagle v. Nagle</u>, 941 P.2d 1, 3 (2005).

4. In PARENTHETICALS.

State the holding as it relates to the use of the cases.

> **Artists must look outside the moral rights doctrine for protection. <u>See Peabody v. Percival</u>, 999 F.2d 17 (9th Cir. 2004) (holding that moral right is limited in the U.S., so breach of contract can be used to compensate artists whose work is mutilated).**

HOLDING OR *RULE?*

A holding is the outcome in a specific case, such as the following.

> **The Court awarded custody to the father because he was able to spend more time with and provide more of a safe environment for two children, ages 10 and 12.**

Although you may accurately use "the court held" to introduce a holding, this phrase usually is unnecessary. A rule is the law that was used to reach the holding, such as the following.

> **In this jurisdiction, the court awards custody to the parent who can better serve the child's best interests.**

Use the rule to establish the foundation of your analysis or argument. Use the holdings to define and illustrate how the law works, and to demonstrate the parameters of the law as applied previously.

HOPEFULLY

Use *it is hoped* or *I hope*. Use *hopefully* only when you mean that something was done in a hopeful way.

> **The Pilgrims sailed hopefully for America.**

It is rare that you will mean this. While *hopefully* is used widely in speaking, it is not yet accepted as meaning *it is hoped* in formal writing.

HOWEVER

However has two different uses: as a transition and as an adverb. Each use can cause problems for the legal writer.

1. As a transition.

However is a concise way of saying something roughly equivalent to *on the other hand*; it signals a shift to the other side or a contrasting subpoint. One way this may be done is to place *however* right after a semicolon joining two sentences.

The defendant has testified that he was not present at the scene of the crime; however, two witnesses have contradicted this.

When using *however* this way, do not use it with only a comma. You must put a semicolon before *however* and a comma after. The semicolon is necessary because however is not a conjunction, like *and* or *but*.

The court remanded the case; however, the plaintiff did not receive an appreciably higher reward.

rather than

The court remanded the case, however, the plaintiff did not receive an appreciably higher reward.

Another way *however* may be used as a transition is to place it a few words into a sentence.

The defendant has testified that he was not present at the scene of the crime. Two witnesses, however, have contradicted this.

2. As an adverb.

As an adverb, *however* modifies a part of the sentence rather than serving as a transition between sentences.

However it happened, the fact remains that the defendant lost use of his arm as a result of this accident.

Often this use of *however* sounds awkward in formal writing. In this situation, you may substitute another phrase.

No matter how it happened, ...

or

Regardless of the cause of the accident, ...

Avoid overusing the word. If, for example, you see *however* appearing in every paragraph you write, you are probably overusing it. To correct the problem, first check your organization: Are you trying to cover two points that would be better presented in two separate paragraphs? Are you wavering between two views, avoiding taking a stand when it is your job to take a stand? If so, see ORGANIZATION and PARAGRAPHS for possible solutions. Second, check the accuracy of your word choice: Are you using *however* when you really mean *nevertheless, additionally*, or something else? See TRANSITIONS for a list of transition words that may communicate your point more accurately. Usually the answers to these questions will show you how you must revise. If not, consider using synonyms for *however* to avoid overusing it.

HUMOR

Effective humor is a deft and welcome stroke in legal writing, but it requires a precise choice of location and time. Some judges may find humor a welcome relief when working on a case, so it may be effective to file a complaint in the form of poetry or to make light of a minor point in a brief. Be particularly sensitive, however, to all audiences; the client may not be amused. Also do not use humor with a serious topic, as with any behavior causing serious harm to someone. When legal writing is reaching an audience not so immediately involved in the topic, such as in scholarly writing, you may use humor to underscore your point or perk up interest. Do not, however, insert humor that does not assist in your purpose. For related information, see VOICE and PURPOSE.

HUNG OR HANGED?

See *HANGED* OR *HUNG*?

HYPERBOLE

Hyperbole is an excessive exaggeration used as a figure of speech; avoid it generally, because its excesses often reduce the writer's credibility, as in the following examples.

Defendant was dying to get out of the courtroom.

The judge hung the defendant out to dry.

HYPHENS

Hyphens have three uses: (1) dividing words at the end of a line, (2) joining MODIFIERS that work together, and (3) connecting some prefixes to words.

1.   Dividing words at the end of a line.

You may use a hyphen to divide a long word coming at the end of a line. Check the dictionary if you are not sure where the hyphen should go. Do not hyphenate proper names and avoid hyphenating at the end of a page, as a favor to your reader. With word processors that allow proportional spacing, however, hyphens are seldom used in this way.

2.   Joining modifiers that work together.

Use a hyphen to signal that the words hyphenated work together to modify a subsequent noun: *bone-jarring blow, high-pitched voice, work-related expenses, owner-occupied housing, thirty-seven-year-old male*, or *three- to five-year sentence*. There are two exceptions to this rule. Proper names are not hyphenated: *Southeast Asian conflict, Supreme Court opinion, West Coast phenomenon*. Also, modifying words are not hyphenated when they follow a linking verb, rather than preceding the word they modify.

The blow was bone jarring.

rather than

The blow was bone-jarring.

183

For more examples, see ADJECTIVES AFTER A LINKING VERB.

3. Connecting some prefixes to words.

    Also use a hyphen to connect some prefixes.

    (a) You may use a hyphen when adding a prefix to a proper name: *un-American, ex-President Clinton.*

    (b) Use a hyphen when the prefix ends with the same vowel that begins the main word: *re-examine, semi-independent.*

    (c) Use a hyphen with *self-* as a prefix to another noun: *self-employed, self-sufficient.* For more examples, see *SELF-* OR *SELF?*

    (d) Use a hyphen with ex- when it means former: *ex-wife.*

    (e) Use a hyphen whenever omitting it will confuse readers.

    He wanted to re-lease the apartment.

    Or reword the sentence to avoid the problem.

    He wanted to lease the apartment again.

I

Use this pronoun when referring to yourself doing your job. Thus in a letter to a client, write the following, rather than resorting to passive voice.

I have forwarded the forms to the IRS.

But do not use *I* in other circumstances. Keep the focus on the content, not the writer. So in a brief you might conclude as follows:

The defendant was fairly treated.

But you would not write this sentence because your point of view is implied and the court will do the concluding.

I therefore conclude that the defendant was fairly treated.

For a general discussion of the reasons behind this use of *I*, see TONE, subsection 1(b).

IDIOM

An *idiom* is an expression or phrase that is acceptable English even though it cannot be understood by interpreting the literal meaning of its elements.

We gave them up.

or

How do you do?

Idioms are often metaphors that have become so common that the original metaphorical image is lost: *to catch a cold* or *to strike a bargain.* Avoid idioms that are ambiguous in context or that sound too informal.

He dropped off the package.

He was reeling from the bad decision below.

The judge caught the drift of his argument.

Many idioms are informal, and thus should be avoided in documents such as briefs to the court, contracts, and other public documents.

I.E.

The abbreviation *i.e.* stands for *id est*, or *that is*. As an abbreviation, you may use *i.e.* in place of those two words, particularly in the context of further explanation, as in an explanatory footnote.

The 12(b)(6) motion succeeded, i.e., the case was dismissed.

Avoid using *i.e.* in text, such as a business letter or formal documents, such as wills, because it can create ambiguity. Use *that is* or another appropriate phrase instead, surrounded by commas.

On June 4, 2005, she initiated the action, that is, filed the motion.

rather than

On June 4, 2005, she initiated the action, i.e., filed the motion.

He agreed to the condition when he signed the waiver.

rather than

He agreed to the condition, i.e., he signed the waiver.

Avoid confusing *i.e.* with *e.g.*; *i.e.* introduces a phrase that explains in other words, but *e.g.* introduces an example.

IF

If is useful in legal writing because *if* has only one meaning, and therefore provides a precise transition between clauses. Because *if* is precise and because you will often be writing about points that logically are *if . . . then* situations, do not worry too much about overusing *if*. Worry only when several sentences in a paragraph contain *if* and when those *if's* are not logically parallel. For related information, see SENTENCE STRUCTURE, subsection 3 and TRANSITIONS.

If the *if* phrase is quite long, use a *then* after the comma at the end of the *if* phrase.

If the court extends this reasoning to include all victims of industrial accidents, then Harris can establish a cause of action.

IF AND WHEN

Delete the *and when; if* says it all.

IF OR *WHEN?*

Use *if* when you are suggesting that something may or may not happen.

If the bill is not paid within 60 days, the refrigerator will be repossessed.

Use *when* when you are discussing something that will happen.

When the electricians complete their work, the inspector will set up an appointment to see the house.

Thus, on some occasions, you may choose between *if* and *when* to suggest pessimism or optimism about the likelihood of something happening.

When our candidate is elected, the convention center will be built.

or

If the campaign were to fail, the convention center would remain on the drafting board.

When using *if* to suggest that something will not happen, also shift the verb to the subjunctive mood. For more explanation, see VERBS, MOODS.

IMAGERY

Imagery has as much power in legal writing as it does anywhere else. Giving a reader an image that captures a legal situation can be more persuasive than pages of traditional legal proof. Imagery can also be memorable for its misuse and can suggest other arguments or responses that detract from the main issues. Use imagery sparingly, then, to capture what cannot be done in a better way.

Defendant's actions conform to every element of the statute.

rather than

Defendant went out in a blaze of glory.

but

Defendant landscaped his tax garden with a variety of perennial loopholes.

rather than

Defendant violated many tax laws.

When using imagery, focus your fire. Develop one image that can remain in the reader's memory. If your creative juices are flowing and you create many wonderful images, resist the urge to include them all. Choose the one best image and save the others for another day.

IMPACT

Use *impact* as a noun.

The impact caused extensive damages to defendant's vehicle.

The impact of such a decision would be far reaching.

Although *impact* is sometimes used as a verb, as in *to impact a decision*, this use is not yet acceptable in formal English, and its meaning is vague. As a verb, *impact* should refer only to such things as teeth.

His wisdom tooth was impacted.

IMPERATIVE MOOD

See VERBS, MOODS, subsection 3.

IMPLY OR *INFER*?

These words are not interchangeable. *Imply* means to *suggest* or to *express indirectly*. *Infer* means to *surmise* or to *derive a conclusion from the information*. As a result, use *imply* when the subject is a piece of writing, a thing, a speaker, or a writer.

This reasoning implies that . . . .

Use *infer* when the subject is a reader or a listener.

The court inferred from this phrase that . . . .

IN ADVANCE OF

Use *before* for a cleaner, more concise sentence. For a discussion of the general principles behind this, see CONCISENESS, subsection 9.

INCLUDING, BUT NOT LIMITED TO

Including is usually sufficient because it indicates, by definition, that something is a component part of a whole. In modern usage, *including* is replacing the more traditionally explicit phrase *including, but not limited to* when introducing lists in drafting. Nevertheless, many lawyers prefer the latter because it is safer. You may want to check with your audience to decide what to use.

INDENTED QUOTES OR QUOTATION MARKS?

Use quotation marks around direct quotes of forty-nine or fewer words and around titles of articles. When a direct quote is longer than forty-nine words, indent it, single-space it, and omit quotation marks. The only time you will use quotation marks in an indented, single-spaced quote is when there is a quote within the indented quote. For related information, see QUOTATIONS, HOW TO PUNCTUATE.

INDENTING

See QUOTATIONS, HOW TO PUNCTUATE.

INDEPENDENCE IN LEGAL WRITING

You have it; the question is when and how to exercise it. Because legal writing is so dependent on audience needs and preferences, you must ascertain what will be best meet those concerns. As a good architect learns about a client's lifestyle before designing a home, you must learn as much as you can about who will use your document, how often, and how long the document is expected to last, and then build accordingly. You are not building your dream house with each document, so you cannot exercise total independence; rather, you are building something for others to use, so your creativity and independence are exercised in the way you design the document and make it work for your audiences.

You may be writing a quick email response to a colleague, so you can be quite independent. But if you are drafting a contract for two businesses, the contract must last much longer than the current negotiation and must include the results of that negotiation. Similarly, if you are part of a team drafting an appellate brief, your independence is less important you're your teamwork abilities. As a good architectural team, you will need to negotiate everything from the theory to the word choice in order to reach common agreement for the best way to meet the audience's needs. For related ideas, see CHOICES IN LEGAL WRITING, EDITING OTHERS' WRITING, and STYLE.

INDEPENDENT CLAUSE

See CLAUSES or SENTENCE, PARTS OF, subsection 8.

INDICATIVE MOOD

See VERBS, MOODS, subsection 1.

INDIRECT OBJECTS

See SENTENCE, PARTS OF, subsection 5.

INFER OR *IMPLY*?

See *IMPLY* OR *INFER*?

INFINITIVE VERBS

See VERBS, TENSES, subsection 13.

INFORMAL LANGUAGE

See COLLOQUIALISMS.

–ING WORDS

See GERUNDS.

IN, INTO, OR IN TO?

In means *inside of, during, as part of the act or process of,* or *among other things.*

He is in the room.

Into means *to the inside of* or *to the action or occupation of.*

She will go into law.

In to is used when an infinitive verb is used in a prepositional phrase.

My supervisor came in to introduce me to a new client.

The idiom *in to* is too informal for legal writing.

My friend is in to body building.

For related information, see PREPOSITIONS.

INITIALS

When initials are used in a person's name, put a period after the initial.

Helen C. Walrich

When several initials are used in place of a person's first name, use periods after each initial, with no spaces between initials.

D.H. Lawrence

When initials are used in place of a name, use periods with no spaces between initials.

J.F.K.

The name United States is abbreviated when it precedes the word *Government* or when it precedes the name of a government organization. Use periods after the letters, but no spaces.

U.S. Navy

Initials are often used when they are more familiar to the readers than the full written title. When initials are used in place of the full name of a company, organization, or government agency, use no periods and no spaces between the initials.

IBM

NLRB

MIT

NAACP

TVA

But remember the audience. If some of your readers cannot readily decipher the initials, avoid using them, or place the written name in parenthesis after the first use of the initials.

IN ORDER TO OR *TO*?

In legal documents, you can usually skip the first two words. They do not add to the meaning.

Counsel shifted his reasoning to ask for a different remedy.

rather than

Counsel shifted his reasoning in order to ask for a different remedy.

IN QUESTION

This phrase is often used to describe issues under consideration in the present legal analysis or discussion. It is legal jargon. If used frequently, this phrase robs the text of CONCISENESS. Therefore, when possible, avoid this phrase by using *these* or *this*: *these facts*, rather than *the facts in question; these parties* rather than *the parties in question*, or *this issue* rather than *the issue in question*.

INSERTED PHRASES

See INTRUSIVE PHRASES.

INSTANT MESSAGING

See TEXT MESSAGING AND INSTANT MESSAGING.

INSTRUCTIONS TO THE JURY

See JURY INSTRUCTIONS.

INSURE OR *ENSURE*?

See *ENSURE, INSURE,* OR *ASSURE*?

INTERJECTIONS

Interjections are just that, interjections of exclamation.

Outstanding!

Because they are emotional and informal, do not use them in legal writing, except as part of a quote.

IN TERMS OF

Reword to avoid this phrase, because it often invites imprecision.

This court has previously addressed the issue of when adult invitees are responsible for their actions, but not whether minor invitees have equivalent responsibility.

rather than

> The issue is resolved in terms of the responsibilities of adult invitees for their actions, but not of minors for theirs.

INTRUSIVE PHRASES

Intrusive phrases are phrases inserted into a sentence in a way that interrupts the sentence's ordinary flow.

Anorexics, <u>by failing to eat</u>, passively expose themselves to harm.

You may use short intrusive phrases to emphasize a point because the reader will naturally pause to understand and integrate the point in the intrusion.

These facts, which are not common knowledge, illustrate the kind of information expert witnesses can provide.

These issues, controversial and crucial, must nevertheless be resolved.

Dr. Janssen, who attended the defendant in the emergency room, testified that her injuries were caused by the faulty design of the steering wheel.

Do not use phrases longer than approximately seven words, however, because phrases that long will cause the reader to lose track of the point the rest of the sentence was making.

Without realizing she would be punished by this court for her action, the defendant committed perjury.

rather than

> The defendant, without realizing she would be punished by this court for her actions, committed perjury.

Avoid using intrusive phrases if you do not want the reader to stop. Also avoid overusing intrusive phrases because they can make your style too cumbersome. For the larger context, see SENTENCE STRUCTURE, subsection 7.

INVERTED ORDER

See SENTENCE STRUCTURE, subsection 4.

IRREGARDLESS OR *REGARDLESS?*

Use *regardless*, always.

ISSUE STATEMENTS

An issue statement frames the question to be decided in a legal argument. Its answer determines the outcome of the case. In complicated cases including several issues, the synthesis of those answers determines the outcome. The issue is the lens of the legal analyst's camera, so focusing it is of utmost importance. Even when a formal issue statement is not required in the final document, frame the issue for research purposes. You may also want to include an issue statement in the opening of your argument to help the reader focus.

To begin this focusing process, first identify the three parts of each issue. Work these three parts into a single statement, which provides a preliminary issue. Then, as you develop your document, refine this issue to reveal how these parts fuse together to form the essential question to be resolved, in light of your theory of the case.

1. Parts of the Issue.

    Any legal Issue can contain three parts:

    ● a reference to the law under which the question is being asked;

    ● the legal question, which combines the law and the facts of this case; and

    ● the facts that gave rise to this question and affect its outcome, which are the legally significant facts.

The following rough Issue illustrates these three component parts.

Law

Under Sec. 102.03(1)(f), Stats. Worker's Compensation,

Legal question

was the plaintiff going to and from employment while on the employer's premises

Legally significant facts

when (1) he was a produce buyer for a market, (2) he went to the public library to research current crop conditions, and (3) he was injured while on his way from the library to the market?

2. Drafting the Issue.

    When first drafting the Issue, you may begin by drafting each part separately. This separation in the preliminary stages reveals each significant segment of the legal analysis. Unify each of the three parts internally.

    ● Make sure the law is coherently framed. You may identify they law by naming the statute, identifying the area of case law, or summarizing the rule being applied.

    ● Phrase the legal question using terms that are central to your analysis, which often means you will use terms of art or descriptions of a key concept or fact.

    was the plaintiff going to and from employment

was an employee deviating for a private purpose.

To aid readability, try to keep your subject and verb close together. This usually means that the legal question forms the subject and verb. (For reasons why this is best, see INTRUSIVE PHRASES.)

- Group the facts together in the preliminary statement, rather than commingling the law and facts. This separation allows you to sort legal points more easily at the beginning of your process and keep the issue readable at the end. Also place the longest of the three parts at the end of the preliminary issue statement, after the subject and verb. Because the facts are often the longest part, these can go at the end of the draft issue. That leaves one component to be placed in the sentence, the reference to the law. Try writing this as an introductory phrase coming before the subject and verb.

This order of law, question, and facts is not required. It is, however, a good place to start when drafting your Issue, because it is generally readable and clear for the purposes of checking it against your research, themes, and purposes. You can then revise the order later as needed for strategic or other reasons.

> **Under Wis. Stat. § 102.03(1)(c), which allows compensation for workers injured while going to and from employment to perform a service, was a produce buyer performing a service when, after researching current crop conditions at a library, he was injured while traveling to the Market that employs him?**

or, for the opposition

> **Under the Workers Compensation Statute, which excludes compensation to employees injured while engaged in a deviation for a personal purpose, was an employee deviating for a private purpose when he stopped at a local bar before going from the library to the warehouse?**

3. Refining the Issue.

As you research and develop your theory of the case and your legal document, you will be able to focus your issue more precisely. Your law may zero in on a particular area, such as *Workers Compensation Statute*. Your legal terms may become more explicit and move your core question beyond *is the defendant liable* to *was a produce buyer performing a service*. Your facts may be rephrased to clarify the legally relevant aspect of that fact, *when he stopped for a drink in a local bar before going from the library to the warehouse*. Move back and forth as needed between drafting the issue and other parts of your writing process. Do not expect the issue to be completed as one unified step in isolation from the rest of your writing process.

193

Furthermore, allow for the possibility that your Issue's sentence structure may change. If the phrasing describing the law becomes lengthy, you may move that component to the end of the sentence. If the law becomes brief, it may merge with the legal question. Similarly, a key fact may move into the legal question, becoming the subject of the sentence. This kind of development is natural and desirable. The form of the sentence stating the issue must reflect the organization of the content, rather than being imposed arbitrarily. Thus the initial three-part structure here offers a beginning point, but not a required format for the final structure of the Issue. For example, the following sample issues, filed in a case before the U.S. Supreme Court, do not follow standard form yet are still effective.

Petitioner's Issue

Is a large law firm exempt from Title VII of the Civil Rights Act of 1964, and therefore free (1) to discriminate on the basis of sex, race, or religion and (2) to discharge those associates whom they did not admit to partnership based on reasons of sex, race, or religion, merely because the firm is organized as a partnership and has an established "up-or-out" policy?

Respondent's Issues

1. **Are law partners organized for advocacy entitled to constitutionally protected freedom of association?**

2. **Through Title VII of the Civil Rights Act of 1964, did Congress intend to give the Equal Employment Opportunity Commission, a politically appointed advocacy agency engaged in litigation, jurisdiction over invitations to join law firm partnerships?**

4. The Issue's role in various documents.

Issues are part of case briefs, Memoranda of Points and Authorities, pretrial briefs, trial briefs, or appellate briefs. The Issue is often the first part the reader consults to focus on the law, the facts, and the question their combination raises.

In objective writing, Issues focus the reader without persuading.

Under Iowa Code Section 99.99.99, Custody of children, is it in two children's best interests to award their mother custody when she has been their main care provider and has never been known to physically punish them, but when she has a history of alcohol abuse and has been overheard shouting at other adults?

In persuasive writing, the Issue must not only focus, but also persuade the reader. This persuasion is usually achieved by framing the law to reveal its favorable aspects, by making subtle changes in the wording of

194

relevant facts, and by using sentence structure techniques to put structural emphasis on favorable and significant aspects of the facts. In sum, creating a persuasive Issue involves making subtle changes to the objective base issue, not wholesale changes in substance.

> **Under Iowa Code Section 99.99.99, which establishes "best interests of the children" as the basis for custody decisions, is it in two children's best interest to award their mother custody when she has a history of alcohol abuse, has shown no signs of abstention from alcohol, and is given to emotional outbursts?**

For related information, see QUESTION PRESENTED and MEMORANDUM OF POINTS AND AUTHORITIES.

IT

Minimize the use of this pronoun as a subject because too often its antecedent is unclear. See AMBIGUITY, WAYS TO AVOID, section 2. For related definitions, see ANTECEDENTS and PRONOUNS.

ITALICS

Italics provide a graphic aid for the reader, often replacing the underlining used by typewriters. Like underlining, italics should not be used to add emphasis in the general text of formal legal writing. Instead they should be used:

- to indicate emphasis added to quotes;
- to highlight some words in some legal documents, such as *resolved* in a bill and *ordered* in a court order;
- to indicate defined terms, as in a contract, or for signals and cases in footnotes; and
- to mark words from a foreign language, like *savoir faire*.

In law review footnotes, use italics rather than underlining for case names and article titles. You may also use italics instead of underlining for case names in briefs. For related information, see BOLDFACE TYPE and UNDERLINING.

IT IS SAID THAT, IT WOULD SEEM THAT, IT MIGHT BE SAID THAT

If you have reservations about the point you are making, state them. Do not rely on these phrases, because they make you seem uncertain without indicating the sound reasons for your lack of certainty.

IT IS ... THAT

Often this phrase can be omitted for a stronger, more concise sentence.

The attorney must prepare a thorough and accurate statement of fact.

rather than

It is important that the attorney prepare a thorough and accurate statement of fact.

For related information, see CONCISENESS, subsection 10.

IT OR *THEY*?

For COLLECTIVE NOUNS, which treat a group as one functional entity, use *it*.

As the crowd grew in size, it inched toward the cordoned-off area.

For a group of many individuals, use *they*.

As people crowded into the area, they moved closer to the cordoned-off area.

For related, specific questions, see COURTS, IT OR THEY? and COLLECTIVE NOUNS.

ITS OR *IT'S*?

It's = it is.

Its = belonging to it.

Legal readers are annoyed if one is confused with the other.

JARGON

Jargon is a pejorative term for technical language that the reader does not understand, such as *price/cost elasticity*, although the writer and others in the writer's field of expertise would understand it. *Legalese* is jargon used by lawyers. Legalese includes both specialized words unfamiliar to nonlegal readers, such as *estopped*, and flowery words that (1) are unfamiliar to the reader, such as *abovementioned* and *heretofore*, and (2) could be avoided by using a more familiar word, such as *this* or *previously*.

Because you as a writer are trying to communicate to the reader, you want to avoid using jargon. Remember that nonlawyers are not the only ones who will resent jargon; judges are just as likely to resent an unfamiliar or unnecessary technical term.

Therefore, if you must use the technical word to make your point, add a definition in text so the reader does not have to look it up elsewhere. See UNOBTRUSIVE DEFINITIONS for ways to do this. For related information, see LEGALESE.

JUDGES, HOW TO ADDRESS

Use *your honor* when speaking to a judge. When writing or speaking about a judge, use *the honorable Judge [name]* for lower court judges and the *honorable Justice [name]* for higher court justices. Always precede the judge's name with *Judge* or *Justice*. This is what the *J.* following a court's name in an opinion represents.

JUDGMENT

A judgment is a court's final determination of the parties' rights in a legal controversy. In the United States, judgment has only one *e*:

judgment

rather than

judgement

JUDICIAL OR *JUDICIOUS*?

Use *judicial* when you want to refer to the courts; use *judicious* when you mean using sound judgment.

Determining the length of the sentence was properly left to judicial discretion.

but

The court appreciates a more judicious use of objections during a trial.

JUMP CITES

See PINPOINT CITES.

JURISDICTION

Jurisdiction describes the boundaries of authority in any given legal matter. When a court has jurisdiction over a given matter, that court has authority to decide the outcome of a dispute. Jurisdiction can be limited by geographical or legal boundaries. For example, Virginia state courts have jurisdiction over legal issues within the geographical boundaries of the state of Virginia and within the legal boundaries of state questions. But the federal district courts in Virginia, the Fourth Circuit Court of Appeals and the U.S. Supreme Court have jurisdiction over federal questions that arise within the state of Virginia.

Jurisdiction affects your research and reasoning, especially in persuasion as you use it to define the law and support your arguments. For example, you may be able to get a case dismissed because you can argue that the court does not have jurisdiction in the matter. You may be able to limit the scope of a court's authority by arguing that a court has only limited jurisdiction in the matter. Or you may be able to write new law by inventing jurisdiction over a matter not yet decided. In any case, make sure you are aware of all jurisdictional boundaries for any legal issue you are analyzing. For related information, see MANDATORY AUTHORITY, PERSUASIVE AUTHORITY, and RESEARCH STRATEGY CHART, step 4.

JURY INSTRUCTIONS

Jury instructions are read aloud by the judge to the jury to explain how the jury should view the evidence and reach a decision. Sometimes the jurisdiction has form instructions that cover each point the judge needs to explain; when no form instruction exists, the judge prepares the needed instruction. In many jurisdictions, attorneys for both parties draft jury instructions and submit them to the court; by doing so, each side is asking the court to use their instructions during the trial. The courts chooses which set to use, a choice that can be reviewed on appeal. If your instructions are chosen by the judge to be read, you have gained a great deal, because the law will be explained in a way that is congruent with the case you have prepared.

To write effective jury instructions that the court will accept, you need to understand not only the general legal issues but also the ways in which those issues can be framed to be accurate yet persuasive. To accomplish that, you can use a checklist of specific techniques to make your instructions clearer.

1. General issues when drafting jury instructions.

When drafting jury instructions, you must reconcile conflicting matters in two areas. First, you must strike a workable balance between two audiences. Jury instructions explain the law to jurors, yet they have to be accepted by the judge. As a result, you need to use some legal terms but also explain them in everyday language.

Second, you must conform patterned jury instructions to the specifics of your case. Most states provide patterned jury instructions that are established general statements of the law. Check your jurisdiction for any specific requirements. Although the model instructions provide a good starting point, they usually need editing to be relevant to the particular facts involved in your case. For example, you may have to delete statements addressing issues settled before trial or you may have to combine several instructions to address the multiple issues in your case. Check your jurisdiction's requirements; some states do not allow any modification of model jury instructions, but others encourage it.

2. Drafting checklist.

The following checklist can help you balance these factors when writing jury instructions.

(a) Use elements of the standard jury instructions.

For example, you might keep the wording of the standard instruction but break it into several shorter sentences to make it more readable. Similarly, you might retain the legal terminology in the instructions, but increase understandability by adding definitions if you think they are needed. For help here, see UNOBTRUSIVE DEFINITIONS and READABILITY, subsection 1.

(b) When appropriate, include support.

Providing citations or explanations with your submitted instructions can let the judge knows there are legitimate reasons for your changes.

(c) List all the legal questions the jury must resolve to decide in your client's favor.

When choosing the instructions you will use, you need to lay out the specific law the jury will need to resolve all the legal questions in your case. This thorough preparation can help you avoid gaps and present a logical overall package.

(d) Revise the instructions for clarity.

The jury often hears but does not read the instructions. As a result, you must reorder your priorities to meet the needs of the listener: you must worry more about CLARITY and less about conciseness. The following techniques can help you.

  (i) Use understandable words.

- Use words that will be familiar to the jury. For example, use *automobile* rather than *motorized vehicle*.

- Use verbs instead of nouns whenever possible.

> **You should <u>consider</u> all the evidence as a whole**.

rather than

> You should give <u>consideration</u> to all the evidence as a whole.

- Avoid using several negative words in one sentence.

> **Mr. Allen should have come to a complete stop at the crosswalk.**

rather than

> Mr. Allen must <u>not</u> have <u>failed</u> to come to a complete stop at the crosswalk.

- Use transitions or phrases that precisely communicate the logical relationship between two points.

> **<u>Even if</u> Mr. Allen did stop at the crosswalk, he should have also stopped again at a point where his view was not obstructed**.

rather than

> Mr. Allen should have also stopped at a point where his view was not obstructed.

For more information, see TRANSITIONS and CONNECTIONS, MAKING THEM.

(ii) Use understandable sentence structure.

- Keep sentences simple by making only one legal point per sentence.

You may decide that the testimony of one witness is entitled to greater weight than that of another witness, or even of several witnesses. In weighing the evidence, you may consider your own knowledge, observations, and life experiences.

rather than

In weighing the evidence, you may consider the testimony of one witness as entitled to greater weight than that of another or several others, your own knowledge, what you have observed, and the experiences you have had in life.

- Use only one word for one idea. For example, use *capable* rather than *capable and able*.

- Place lists at the end of a sentence.

In weighing the evidence, you may consider your own knowledge, observations, and life experiences.

rather than

You may consider your own knowledge, observations, and life experiences in weighing the evidence.

(iii) Personalize the instructions if permissible in your jurisdiction. You can still remain objective by using only objective, factual terms.

If Mr. Ellis had a gun concealed . . . .

rather than

If the defendant had a weapon concealed . . . .

3. Drafting jury instructions when no model exists.

Sometimes you will need an instruction for which your state has no model. When that happens, simply draft an explanation of the law, making sure you are stating the law accurately. Then revise that draft using the techniques listed in subsection 1.

4. Making jury instructions part of your advocacy.

To help make your instructions an extension of your advocacy, consider framing the instructions early in the litigation process, when you are drafting your brief, or at least before the start of the trial. Then

200

you can word your arguments so that they lead to the conclusions you want to reach, based on the law laid out in the instructions.

JURY, PLURAL OR SINGULAR?

Use a singular verb with *jury* when it is a collective noun, which it usually is.

The jury receives instructions at the end of the trial.

Use a plural verb only when you refer to the jury as a collection of individuals.

The jury appear nervous.

Better yet, avoid this awkward-sounding phrase by using *members* of the jury *or another similar phrase*.

The members of the jury appear nervous.

or

Each jury member appears nervous.

KEYCITE

See UPDATING THE LAW.

KEY TERMS

Key terms are words describing concepts or facts crucial to an issue. As such, key terms work in tandem with TERMS OF ART to define and discuss legal issues. As terms of art are derived from the law, key terms are derived from LEGAL ANALYSIS, POLICY, BACKGROUND FACTS, EMOTIONAL FACTS, and LEGALLY SIGNIFICANT FACTS. Thus, key terms may be definitions, facts, or descriptions of desired results, among other things.

For example, in a custody dispute where *best interests of the children* is a term of art from the statute, the key terms in the discussion or argument might be *custody dispute, father-son relationship*, or *son's wishes*. For related information, see ISSUE STATEMENTS or QUESTIONS PRESENTED.

LARGE–SCALE ORGANIZATION

See ORGANIZATION, LARGE–SCALE.

LATIN PHRASES

In general, limit your use of Latin to those phrases that enjoy widespread usage. Some of these phrases are more concise and are easily understood by lawyers, but not by nonlawyers. For example, you may need to use *res ipsa loquitur, habeas corpus, prima facie, stare decisis, res judicata*, and *sui generis*. But in almost all other cases, rewrite using the English equivalent; Latin phrases are jarring to the modern reader, even when that reader is a lawyer.

The defendant pleaded no contest.

rather than

The defendant pleaded *nolo contendere*.

No one would be impressed by this use of Latin; it would risk losing nonlawyer readers and irritating legal ones. For more information, see WRITING TO OTHER ATTORNEYS. For specific questions, see AD HOC, I.E.,DICTA, PER, VIZ., and ETC.

LATTER

See FORMER.

LAW REVIEW ARTICLES

See ARTICLES, PUBLISHED and SCHOLARLY WRITING.

LAWYER OR *ATTORNEY*?

See *ATTORNEY* OR *LAWYER*?

LAY OR *LIE*?

Lay means *to place or set down* or *to deposit*, among other things. It is a transitive verb that always takes a direct object.

Today I am laying out my strategy for the trial.

The attorney laid the exhibit carefully on the bench before the bailiff.

She had laid her briefs down on the desk before she left the office.

Lie means to *recline* or to *remain in a specific condition*, among other things. It is an intransitive verb that never takes a direct object.

The site of the crime lies between Fargo and Grand Forks.

When I lay down yesterday, the phone rang.

The gun had lain in the snow before months before it was discovered.

LEGAL ANALYSIS

Literally, *analysis* means understanding something by studying its parts. Functionally, legal analysis means studying the parts of a legal problem and combining them into a coherent explanation of how the law in a specific area addresses or solves that problem. The more component parts, the more possibilities exist for permutations and combinations of those parts. In each legal culture, traditions and practices have developed about how to combine those parts into a cogent legal analysis.

In the United States, the law is not based solely on established statutes or codes, but also on traditions derived from cases and U.S. legal history. Rather than starting from an assumption that legal analysis can be written to cover everything, U.S. law starts from the assumption that lawyers and judges will have to face unanticipated situations and will have to develop new law based on what has been done before. For example, because of the doctrine of *STARE DECISIS*, traditional legal analysis often includes deference to precedent, which requires careful research into how previous situations have been analyzed. The legal writer must anticipate these new developments in his or her analysis. Legal analysis thus requires legal writers not only to follow past patterns but also to improvise. This tradition and improvisation can occur in every legal document, including not only judicial opinions and appellate briefs, but also memos, opinion letters, and contracts. In nontraditional legal analysis, improvisation can overtake tradition, and the law and precedent may be modified or replaced to suit the current situation.

With so much research to gather, each ingredient with its own component parts, the possibilities for legal analysis are many and varied. Traditional legal analysis thus requires mastery of the following, not necessarily in this order:

(1) selecting raw legal materials for a particular situation,

(2) dividing those materials into their component parts,

(3) determining which components are relevant to the analysis,

(4) applying relevant components to correlating components in the problem to be solved,

(5) recombining components in an appropriate way,

(6) accounting for both strengths and weaknesses, and

(7) demonstrating how the combination leads to a particular conclusion.

1. Selecting raw legal materials.

Your selection of the materials for your legal analysis depends on your client's situation. To clarify this focus, you may want to frame your preliminary legal question first. Also remember your client's budget and your audience. When you begin researching, you can select materials according to that situation. For example, you may need only the relevant Illinois cases for a short memo on Illinois tort law directed to a partner. You may need statutes, cases, rules, and regulations for a tax appeal to an IRS agent on behalf of your client. Or you may need cases, previous office memos, and several sample contracts for a transactional document designed for a corporate client. Avoid shopping for sources; instead frame your search carefully. For possible methods, see RESEARCH

STRATEGY CHART and RESEARCH AS WRITING. Your preliminary sense of ISSUES, PURPOSE, and AUDIENCE will also assist you in selecting while you read.

2. Dividing materials into component parts.

You divide a source into components by identifying its legal sub-parts. You can use the legal doctrine itself to identify the categories, such as when you divide a tort or criminal statute into elements. You can impose categories that help you sift through the material, such as when you brief a case by facts, procedural history, issue, holding, and so on. Or you can use components emerging from your situation, such as when you take notes according to your client's issue, or research parts of a contract by identifying your client's goals. Most law students learn some categories for components in the early months of law school. Your ability to divide effectively will grow as your knowledge of the law and its corresponding categories grows.

3. Determining which components are relevant.

After you have listed the components parts, determine which parts are central to the outcome of the analysis by comparing them to your situation. A statute may list the elements for a cause of action, but, in your situation, the third element is not disputable. So for example, in a negligence question, when no one disputes that there was a *duty*, no lengthy discussion of duty is necessary. The essential components that define, identify, and establish the duty are enough. If the *breach* of that duty is disputed, then more components from other sources may be necessary to define what a *breach* is, is not, or may be. Thus your issue and your facts help you determine what rules, holdings, policies, arguments, counterarguments, and equities to pull from other sources.

4. Applying relevant components to correlating components in the problem to be solved.

When you have determined what the relevant components are, you can select sources with similar components and correlate those components with your situation. Details will be needed about the relevant components, although which detail is needed from precedent cases or other sources will vary depending on which components of the source you are using. Depending on which components you have determined to be relevant, those details may include the rule, the rationale, the holding, the legal significant facts, or dicta central to understanding the case's significance. When writing your analysis, describe those essential details sufficiently. Whenever the comparison is essential to the analysis, make sure that you include enough material to allow the reader to analogize the law to the relevant details of your client's situation.

As you apply the components, avoid including unnecessary detail. If the doctrine requires that you analyze three elements, you can determine what in your situation can be discussed under each element, rather than including everything under each element. A component's legal significance is what triggers the correlation: do not dwell on whether a *vehicle* was a *private vehicle* unless you have determined that that particular difference is legally significant; do not describe the history of a tax regulation unless that history affects the analytical outcome. Remember that your application goes beyond the facts; you may be using or comparing equities, policies, outcomes, parties' goals, statutory construction methods, and so on.

5. Recombining components to reveal your reasoning.

As you decide which components are most important, you will begin to determine how to recombine those important components in your presentation of your reasoning. Sometimes you will follow the order used repeatedly by all courts analyzing these issues because that will be familiar to your readers. Sometimes, especially in persuasive writing, you may want to put the most favorable components first. If you are presenting a new legal theory, you may recombine components to show the relevance you are advocating.

Often you will apply the law according to its own structure. If your rule evokes a balancing test, you may apply the rule to the facts by showing one part of the test, then the other part, then how they balance against each other. If the doctrine requires analysis of three elements, you may apply each element to your situation before presenting the next. If the analysis requires a balancing test, divide components into the two sides. Or if the theory of the case requires a threshold issue to be discussed, you may cover those components first. For greater organizational clarity, order components by their legal relationship, rather than the outcome of the comparison. Thus you will seldom first compare all the similar components and then contrast all the differing ones.

You may find it useful to use expository writing devices, such as definition, cause and effect, or enumeration. If you want to show that your client did not violate a restrictive covenant, for example, you can first show the rules on restrictive covenants and then define violations of that covenant by showing what actions the courts have held to be violations in previous cases. Then you can compare or contrast your client's situation with those of the previous cases. For some ideas for presenting reasoning, see SYLLOGISMS. For a more detailed approach to reasoning see Pierre Schlag and David Skover, Tactics of Legal Reasoning (1986) and Jill J. Ramsfield, The Law as Architecture: Building Legal Documents (2000).

6. Accounting for both strengths and weaknesses.

In memos, examine both the strengths and weaknesses of your client's case and balance them against each other. The reader should know how the rules, policy, equities, economics, or practicalities can be used to build or challenge your arguments. Then the reader should know how and why these factors tip the balance in one direction. For example, if you are arguing that your client's actions did not violate a restrictive covenant, you must address similar actions by others that did violate the covenant.

When examining the strengths and weaknesses, do not limit your analysis to an explanatory list. Instead, weave these parts together as dictated by the law and facts themselves. A mechanical listing would defeat the analytical purpose. A thorough analysis requires a careful consideration and construction of the subparts. Provide this analysis to give your readers the confidence that you have included all relevant components, examined all arguments thoroughly, and constructed a coherent progression for the reasoning. For related information, see ARGUMENT SECTION, DISCUSSION SECTION, RULES, and APPLICATIONS.

In briefs, present your strong arguments by structuring the brief around them. Address the other sides' arguments within that structure as necessary. Omit arguments that are irrelevant to your theory. In some cases, you may wait to address the other sides' arguments in a reply brief. In negotiations, anticipate the various positions each party can take and decide how you will present, address, or avoid those positions in the negotiation process. Remember that there are always more than two approaches to issues and that a strong legal analysis not only accounts for all approaches but also presents them in a way that demonstrates their relation to each other.

7. Demonstrating how the combination leads to a particular conclusion.

However you recombine the components, you need to explain to your reader why each step in your reasoning is valid. Do not jump to any conclusions. Instead, explain your reasoning for each step and explain how each component is connected to the others. Leave no assumptions to the reader. For example, if you do not need to develop one element of a doctrine, explain why it is not needed. Rearrange it or give it shorter treatment, but do not eliminate it without explanation. If you are comparing your client's situation to others, use previous holdings to define a doctrine's elements and then show where your client's situation fits into this definition. One comparison usually does not make an analysis.

Often you will need to characterize more specifically the components of your client's situation to reveal your reasoning fully. To do this, describe the component using words that are narrower than those used in the rule of law but broader than the actual specific details. This characterization forms the bridge that spans the gap in your reasoning. The following two examples illustrate different ways components can be characterized to reveal different lines of reasoning. Note how the underlined phrases characterize the components differently and suggest the different combinations.

Rule

Commercial drivers are held to a higher standard of care.

Fact

Client offered to drive his friend to the airport for $20 on two different occasions.

Characterization

Client, like a commercial driver, <u>offered to provide a service for payment</u>.

Conclusion

Client will probably be held to the higher standard.

For a different conclusion,

Characterization

Client, unlike a commercial driver, <u>was not offering services to the public</u> for payment.

Conclusion

Client will probably not be held to the higher standard.

This characterization and combination of components is the essence of your legal analysis. It also is the place where many legal debates have their center. Therefore, be flexible when considering all the reasonable possibilities, so that you do not overlook the best argument because you settled for the superficial one. Also be rigorous in your thinking, so you do not follow a line of reasoning that will not stand under a court's or other legal reader's scrutiny.

LEGAL ANALYSIS CHART

CASE BRIEF	OPINION LETTER or EMAIL	OFFICE MEMO	BRIEF
Citation	[Letterhead]	Caption:	Caption
	[Date]	INTRODUCTION	INTRODUCTION or
Parties	[Salutation]		SUMMARY OF ARGUMENT
Prior Proceedings		or	STATEMENT OF THE CASE
Theories/Objectives	Introduction		Procedural History
FACTS	FACTS	STATEMENT OF FACTS	Facts
ISSUE	ISSUE	QUESTION PRESENTED	ISSUES
		BRIEF ANSWER	
HOLDING	ANSWER	DISCUSSION	ARGUMENT (by issue or remedy)
		For each issue:	Point heading
REASONING	EXPLANATION	Rule	For each issue:
Rule	Rule	Application	Rule
Application	Application	Conclusion	Application
Conclusion	Conclusion		Conclusion
		CONCLUSION	
DICTA	Prediction	Prediction	CONCLUSION
Comments	Recommendation	Recommendation	Short request for remedy
	Specific directive Closing		

LEGALESE

Legalese is a pejorative term for technical legal words or phrases, and it implies that the legal words are unneeded. To avoid the problem, avoid legal terms whenever common language terms can convey the meaning.

> **The testator, William James (James) then signed the will, which was witnessed by Ellen Brady, Katrina Birchler, and Mella White**.

rather than

> The *said* testator, *one* William James, *(hereinafter referred to as James)* then *duly* signed the *aforementioned said* will, *in witness whereof* were Ellen Brady, Katrina Birchler, and Mella White.

Similarly, although you will find that you do need to use many technical legal terms, you do not need to overuse them. You will be able to keep your writing style more direct and concise if you do the following.

Replace this phrase	with this version.
the <u>above</u> Client	**the Client**
the <u>aforementioned statement</u>	**this statement**
a <u>priori</u>	**therefore**
<u>as per</u> your request	**at your request**
the court <u>deemed</u> that	**the court held that**
the <u>duly</u> designated person	**the designated person**
now <u>comes</u> the Plaintiff	**the Plaintiff**
<u>(hereinafter referred to as</u> Plaintiff)	**(Plaintiff)**
i.e.	**that is**
in re	**regarding**
defendant pleaded nolo contendere	**defendant pleaded no contest**
the <u>said</u> Plaintiff	**the Plaintiff**
the <u>signers</u> whereof	**the signers**
provides	**states**
pro forma	**a formality**
per diem	**daily, per day**
the client decided sua sponte	**the client decided on his own, the client decided**
supra	**previous**
viz.	**namely**
whereas the owner has	**because the owner has**
in the event that	**if**

If you must use a technical term and you are not sure the reader will know the meaning, add a definition.

> **The tortfeasor, who is the person committing the tort,** . . . .

For ways to do this, see UNOBTRUSIVE DEFINITIONS. For a discussion of a related problem, see JARGON.

LEGALLY SIGNIFICANT FACTS

Legally significant facts are facts that, if they were changed or deleted, would affect the outcome of the case. Although you may have initial ideas about what facts are legally significant, you need to read the law to verify those ideas. As you compare the law to your situation, certain facts will emerge as significant, just as white emerges under a black light.

For example, a case may state that the waving of a loaded gun in someone's face is an assault. In the fact situation being analyzed, Michael waved a gun that was not loaded. As part of your analysis, you must decide whether the fact that it was unloaded is legally significant because that difference may mean Michael is not guilty of assault. In another situation, you may read that an accountant cannot exercise an accountant-client privilege, but your client is both an accountant and a tax attorney. This fact is legally significant because it may mean that your client can exercise the privilege.

In a memo, legally significant facts should appear in the statement of facts, in the question presented, in the Brief Answer, and in the application part of the Discussion Section. Any legally significant facts used in the application should appear in the Statement of Facts first, in detail. No surprises. Similarly, in briefs, legally significant facts should appear in the Statement of the Case, the Issue Statements, the Point Headings, the application in the Argument Section and in abbreviated form in the Conclusion. In an opinion letter, include legally significant facts in the separate section on facts, in the application during the explanation, and in the recommendation.

For an explanation of other kinds of facts, see BACKGROUND FACTS and EMOTIONAL FACTS. For related information, see ISSUE STATEMENTS and BRIEF ANSWERS.

LEGAL WRITING CHECKLIST

The following checklist is designed to give you a point of departure in checking your document. Edit the list according to your readers' preferences and your project's purpose. You might also use some of these questions as a guideline for asking questions of the assigning attorney when the project is first given to you. For more detailed questions to ask at each stage in the writing process, see WRITING PROCESS CHECKLIST.

1. PURPOSE.
   - Is the document's purpose clear?
   - Is it stated within the first two paragraphs?
   - Is the issue stated?
   - Is the answer stated?

2. CONTENT.
   - Is the law itself quoted or accurately paraphrased?

- Are the elements clearly delineated by the writer? Are the elements consistent with the law?
- Are the principles of statutory interpretation accounted for?
  - Plain meaning?
  - Legislative intent?

    Purpose?

    Previous interpretations?

    Policy?
- Are your client's arguments included?
- The other side's arguments?
- Are the arguments balanced, using principles of interpretation?
- Is a "mini-conclusion" reached on each element?
- Are elements connected to each other, where appropriate?
- Are all conclusions synthesized in the last paragraph?
- Is a recommendation made?

3. ORGANIZATION.

- Is the organization consistent with law and appropriate to these readers and this purpose?
- Does the organization lead logically to the recommendation?
- Can any legal reader not misunderstand the scheme?
- Do the first sentences of each paragraph guide the reader through the document?

4. READABILITY and CLARITY.

- Is the tone appropriate to this audience? Are terms of address appropriate?
- Is sentence length varied to create a readable rhythm?
- Is the document free of legalese?
- Are terms of art used accurately?

5. MECHANICS.

- Are the citations accurate in form and substance?
- Is the grammar correct?
- Is all technical material accurate?
- Are all typographical mistakes corrected?

LEGISLATION

Drafting legislation requires particular skill, for legislation must bear up under generations of scrutiny. Consider those generations of audiences, as well as the current audience of legislators. The following guidelines can help you do this when drafting legislation. For the broader context, see AUDIENCE.

1.   Draft the original idea you have in mind as clearly as you can, in your own words.

2.   Consider all the legal problems raised by the legislation, both the original problem and any previously unanticipated corollaries. Run the draft past several readers from different audiences if possible.

3.   Check the draft against other sections within that part of the statute to catch any possible inconsistencies, ambiguities, or other problems that may arise in this larger context.

4.   Similarly, see if any terms used in your legislation are defined elsewhere in the statutes and keep your use consistent with those definitions.

5.   Adjust the language to accommodate any ancillary problems created in the process of revising the legislation.

- Avoid extra phrases that raise, rather than answer, problems. For related information, see ACCURACY, subsections 1 and 2.

- Use PLAIN ENGLISH.

- Use clear, familiar words. See LEGALESE.

- Replace or define all terms that might lead to ambiguity. For help here, see AMBIGUITY, WAYS TO AVOID and UNOBTRUSIVE DEFINITIONS.

6.   Unify style when the legislation has been drafted by more than one person. For ways to do this, see REVISING CHECKLIST.

7.   When using quotation marks in legislation, put other punctuation marks, such as periods or semicolons, outside the quotation marks unless that punctuation mark is part of the quote.

"Dwelling", when used in this section, means . . . .

This differs from the use of quotation marks in general writing, where commas and periods always are placed inside the quotation marks. Because there are so many audiences to please and so many things to consider in drafting legislation, do your best under the circumstances to create the clearest results.

LENGTHY QUOTES

See EXTENDED QUOTES.

LESS OR *FEWER?*

See *FEWER* OR *LESS?*

LETTERS

In letters, your information is not the only thing you communicate to the reader. Just as the clothes you wear to an interview communicate something about your general personality, the way you put together a letter communicates your attitude. Fortunately, you can use three basic writing tools to establish the appropriate impression by establishing the appropriate tone: WORD CHOICE, SENTENCE STRUCTURE, and overall structure. For details about how to structure your letters, see specific kinds of letters: GENERAL CORRESPONDENCE LETTERS; OPINION LETTERS; BAD NEWS, GIVING IT; BAD NEWS, SOFTENING IT; and LETTERS REQUESTING PAYMENT. For help in choosing and creating the appropriate tone, see TONE IN LETTERS. For related information, see EMAIL.

LIE OR _LAY?_

See _LAY_ OR _LIE?_

LIKE OR _AS?_

See _AS_ OR _LIKE?_

LINKING VERBS

See VERBS, LINKING.

LISTS, STRUCTURE OF

The following rules can help you use lists effectively and correctly.

1. Make sure the items in the list are both logically and grammatically parallel.

> **You may decide that the testimony of one witness is entitled to greater weight than that of another witness, or even of several witnesses. In weighing the evidence, you may consider your own <u>knowledge, observations, and life experiences</u>.**

rather than

> In weighing the evidence, you may consider the testimony of one witness as entitled to greater weight than that of another witness or several others, <u>your own knowledge, what you have observed, and the experiences you have had in life</u>.

In the first example, two ideas (_weighing evidence_ and _using personal experience to weigh the evidence_) are divided into two sentences. Additionally, the list of kinds of personal experience in the second sentence is revised to be grammatically parallel. For related information, see PARALLEL STRUCTURE.

2. Use commas to separate items in the list.

The defendant moved his car into the left lane to pass, lost control on the snow-packed pavement, slid back into the right lane, and collided with the plaintiff's truck.

When writing a list in legal writing, it is prudent to put a comma before the *and* or *or* that introduces the final item in the list. For example, in the following sentence, the comma before the *and* makes it clear that there are four shares, not three.

My estate is to be divided equally among my nephew, my son, my daughter, and my son-in-law.

3.   Do not use semicolons just because the list is set off from the text.

Use semicolons only when there is a comma within one or more item in the list. See subsection 4.

"Remanufacturing equipment" includes the following processes:

(1) disassembly to a predetermined standard established by the manufacturer for each model,

(2) cleaning,

(3) refinishing,

(4) inspecting and testing to new machine test standards,

(5) installation of all retrofits, and

(6) operational testing.

If the sequence of the items is not critical, you may use bullets instead of enumeration.

"Remanufactured equipment" includes the following components:

- **motors,**
- **transmissions or gear assemblies,**
- **linkages,**
- **switches and levers,**
- **thermostats,**
- **chassis, and**
- **exterior frames**

4.   Use semicolons only if there is a comma within one of the listed items.

When there are no commas within individual items, there is no need to use semicolons, no matter how long each item in the list is. See subsection 3 for an example of the correct use of commas. The following examples show the correct use of semicolons with commas.

The Company warrants for one year that its compressors (1) are free from defects in material and workmanship; (2) have the capacities and rating set forth in the Company's catalogs, provided that no warranty is made against corrosion, erosion, or deterioration; and (3) meet all relevant federal safety standards.

The Company is not liable for any delay in performance because of any of the following:

(1) any act of God, including but not limited to floods, epidemics, fires, storms, or earthquakes;

(2) any acts of others beyond the reasonable control of the Company, including but not limited to strikes or other labor disturbances, riots, wars, acts of civil or military authority, or acts of the Customer; and

(3) any cause beyond its reasonable control, including but not limited to delays in transportation, inability to obtain necessary materials or components, or labor shortages.

5. Whenever possible, put the list at the end of the sentence.

Lists are easier to read at the end of a sentence, after the reader has the main framework of your idea in mind. With that framework clarified, the reader can then attach all the details included in a list.

In justifying the exclusion of expert psychiatric evidence, the court listed three concerns: maintaining the integrity of the bifurcated trial procedure, avoiding allowing the guilty to go free, and preserving the defendant's right against self-incrimination.

rather than

The concerns of maintaining the integrity of the bifurcated trial procedure, avoiding allowing the guilty to go free, and preserving the defendant's right against self-incrimination justify the exclusion of expert psychiatric evidence.

6. Choose the format for your list by considering the complexity of the list.

In general, as items become more complex or the list becomes longer, you need to use more graphic aids to help the reader. Use your common sense and consider the following guidelines.

(a) Run the list in text if each item is one to three words long and there are two to five items in the list.

The plaintiff paid the defendant $2,550 in installments of $510, $700, $850, and $490.

(b) As this sentence illustrates, run the list in text and insert parenthetical numbers before each item if (1) each item in the list is several words long and (2) the list includes three or fewer items. This can be useful in those awkward situations when you need to include a list within a list.

> **The defendant agreed (1) to provide the roofing materials needed and (2) construct the new roof or subcontract the job to a bonded roofer.**

(c) Introduce the list with a colon and insert parenthetical numbers if the list does not occur in highly formal writing and if most items are more than three words long or there are more than five items in the list.

> **Before drafting this warning letter, I will need the following information: (1) copies of all previous written correspondence you have had with Mr. Jones regarding this matter, (2) any information you may have forgotten during our interview regarding your conversations with Mr. Jones, and (3) copies of the relevant pages of your bookkeeper's records on accounts receivable.**

(d) Introduce each item on the list with the same word (1) if you want to remain more formal, (2) if the items on the list are more than three words long, or (3) if the repeated word contains an idea you want to emphasize.

> **A doctor may forego disclosure to his adult patient if any of the following situations occur: if the patient is unconscious, incompetent, or otherwise incapable of understanding the information; if in the doctor's opinion the information would have a disproportionately adverse reaction on the patient's ability to make a rational decision; or if an emergency exists which allows no time to safely consult with the patient.**

(e) Use a colon and parenthetical numbers and also tabulate the list if (1) most of the items on the list are more than ten words long, (2) the items are phrases but not complete sentences, and (3) there are more than three items in the list.

> **The Company's liability does not include any of the following:**
>
> **(1) any damage occurring in connection with the use of the equipment in any nuclear facility;**
>
> **(2) any consequential or incidental damages, including but not limited to loss of profit, damage to associated equipment, cost of capital, and cost of substitute products;**

216

(3) any costs beyond the price of the product and service that gives rise to the claim; or

(4) any claims arising from advice or assistance given by the Company without separate compensation for that advice.

(f) Set off complete sentences in a list, each introduced with a number, if each item is a complete sentence of more than ten words, there are more than two items, and that format is appropriate in this writing situation.

> During the period of this maintenance agreement, if the Company determines that it cannot maintain the equipment in good working order, then the Company must replace the equipment with another unit in good working order. This requirement is subject to the following provisions.
>
> 1. If the Company replaces the equipment within two years of the warranty expiration date, then the replacement unit must be one that is newly manufactured, remanufactured, or reconditioned.
>
> 2. If the Company replaces the equipment more than two years after the warranty expiration date, then the replacement unit will be one that is refurbished in accordance with the process used to refurbish rental units.
>
> 3. If the Company cannot replace the equipment with another unit of the same model, then the replacement unit will be substantially similar or will have greater capabilities.
>
> 4. ....

6. Set off complete sentences with *first, second*, and so on.

Separate sentences are the appropriate structure when the items in the list introduce points that will be discussed at length or when you are writing in a situation where a set-off list seems inappropriate.

> The appellate process has two major objectives, both critical to success. First, the appellate process must give litigants a fair opportunity to have legitimate claims resolved by a court of law. Second, the appellate process must provide a framework within which the common law can develop in an orderly manner.

For related information, see PARALLEL STRUCTURE and LISTS, WHEN TO USE.

LISTS, WHEN TO USE

Use a list whenever you have three or more items that are logically parallel. Also use a list when you have a lot of information that the reader needs to remember, because grouping items into a list makes both reading and remembering easier. For help doing this, see LISTS, STRUCTURE OF. Two particular problems with lists are handling multiple lists and long lists.

1. Handling multiple lists.

Avoid using too many lists at once. For example, avoid using more than one list in a sentence. If you need to include several lists, try to put each lengthy list in a separate sentence. Also try to separate clearly any small lists of two or three items.

> **Seller is to comply with all requirements of laws and regulations, whether federal, state, or local. For example, these requirements include but are not limited to compliance with laws and regulations relating to labor, worker's compensation, wages and hours, unemployment compensation or insurance, old age benefits, other social security and welfare laws, and payment of payroll taxes.**

rather than

> Seller is to comply with all requirements of federal, state, and local laws and regulations, including, for example, but not limited to, compliance with laws and regulations relating to labor, worker's compensation, wages and hours, unemployment compensation or insurance, old age benefits, any other social security and welfare laws, and all requirements concerning the payment of payroll taxes.

2. Handling long lists.

If you can reduce the number of items listed, do so, because lists are hard to read if they run long, such as more than five items. The reader has difficulty remembering that many items at once. But, because often you cannot shorten the list in legal writing, you may have to try some other techniques. Try grouping the listed items into logical subgroups. For example, four lists of four items each is much easier to read than one list of sixteen items. If subdividing is not possible, use graphic devices to make the list easier to follow. For samples of these see LISTS, STRUCTURE OF, subsection 6.

LITERAL LANGUAGE

Literal language is used almost exclusively in legal writing because it is precise and accurately defines things. For a definition, see LITERAL MEANING. For some uses of figurative language, rather than literal, see FIGURATIVE MEANING.

218

LITERALLY

Literally in a strict sense means *really* or *actually*. *Literally* is often misused to mean *figuratively*. The following sentence uses *literally* correctly.

There were literally three hundred people in the courtroom.

This means that there were actually three hundred people there. The following example uses *literally* incorrectly.

I am literally dying of boredom.

I am dying of boredom is sufficient to communicate the hyperbole; boredom does not literally cause death. For related information, see LITERAL MEANING and HYPERBOLE.

LITERAL MEANING

A word's literal meaning is its actual or exact meaning. Its meaning is not generally debatable. Literal meaning avoids exaggeration, metaphor, or embellishment; it therefore conveys the explicit meaning of the word or words.

Four witnesses gave statements after the accident.

rather than

A handful of witnesses painted a vivid picture of the tragedy.

Legal writers expect literal language, particularly in drafting and objective writing. Save FIGURATIVE MEANING for persuasive or scholarly style.

LOGICAL FALLACIES

Logical fallacies are those patterns of thinking labeled in classical western thought as improper methods of reaching conclusions. These patterns reach invalid conclusions. For related information, see SYLLOGISMS.

LOGICAL LINKS

Logical links are those clues that show the reader how your sentences and paragraphs fit together logically. For ways to show the logical links in your argument, see CONNECTIONS, MAKING THEM; TRANSITIONS; and PARAGRAPHS.

LONG QUOTES

See EXTENDED QUOTES.

LOOSELEAFS

This term refers to looseleaf services, which are research tools especially valuable for specialized research in areas such as tax, patent law, and environmental law. Looseleaf services collect and integrate information from several sources, including courts, executive agencies, scholars, and practitioners. Looseleafs can provide quick, current overviews of specific issues; offer related information; and update the law. For related information, see UPDATING THE LAW.

LUCIDITY

See ACCURACY and READABILITY.

–LY OR NOT?

The suffix *-ly* is used to make adverbs out of adjectives, such as *carefully* from *careful* or *generously* from *generous*. When using *-ly*, make sure that the word is being used as an adverb, that is, it modifies a verb, an adjective or another adverb.

Taxpayers must file directly with the IRS on these matters, rather than through another service.

The Code is carefully constructed to be readable to users.

If the word is modifying a noun or pronoun, there should be no *-ly*.

The statute's careful construction makes it immediately understandable.

For related information, see ADVERBS and ADJECTIVES.

MAIN SENTENCES

See TOPIC SENTENCES.

MANAGING WRITERS

Good management creates active, engaged, continually improving writers; bad management creates passive, hostile, unresponsive ones. To create active, not passive, writers, comment in a way that engenders a thoughtful response from the writer both for this document and for future documents. To do this, you have to get to the *why* behind the comment so that the writer sees how the change matters in this context and how to make a similar decision in the future. If you instead edit only the paper, you are dooming yourself to edit every future paper from that person. If you instead teach that person to be her own editor, you create an independent writer. You can do the latter only if you explain yourself and justify your advice.

As a manager, you can increase your efficiency, increase the quality of the writing, and reduce stress for both you and the writers. Managing writers effectively requires

- a focused vision of the final goal,

- clear directions at the start,

- effective and timely feedback, and

● attention to writers' needs.

If this focus and attention are not communicated, writers may be unable either to meet your needs or to improve over time. Most writers do not respond well to vague directions and little feedback during the process. They are mystified by unexplained changes or cuts, and cannot improve when they see excessive red-lining that obliterates their work and does not relate to clearly defined goals. Good management can meet both your needs and theirs. In addition, good management saves you time.

To increase both your writers' effectiveness and your efficiency, evaluate how you distribute your projects and follow through on their progress. To do this, consider the following ideas.

1. Give written directions.

These directions are particularly useful at the start of the project. Most writers respond well to clear directions, so give the writer a clear idea of the document's PURPOSE, AUDIENCE, ISSUES, possible results, and PROFESSIONAL POSTURE.

2. Set realistic deadlines together.

As you set deadlines, include interim deadlines to check issues, organization, and overall structure so you and the writer do not find yourself panicking as the final deadline nears.

3. Meet for clarification.

After the writer's initial research has clarified the issues, have the writer return them for your review. Make sure the focus is specific enough, yet not too narrow, and that it is substantively accurate. Use these written issues to ascertain whether the writer is following directions and remaining within the scope of the project. The time this takes will save both of you more time later. If you have thought of new ideas since you gave directions, use the issues to help the writer incorporate those ideas. As you comment on the issues, and in all your later comments, remember to teach rather than to tell. Explain the how and why behind your changes, so the writer can learn to see make these changes on his or her own in the future.

4. Meet to plan the overall document.

After this initial research, meet to discuss approaches to planning the overall document, especially if it is a big one. Together, choose the best approach or organizational scheme. This helps keep the writer invested in the project and helps the writer understand your reasons for suggesting specific structural approaches. To unify the organization and help the writer build the structure, tie your suggestions to the overall purpose and audience.

5. Rewrite before you revise.

When you receive the first draft, assist the writer by addressing rewriting concerns rather than revising ones. Look at the writing with a telescope, not a microscope. For example, avoid editing for tone, wordiness, or other small-scale concerns, which lead you to appropriate the text and alienate the writer. Editing extensively at this stage would be inefficient, in any event, because some of the sentences you edit will disappear in later drafts. Rather, describe the objective the rewrite should meet, and then evaluate the structure and content against that objective. Help the writer see what rewrites are necessary, rather than doing the rewrites yourself. Give comments that foster their continued progress, encourage excellent analysis, and increase the product's usefulness. Thus your comments will focus on substantive changes and their reasons. This process will minimize editing time, reduce frustration, and maximize benefits to the writer and the document. For specifics, see EDITING and REWRITING CHECKLIST.

6.   Give reasons for your edits.

Include your reasons for making changes. These can be brief, just *to clarify* or *for conciseness, try this version*. Reasons are important; the writer will respond better if he or she knows why you have changed something.

7.   Identify patterns.

If you need to edit in detail, edit only one page or paragraph. Then identify the PATTERNS in the writer's expression. For example, you may notice unusually long sentences, legalese, or weak topic sentences; identify these and ask the writer to edit the document throughout for similar examples.

8.   Set an example of timeliness.

Return the drafts at the agreed-upon time so your writers get a strong sense of the importance of meeting deadlines.

9.   Revise and polish.

In later drafts, move to revising, then polishing concerns. For guidance here, see REVISING CHECKLIST, and POLISHING CHECKLIST. Give unambiguous, consistent comments that help the writer move swiftly to the desired results. Continue to tie comments to the document's purpose and audience, not your personal preferences. Avoid changing words just to change them; if the writer has captured the concept so that any reader would find it unambiguous, leave it. Try to be as precise, organized, and specific as you expect the writer to be. For specific commenting techniques, see EDITING.

10.   Take a long-term view.

To create long-term improvement, help your writers determine their respective strengths and weaknesses overall. You might want to discuss those at the start of their tenure with you by having each writer self-evaluate. Then, together, you can design a long-range program that develops their writing and evens out their abilities. As each project closes, or at the end of a group of projects, relate the writer's development to the long-range plan.

Similarly, determine your strengths and weaknesses as a manager. Periodically, you may want to ask for feedback on your management techniques so that you can increase your effectiveness. Receiving feedback openly and implementing good ideas will give a strong message to your writers that you can help each other.

MANDATORY AUTHORITY

Mandatory authority is the primary source of law for a specific legal question in a specific jurisdiction. Mandatory authority includes the statutes, the constitution, regulations, and cases that have been created in the specific jurisdiction in which your client's legal issue arises. This authority is "mandatory" because it must be followed in that jurisdiction. The legal issue places the research in a specific jurisdiction. For some issues, state law is mandatory. For example, mandatory authority for a tort law issue in Illinois includes the statute passed by the Illinois legislature, the Illinois cases construing that statute, and any regulations promulgated under the statute. It also includes the state constitution because all statutes must be constitutional.

For federal issues, only federal law is mandatory, and only within the federal jurisdiction within which the question arises. For example, mandatory authority for a federal income tax dispute in California will be the IRS Code, the regulations promulgated under that code, the decisions of the IRS, the case law in the federal district court where the suit is brought in California, the case law in the Ninth Circuit, case law in the U.S. Tax Court, and any decisions made by the U.S. Supreme Court on the matter. Finally, the U.S. Constitution is mandatory because all laws must be constitutional.

Some issues involve both state and federal law. For example, mandatory authority for an environmental issue in New Mexico includes federal law, environmental statutes passed by Congress, regulations under those statutes, federal cases in the New Mexico district court and the Tenth Circuit Court of Appeals, and regulations in that jurisdiction because most environmental issues are considered federal; and the law must be constitutional. There may also be state laws that fill in gaps left by the federal law on the issue. In that situation, New Mexico's environmental statutes, cases, and regulations are also mandatory authority, and they must be constitutional within both the state and federal constitutions.

Lawyers are bound to find, analyze, sort, and use all pertinent mandatory authority. For related information, see PERSUASIVE AUTHORITY and RESEARCH STRATEGY CHART. Check your local jurisdictions because some have rules that affect what is mandatory and persuasive, particularly among appellate court divisions.

MATTER OF FACT, AS A

See AS A MATTER OF FACT.

MAY

Use *may* to communicate permission from an authority.

Under this statute, the corporation may defer payment of income taxes for one year if three criteria have been met.

You can also use *may* to communicate possibility.

The outcome of the trial may depend on the credibility of the two attorneys.

In contrast, *can* suggests capacity or ability.

The corporation can file its return on either of two dates.

Because it has two possible meanings, watch for potential ambiguities when using *may* in drafting. Sometimes, but not always, the meaning of *may* will be clear in context. When ambiguity is possible, use *might* for possibility and add some phrase like *if he or she chooses* for permission.

For related information, see VERBS, AUXILIARY and MIGHT.

MAY OR CAN?

See *CAN OR MAY?*

MEANING OF WORDS

For topics in this area, see LITERAL MEANING, FIGURATIVE MEANING, CONNOTATION, PRECISION, subsection 2, and WORD CHOICE.

MEMORANDUM OF POINTS AND AUTHORITIES

A Memorandum of Points and Authorities outlines the legal arguments to be made on a narrow legal issue. In some jurisdictions, this terminology is used because the format requires the writer to make each legal point separately and give authority for it. Check your jurisdiction for the appropriate terminology and format. For an example of one kind of format, see BRIEFS. For related information, see PERSUASIVE WRITING.

MEMOS

Memos are intraoffice communications that convey information from researchers to decision-makers before, during, and after litigation and negotiations. Memos usually inform the reader, who is often the decision-maker, of how the law measures the strengths and weaknesses of the client's position, predict the court's decision or the negotiation's outcome, and advise the reader on what decision to make. Because the memo is the vehicle for making in-house decisions, the reader's professional reputation is on the line. In effect, the reader must trust the writer with the reader's reputation because the reader will use the memo to decide about the situation and in turn communicate advice to a client, draft a brief, or begin a negotiation. Thus the memo is not a test of the writer by the informed reader but rather a way for the writer to communicate to the reader the law, analysis, objectives, alternatives, and possible results. The writer's reputation is on the line, too, because it is often through memos that the writer demonstrates research prowess, analytical ability, intellectual flexibility, and creative problem-solving techniques. The memo is used in most areas of legal practice. For related information, see OBJECTIVE WRITING. The usual format for a memo follows.

MEMO

The caption contains information that gets the memo filed accurately and makes it useful for future reference. For more information see CAPTIONS.

To:
From:
Date:
Re:

INTRODUCTION

An Introduction may be included to remind the reader of the assignment and to summarize the memo's purpose and scope. It should be a short paragraph.

Some readers prefer including this section in place of the Statement of Facts, Questions Presented, and Brief Answers. In this variation, the Introduction will be longer and will include the information that is otherwise included in the three sections below. It also includes a transition to the Discussion.

STATEMENT OF FACTS

The Statement of Facts explains the situation that led to this legal problem. In doing this, it summarizes the procedural facts, legally significant facts, and needed background facts. If the memo is written in the context of a dispute, it might explain the facts in dispute and the claims made by each side. The Statement may also note what information must still be obtained. The Statement of Facts may precede or follow the Questions Presented and Brief Answers, so check with your reader to determine the order. For more detail, see STATEMENT OF FACTS. For related information, see LEGALLY SIGNIFICANT FACTS and NARRATIVE WRITING.

QUESTION PRESENTED

This section tells the reader the legal question that, when answered, will determine how this problem is resolved. Because this is the analytical focal point of the document, the Question Presented should distill the legal question, or questions, into a form that allows the reader to prepare for the analysis that follows. To do so, it should contain some version of the following three elements: the general law governing the situation, the specific legal question being answered here, and the legally significant facts on which the situation turns. These three aspects of the legal analysis give the reader the general legal context for the situation, the specific question that arises from this situation, and the specific facts on which the reader should focus. To arrive at this final Question Presented, begin with the preliminary Question Presented as it was formulated in Step 3 of the RESEARCH STRATEGY CHART.

Under [general rule of law],

did (or was) [legal question]

when [legally significant facts of this case]?

Under Wyoming law on false imprisonment, did Orth falsely imprison Leitner when she drove him around in her car without letting him out?

Then refine the question as your research develops.

Under Wyoming Stats. § 432.17, did Orth falsely imprison Leitner when she forced him into the car, drove him around for seven hours without stopping, and refused his request to be let out of the car?

Check with your reader to see if the Question Presented should be worded generally or focused on the client's situation. Your reader may prefer that the facts be stated in general terms so the memo is easier to use as a reference in future cases, such as in the following example. Note that this form can take the present tense.

Under Wyoming Stats. § 432.17, does the driver of a car falsely imprison a passenger when she forces him into the car, drives him around for seven hours without stopping, and refuses his request to be let out of the car?

Some readers may prefer a question beginning with *whether*, but this is generally a less readable format. For examples and more discussion, see QUESTIONS PRESENTED. To see how to format the question, see steps 1–3 in RESEARCH STRATEGY CHART and ISSUES. To put the question in analytical perspective, see LEGAL ANALYSIS.

BRIEF ANSWER

The Brief Answer gives the writer's prediction of how a court would answer the question and encapsulates the reasons for this answer.

Yes. Orth falsely imprisoned Leitner because she intended to confine him in the car, because Leitner was actually confined in the car, and because Leitner was aware of his confinement.

The Brief Answer can also foreshadow the organization of the upcoming Discussion by using language that communicates the legal criteria required in this area of law and by listing those criteria in the order in which they will be discussed. Here, the Discussion should have three parts, each discussing an element of false imprisonment: intention, actual confinement, and awareness. The Brief Answer can serve as an executive summary of the document, the place where the reader will find the reasons for the writer's legal conclusions.

DISCUSSION

Purpose

The Discussion explains the legal reasoning that supports the writer's answer, allowing the reader to be assured that the answer is based on reliable reasoning. This section is generally substantially longer than the other parts of the memo, with good reason. Its content is crucial to the usability of the entire documents. The reader will be using the memo to advise a client about how to proceed, draft a brief in the midst of a case, or establish an approach to negotiations.

A good Discussion explains, concisely and precisely, how the law supports the answer. When the Discussion is well written, the reader knows that the legal conclusion is valid, barring a substantial misstatement of the law. The reader can understand the logic behind the answer, which helps the reader in turn explain the answer to the client.

A good Discussion also eases the writer's nerves. As a new employee on the lower rungs of the career ladder, you may find it difficult to commit yourself to a specific and useful answer to a legal question. As you lay out your reasoning in the Discussion, however, you are able to justify your recommendations. If your Discussion lays out the full analysis, misses no logical steps, considers viable alternatives, fully explains reasoning, and predicts possible and practical results, then your memo is likely to be useful to the reader. Be sure that the Discussion fulfills the PURPOSE discussed in the initial assignment.

Organization

Two factors play the biggest role in determining the best organization of the Discussion: the structure of the law you are using and the interests of your reader. Often these two factors converge to create the Discussion's organization. Your reader most often is an attorney who understands that the first step in predicting how a court will resolve an issue is determining what legal standards the court will use. Thus the legal reader's first question naturally is, "what is the governing law on this?" You can begin by addressing that question.

For example, to organize the Discussion explaining the previous sample Brief Answer, you could look first to Wyoming law on false imprisonment. If that law established a three factor test, then you could begin the Discussion by presenting those three factors.

> **When determining whether false imprisonment exists, the court considers three factors**. . . .

or

> **To establish false imprisonment in Wyoming, the plaintiff needs to establish that (1) the defendant** . . . **, (2)**. . . **, and (3)**. . . .

The opening paragraph of this traditional approach could then explain the components of the law, or the RULES, that resolve this issue and how those rules fit together. This overview prepares the reader to follow the organization of the rest of the Discussion.

But this overview alone does not provide the reader with enough information to determine whether that overview is correct, or that the law implies anything specific. The following paragraphs will address those details. As you explain the law, you need to explain what each element or component of the law means and how it is actually used. That may involved enacted law, case law, or both. If a statute or administrative rule establishes a legal rule, begin by explaining that law. When you do this, focus on accuracy. Thus you usually do not just cut and paste the statute into your Discussion, because that would leave to the reader the task of sorting out the relevant language. Neither do you go to the other extreme, paraphrasing the law so broadly that the TERMS OF ART and accuracy are lost. Find a workable balance by identifying the key phrases you need, often including terms of art, and paraphrasing the background parts of the rule. For help doing this, see QUOTATIONS, WHEN TO USE. Also focus on the law that is relevant to the particular component at hand. This will help you avoid presenting unreadably long passages of law.

In a traditional approach, you also need to place the components in a logical order. Sometimes the components logically require a given sequence. For example, depending on how Wyoming law was structured, you might need to discuss first whether Leitner was actually confined before discussing whether Leitner was aware of the confinement. If no confinement existed, the question of awareness would be moot. If, however, the factors did not logically require a particular sequence, you could choose the sequence that made more sense given your facts. For example, if the actuality of Leitner's confinement were not debatable but Orth's intent and Leitner's awareness were both less clear, you might address the actuality of confinement first, covering it quickly and then moving to the more debatable components. If, however, both the actuality of confinement and Leitner's awareness were not debatable, you might cover intent first, resolving that issue before addressing the two straightforward points.

For each component, the Discussion Section often begins with the general rules of law and amplifies the meaning of the rules through analogous cases. That rule usually begins with the governing statutes. When including case law in this traditional approach, be mindful of your jurisdiction. Use cases from your jurisdiction when they exist, going to persuasive authority only after you are sure your jurisdiction has not resolved the issue. Also be mindful of using only that portion of the statutory and case law that addresses the component you are discussing. Your reader wants to know how mandatory and relevant law addresses that component, not to read a book report on the whole case. Therefore include only the detail needed from the relevant case to explain the component, whether it is facts, reasoning, policy, or any other aspect. Rather than just reporting details from the precedent case, explain their significance. Omit any details that may have been important to the original case but that are not relevant to the rule you are discussing. For related information, see RULE, REASONING, and LEGAL ANALYSIS.

After you have explained the rule of law in this traditional approach, you need to explain how you believe that law will be applied to your situation. To do this, do not simply compare your facts to those of precedent cases. The factual comparisons may or may not be significant. Instead, just as you explained how the precedent case's components were significant, now you explain how any similarity, difference, or quality in any of the components is significant enough under the law you are applying to affect the analytical outcome. For related information, see APPLICATION.

Finally, you need to decide how to present the law and its application. If each element can be applied independently, then you may apply the law after each element. If, however, the law really must be applied as a whole unit, you may need to present all the law on an issue before applying it. Thus you will not necessarily have all the law in one place and all the application in another, but rather for each point of the analysis, you might state the law and then apply it. For related information, see LEGAL ANALYSIS and PRINCIPLES OF GOOD LEGAL WRITING. For more help, see ORGANIZATION, LARGE–SCALE and ORGANIZATION, SMALL–SCALE.

CONCLUSION

This section summarizes the main points made in the Discussion, giving a capsule of the reasoning that led to the Brief Answer. Just as the introductory paragraph provided an overview of the law, the conclusion can provide an overview of the application of that law. The reader is thus reminded of how the previous components do indeed, when taken together, answer the question. Sometimes the conclusion may also contain recommendations to the reader. It does not, however, include any information or reasoning not covered in the Discussion.

MERELY ·

Avoid this word, especially in PERSUASIVE WRITING. Most legal matters would not be *mere* or you would not be writing about them. Additionally, this word is often substituted for LEGAL ANALYSIS: rather than proving the proposition, the writer relies on a label. Avoid this shortcut and make your point directly.

Defendant was not at the scene of the crime.

rather than

Plaintiff merely guesses where defendant was at the time of the crime.

MIGHT

Might is used to suggest the possibility of the action occurring, often if a condition is met.

If we drop this third cause of action, the court might grant a summary judgment on the first two.

It is also sometimes used with suggestions to help create a tone of deference.

When deciding whether to accept this settlement, you might want to consider the legal cost you will incur by proceeding with the lawsuit.

For related information, see VERBS, AUXILIARY.

MISSPELLINGS, HOW TO AVOID

You cannot avoid misspellings just by running a spell check program. Sorry. While spell checkers reduce the numbers of misspellings that appear in most documents, they do not catch homonyms or cousins to your selected word, like *trail courts* or *witch all due respect*. You have to pay attention and proofread meticulously. For help with this process, see POLISHING.

If you want to improve your spelling, you can use several relatively painless measures.

1. Record your problems.

Take a 3 × 5 index card and write on it three words you need to use frequently but have trouble spelling, such as *defendant* or *conceive*, and underline the part that gives you trouble. Then put the index card somewhere where you will see it frequently, such as on your bath room mirror or inside your brief case. Do nothing more for two or three weeks. By that time, you will probably find that you can close your eyes and see the card in your mind, thus seeing how to spell the problem words. As you gain confidence with these three words, substitute new ones on the list.

2. Make a list.

Make an alphabetized list of words that commonly give you trouble, but keep the list to one page. Then carry this list with you and look up the problem word any time you need to write it. With this technique, you are not trying to learn to spell the words; you are finding a way around the problem, which is a practical alternative.

MODELS, USE OF

See FORMS, USE OF.

MODIFIERS

A modifier adds information about a noun or verb; this modifier can be either a single word or a group of words. Avoid using too many modifiers because they weaken the sentence. Particularly avoid using two modifiers that mean the same thing, such as *first and foremost* or *separate and apart*. Also avoid modifiers that have little substantive meaning, such as *in this manner, very,* or *obviously.*

> **These are the specific words of Minnesota lawmakers; consequently, the words must be given special significance.**

rather than

> Clearly these are the specific and precise words of Minnesota lawmakers regarding the issue; consequently, the words must be given special significance and appropriate attention.

> **Higgins does not establish a standard for viability other than the fetus' ability to exist separately from its mother**.

rather than

> Obviously, the court in Higgins appears to fail to definitively establish an unambiguous and undebatable determining standard for when a fetus reaches the medical state of viability that seems to be any more clearly specific than ascertaining medically the fetus' ability to exist separately and apart from its biological mother.

For more general information on modifiers, see ADJECTIVES, ADVERBS, and PREPOSITIONAL PHRASES. For more on problems associated with the use of modifiers, see MODIFIERS, DANGLING; MODIFIERS, MISPLACED; and MODIFIERS, SQUINTING.

MODIFIERS, DANGLING

A dangling modifier is a modifying phrase that does not modify any word in the sentence. This situation invites ambiguity. Usually these dangling modifiers occur at the beginning of a sentence.

To argue contributory negligence, all elements of negligence must be shown.

It is not clear here who will be doing the arguing. In contrast, see the following revision.

To argue contributory negligence, the defense must show all elements of negligence.

You can avoid this problem by doing the following: when you start a sentence with an introductory phrase beginning with a verb, such as *to argue* or *arguing*, make sure that the subject of that verb is also the subject of the sentence following the introductory phrase. For related information, see AMBIGUITY, WAYS TO AVOID, subsection 1; MODIFIERS, MISPLACED; and MODIFIERS, SQUINTING.

MODIFIERS, MISPLACED

Sometimes a modifying phrase, because of its position, modifies the wrong phrase in a sentence.

The defendant refused to service the car belonging to the man who insulted him with good reason.

Here *with good reason* should modify *refused* rather than *insulted*. To avoid ambiguity, place the modifying phrase right next to the word modified, such as *refused* in this example.

The defendant, with good reason, refused to service the car belonging to the man who had insulted him.

For other problems associated with modifiers, see MODIFIERS, DANGLING and MODIFIERS, SQUINTING.

MODIFIERS, SQUINTING

Squinting modifiers create ambiguity because they can modify terms either before or after the modifier.

Ms. Sparks only suggested filing a suit for adverse possession.

To correct this problem, either move the modifier to an unambiguous location in the sentence or reorganize the sentence.

Only Ms. Sparks suggested filing a suit for adverse possession.

or

Ms. Sparks suggested but did not recommend filing a suit for adverse possession.

For a discussion of related problems, see MODIFIERS, DANGLING; MODIFIERS, MISPLACED; and ONLY.

MOODS

See VERBS, MOODS.

MOST IMPORTANTLY

Avoid it. This phrase both gratuitously points a finger at this part of the document and diminishes the importance of the rest of the document. Instead, use positions of emphasis, word choice, and terms of art to show your point's inherent importance. If you must, use *most important*. For alternative techniques, see POSITIONS OF EMPHASIS and TERMS OF ART.

MOTIONS

A motion is a request to a court to rule or issue an order in the moving party's favor. Motions may be made orally, as an objection during trial, or may be written, as a motion to dismiss a claim. In most jurisdictions, the motion must be filed with the court as a separate document. In some jurisdictions, it is combined with a notice of motion, which tells the opposition when the court will hear the motion. Check your jurisdiction for specific format and filing requirements. The motion is usually just one or two pages long. It includes a CAPTION, references to the statute or common law supporting the motion, the reason the motion is justified, and the specific request for relief.

Often you will file a brief in support of the motion. This brief is designed to persuade the court to rule in your client's favor. When the opposition responds to the motion, it will usually file a brief in opposition to the motion. For a basic format, see BRIEFS. For related information, see PERSUASIVE WRITING and NOTICE OF MOTION.

MS., MRS., OR *MISS*?

If possible, find out from the person addressed what she prefers. If this is not possible, use *Ms*.

MUST

Must communicates a requirement,

Whenever a pedestrian is in a school crosswalk, all drivers approaching that crosswalk must stop . . . .

Must is a clearer indication of requirement than *should*, which in general speech can mean either must or ought. *Shall* is sometimes used instead of *must* in legislation, but is not more precise grammatically. For related information, see LEGISLATION and VERBS, AUXILIARY.

MUST OR *SHOULD?*

Use *must* to indicate requirement, inevitability, or legal obligation. *Must* has a more absolute connotation than *should*. Use should to indicate moral or ethical obligation, probable occurrence, or uncertainty about a future event.

You <u>must</u> register before you can vote.

but

You <u>should</u> vote in the coming election.

NAMES OR GENERIC DESCRIPTION?

There are two schools of thought on whether or not to use clients' names in any piece of legal writing. The first school holds that names are appropriate because they focus the reader on the specific outcome of the case being analyzed. The second school prefers using more general terms because the reader can get a concept of the legal question being analyzed, which in a memo will also be of use in future cases. Consider your audience, and write accordingly.

Under Washington law on false imprisonment, did Orth falsely imprison Leitner when he drove Leitner around in the car for seven hours without letting him out?

or

Under Washington Law on false imprisonment, does the driver of a car falsely imprison a passenger when he drives the passenger around for seven hours without stopping and letting him out of the car?

Whichever format you use, remain consistent throughout any piece of legal writing. If you choose to use names in objective writing, use them in each subsection of the memo or opinion letter. Choose the form of name most appropriate to the setting, such as *Mr. Jones, Theodore Jones*, or *Ted*, depending upon your familiarity with the party and the formality of the document you are writing. Similarly, if you choose to use names in persuasive writing, use them in each part of the brief or opinion letter. Choose the form of name most favorable to your client. For example, use *Mr., Ms., Miss,* or *Mrs. Smith* if you wish to dignify the party by using a formal tone. In briefs, use first names only if needed for clarity or if referring to a juvenile. For example, if two brothers were contesting a will, you might use first and last names, such as *Allen Anderson* and *Andrew Anderson*, to distinguish the two. If one party was an eight-year-old girl, you might use the first name only, such as *Betty*, to underscore the sympathy the court might feel for the child.

Avoid using names of anyone other than the parties, such as the names of opposing counsel. Such references detract from the purpose of your argument.

NARRATIVE WRITING

In contrast to expository writing, narrative writing tells a story. When well-constructed, it can also present or support an argument. In legal writing, narratives appear in Statements of Facts, illustrative anecdotes, and longer hypothetical examples. As a form of argumentation or scholarship, narrative writing seeks to convince the reader or listener that the story itself is compelling enough to suggest a certain legal result or mode of thinking.

Although chronological organization may be used in narration, narrative writing is not equivalent to chronological organization. For example, a Statement of Facts might start with the first event of significance to the issues rather than the first chronological event. Thus in a divorce case, the Statement of Facts might begin as follows.

After thirty years of marriage, Edgar Plantagenet has decided he wants to divorce his wife.

rather than

Edgar and Mary Plantagenet were married on June 9, 2001.

Often an organization other than a strict chronology is more effective for emphasis or clarity in the narration. For example, you might begin with a statement of the problem so the audience will read the subsequent details in light of the legal question involved.

This case arises from an arrest of Defendant after the warrantless search of her house.

This is particularly useful when you need to minimize the effect of some facts that occur early in the chronology but are not sympathetic to your client. If the narration will be extensive or complex, you may begin with a summary of the situation.

Veldmar, Inc. and Thanco Corporation both agreed to a merger plan in July 2007. Since that time, however, a complex series of events has made this merger economically impossible for Veldmar.

This overview provides a framework so the reader understands why he or she is reading the subsequent details.

For persuasion, you may begin with a fact that deserves emphasis and that can make sense to the reader even out of the larger context of the other facts. Then move into your chronological narration after that dramatic statement.

Alexander Oliaka, who used to run three miles each morning, will never run again. He will spend the rest of his life in a wheelchair as a result of spinal injuries he suffered in an automobile collision. The collision occurred on August 17, 2004.

This opening allows the reader to focus fully on one dramatic, sympathetic fact. The impression is made, then the rest of the narration then adds the other facts needed to fill in the rest of the picture. For ways to emphasize key facts through word choice or sentence structure within a narration, see EMPHASIS. For related information, see EXPOSITORY WRITING.

NEGATIVES

Negative statements are harder to understand than positive ones, so state things positively whenever possible.

Come to the meeting at 3:00 p.m. or later.

rather than

Do not come to the meeting before 3:00 p.m.

The negative statements that are hardest to read are those including *unless, neglect to, not unlike, hardly, scarcely,* and other such words. These negative words can be easily misread and so should be avoided when possible. Multiple negatives are also hard to read, so avoid them.

Come to the meeting only if you are required to do so.

rather than

Do not come to the meeting unless you are told not to neglect to come.

NEITHER

Use *neither* only when listing two items. Like *either, neither* is a helpful signal for the reader when it is followed by two listed items; it is much less helpful when it is followed by a list of more than two items, because *neither* leads the reader to expect only two. Therefore, if you are introducing a list of more than two items, try using *none of the following,* which will prepare the reader for a longer list.

Further, make sure that the terms after *neither* and *nor* are logically and grammatically parallel.

Neither the defendant's own testimony nor her written records support this assertion.

rather than

Neither the testimony offered by the defendant nor the defendant's own written records support this assertion.

For related information, see PARALLEL STRUCTURE.

NOBODY

Nobody takes a singular verb.

Nobody has arrived for the hearing yet.

Nobody knows the trouble I've seen.

Nobody sounds slightly informal, so you may prefer *no one* in most legal writing.

NOMINALIZATION

Nominalization refers to the process of turning adjectives, adverbs, and verbs into nouns. Nominalizations are grammatically correct, but their overuse can make the writing stodgy or hard to read. When possible and appropriate, replace a nominalization with the verb, adjective or adverb form.

Use the following phrases	rather than these.
stated	made the statement that
coin-operated machines	machines operated by means of insertion of a coin
Counsel objected to the expert's testimony.	Counsel made an objection to the expert's testimony.
He was devoted to his father.	He showed great devotion to his father.

But use nominalizations where they make more sense, such as when the noun forms are terms of art.

He is accused of alienation of affection.

rather than

He alienated her affections toward her husband.

NONE, SINGULAR OR PLURAL?

None means *no one of*, and so is singular.

None of the reasons given is valid.

NO ONE

No one takes a singular verb; related personal pronouns and adjectives must also be singular.

No one has testified to plaintiff's innocence.

No one has all of his or her [not their] **pretrial discovery ready.**

NON OR *NON–*?

Attach the prefix *non* without a hyphen when it is part of the word.

nonentity, nonnegotiable, nonprofit

Use a hyphen when it modifies the original word but is not really part of the word.

non-lawyer, non-Russian, non-Euclidean

Use *non* followed by the space when it is used as a Latin term as part of a phrase.

non sequitur, non pro tunc, non troppo

When in doubt, consult a dictionary or the U.S. Government Printing Office Style Manual (2001).

NONRESTRICTIVE PHRASES

Nonrestrictive phrases describe, but do not limit, the words preceding them. They are surrounded by commas, which act as a kind of parentheses, because if the nonrestrictive phrases were taken out of the sentence the sentence would still be accurate. Nonrestrictive phrases often begin with *which* or *who*.

The defendant, who thinks he is innocent, looks terrified.

The Fourth Amendment, which protects citizens against unlawful searches and seizures, provides the foundation for this suit.

For related information, see THAT OR WHICH?

NOR

Nor is a conjunction that continues the negative force of *neither, never,* or *not,* and therefore can be used effectively in persuasive writing.

The defendant was never read his rights, nor was he allowed to make a phone call, nor was he allowed to talk with an attorney within the first twenty-four hours of his internment.

The respondent objected neither to cross-examination nor to introduction of the evidence at trial.

The statute has never been construed to have such a result, nor is such a result possible under the Constitution.

When using *nor*, as with any conjunction, make sure the parts you are coordinating are grammatically and logically parallel. For related information, see PARALLEL STRUCTURE.

NOT

Not is a small word that changes the meaning of a whole sentence. Therefore, proofread your text to make sure *not* is placed accurately. Additionally, whenever possible, try to write so the point will not be lost if the reader overlooks the *not*.

NOTES

Develop an effective system of note taking so that prewriting is comfortable for you. Your system is personal, of course, but taking effective notes throughout research and prewriting will make writing and rewriting go much faster. In developing your own system, consider the following.

1. Play to your strengths.

Whatever form you use, make the most use of that approach. If you prefer to write by hand because you remember more that way, then use note cards, legal size paper, or cut-and-pasted scraps of paper. Write on only one side of the paper so that information can be moved easily. If you take notes on a computer, organize your files so notes can be easily located and retrieved. You may wish to make separate files for each source, naming them so that they will be alphabetically organized within a subdirectory. Or you may wish to type in the Bluebook or ALWD citation as you take the notes, so that the sources are immediately retrievable in formal citation form. Or you may wish to separate notes by substantive issue, then subdivide according to sources, your own notes, your emerging outline on that issue, and your questions.

2. Save the citation.

If an authority looks at all usable, record the entire correct citation right at the beginning. This will save you time when you use that authority later; you can transfer the correct citation directly into your document rather than return to researching the citation.

3. Save the pinpoints.

When using quotes, rules, propositions, reasoning, or holdings from any case, note the exact page number so that you can incorporate pinpoint cites in the final draft without returning to the original source. Consider printing out hard copies of any quotes you plan to use or saving the original excerpt in a separate file. You may then paste the quotation into your document where needed, and use the original version to verify the details of punctuation and wording.

4. Organize a system.

Try to develop a system that organizes notes by topic, such as one using headings, using colors, or using tabs, so the notes can be easily organized according to issue. In a complicated project, keep a record of your research path, listing all the sources checked, even if they are not fruitful, so you do not retrace your steps.

5. Be legible.

Type thoroughly enough or write legibly enough that you will not waste time later trying to decipher your notes.

6. Avoid distracting sidelines.

Focus on the legal issue or theme that you are researching by translating your notes into relevant terms of art. After you have formulated the question presented or theme in step 3 of the research process described in the RESEARCH STRATEGY CHART, begin reading your sources with that issue or theme in mind; then record holdings, propositions, rules, and concepts by translating them into the terms of art important to that issue. For example, if you are researching whether or not your client committed an intentional tort, use *intend* as your main verb when stating the holding.

> **A five-year-old boy could not intend to injure an elderly woman because five-year-olds are not capable of forming intent.**

rather than

Five year old not held responsible for elderly woman's fall.

7. Record your ideas.

Add your own notes as you continue thinking about the problem. Those notes may include either cross-references or your own thoughts as the research and writing process progresses.

8. Discover the big picture.

Work the notes and your own thoughts into your theory of the case or theme, whatever you are writing. Your own synthesis of the information and ideas will help you begin to organize and understand the significance of your research and will help you build your case, explain your answer, or suggest your advice.

9. Remain flexible.

Experiment with different approaches. Your laptop may be your best companion as you read a variety of sources. You can cut and paste, translate by typing, or refashion accurately what you are collecting for a specific purpose. But you may be tempted to simply retype, or cut and paste without thinking. This is a form of PROCRASTINATION, postponing the real thinking until later. To break that habit, you may want to switch to some handwritten notes, combine hand writing and typing, or keep two separate files, one for the literal note taking and another for the general translation of the concepts into a coherent whole.

NOTICE OF MOTION

A Notice of Motion accompanies a Motion, which is a document submitted to a court to obtain a specific result. The Notice's purpose is to notify the other party of the time and place the motion will be heard. Often a brief in support of the motion also accompanies the Motion and Notice.

In some jurisdictions, you may incorporate the Notice into the Motion's preamble, as shown in the following example. Combining the two, however, may create an awkwardly long sentence. When deciding which form to use, base your decision on your court's preferences, rather than your own. For related information, see MOTIONS and BRIEFS.

STATE OF WISCONSIN   CIRCUIT COURT   DANE COUNTY

OLAF PETERSON, HENRY PETERSON and DOROTHY PETERSON,	))))	NOTICE OF MOTION AND MO-TIONS AFTER VERDICT
Plaintiffs,	)	Case No: 000–999
vs.	)	
BUDGET INSURANCE COMPANY, et al.,	))	
Defendants.	)	

TO: Attorney David A. Salverson
     Salverson & Johnson, S.C.
     Suite 6032
     9101 West Wisconsin Avenue
     Milwaukee, Wisconsin 53203

PLEASE TAKE NOTICE that on September 29, 2004, at 10:30 A.M., at the Courthouse in the City of Madison, Circuit Court, Branch IX, the Honorable Albert Purdy, presiding, the Defendants, by their attorneys, will move the Court on Motions After Verdict as follows:

1. For judgment notwithstanding the verdict, dismissing the Complaint of the Plaintiffs, for reasons evident in the record and stated in these Motions;

2. In the alternative, to change the answers to Questions No. 1 and 2 from "Yes" to "No", dismissing the Complaint of the Plaintiffs on the ground of insufficiency of the evidence to sustain the answers;

   . . .

8. In the alternative, to set the judgment aside and order judgment in favor of the Defendants, dismissing the Plaintiffs' Complaint on the ground that the Plaintiff's negligence was a superseding cause of his injuries.

Dated August 15, 2004.

POTTERS, PEARSON, PEEPLES, & PRINCE

BY: _____

     JOSEPH E. POTTERS,

     Attorney for Defendants,

     Budget Insurance Company

     and Far Horizons Foundation, Inc.

     P.O. Box 6666

     Madison, Wisconsin 53701

NOT ... BUT

These two phrases can be partners as conjunctions. In persuasive writing, use the pair to emphasize the contrasts between two points.

> **Not one, but three times has Mr. Perry denied that he made an offer on the property.**

In objective writing, use the pair to make a point about the specific relationship between two points.

> **Borders are not significant in immigration patterns for their literal placement, but for their figurative power to prevent potential immigrants from attempting to cross them.**

In using this pair of conjunctions, remember to use *but* after *not*. Do not confuse *not ... but* with *not only ... but also* because *not ... but* means almost the opposite of *not only ... but also*.

> **The defendant abused not only the privileges offered him, but also the procedure designed to protect him.**

rather than

> The defendant abused not the privileges offered him, but the procedure designed to protect him.

For related information, see NOT ONLY ... BUT ALSO.

NOT ONLY ... BUT ALSO

These two phrases belong in partnership as conjunctions. In persuasive writing, use the pair to foreshadow and emphasize the logical parallels of two arguments.

> **Not only has the plaintiff failed to show that the father gave the son implied consent, but the plaintiff has also failed to show that the father provided the car for the son's use.**

In objective writing, use the pair to connect legal concepts clearly.

> **The plaintiff must show not only that the father gave implied consent, but also that the father provided the car to the son.**

In using this pair of conjunctions, remember to use *but also* after *not only*. Do not use *not only ... but*. The mismatched *not only ... but* is particularly confusing to readers because *not ... but* means almost the opposite of *not only ... but also*.

Also make sure that the term following not only is structurally and logically parallel to the term following but also.

> **The defendant abused not only the privileges offered him, but also the procedure designed to protect him.**

For related information, see NOT ... BUT and PARALLEL STRUCTURE.

NOT SO MUCH ... AS

Like *not only ... but also*, these words work together as conjunctions and should be used together. This conjunction suggests a comparison based on degree, rather than category. Thus it is useful when suggesting one factor outweighs the other.

The key is not so much the existence of central authority as the frequency with which that authority is exercised.

rather than

The key is not so much the existence of central authority but the frequency with which that authority is exercised.

NOUNS

To lawyers, nouns are probably second only to verbs as the most important part of speech. Nouns name clients, theories, causes, damages, results, and rights. Thus legal writers must choose nouns with care and use them with precision. To do so (1) understand the uses of the various noun classifications and (2) avoid the common problems associated with the use of nouns in legal writing.

1. Classifications of nouns and their uses.

    (a) Proper nouns name specific persons, places, or things, and are capitalized.

    San Francisco, Sandstrom, Bill of Rights

    (b) Common nouns do not refer to specific persons, places, or things, and thus are not capitalized.

    lawyer, courtroom, fairness, alienation

    (c) Abstract nouns name concepts or ideas, rather than tangible things.

    fairness, right, protection, weapon

    Abstract nouns are necessary and useful in legal writing, but if misused or overused they make the content less memorable for the reader. Therefore they need to be used with precision.

    Equity dictates that the plaintiff be reimbursed for this loss.

    rather than

    Fairness dictates that plaintiff's rights should be protected.

    (d) In contrast, concrete nouns name tangible things.

    lawyer, courtroom, Doberman, knife

    These concrete nouns are easier to remember and are thus more helpful to the legal reader. Therefore, use concrete nouns often, especially to emphasize a point.

The testimony of four witnesses proves Mr. Noble was mentally incompetent, and should therefore be spared the death penalty.

rather than

Fairness dictates that my client's mental state should absolve him of guilt.

(e) Vague nouns include so many possible items that the reader gets no clear picture of any one item. A noun can be concrete, but still vague.

vehicle, money, building, person

In legal writing, vague nouns can cause ambiguity when they force the reader to break them down and supply his own meaning to the various items to which the vague noun might refer. Be specific as to which item you are referring.

Plaintiff should have filed the motion by December 15.

rather than

Plaintiff should have followed the procedure.

For more examples, see EMPHASIS, subsection 2.

(f) Collective nouns name groups that are to be treated logically and grammatically as a single unit.

The Supreme Court holds . . . .

With collective nouns, use the singular form of the verb, such as *holds*, even though the noun refers to a group, such as a court made up of several justices.

(g) GERUNDS are nouns formed from the *-ing* form of a verb. Often using gerunds makes a sentence more concise.

Imagining alone does not constitute intent.

rather than

The act of imagination alone does not constitute intent.

(h) Although not a grammatical term, many nouns provide a general reference to a broad category of concrete items. These words are not necessarily abstract nouns, but often have the same effect.

plants, animal, person, vehicle

Use these general nouns with restraint because they can make your meaning vague and less memorable. Often your better choice will be a more specific term.

shrubbery, squirrel, toddler, motorcycle

2.   Common problems with nouns in legal writing.

Two common problems occur with nouns in legal writing: they are used imprecisely and inconsistently. Therefore, consider your choices carefully. First, choose the noun that most precisely states your meaning. To paraphrase Mark Twain, "the difference between the right word and the almost right word is the difference between *internment* and *interment*." Second, do not change a noun solely for variety. The legal reader will assume a different noun represents a different idea. For more explanation and examples, see WORD CHOICE and REPETITION.

NOUN STRING

This phrase describes three or more nouns placed together without any connecting words between them to signal their interrelationship. Noun strings are concise, but often hard to understand.

Operations Reduction Contingency Plan Agreement

The difficulty occurs because the reader has to fill in the connecting words to understand the meaning. When the noun string is unfamiliar to even one of your readers, fill in at least some of the prepositions and other helpful structural signals.

Agreement to a Contingency Plan for a Reduction in Operations

or

They agreed to use a contingency plan to reduce operations.

Noun strings are often a form of jargon, and as such may be familiar to some readers. They are also common in bureaucratic language. But use these noun strings only when they will be easily understood by all of your readers, as when all the words in the string are familiar

unemployment benefits claim

or when the string is a term of art.

work product privilege

Confrontation Clause issue

Do not use noun strings out of habit, but rather when they are the most readable way to present the idea. For related information, see JARGON, TERMS OF ART, and CLARITY.

NUMBERS

See NUMERALS.

NUMERALS

The common question here is whether a number should be spelled out in words or written as a numeral.

1. Spell out a number that begins a sentence.

    One hundred twenty-five pieces of evidence were admitted at trial.

The one exception to this rule is years.

    1984 was not what we expected.

2. Spell out zero to ninety-nine in text and zero to nine in footnotes in law review articles.

    Different sources list different upper limits on spelling out numbers. Check your citation manual. According to the <u>U.S. Government Printing Office Style Manual</u> (2001), units of measurement are an exception. See subsection 9 below.

3. Spell out *million, billion*, and so on, rather than using zeroes, because they are easier to read.

    127 million

Also spell out numbers in indefinite expressions.

    The plaintiff is in his seventies.

Similarly, spell out round numbers larger than ninety-nine, if you choose, as long as you are consistent throughout the text.

4. Add parenthetical numbers only in drafting.

    Spell out numbers and then insert numerals in parentheses only in legal drafting, and then only when the duplication is needed to avoid the possibility of a critical inaccuracy caused by a mistyped numeral.

    In consideration for these agreements, Howard Industries agrees to pay Liveson Construction the sum of four thousand dollars ($4,000).

5. Use numerals for numbers larger than ninety-nine.

    The prosecution introduced 173 separate documents to support this claim.

6. Use numerals if, in one series, you have numbers both over ninety-nine and ninety-nine or under.

    The numbers of computers taken in these four robberies were 7, 25, 102, and 130.

7. Use numerals for sections.

    Use numerals when you are referring to a section of a document and that section itself is identified by a numeral.

    This exception is covered in subsection 5.

8. Use numerals for fractions and decimals.

    The total purchase price was $10.4 million.

    The production cost is now 2 ½ times greater than it was when the contract was signed.

9. Use numerals for units of measurement, such as for age, weight, money, and time.

6 years old, 95 pounds, 2700 yen, 4:30 p.m., 1.3 liters

Be sure to proofread all numerals to make sure they are accurate and equivalent to the written version.

OBJECT

See SENTENCE, PARTS OF, subsections 3, 4, and 6.

OBJECTIVE WRITING

1. General principles.

Objective is the term used by some to refer to legal writing that informs and predicts, using a neutral point of view. For example, objective writing in memos can inform the reader of the current status of the law; in opinion letters, it can inform the reader of the current status of a case. In either situation, the reader is looking for a relatively unbiased assessment of the circumstances. The legal reader may also expect objective writing to include a prediction of the outcome of the case. This prediction should be based on objective analysis of the law that measures the strengths and weaknesses of the client's position and balances them. Objective writing does not minimize the weaknesses of the argument, as persuasive writing does.

The majority of states draw the viability line at around six months; only two states have drawn the line earlier.

rather than

Not one, but two states have fully considered the valid arguments for drawing the viability line earlier and have thus accepted those arguments.

Many lawyers believe that objective writing does not exist because even a fairly neutral assessment of the circumstances requires the analyst's point of view. And many legal readers will expect this assessment to be strongly informed by the writer's individual analytical abilities. Nevertheless, the term "objective writing" has come to refer to most forms of legal writing that are not formally persuasive, such as BRIEFS or OPINIONS.

2. Checklist of useful techniques.

Consider the following in preparing any objective writing, such as a memo or an opinion letter.

(a) Keep an objective point of view, as a reporter would. Separate the facts into *who, what, where, when, why,* and *how,* as suggested in the RESEARCH STRATEGY CHART. This separation allows you to evaluate the scope and interrelationship of the information before connecting it to the law.

(b) As you read the law, take notes on its parameters, history, and trends. This will allow you to develop and evaluate the arguments available to all parties involved in the situation.

(c) As you report on the law, frame it so that the reader sees how the law works, regardless of the upcoming arguments. For example, you may report a statute's specific language, or you may synthesize a general rule of law from several cases. Report what the law or the status of the case is by giving an objective summary of the law.

(d) Clarify both the strengths and weaknesses of the client's arguments. Make sure the information in the memo is complete, despite your personal bias; do not omit unfavorable points the other side may raise. Account for them and work them into your analysis.

(e) Balance those strengths and weaknesses. That is, evaluate the relative weight that such matters as the law, precedent, practical circumstances, social and legal trends, economics, general policy, and overall equity should be given in this situation.

(f) Offer your assessment of how you think the situation will be interpreted and why. The reader is usually interested in your synthesis of all of the information, arguments, and possibilities.

(g) Avoid overuse of modifiers, because such words add interpretation more than analysis, objective writing informs but does not persuade. Concentrate instead on precise use of nouns and verbs.

> **The majority of states draw the viability line at around six months; only two states have drawn the line earlier.**

rather than

> The vast majority of states have clearly decided to draw the viability line at approximately six months, although two dissenting states have deviated somewhat from that popular course.

When using modifiers, also avoid those that argue, such as *unjust* or *unmistakably*; use only those modifiers that are factually based, such as *unsettled* or *previously*.

For related information, see OBJECTIVITY and POINT OF VIEW, OBJECTIVE OR PERSUASIVE? For explanations of related concepts, see POLICY and EQUITY.

OBJECTIVITY

Objectivity is essential to all forms of legal writing at some stage. You must remain particularly objective when assessing your client's situation so that you can correctly anticipate all possible arguments on all sides of the issues. Equally important, you must remain objective in any oral presentations designed to inform the court or another attorney of the law, such as in pretrial or intraoffice conferences.

Objectivity is paramount in negotiations and in pretrial work because, to advise your client, you must accurately assess the relative strength of the arguments. This objectivity paves the way for accurate use of law, facts, practical circumstances, economics, social concerns, and POLICY to persuade the court in briefs and oral arguments or to help your client to negotiate satisfactory results. Therefore, in intraoffice documents, such as memos, present information objectively. For related information, see OBJECTIVE WRITING.

OBJECT OF A PREPOSITION

See PREPOSITIONS and SENTENCE, PARTS OF, subsection 6.

OBLIVIOUS OF OR OBLIVIOUS TO?

If you mean *unaware*, use *oblivious of*. If you mean *forgetful*, use *oblivious to*. Of the two, *oblivious of* is the narrower meaning. To avoid confusion, consider using another word, such as *unaware* or *unmindful*.

The defendant was unaware of the significance of this waiver.

rather than

The defendant was oblivious of the significance of this waiver.

The defendant was unmindful of her duty to see that all the children's seat belts were properly fastened.

rather than

The defendant was oblivious to her duty to see that all the children's seat belts were properly fastened.

OBVIOUSLY

Use *obviously* only when the point is indeed obvious. Use *obviously* sparingly in legal writing, because you seldom state an obvious point, and even when you do state it, you seldom want to underscore its obviousness. If the point is not obvious, labeling it as such insults your reader and impairs your credibility. For related concerns, see LITERAL MEANING.

OF COURSE

This phrase is best avoided in legal writing; *of course* implies that the point is obvious, but the legal reader may not see your point as being this clear cut. Do not use *of course* to gloss over assumptions that need to be supported. For related problems, see IT IS SAID THAT, OBVIOUSLY, and MODIFIERS.

OK, O.K., OR *OKAY?*

None of the above is common in formal writing, so avoid using them. If you need to use one of the three, *OK* is the most widely used form.

OMITTING WORDS FROM QUOTES

For when and how to do this, see QUOTATIONS, HOW TO PUNCTUATE, subsections 7, 8, and 9. Also see EDITING QUOTES.

ONE

One as a pronoun indicates a single person, a single unit, a single thing. It takes a singular verb.

One of the defendants is moving to have the case dismissed.

One of the problems with teaching legal analysis is that not all professors agree on the best way to teach it.

ONE–SENTENCE PARAGRAPHS

Use one-sentence paragraphs for EMPHASIS or transition, but only occasionally. If you have several in one brief or memo, you are probably overusing them. The following one-sentence paragraph, coming after a detailed explanation of a Congressional policy statement, effectively emphasizes a point and leads into the next discussion.

While this Congressional policy does not directly affect commerce regulations, it may be so strong that future Presidents will think twice about restricting scientific transnational communications.

For problems one-sentence paragraphs may signal, see PARAGRAPH LENGTH, subsection 2. For related information, see PARAGRAPHS and ORGANIZATION, SMALL–SCALE.

ONLY, WHERE TO PLACE

Each time you use *only,* check its placement; in general, place it immediately before the word it modifies. A misplaced *only* can create ambiguity, and often in legal writing that ambiguity is serious. For example, the following sentence is not clear.

Shares are sold to the public only by the parent corporation.

Are shares sold *only to the public,* or *only by the parent corporation*? Although the reader might be able to reason out the meaning in context, the sentence should be written so the meaning is unmistakable. Often ambiguity occurs because *only* comes too early in the sentence.

You should only introduce this evidence if the defendant chooses to testify.

The writer did not mean to say that the reader should *only introduce* this evidence and do nothing else with it. To avoid this ambiguity, try placing *only* as late in the sentence as possible without creating an inaccuracy.

> **You should introduce this evidence only if the defendant chooses to testify.**

For related information, see also ACCURACY, subsection 2; MODIFIERS, SQUINTING; and AMBIGUITY, WAYS TO AVOID, subsection 1.

ON THE CONDITION THAT OR *WITH THE CONDITION THAT?*

The most likely option here is a shorter, clearer phrase that avoids the question. Try replacing the phrase with the most accurate choice from the following list.

if	**when**
only if	**only when**
but only if	**but only when**

For example, you might write the following

> **The seller agrees to replace any defective widgets, but only if the buyer notifies the seller of the defect within forty-eight hours of delivery.**

rather than either

> The seller agrees to replace any defective widgets on the condition that the buyer notifies the seller of the defect within forty-eight hours of delivery.

or

> The seller agrees to replace any defective widgets with the condition that the buyer notifies the seller of the defect within forty-eight hours of delivery.

For related information, see IF OR WHEN?

OPENINGS FOR LETTERS

In general, open with a sentence or two explaining the point of your letter or why you are writing.

> **In response to your inquiry, I am enclosing** ....

or

> **Last Monday, we met to discuss** .... **This letter formalizes our agreement that I would act as your attorney concerning**
> ....

This is usually preferable to starting with a sentence explaining who you are; that opening tempts the reader to say, "Who cares?" You can, however, explain who you are in the second or third sentence, after the reader has some reason to care, or you can add an explanatory reference as part of another sentence.

As your attorney, I want to notify you of some recent changes in the tax law that may require a change in your record-keeping practices.

In some cases, you may want to be slightly less direct, including a brief explanatory paragraph before your point. See BAD NEWS, GIVING IT and PERSUASIVE LETTERS for ways to handle these situations. For more detail on ways to structure other letters, see GENERAL CORRESPONDENCE LETTERS.

For opening routine letters, have stock phrases so that you avoid reinventing the wheel. But take care in selecting these stock phrases, because these opening phrases give the reader an impression of your personality, just as your demeanor creates an impression when you meet someone for the first time. In general, avoid stuffy openings, like *Pursuant to your request*, and long-winded ones, like *In regard to the matter of your request....* When you receive a letter that appeals to you, notice the opening. If you like it, modify it as needed and add it to your own collection of stock openings. For related information, see SALUTATIONS.

OPINION LETTERS AND EMAIL

1. General considerations.

Opinion letters serve the client in two ways: (1) they inform the client of the writer's legal analysis of the situation and any updating information and (2) they predict a possible outcome or recommend a certain path. In order to do both well, consider carefully your

- point of view,
- context,
- tone, and
- audience.

Choose objective writing if you are merely informing the client of the situation. Choose persuasive writing if you are trying to convince the client to do something, such as settle out of court or pay a bill. For more information on handling bad news, see BAD NEWS, GIVING IT and BAD NEWS, SOFTENING IT.

Likewise, choose the tone appropriate to your audience. If you know the client well and it seems appropriate, use a friendly tone; if you do not know the client well, be more formal but not stuffy. Choose a style that considers the client's experience in law and the client's needs. For examples and techniques, see TONE IN LETTERS.

Finally, be sure to address the needs of your audience. Because your client has asked a legal question, do make sure you answer the question. Do not write an abstract essay or a law review article on the general topic, but instead answer the specific question as best you can. Write in clear and understandable language unless you know the client prefers you do otherwise. Clients who want legalese may exist, but they are rare. For related information, see AUDIENCE, LEGALESE, and CLARITY.

2. Organization.

Opinion letters should contain any or all of the following, depending upon the status of the case.

(a) A heading, including the date.

RE: Merits of Pursuing 4/05 Claim Against Polewski

(b) A salutation.

Dear Dr. Brand:

For more information, see SALUTATIONS.

(d) An opening or introduction.

In the opening paragraph, state the question the letter will answer and refer to the request you received. Be sure to set the appropriate tone in this paragraph.

If the news is good, you may want to include the conclusion and recommendation to the client here. If the news is bad, you may state the conclusion later. (See subsection e.) Either way, include a caveat stating that the validity of the answer depends on the accuracy of the facts you were given. This caveat can serve as a transition into the next section. For related information, see OPENINGS FOR LETTERS.

(e) A summary of the facts.

Include the legally significant facts, the background facts, and any other facts the client and other potential readers should know that could affect the case. If the letter is long, set this section off with a subheading, such as the following.

FACTS OF THE CASE

or

RELEVANT FACTS

or just

FACTS

Clients may omit facts unfavorable to their position, so before writing you may want to probe to get those unfavorable facts that might influence your opinion. If appropriate, you may even draft the facts section and get the client to review it for accuracy before drafting the opinion itself. In the letter, ask the client to advise you of any additions or corrections needed in the letter, because your analysis depends on the accuracy of these facts. For related information, see LEGALLY SIGNIFICANT FACTS.

(f) Your conclusion, if this was not included earlier.

Make sure you answer the client's question. If the conclusion is long, you may set if off by using another subheading. See CONCLUSIONS.

(g) An explanation of your conclusion.

With your explanation, include a summary of the law and explain how the law applies to the client's facts.

(h) Clear signals of our organization.

If you are using subheadings, include one for this section. In the explanation section, lay out your reasoning step by step (see ORGANIZATION, LARGE–SCALE). Also take care to avoid using unneeded legal terms (see LEGALESE) and to define those legal terms that are needed (see UNOBTRUSIVE DEFINITIONS). Whether and when you include CITATIONS is a matter of judgment, depending on the sophistication of your reader, the extent to which your opinion rests on the case cited, and the possibility of the client misunderstanding the significance of the cites. Including citations, however, does not greatly affect readability; readers can skip over citations easily if they so choose.

(i) If relevant, a prediction or recommendation.

You may include a prediction of the outcome of the case, based on the overall balance of the strengths against the weaknesses in the application of the law to the facts.

When making a recommendation, you will be balancing here your professional responsibility to inform the client fully and your need to protect yourself against potential malpractice problems. Do cover yourself, but do it by explaining the specific caveats and reasons behind your opinion, not by using spineless, general phrases that only create ambiguities. Avoid phrases like *in effect, it is said that*, and *of course*. For example, the following paragraph hedges by explaining the writer's position rather than by inserting spineless phrases.

It is my opinion that you should try to settle this claim because litigation would not be economically worthwhile. My research indicates that New York law may favor Mr. Polewski's position, and that your legal position is therefore unclear. As a result, although the outcome of a trial is not certain, you would be running a substantial risk of losing this claim even after investing the substantial amount required to litigate the case.

Sometimes you will have to say that the client cannot do what he or she wants. When possible, make this bad news more palatable by offering alternatives that lead to the same objective or to similar ones. For example, you may have to state that a lawsuit would probably be financially unfeasible, but may be able to add that negotiation might bring about some of the desired result. When your answer is no, also include in your conclusion a brief outline of your strong reasons for the no, in case an unhappy or angry client skips reading the reasons section. For related information, see BAD NEWS, SOFTENING IT.

(j) A specific directive to the client to call or come in to discuss the matter further.

Unless the letter is meant to do so, add a sentence explaining to your reader that your letter does not create any legal rights. For related information, see OPINION OR ADVICE?

(k) A closing.

Sincerely yours,

or

Yours truly,

For related information, see CLOSINGS FOR LETTERS.

For a discussion of letters in general, see GENERAL CORRESPONDENCE LETTERS. For related information, see TONE IN LETTERS.

OPINION OR ADVICE?

When writing an opinion letter or conferring with a client, an attorney may give a client a legal opinion on a matter as long as that opinion is based on the law and the reasonable boundaries of the law. An attorney may also advise a client to pursue a certain legal course. Be careful, however, of personal, as opposed to legal, advice that could cross the line from professional opinion to coercion. Such advice could violate the *Model Code of Professional Responsibility*, a question beyond the scope of this book. For related information, see OPINION LETTERS, subsection 2(i).

OPINIONS, READING THEM

When reading a judicial opinion, consider the steps listed below to increase both your effectiveness and your efficiency.

1. General considerations.

Keep in mind the purpose for which you are using that opinion. For example, if you are reading an opinion to learn about a particular subject for class, such as personal jurisdiction, read the opinion for what it offers to enhance the analysis of personal jurisdiction. If you are reading the opinion for research, read with the thesis or issue of your memo, brief, or paper in mind.

Also understand the purpose for which the opinion was written, which differs from your purpose as you read the opinion now. Opinions are written, first, to explain the court's decision to the people who brought their problem to the court for resolution. The judge wants both parties to see the fairness of its resolution. For the winning party, this task is not so difficult; the winner, after all, believed the law favored his or her position. The winner is not likely to scrutinize the opinion for every error. The losing party, however, will scrutinize that opinion and will not be inclined to accept the court's reasoning.

The judge understands the loser's position, and often writes the opinion with that position in mind. For example, after explaining the facts of the case, the judge often presents the losing party's arguments and explains the flaws in those arguments. Then, after explaining the arguments that did not prevail, the judge presents the reasoning upon which the court relied. Thus the court often does not start with its winning argument, even though in other legal writing the strongest argument usually goes first.

2.   Specific techniques.

Because you, however, are looking for something more specific, your purpose differs from that of the opinion writer. Therefore, you may want to read through the opinion once to get the gist of it, without marking the text or taking extensive notes. This aids your understanding by helping you see the overall framework of the case before you begin dealing with the details. Note who won the case and why. You may even want to begin by reading the end of the opinion to see the results; then go back to get an overview of how the court reached that result.

Then read more specifically for your purpose. Focus on the holding, the result of the case, and relate that holding to your topic or issue. For example, if a new trial was granted because evidence was not properly suppressed, then study the case to extract a definition of when evidence should be suppressed.

Then reread the case, briefing it according to your preference. Note how the court uses the law, facts, trends, reasoning patterns, and social context to reach its result. Determine, or brief, the following:

- the procedural posture, or where the case is in the judicial process
- the holding, or what result the court reached and why
- the legal rule, or how the court established fundamental rule or legal basis for the opinion
- the court's reasoning, including
  - how it proceeded from its basis to its conclusion;

- how it put the arguments in context and accounted for practical circumstances;
- how it addressed specific arguments, including policy arguments;
- how it adopted specific types of arguments, such as law and economics, critical race theory, judicial economy, and statutory construction; and
- how it eliminated or omitted other possible results.

• which facts were critical to the outcome

For suggestions on how to do this, see CASE BRIEFS.

3. Appellate briefs.

If you are working on an appellate brief, also note the standard of review, because this may affect your use of the case.

OPTIMAL OR *OPTIMUM?*

Most legal readers prefer *optimum*, although either is correct.

This is the <u>optimum</u> situation for the plaintiff, who would prefer to settle rather than file suit.

or

This is the <u>optimal</u> situation for the plaintiff because we settled for more than she had asked.

Optimum refers to the best condition, amount or degree for a particular situation. For PRECISION, do not use it to mean best in an absolute sense.

OR

Or is a conjunction that signals to the reader that you mean *any one of the listed items*, rather than *all of them*. Thus *or* is disjunctive. In legal writing, misuse of *or* can create ambiguity in two situations.

1. *Or* alone is not always enough to communicate your meaning.

Often you must clarify by adding other explanatory phrases, such as

by any of the following means

or

any of the following subsections.

2. *Or* alone is usually not enough to signal clearly that a long list is disjunctive.

When you rely solely on *or* to show the structure of the list, the reader has to read through most of the list before finding out whether this is an *and* or an *or* situation. Therefore, if your list is very long, let the reader know before the list that this is an *or* situation.

> **Either party may notify the other of a delay <u>by any of the following means</u>:** telephoning the other party, sending an agent with a written message, sending an agent with an oral message, sending a telegram addressed to the other party personally, sending a certified letter, or meeting with the other party in person.

rather than

> Either party may notify the other of a delay by telephoning the other party, sending an agent with the message, sending a telegram, sending a certified letter, <u>or any combination of these</u>.

For related information, see CONJUNCTIONS; AND/OR; and LISTS, STRUCTURE OF.

ORAL OR *VERBAL*?

Verbal refers to any communication using words, whether spoken or written; *nonverbal* refers to gestures, actions, and other unspoken communication.

> **A successful lawyer is usually a master of verbal communication.**

Oral refers to any communication that is spoken, rather than written. Do not use *verbal* when you mean *oral*.

> **The contract was based on an oral agreement made July 6, 2001.**

rather than

> The contract was based on a verbal agreement made July 6, 2001.

ORAL PRESENTATIONS

Oral presentations must convey the essence of written presentations, but in less time and more simply. Whether it is an objective presentation to a senior partner or a persuasive argument before a court, the presentation should focus on

- the issue to be resolved,
- the answer, and
- a clear explanation.

The following techniques can help you present this content effectively.

1. In an objective oral presentation.

    (a) State the issue to which the listener wants an answer. Incorporate the same three parts used in Issue Statements: the general law under which the question is being asked, the legal question, and the legally significant facts pertinent to that question. For examples, see ISSUE STATEMENTS and QUESTIONS PRESENTED.

(b) Give the answer. Do not make the listener wait for this. For examples, see BRIEF ANSWER and CONCLUSION.

(c) Make sure your listener is familiar with the facts of the case; if you are not sure, ask the listener. If facts are needed, give a succinct presentation of the legally significant facts, the background facts, and any significant emotional facts, if they relate to the issue and answer and are necessary to make your point. Keep this summary as short as possible.

(d) Explain your analysis as succinctly as possible. Make sure extraneous detail is omitted and remaining details are clearly connected to each other and to your conclusion. The listener wants an explanation that justifies your main message and sound reasoning that supports your position. The listener also wants to know that accepting your position will not precipitate any negative ramifications. These goals exist in any kind of oral presentation, whether to a supervising attorney, to a client, or to a colleague.

(e) Be extremely flexible in answering questions. It is likely that you will get interrupted by any legal listener, so use the questions to explain to the listener what the answer is and to move gracefully through the pre-planned parts of your presentation. For example, if you are asked a question about the third issue you wanted to discuss while you are discussing the first, answer the question about the third issue and move gracefully back into the first. You can do this by saying something like *which is why we are arguing under the first issue that* . . . .

2. In persuasive oral presentations.

(a) State the issue to be resolved and your answer to that issue. State it first, so you can get this information out before you are interrupted.

(b) Explain the plan of your argument to defer questions about later issues.

(c) Make sure the listener knows the facts. If you are the moving party, you must give the listener the facts of the case. But if they so choose, let the listeners waive that presentation of facts.

(d) State the conclusions the court should reach, including a brief statement explaining that a decision in your client's favor is consistent with principles of law and fair under these facts.

(e) Know the record and the law thoroughly. There is no substitute for this. If you are comfortable with the record and the law, there will be no hesitation or weakness in your argument. Your confidence should then come automatically.

(f) Address the case's impact on the law in general, especially if addressing an appellate court. The listener wants to know how the decision in this case will affect subsequent cases.

(g) Be candid and flexible; deal with weak points directly and welcome questions as an opportunity to explain the answers to the listener.

(h) Be respectful, showing good manners and good humor and keeping personalities out of the argument.

ORDERS

Orders are brief documents issued by the court that state a decision on a motion and any action that the court is ordering as a result of that decision. For the court's convenience, attorneys are often expected to draft the orders they want the court to sign if their sides prevail. Your main goals when writing orders are to include all needed information precisely and to avoid unneeded verbiage and legalese. As with all court documents, be sure to check and follow any rules in your jurisdiction.

1. Parts of an Order.

An order includes the caption, the body, and the signatures. The caption follows the same form as the caption on the complaint, motions, and other documents in the case. The word *order* simply goes in the location where the names of the other documents were. For examples, see CAPTIONS.

The body often begins with a reference to the procedure preceding the order, to show that proper procedure has been followed.

The defendant filed a Motion to Dismiss the complaint on the ground that it failed to state a claim upon which relief can be granted. After hearing oral arguments and receiving briefs, the court rendered its ruling to dismiss the complaint on January 9, 2000, which is incorporated here by reference.

It then includes the detail of the order itself.

IT IS HEREBY ORDERED that plaintiffs' complaint and all causes of action arising under it are dismissed against the Defendant on the merits with cost.

If the order involves several items, they can be tabulated to make the content easier to read. The signature line should then follow the form in your jurisdiction, leaving a line for the judge to sign.

2. Avoiding unneeded legalese.

Use terms of art when needed, but avoid legalese. For examples of both, see TERMS OF ART and LEGALESE.

ORGANIZATION

Effective organization guides the reader through the text, just as a map guides a traveler through the country. This organization is not easy to achieve, but it is worth the effort. Clear and logical organization distinguishes excellent writing from mediocre.

1. When to organize.

You must organize any piece of writing, but you need not do it at one particular point in the writing process. Instead, you may develop your organization at any of several stages. For example, you may organize by outlining during prewriting. Alternatively, you may first collect your thoughts or even write a loose set of notes or rough draft before you develop your organization. For further help, see PREWRITING, OUTLINES, and ORGANIZATION FOR THOSE WHO CAN'T OUTLINE.

2. How to organize.

Clear organization is easier if you think carefully about the information you want to convey. If you have expressed your message clearly to yourself, you are likely to communicate it more clearly to your reader. This is why some writers need to develop notes or create a rough draft before outlining.

As you think about your organization, consider the following questions.

- What is the main theme or message?
- What content must be included to convey that message to these audiences?
- What are the logical categories or groups into which that content falls?
- Which of these groups are most relevant to my issue?

After determining the answers to these questions, you should find it easier to determine your major points and the most logical order for those points.

Plan for and take the time you need to include all the parts needed in your document and develop a good sense of the overall interrelationship of those parts. Then consider several ways of expressing that relationship. Determine which ideas are major steps in your analytical progression and which ideas are subordinate, supporting those major steps.

Experiment with different major steps and different orders, if the structure of the law allows variations. There are usually several coherent ways to organize, each of which can still please your audience and conform to your purpose. Sketch many versions, at least three, even if some of them seem absurd. By comparing them all, you will get a stronger sense of which one is best. Consult with your reader, if possible, or with others at this stage. Then choose the organization that best fits your purpose, audience, and scope. For related information, see PUR-POSE and AUDIENCE.

Start at the micro-, middle or macro-levels of the project and work through to the rest. Depending on your preferred writing process, your thinking may be facilitated by starting with any of the following approaches to organization.

(a) You may find that you work best by starting at the macro-level with one overall statement of your theme or message. This is often useful when the scope seems too broad or you need a sense of specific direction. To do this, write out your purpose and list your main audiences; then write out your message. Then relate all sections of the document to the purpose and the substantive message. Use parallel structure, parallel word choice, and whatever other devices are appropriate to reflect that organization in your message. Then ask yourself what is needed to support that message. Answering this question will help you identify issues, subissues, answers, remedies, needed sources, and other details. From these you can see what must be included in the organization.

To complete your organization, connect these points coherently, determining which points are subordinate to others and identifying all the support needed for each point. For help doing this, see OUTLINES, LEGAL ANALYSIS, PARALLEL STRUCTURE, WORD CHOICE; and CONNECTIONS, MAKING THEM.

(b) You may find that the middle level of your document appears first to you: you know what three or five points you have to cover. From those points, you can work to figure out what your theme or message is, what broader context your points fit into, as well as what support is needed to fill in the details.

To organize this way, list all the points that you think you need to include in your paper and then group each individual point with others that seem related. Experiment with different groupings until you find the scheme that seems logical and provides a place for each point you have listed. When you have settled on a grouping, ask yourself why those groups make sense, and write down your reasons. This process should help you determine the logical connections among the various points you will be including, so the points knit together in ways that help you to choose the best organization for the readers.

(c) If you prefer to start at the micro-level, gather all that you need on paper, electronically, or both. Then, when your content is captured on paper, start to look for ways to group that content coherently. You can begin by grouping items you know belong in a list. Look at each piece of content to find logical links to other pieces of content. Write down labels for the groups as they occur to you.

Gradually you will build a sense of the larger units in your material, and you will begin to get ideas about headings for those groups. These headings become major organizational units for your outline. Once you have extracted these main points, you can begin to see ways to connect each to the theme and to each other, always keeping your purpose and your audience in mind.

See what organization works: try three or more plans, thinking how well each would work to suit your purpose. Let all of them rest and later choose the one that best suits your purpose and your audience.

For further help, see HABITS, WRITING and WRITING PROCESS. For various ways to organize, see OUTLINING, ORGANIZATION FOR THOSE WHO CAN'T OUTLINE, GETTING STARTED, and PRE-WRITING.

3. How to present your organization to the reader.

In legal writing, worry more about making your organization clear to the reader, less about being too obvious. For example, use enumeration, such as *first, second, third,* or *(1), (2), (3).* Use transitions, such as *additionally* or *in contrast.* Use headings and subheadings. For help here, see TRANSITIONS; CONNECTIONS, MAKING THEM; and HEADINGS.

Use focused paragraphs that include topic sentences, usually at the beginning of the paragraph, and that include support for that point only. Those topic sentences can relate to the overall theme, to the previous paragraph, to the current paragraph, or to all three. See PARAGRAPHS and TOPIC SENTENCES. Remember that the reader needs guidance, reminders, and a sense of the whole, so present your analysis or argument in a way that will keep the audience engaged throughout the document.

For more information, see ORGANIZATION, LARGE–SCALE; ORGANIZATION, SMALL–SCALE; TOPICAL ORGANIZATION; and CHRONOLOGICAL ORGANIZATION.

ORGANIZATION FOR THOSE WHO CAN'T OUTLINE

The following steps can help you organize successfully, even if you have never been able to master outlining.

1. Brainstorm.

Try listing all the points you want to make or might want to make, or just list everything you can think of. Do not worry about order, quality, or anything else at this stage except coming up with ideas. This stage could take the form of free writing, or drafting without stopping to look at notes or revise even spelling. Or it could take the form of note taking, jotting down all sorts of ideas in a list or on cards. The form does not matter here so much as the result. Do not stop to delete or revise any ideas; editing at this point can distract you from the primary task of generating ideas. You want to seek out many options, so that you have more to choose from later.

2. Group your ideas.

Read through all your drafting or all your listed points and see if they fall into any logical groups. See if some major ideas emerge from the list. Try grouping the points several different ways before you settle on one way that makes the most sense to you. Often the organization that occurs to you first will be adequate, but not optimal. Alternatively, if your list of points includes six or fewer items, you may already have your logical groups. If so, fill in more supporting points on those items and then check to see if you are still satisfied with those groups.

3. Organize the groups.

Look at each group and decide which point is the major one and which are subordinate, or supporting, points. At this stage you may still find some errors in your grouping, but you can revise those groups as needed. You may also find that you have stated the same thing in two different ways, so that you can strike out redundant points. You may also delete points that are clearly irrelevant.

4. Subdivide further, if needed.

Divide your arguments, and divide the subpoints made in those arguments. Check each item to make sure that it should not be subdivided further. Remember that you need to make only one point at a time. Even though all your points are inextricably interrelated, you must divide them into manageable portions for the reader. For related information, see PARAGRAPHS.

5. Order the groups, points, and subpoints.

After the points are divided, decide how to order them. To determine this order, think about what will be logical to your reader, rather than what seems important to you. To help determine what is logical to the reader, ask yourself the following three questions.

(a) Is there some threshold point that comes first? For example, if your case involved a jurisdiction question, that question would logically come first because the court will not look to any other issues until they have determined that it is the court's job to decide those issues.

(b) Is one point more significant than the others? For example, if your case involves clear-cut violations of freedom of speech and also involves some technical violations of proper notice, you may want to start with the violation of the freedom of speech. This point may convince your reader that justice favors your side, and will probably make more compelling reading. The technical point may then provide a convenient peg upon which to hang the hat of justice.

(c) Is one point stronger than the others? For example, if your case involves a clear-cut violation of proper notice but also involves a potential-but-debatable violation of freedom of speech, you may start with the violation of proper notice. This way you can establish some justification for your client's position before you present more questionable justifications.

6. Write.

At this point you will have all the information provided by a traditional outline, and you can rewrite it in outline format, if you wish, or go directly to writing your rough draft. If you had started trying to outline by writing a roman numeral at the top of the page, you would have been expecting yourself to do all of these previous steps in your head, which is why trying to write a traditional outline is futile for many people.

7. Check the organization.

Once you have written your full draft, recheck your organization. In fact, many successful writers write a rough draft first and then outline or go through the organization steps listed above. One way to check your organization is to read the first sentence of each paragraph throughout the document. This should give you a summary of the points of the paper, although it will not document the proof of those points.

If you find it difficult to approach organizing, see ORGANIZATION, LARGE–SCALE and WRITING PROCESS. For related information, see GETTING STARTED.

ORGANIZATION, *THEY* OR *IT*?

See CORPORATIONS, *THEY* OR *IT*?

ORGANIZATION, LARGE–SCALE

Large-scale organization conveys the overall coherence of any piece of writing. Large-scale organization is communicated throughout the document. It is communicated in tables of content, summaries of argument, executive summaries, headings, topic and thesis sentences, introductions, and conclusions. The logic of this organization should flow from a careful balancing of many factors, including audience, purpose, content, legal analytical patterns, and local traditions.

1. Audience.

Adjust the organization to fit the way your audience may think of the content, or the way you would like your audience to think of the content. When writing briefs to a court, always check the procedural posture and the procedural rules, which will help you understand how the court will approach the issues in your case. For example, when organizing a brief for a court, consider what question will be first in the court's mind, and try to begin with that, such as whether this court has jurisdiction over the issue. That procedural issue would probably be discussed first; if the answer is no, the substantive questions will not matter. When organizing an opinion letter, you may need to begin with the client's question because he is expecting an answer to that, even if it is not the main legal question.

2. Purpose.

Also adjust the organization to fit the document's purpose. If you are organizing a memo that exposes weaknesses in your client's case and you want to discourage the client from proceeding, you may begin with those weaknesses. But if the client wishes to proceed, you will organize the brief differently, probably beginning with the client's strongest arguments because your purpose then will be to win. Similarly, you may organize a contract chronologically, exposing the steps in the transaction if your purpose is to comfort the other party by spelling out each step. But you may organize the contract topically if your purpose is to encourage the non-represented party to sign, and thus place affirmative statements of duties before descriptions of penalties incurred by breach.

3. Content.

Content affects your organization when the law is strongly, consistently discussed in particular patterns. A statute may have four elements, all of which courts consistently discuss in the same order. Rather than disrupt that scheme, you may choose to present your document by following it. Or when particular arguments appear consistently in a string of cases, you may choose to group your analysis of those arguments similarly. If a trend is emerging in a series of cases, you may want to pick up that trend in your analysis. Or if the content of a transaction is suggesting its own unique scheme, you may fashion the contract accordingly and reject more traditional structures. The law usually offers several possible structures for a document. It is up to you to decide how much that law will actually inform your document's structure.

4. Local Traditions.

Local traditions may also affect your organization. Your local court, or your firm, may organize certain documents or doctrines in prescribed ways to which all local readers are accustomed. Research those traditions as you make your final organizational decisions.

5. Analytical Patterns.

Analytical patterns also influence your organization, and these may be the richest and most subtle adjustments you make. From your general legal reading, you will extract a range of analytical patterns used in U.S. legal practice. Those patterns range from traditional deductive and inductive patterns to post modern structures. As you read the pertinent materials for any project, you will note analytical patterns such as general-to-specific, rule-to-conclusion patterns or inductive examples-to-generalities patterns. You will also note the balancing tests used in constitutional issues or in law and economics arguments. In some judicial decisions, you will see a post modern array of opinion, concurrences, and dissents, out of which you must extract the law. All of these patterns and more are available to you, too. You may see several that will work.

Choose the pattern that best allows you to convey your message to your audience. If the reader's thinking would differ from the traditional organization, as in an innovative law review article or an unusual case, compensate. If you can reorganize the content for the reader without violating your thinking, do so. If you cannot, then inform the reader early and clearly of your organization, so the reader can adjust his or her thinking to follow the document. For help choosing the organization, see LEGAL ANALYSIS, MEMOS and PROCEDURAL OR SUBSTANTIVE?

Always communicate your document's overall large-scale organization, so that your choice of organization communicates to the reader how each subpart fits in the whole. For example, if there is a question of governmental immunity in your memo and two subissues must be raised to answer the larger issue of immunity, organize both the question presented and the discussion section so that the reader sees how the subissues fit into the larger question of immunity. For techniques to help communicate the organization, see HEADINGS, TOPIC SENTENCES, and CONCLUSIONS.

Work on the large-scale organization as early in the writing process as you can and keep working on it until it is clear to you. Most issues can be organized in several ways, and your paper must be organized in a way that makes sense to you. Consider your possible large-scale organization as you gather research in prewriting, as you outline, and as you rewrite. If the large-scale organization is not working at any of these three points, try rearranging. If you wait until revising or polishing, it may be too late and too frustrating to change. For related information, see WRITING PROCESS, OUTLINES, ORGANIZATION FOR THOSE WHO CAN'T OUTLINE, and REWRITING. For more extensive discussion of different ways to organize, see Chapter 9 of Mary B. Ray & Barbara J. Cox, Beyond the Basics: A Text for Advanced Legal Writers (2d ed. 2003), and Chapters 4 & 5 of Jill J. Ramsfield, The Law as Architecture: Building Legal Documents (2000).

ORGANIZATION, SMALL–SCALE

Small-scale organization refers to the organization between and within paragraphs and sentences; it communicates the logical links between those paragraphs and sentences. In contrast, large-scale organization refers to the overall format of the analysis or explanation. Small-scale organization involves six aspects of writing, each of which is explained in detail in a separate entry. These include

- using effective topic sentences (see TOPIC SENTENCES),

- putting sentences in logical order (see SYLLOGISMS),
- clarifying logical connections (see CONNECTIONS, MAKING THEM),
- choosing the most effective sentence structure (see SENTENCE STRUCTURE, subsections 6 and 7),
- communicating the links between sentences (see TRANSITIONS and CONNECTIONS, MAKING THEM), and
- making lists readable (see LISTS, STRUCTURE OF).

The revision for small-scale organization should take place after writing and rewriting, so that you are not struggling with fundamental ideas at the same time you are straightening out the expression of those ideas. For related information, see WRITING PROCESS and REVISING CHECKLIST.

ORNATE LANGUAGE

See FLOWERY LANGUAGE.

OTHERWISE

Otherwise means *in another way* or *apart from that*.

We cannot locate our expert witness, but otherwise the case is in good shape.

It can sound rather informal, so use it sparingly. Also avoid overusing *otherwise* or using it loosely.

If they accept this offer, we will settle. If they refuse, we will sue.

rather than

If they accept this offer, we will settle. Otherwise, we will sue.

OUTLINES

Outlines can help writers before or after writing a draft. Outlines can take any form: lists, barely legible scratching, flow charts, webs, Venn diagrams, or traditional outlines. Whatever the form, outlines help the writer make sure any reader can understand the document's organization. Make an outline, either before or after writing, by sketching a general portrait of the large-scale ideas, such as the following.

Custody disputes

    Was "tender years"

    not any more

    ERA contributed

    changed in 1973

Now statutory—five factors + 1 = "best interests"

Apply here—probably mother

Conclusion

Then fill in the details as you reread authority and rethink your ideas.

Custody disputes

    Was "tender years"

        "best interests of child" paramount then <u>Jones</u> at 48, 50.

        Mother used to be thought best <u>Id</u>.

        ERA, general social changes say father or mother can "mother" <u>Smith</u> at 97

        Led to partial codification, some changes in 1973

    Statute R.C.W. 29.09.999 (quote)

        Court must show they looked at factors <u>Smith</u> at 85, all five + anything else relevant

        Broad discretion, but must be more structured now. <u>Id</u>.

Apply here

    Factor 1—wishes of parents

        both want, but both will give visitation rights

    Factor 2—wishes of child

        nothing expressed

    Factor 3—Interrelationship of children w/parents

        mother drinks (<u>Johnson</u> mom drank too—distinguish)

        father strict (<u>Pines</u>—father got son—same?)

        mother stable? (see <u>Schwartz</u>—not as crazy as this woman: distinguish)

    Factor 4—Child's adjustment to home & community

        with mom now, no adjustment

        father will live in same city, but move required

    Factor 5—Mental and physical health

        mother stable? (see <u>Schwartz</u>; distinguish this mother, not that crazy)

        father unemotional

    Other factors—adultery, moral character

father having an affair, missed meeting with kids

cf. Hildebrand—doesn't mean he can't "mother"

Conclusion

Mom probably gets them because she is more responsive to their needs, has them now, hasn't missed any time with them.

Sketch out several versions. Use these sketches to make sure you come to understand your major points. As you develop your outline from these sketches remember your document's purpose, audience, and scope. For example, the preceding outline takes its major cue from the statute itself, following the elements in order. But it may be too long and may not have enough persuasive impact. You can experiment by writing point headings that group the components differently, such as putting together all the factors that are not in dispute.

I. THE TRIAL COURT SHOULD AWARD CUSTODY TO MRS. DAVIS BECAUSE IT IS IN THE CHILDREN'S BEST INTERESTS TO STAY IN THEIR FAMILY HOME.

Factors not in dispute

A. Interrelationship strong

B. No adjustment needed

C. Mental and physical health optimal

II. THE TRIAL COURT SHOULD NOT AWARD CUSTODY TO MR. DAVIS BECAUSE HE CANNOT DEVOTE ENOUGH TIME TO THE CHILDREN.

A. Interrelationship weak

B. Adjustment too hard

C. Mental and physical health will be impaired

D. Affair will be devastating

Do several different versions to test the strength of how all the ingredients combine, affect one another, and interrelate. If you can, test the versions by showing them to another reader or two. Ask which one makes the most sense in this context. From that input, recombine the ingredients to arrive at the strongest organization. This process will help you avoid falling in love with your first outline, which is often writer-based: the first outline may make sense to you, but not necessarily to anyone else. Experimenting will broaden your thinking and your analytical approach enough to transform it to be more reader-based. If you reach a decision on the outline before writing the first draft, then at the writing stage you can just fill in the blanks left in the outline. Make lots of notes in the margin to remember details about each point; this will make writing easier.

If you outline after writing, you can use the outline to check logic and details. Any reader should be able to write your outline after reading your writing, so you can make sure your writing is clear by outlining it yourself. To do this, print out the draft and highlight the initial sentence of each paragraph. Then read those sentences aloud, checking for logical flow. Read critically, making sure each step of your presentation is congruent with the overall logic. A problem with this approach, as with any other, is that it can remain writer-based, making sense to only you. Try reading the draft in bad faith, as many of your audiences will. Criticize its structure and ask what would make it clearer. Or ask another reader or two to outline it from the draft. From their responses, clean up the outline and move parts accordingly.

If ORGANIZATION is a problem for you, outlining may offer a solution. If outlining does not work for you, see ORGANIZATION FOR THOSE WHO CAN'T OUTLINE. For other aids to organization and related problems, see WRITING PROCESS; WRITING BLOCKS; and ORGANIZATION, LARGE–SCALE.

OVERDONE

See FLOWERY LANGUAGE, MODIFIERS, and EMOTIONAL LANGUAGE.

OVERREFINEMENT

This term refers to the kind of errors writers commit when they are trying hard to be correct but do not quite understand the rules. For example, a writer might use *I feel badly* even though *I feel bad* is correct. For other common overrefinement problems, see *GOOD* OR *WELL?*, *BETWEEN YOU AND ME* OR *BETWEEN YOU AND I?*, *CAN* OR *MAY?*, *PRIOR TO, IN ADVANCE OF*, and *WHO* OR *WHOM?*

In a broader sense, *overrefinement* refers to the tendency some writers have to revise their writing too much. For example, a writer might remove important transitions in the name of conciseness, or create figurative language when literal language conveys the point better. Fight the temptation to overrefine, which can rob your STYLE of its spontaneity and READABILITY. Overrefinement can also add unnecessary time to your schedule. For help with this problem, see DEADLINES, MEETING THEM. For ways to refine effectively, see REVISING and POLISHING.

PADDING

In legal writing, avoid padding, or adding content not because it is needed but solely to increase length. Legal readers prize CONCISENESS; padding will not impress them.

PARAGRAPH BLOCKS

A paragraph block is a group of paragraphs that fit together as a visual and substantive unit, just as sentences fit into the unit of a single paragraph. It is created by adding an extra space before the first and after the last paragraph in the block.

1. When to use.

Paragraph blocks are most likely to be useful when your analysis requires a sub-subsection of explanation in the text; in this situation, you often will not want to add another level of heading because you already have headings and subheadings, and a third level might fragment the organization too much. The visual separation of a paragraph block is not as strong as that created by a subheading, and thus it is useful without distracting from the headings already in place. The paragraph block is most likely to be useful in longer documents. In shorter documents, headings, subheadings, and paragraphs should provide sufficient organizational tools. For related information, see POINT HEADINGS, HEADINGS, PARAGRAPHS, and TRANSITIONS.

2. How to use.

To create a paragraph block visually, put an extra blank line between the previous text and the first paragraph of the block. At the end of the paragraph block, again add an extra blank line. Paragraph blocks work best if they are limited to three to six paragraphs; if the blocks are longer, the reader forgets about the paragraph block and its organizing value is lost. If the block consists of only two paragraphs, the reader may think that the blank lines are typographical errors.

Remember that substance dictates the form of your writing. Therefore, avoid creating a paragraph block solely for looks. Create one only when your analysis requires the sub-subsection.

PARAGRAPH LENGTH

In a brief, memo, or longer opinion letter, you should average two or three paragraph breaks per page. In business letters or email, you will have more paragraphs per page. Whatever the setting, however, you should divide paragraphs logically rather than periodically. Therefore, first divide paragraphs logically and then in revision change this paragraph division, if needed, using the following guidelines.

1. Long Paragraphs.

If you find one paragraph that runs about half a page, leave it undivided if it is logically one unit. If you have one paragraph that runs for more than two-thirds of a page, try to divide it, because the reader needs a visual break. If you have many paragraphs that run two-thirds of a page, check for general organization problems. You may be focusing on the connections between points but ignoring subtler distinctions, which will make the overall organization muddy.

2. Short Paragraphs.

If you have written a one-sentence paragraph or many short paragraphs, check to see if you have supported your points adequately. Also check for paragraphs that present fragments of a full development, and so should be unified for logical flow.

Occasionally a one-sentence paragraph can be used for emphasis, but not more than once in six pages. Occasionally a one-sentence paragraph also serves as a transition or an introduction, but again it should not occur too often. For more on this, see ONE–SENTENCE PARAGRAPHS. For related writing problems, see SENTENCE LENGTH.

PARAGRAPHS

In legal writing, each paragraph should focus on only one point, and each should have a topic sentence that states that point, usually at the beginning of the paragraph. In other disciplines, such as literary criticism, this more obvious form of logical organization is often disfavored. Obvious organization, however, is rarely criticized in legal writing. Instead, your reader will be grateful to you for making it easy to see the point.

For example, in the following paragraphs, the points are much clearer when two paragraphs are used, one for each point made, and when each point is stated in a topic sentence at the first of the paragraph.

To complain about the illegality of a search, the defendant must, as the State correctly asserts, have an expectation of privacy in the place searched. United States v. Park, 999 U.S. 314, 316 (2009); United States v. Toyle, 999 U.S. 115, 118 (2010). The State implies that solely because the defendant's office, desk, and files were within a public building, he knowingly exposed them to the public. This is incorrect. The uncontroverted testimony in this case established that defendant did expect his office, desk, and files to be private because he exercised exclusive use and control over those areas and in things present in those areas. (R. 207–209).

This expectation of privacy must be justified under the law. In this case, the defendant was justified in expecting privacy in his private office. There was no free public access to these areas. The sole fact that a private office is located in a public building does not satisfy the "plain view" doctrine as restated in United States v. Peabody, 999 U.S. 22, 26 (2011). The trial court in this case thus found that defendant had rights guaranteed by the fourth amendment of the United States Constitution and by article I, section 2 of the Constitution of the State of Iowa, and that these rights were violated.

rather than

> The trial court in this case found that defendant had rights guaranteed by the fourth amendment of the United States Constitution and by article I, section 2 of the Constitution of the State of Iowa, which were violated. To complain about the illegality of a search, the defendant must, as the State correctly asserts, have an expectation of privacy in the place searched. United States v. Park, 999 U.S. 314, 316 (2009); United States v. Toyle, 999 U.S. 115, 118 (2010). The State implies that because the defendant's office, desk, and files were within a public building, he knowingly exposed them to the public. This is simply not the fact in this case. The uncontroverted testimony indicates defendant did expect his office, desk, and files to be private and that he exercised exclusive use and control in these areas (R. 207–209). There was no free public access to these areas. The location of a private office in a public building does not satisfy the plain view doctrine as restated in United States v. Peabody, 999 U.S. 22, 26 (2011). Further, the defendant's expectation of privacy in his private office is justified under the law.

For related information, see ONE–SENTENCE PARAGRAPHS, TOPIC SENTENCES, and PARAGRAPH LENGTH.

PARALLEL CITATIONS

See CITATIONS, PARALLEL.

PARALLELISM

See PARALLEL STRUCTURE; LISTS, STRUCTURE OF; and EMPHASIS.

PARALLEL STRUCTURE

Parallel structure means using the same grammatical structure for things that are logically parallel. For example, parallel adjectives can describe parallel qualities.

Defendant was hostile, abusive, and violent.

rather than

Defendant was hostile, abused the officer, and had violent behavior.

Parallel prepositional phrases can also describe parallel qualities.

Plaintiff admits he was driving without his license, without his lights on, and with an open six-pack of beer in the front seat.

Parallel structure creates a grammatically transparent framework that allows substantive points to shine through in clear relation to each other. This structure is extremely useful in legal writing because it simplifies syntax and focuses on substance. Therefore, three common places to use parallel structure are in lists, in comparisons or contrasts of cases, and in persuasive writing to add emphasis.

1.   Use parallel structure in lists.

The plaintiff parked his car, turned the wheels toward the curb, and set the handbrake.

This point was established in the testimony of the defendant, of the police officer investigating the accident, and of a passerby who observed the accident.

Parallel structure is also useful for emphasizing the logical parallels between the items in a list, such as in the following list of facts. See EMPHASIS.

The trial court found that Cox Realty displayed the Realax logo at its office, signs, and forms; that Cox's employees each wear a blue blazer with the Realax logo on it; and that Cox Realty benefits from nationwide advertising identifying Realax franchises as "local professionals."

2.   Use parallel structure to compare or contrast cases.

One place where parallel structure is particularly desirable is in the analogy of two similar cases, as shown by the following example taken from the middle of a paragraph. (Citations are omitted.)

In Rickaby, the plaintiff's reputation in the community was not impaired even though the employer disclosed his reasons for discharging the employee in a judicial proceeding. Similarly, in this case Elmore's reputation in the community has not been impaired merely because the employer disclosed her reasons for discharging Elmore in conferences with union officials.

As this example shows, using accurate transitions, such as *similarly*, can also enhance the point of the parallel.

Parallel structure can also underscore a contrast. By making similarities obvious, parallel structure allows the differences to stand out.

In Rickaby, plaintiff's reputation in the community was not impaired even though the employer disclosed his reasons for discharging the employee in a judicial proceeding. In contrast, Elmore's reputation was impaired, because his employer not only disclosed her reasons for discharging Elmore in conferences with union officials but also disclosed those reasons at an office party and in a reference letter written to Elmore's prospective employers.

For more information on this technique, see COMPARISON.

3.   Use parallel structure to add emphasis. In the following example, two points support the implied point that the defendant deserves no

sympathy. The parallel structure of *failed to schedule, failed to have* and *failed to warn* thus reflects the logical parallels of the content and also allows the writer to use repetition to emphasize a point.

> **The defendant company failed to schedule routine maintenance for the press, failed to have a technician check the press when operators complained of its malfunction, and failed to warn the plaintiff about those malfunctions.**

For related information, see REPETITION, subsections 2–4.

PARAPHRASE

Paraphrasing means restating someone else's ideas in your own words. There is nothing illegitimate about paraphrasing as long as you give credit when you have used a specific source, such as an opinion or article, and as long as you avoid misstating the original point. Paraphrasing is more useful than quoting when the original language.

- is hard to understand,
- is lengthy, or
- incorporates irrelevant information that could confuse your reader.

> **The court stated that it must intervene in this case to resolve the issue of mutuality despite the emotional pleas for freedom of contract.**

changed from the original

> Despite the defendant's emotional plea regarding the centrality of upholding contracts to the free working of a democracy, we cannot ignore the plaintiff's complaint. In this case, the court must intervene; the issue of mutuality, not to mention that of duress, requires that the court examine both the contract's wording and the parol evidence surrounding the signing of that contract.

Quote only when the exact language is needed, as when discussing the interpretation of a phrase in a statute, or when you could not say it better yourself, as with an apt and relevant phrase in an opinion.

In writing memos or briefs, it is sometimes permissible to quote a rule that is worded the same way in multiple cases without quotation marks, as long as you use a pinpoint cite. Often this is true for short phrases that are TERMS OF ART. Occasionally, however, it may apply to a complete sentence. You will be able to identify these phrases when you discover that many sources use exactly the same phrase.

> **Use of a criminal defendant's silence for <u>impeachment</u> purposes violates the defendant's <u>due process rights</u>. Boyle v. Kentucky, 999 U.S. 810, 817 (2005).**

For more information, see QUOTATIONS, WHEN TO USE. For related information, see UNDERLINING, subsection 6 and PINPOINT CITES. For related general information, see MEMOS and BRIEFS.

PARENTHESES

Use parentheses in legal writing only in the situations listed below. If the matter is important enough to be in the text, it should be stated outside the shadow of parentheses. Additionally, avoid overuse of parentheses because it can create the impression that the writer is disorganized. For related information, see PARENTHETICALS.

1. When to use parentheses.

(a) Use parentheses to enclose information useful to the reader if that information is not an integral part of the text itself. For example, use parentheses to refer to the transcript, such as (*Tr. 37*), or an appendix, such as (*See Appendix A*).

> **The defendant testified he had never seen the plaintiff (Tr. 349).**

or

> **The defendant testified that he had never seen the plaintiff (See Appendix A).**

(b) Use parentheses to introduce abbreviations. For example, if one of the parties in your brief is *Leitner Systems, Inc.*, and you want to use *LSI* in the text, write out the complete name the first time you use it and then put the abbreviation in parentheses afterwards.

> **Leitner Systems, Inc. (LSI).**

Do not state *hereinafter referred to as* before the abbreviation. See LEGALESE.

(c) Use parentheses in drafting contracts to enclose a numeral repeating a number spelled out.

> **For the sum of five hundred dollars ($500)** . . . .

(d) Use parentheses to enclose examples when the examples are necessary but do not require a separate definition. See UNOBTRUSIVE DEFINITIONS.

> **Crimes against property (trespass, encroachment, and the like) are usually considered less serious than crimes against persons.**

2. How to punctuate within parentheses.

If they are written inside another sentence (*this is an example of a parenthetical sentence inside another sentence*), parenthetical sentences do not begin with capital letters or end with periods; but when other punctuation marks are appropriate, they are used (*do you understand this rule?*). If they are written outside other sentences, parenthetical sentences begin with capital letters and end with periods inside the parentheses.

Defendant's car was parked in the north lot. (The lots have since been reassigned numbers and this is now lot #3.)

PARENTHETICALS

Parentheticals appear in specific places in legal writing to give the reader information about authority. Proper use of parentheticals saves time and text. Improper use or overuse of parentheticals disrupts the flow of the text and irritates most readers. Parentheticals were invented to supplement citations in scholarly footnotes, not to abbreviate legal analyses or argumentation. Keep that original purpose in mind as you use parentheticals. When you use them, check your citation manual for guidelines. The most helpful uses of parentheticals include the following.

1. Use parentheticals in statute citations to convey the following information.

    (a) Use them to show the code location of statutes cited to session laws or secondary sources.

    Popular Names Act of 2004, Pub. L. No. 102–113, 999 Stat. 111 (codified at 99 U.S.C. §§ 2222 to 2232 (2001)).

    (b) Use them to give the unofficial section when an unofficial code is numbered differently from an official code and when the section does not yet appear in the official code.

    Mich. Comp. Laws § 999.09 (2005) (Mich. Stat. Ann. § 111.01 (Callaghan 2002)).

    (c) Use them to identify useful dates, such as the effective date of a statute.

    Alaska Stat. § 99.09.090 (2007) (effective July 1, 2004).

    (d) Use them to indicate the repeal, amendment, or prior history of a statute.

    99 U.S.C. § 999(b) (2005) (repealed 2007).

    (e) Use them to give any other relevant information about a statute.

    99 U.S.C. § 999(b) (2007) (requiring IRS agents to give proper notice of auditing procedures to those being audited).

2. Use parentheticals after cases to indicate that the holding is not the single clear, holding of a majority of the court, or to indicate the weight of authority.

    State v. Blunt, 999 U.S. 99 (2011) (per curiam) (holding that an "indicia of reliability" is necessary for an informer's information to support a search warrant).

3. Use parentheticals after basic citations to add information about the source.

> **Arnold v. Butters, 999 F. Supp. 111 (W.D. Wis. 2010) (holding that moral right is not cause of action for artist whose painting was separated into four pieces).**

PARTICIPLES

See VERBS, PARTICIPLES.

PARTS OF A SENTENCE

See SENTENCE, PARTS OF.

PARTS OF SPEECH

Parts of speech is the grammatical term used to summarize the eight categories into which all English words are divided. These eight categories include NOUNS, PRONOUNS, ADJECTIVES, VERBS, ADVERBS, PREPOSITIONS, CONJUNCTIONS, and INTERJECTIONS.

PARTY

Use *party* when needed for precision, but avoid using it unless it is really needed. Overuse of *party* is one example of LEGALESE.

PASSIVE OR ACTIVE VOICE?

See VOICE, ACTIVE OR PASSIVE?

PASSIVE VERBS

See PASSIVE VOICE.

PASSIVE VOICE

In general, use active voice rather than passive, in both objective writing and persuasive writing, because the active voice promotes clarity and precision. Use passive voice when it is needed, but avoid using it habitually. The following subsections explain how passive voice creates problems and when use of passive voice is warranted. For help identifying passive voice, see VOICE, ACTIVE OR PASSIVE?

1. Difficulty caused by using passive voice.

Passive voice makes the reader's eye move backwards because the subject of the sentence receives the action, rather than causes the action. In contrast, active voice keeps the reader's eye moving forward and clarifies both the subject and the action. As a result, passive voice forces the reader to stop at the end of the sentence and think back through the sentence to sort out who did what.

The plaintiff was hit by the defendant. [passive voice]

but

The defendant hit the plaintiff. [active voice]

A decision was made by the court. [passive voice]

but

The court made a decision. [active voice]

or

The court decided. [active voice]

Passive verbs also sometimes leave the actor out of the picture.

The plaintiff was hit.

A decision was made.

This use of passive voice often creates ambiguity. For example, the following regulation would be inadequate if it did not specify who has the responsibility for the clean-up.

Any manufacturer who generates toxic waste must dispose of that waste by one of the following means.

rather than

Toxic waste must be disposed of by one of the following means.

2. Uses of passive voice.

Passive voice is useful in four specific situations. In legal writing, use it consciously and for these reasons only; otherwise eliminate it.

(a) Use passive voice to de-emphasize unfavorable facts or law. For example, the attorney for the defense might want to write the following.

The plaintiff was assaulted by the defendant.

The attorney for the prosecution, however, might write the following.

The defendant assaulted the plaintiff.

(b) Use passive voice to hide the identity of the actor.

A decision was made to cut your salary.

rather than

We have decided to cut your salary.

Here passive voice avoids telling who made the decision.

(c) Use passive voice when the subject is very long. In this situation, using passive voice creates a more readable sentence because the active voice would put the subject and verb so far apart that the sentence would be too hard to read.

280

> **This action is required by statutory law, by the common law principle of due care, and by a general sense of justice.**

rather than

> Statutory law, the common law principle of due care, and a general sense of justice require this action.

(d) Finally, use passive voice when the subject is much less important than the object.

> **Freedom of speech cannot be encumbered by concerns of propriety.**

rather than

> Concerns of propriety cannot encumber freedom of speech.

For related information, see ACTIVE VOICE and CONCISENESS, subsection 6.

PAST PARTICIPLES

Past participles are the *-ed* form of regular verbs, such as *decided, moved, assaulted.* Irregular verbs form past participles differently, such as *held, gone,* and *been*. See VERBS, PARTICIPLES and VERBS, IRREGULAR.

PAST PERFECT TENSE

See VERBS, TENSES.

PAST PROGRESSIVE TENSE

See VERBS, TENSES.

PAST TENSE

See VERBS, TENSES.

PATTERNS

Patterns appear in writing as repeated use of favorite phrases, syntaxes, words, or structures. These patterns are the evidence of the writer's habitual writing choices, and they combine to form a significant portion of a writer's style. As you refine and develop your legal writing style, however, do not sacrifice readability. Instead, develop a style that enhances the readability while expressing your own professional personality.

1. Patterns that enhance readability.

As you read writing that you admire, note the patterns used by other writers that make the text more readable. Then, as you write, be aware of your own patterns, keeping those that promote readability and avoiding those that do not. The following patterns, for example, can increase your readability.

Use this readable pattern	to replace this pattern.
• **Subjects and verbs close to each other**	• Subjects and verbs separated by long phrases
• **Parallel structure**	• Lack of parallel structure
• **Strong topic sentences**	• Weak topic sentences
• **Clear transitions**	• Inaccurate transitions or no transitions
• **Precise use of terms of art**	• Vague language
• **Focused, concise quotations**	• Large blocks of quoted material
• **Active voice**	• Passive voice
• **Active verbs**	• Linking verbs and nominalizations
• **Important content within the main text**	• Important content in footnotes or parentheticals

For related information, see PRINCIPLES OF GOOD LEGAL WRITING, READABILITY, and TRANSITIONS.

2. Personal professional style.

To develop a personal legal writing style, also note the patterns and variations used by other writers whose writing you admire. Just as music is pleasant to hear because of the interplay of predictability and variation, writing is pleasant to read when it employs a similar interplay of routine and variety. As you write, use some variations in your routine, readable patterns to enhance an important point and to enhance your professional style. The more conscious you are of the patterns, the more versatile you will be in using them to move your reader.

Variations you can incorporate into your personal style

- Variation in sentence length

- Variation in paragraph length

- Sentence with an intrusive phrase

- Sentence with long introductory phrase and short main clause

- Repetition of key word or unusual vocabulary

- Alliteration or assonance

- Imagery or metaphor

- Slightly more formal or informal vocabulary

- Rhythm

- Short quotations

For related information, see CHOICES IN LEGAL WRITING, IMAGERY, PERSUASION, STYLE, and TONE.

PEOPLE OR *PERSONS*?

Use *people* to refer a group of individuals collectively. Use *persons* when referring to a small and specific number.

All people of this country have constitutional rights.

but

Defendant has assaulted nine persons in the last month.

PER

Per means *for each* and is useful when talking about ratios.

The defendant company promised different rates of pay to different sales personnel, ranging from the $5 per call paid to secretaries who worked in the company headquarters, to $1 per call paid to employees who made the calls from their homes.

Per should not be used, however, in other contexts.

Regarding our previous request for payment, ...

rather than

As per our previous request, ...

PERCENT OR *PER CENT*?

Use *percent*, which is preferred by most authorities.

PERFECTIONISM

Perfectionism can be the enemy of creative thought. Relegate your perfectionism to REVISING, REWRITING, and POLISHING in the WRITING PROCESS. In PREWRITING, contain your perfectionist tendencies by balancing time constraints against scholarship and by concentrating on substantive ideas rather than the methodology of note taking, outlining, and other prewriting tasks.

When WRITING, do not allow your perfectionist editing voice to restrict your creative writing voice. Try not to perfect each sentence as you go, but rather try to write the entire paper without revising. This will allow your ideas to flow as you focus on content, not form. Then go back to perfect your paper in the REWRITING, REVISING, and POLISHING stages. In those stages, let your perfectionism work within your time restraints.

For further help, see WHEN TO STOP. For a discussion of related problems, see PROCRASTINATION; WRITING BLOCKS; GETTING STARTED; and DEADLINES, MEETING THEM.

PERFECT TENSES
See VERBS, TENSES.

PERIOD OR QUESTION MARK?
See QUESTION MARKS.

PERIODS
Periods have three common uses in legal writing.

1. Periods ending sentences.

If your sentences routinely run for more than four lines of text, use more periods. See SENTENCE LENGTH and READABILITY.

2. Periods ending abbreviations.

When an abbreviation comes at the end of a sentence, use just one period.

The meeting is scheduled for 9:00 p.m.

3. Periods in parentheticals.

If they are written inside another sentence (*this is an example of a parenthetical sentence inside another sentence*), parenthetical sentences do not begin with capital letters or end with periods; but when other punctuation marks are appropriate (*do you understand this rule?*), they are used. If they are written outside other sentences, parenthetical sentences begin with capital letters and end with periods inside the parentheses.

Defendant's car was parked facing north. (R.P. 31.)

or

Defendant's car was parked facing north (R.P. 31).

4. Periods with quotation marks.

In the U.S., a period goes inside quotation marks, even if the period is not part of the quote.

The term on which we must focus is "intent."

This rule is the same for both double quotation marks ("—") and single ones ("—"). The rule is not meant to reflect logical concerns, but rather historic ones. In early U.S. presses, the periods and commas kept breaking off. Statutory drafting is one exception to this rule, where periods are treated like all other punctuation marks. For more, see LEGISLATION, subsection 7.

PERSON: FIRST, SECOND, OR THIRD?
First person is *I* or *we*, second person is *you*, and third person is *he, she, it,* or *they.* Because person identifies the reader and writer, your relationship to the AUDIENCE determines which to use. In any given

piece of legal writing, choose one person and use it consistently throughout.

1. First person.

Use first person singular, *I*, when giving a personal opinion. Use first person plural, *we*, when including the reader in the scope of the discussion or when representing the collective opinion of several specific people, as in a letter that speaks for a law firm.

I suggest we try to settle this out of court.

We can argue that a five-month-old fetus is viable, but this issue will probably go to the Supreme Court.

Avoid the editorial or royal *we* because it can be ambiguous. Instead, use *I* or avoid referring to any persons.

I understand your dilemma.

rather than

We recognize your dilemma.

The second element of first degree murder is intent.

rather than

We must next consider the second element of first degree murder.

For an explanation of the particular dangers of using the first person plural incorrectly, see WE.

2. Second person.

Use the second person, *you*, to address the audience directly, when appropriate. For example, GENERAL CORRESPONDENCE LETTERS and other correspondence may include you because they require a more personal TONE.

You asked that I write to you about the legal consequences of your unfortunate accident.

Avoid using second person when addressing a court.

Granting this motion is appropriate for three reasons.

rather than

You ought to grant this motion for three reasons.

3. Third person.

Use third person most often in BRIEFS, MEMOS, MOTIONS, and most formal legal documents. Identify parties in the third person, your clients as well as their opponents.

Defendant pled not guilty; he denies all charges.

The law favors the plaintiffs in this class action, so they will likely move for a summary judgment.

PERSONAL REFERENCES

Personal references are appropriate in legal writing only if the reader and writer are familiar with each other and if appropriate given the document's purpose. Avoid them otherwise; they impair both credibility and meaning.

Although Plaintiff argues that there is a dispute as to the material facts, the affidavits show otherwise.

or

The affidavits show there is no dispute as to the material facts.

rather than

Attorney Cromwell on page sixteen of his brief argues incorrectly again that there is a dispute as to material facts.

For related information, see I, TONE, and TONE IN LETTERS.

PERSONALITY IN LEGAL WRITING

Personality can come through in any kind of legal writing. It is the energy behind the writing that conveys a human voice behind the analysis, settlement, brief, or email exchange. It can carry concern, appreciation, humor, pathos, or dignity. Most important, it may be what helps your reader remember what you are writing. The key to incorporating your individual writing personality in your professional writing is balancing that personality with the reader's practical needs and the requirements of the specific legal task. If your preferred way of explaining the content gets in the way of the reader's understanding, then you need to modify the writing to accommodate the reader's needs. In contrast, your way of explaining the problem, perhaps through IMAGERY or GRAPHICS, may help the reader understand the content. In that situation, your personality works as a professional asset. Therefore allow your professional writing personality to emerge as it can serve the reader and the writing task. But do be careful of allowing your personality free reign, such as when you write in haste. For example, in email, where a pressured or frustrated personality may come through too easily, you may write something you regret later.

Generally, legal readers are less interested in vivid depictions of your personality than in your sincerity and earnestness. Legal writing is functional writing, which means that your readers are interested in a practical result, not in your opinion of the situation. They are often interested, however, in the way in which they sense that you are taking care of them and the situation. So develop your personality through a careful, conscious use of writing techniques that resonate with you and work for your readers. For ways to do this, see CHOICES IN LEGAL WRITING, EMAIL, INDEPENDENCE IN LEGAL WRITING, STYLE, and VOICE.

PERSONS OR *PEOPLE?*

See *PEOPLE* OR *PERSONS?*

PERSUASIVE AUTHORITY

Persuasive authority is a primary source of law from another jurisdiction. It is not mandatory authority, which is a primary source of law from the relevant jurisdiction. For example, a case decided by the Arizona state supreme court might be persuasive in New Mexico state courts, but is not mandatory authority there. Persuasive authority should not be quoted, stated, or analyzed as part of the law on which the decision-maker bases an opinion, but it can be used to advise the decision-maker about how to proceed. Use persuasive authority when the mandatory authority in a jurisdiction is incomplete or in some way inadequate to address the issue. For example, you might use persuasive authority when a newly enacted statute has no cases construing it but another jurisdiction's court has construed a similar statute. Although this authority is not binding on the current decision maker, it can be persuasive when other lawmakers have addressed the issue in similar circumstances.

The value of persuasive authority varies depending on its origin. For example, many states look to New York and California on issues of intellectual property because these states house most U.S. entertainers and therefore have developed more law on this topic. But many states ignore those jurisdictions on local issues, such as tort law, education, or property. Those local issues are more dependent on local demographics, so a state is likely to turn to a neighboring state: Wisconsin might look to Minnesota or Iowa law, and West Virginia might look to Tennessee or Kentucky law. The same is true at the federal level. Federal district and circuit courts are not binding on each other. They will look for persuasive authority in distant jurisdictions for some issues, nearby jurisdictions for others. To discover persuasive authority favored by your decision maker, you might note the jurisdictions used in the authority you find during your research to know what sources of persuasive authority have been cited most frequently in your jurisdiction.

PERSUASIVE LETTERS AND EMAIL

Persuading a legal reader to do or decide something in your favor is a bit like finding your way through a mine field; you are trying to reach a certain point without setting off any unfortunate reactions. For this reason, persuasive letters and email will not be as predictably structured as other correspondence. In all persuasive correspondence, however, you will need to make decisions during three tasks: (1) choosing arguments, (2) organizing those arguments, and (3) establishing your tone. The following guidelines should help you make these decisions.

1. Choosing arguments.

In general, take care in choosing arguments because you must tailor your argument and tone to suit the individual circumstances. Choose not what persuades you, but what persuades your reader. For example, if you are trying to persuade a party to settle out of court, do not use threats if the party might view those threats as a challenge and submission as a weakness. Instead, you might explain how an early settlement could bring better results for the party than a costly trial. Similarly, if you think that the reader is motivated by certain values or goals, try to explain how the action you recommend is consistent with those values or goals. For example, you might argue that paying a bill is essentially the same as keeping a promise. Try to help the reader feel good, or at least not defeated, about taking the action you recommend.

2. Organizing the arguments.

Use the same organization generally for any bad news. (See BAD NEWS, GIVING IT.) Start with a paragraph that sets the tone of the letter. The following example establishes a kind tone.

> **Throughout the years, Everly Auto Parts has valued Morgan Auto as a customer. Because Everly hopes to maintain this solid working relationship, Bob Everly has asked me to write to you concerning the rather large outstanding balance in your account.**

Alternatively, you may choose a tough tone, as in the following example.

> **Despite receiving three statements from my client, Everly Auto Parts, your company has not yet paid the balance of $2,015 owed for parts purchased four months ago.**

Or you may choose something in between.

> **My client, Everly Auto Parts, has asked me to write to you concerning the outstanding balance on your company's account.**

Do not go on too long, however, or your reader may become restless and suspicious.

By the end of the first paragraph or the beginning of the second, state your point. This sentence must be clear.

> **Please pay the amount due promptly. Everly will not be able to extend further credit to your company until this balance has been paid.**

Then launch into your reasons. Make one point at a time, rather than rambling back and forth between several points. See PARAGRAPHS.

> **Everly Auto Parts, as a general policy, limits credit to any company to . . . . Additionally, ...**

In the last paragraph close politely, or at least civilly.

Everly Auto Parts will appreciate your prompt payment of this outstanding balance and looks forward to your continued patronage.

3.   Establishing tone.

In general, use a relatively unemotional, polite tone. When your reader is inclined to disagree with you, the emotions you would arouse would work against you. There are some exceptions to this, such as fundraising letters to sympathetic constituents or email advising clients to do what they want to do already. Even here, however, you will usually want to present yourself as a logical, reasonable person who, even when impassioned about a cause, is still capable of making a coherent, logical argument. For a discussion of related points, see TONE, PERSUASIVE WRITING, and GENERAL CORRESPONDENCE LETTERS.

PERSUASIVE WRITING

Writing persuasively is writing to create a desired outcome with a specific audience. In legal writing, you may be persuading a trial court to rule positively on a motion, persuading an appellate court to remand a case, or persuading a fellow attorney that a settlement will be in the best interests of his or her client. When prewriting a persuasive document, begin with the following three steps.

1.   Clarify your PURPOSE.

Your purpose will guide your choices throughout the writing process, from choosing content, strategy, and organization to revising for emphasis. Generally your purpose will be to engage the reader's cooperation in some way, whether that means using the law you set out or settling a claim out of court. Seldom will your purpose justify criticizing or demoralizing the reader or a third person. Focusing on your purpose can take some self restraint, especially when the other party has behaved unprofessionally or unfairly. To be successful, however, avoid allowing personal or unnecessary goals into the mix.

2.   Focus on your AUDIENCE.

Choose the strategy and content that will persuade the individual readers you are addressing. When writing a brief, ask yourself what questions this court will ask and how the law supports resolving those questions in your client's favor.

Do not assume that the exact arguments that prevailed at one level in the court system will prevail at the next level. For example, trial courts emphasize precedent, appellate courts emphasize legal errors, and courts that review constitutional issues may emphasize long-term effects, precedent, or public policy. So when deciding a criminal case, a trial court might be convinced by a careful comparison of your client's facts to the facts of previous cases. But an appellate court reviewing the same case might be convinced only by arguments that the trial court erred in its reasoning. For related information, see STANDARD OF REVIEW, and AUDIENCE. For a more thorough discussion of persuasion in briefs, see Mary B. Ray & Barbara J. Cox, Beyond the Basics: A Text for Advanced Legal Writers (2d ed. 2003).

3. Structure your argument to convince your audience.

(a) Order of presentation.

Choose the structure that is most coherent and convincing to this audience. When ordering your issues, begin with the threshold issue if there is one; do not violate the reader's sense of logical progression. But if issues are independent, then begin with your most compelling argument. This order creates a strong first impression. If one of three arguments is weaker than the others, place it between the other two so it is not in a position of emphasis. (See POSITIONS OF EMPHASIS.)

When stating and presenting each issue, begin with an affirmative statement of your position.

The plaintiff provided adequate warning. Twice he tried to reach the defendant by telephone before leaving messages when no one answered.

Avoid letting your opponent's arguments dictate your structure; use the structure that best suits your position. See COUNTERARGUMENTS, HOW TO HANDLE.

(b) Communicating your structure.

Within paragraphs and paragraph blocks, subordinate their arguments through careful use of subordinate clauses, subheadings, or paragraphs placed in the middle of a larger paragraph block. Retain your focus on your client's position. Although you may need to refer to your opponent's position in the course of your argument, do not dwell on it. Thus if the opposition is arguing that your client did not provide adequate warning, you might write the following.

The plaintiff gave adequate warning. She telephoned repeatedly, and left messages on the defendant's answering machine on two occasions.

Beginning with a statement of the opposition's position would create a defensive tone and make your organization dependent on the other side's position.

The defense argues that plaintiff gave no warning. This is not the case, however, because the plaintiff left messages on the defendant's answering machine on two occasions.

For related organizational strategies, see BAD NEWS, SOFTENING IT.

4. Revise with persuasion in mind.

Revising persuasively entails the use of many specific techniques, none of which alone makes an obvious difference but all of which, when working in harmony, create a masterful piece of persuasion. Each of these techniques takes practice to master. Therefore, choose two or three from the following list, practice and master those techniques, and incorporate them into your writing habits.

(a) Use subjects and verbs for specific effect.

(b) Use concrete words.

(c) Choose the most appropriate term of address.

(d) Repeat key words.

(e) Repeat sentence or phrase structures.

(f) Adjust sentence length.

(g) Insert information into a sentence with care.

(h) Place key phrases at the beginning or end of a paragraph or a sentence.

(i) Use subtly emotional language, rather than overly emotional.

(j) Play one persuasive technique against another.

(k) Avoid overdoing.

Each of these techniques is discussed in the following subentries. Study them and choose the techniques that you understand now. Then, as you master those, add new ones to your repertoire.

(a) Use subjects and verbs for specific effect.

Put your main point in the main subject and verb in your sentence. Conversely, de-emphasize points by putting them in dependent clauses. For example, the following sentence emphasizes *he had slowed and was not accelerating* by making that the main subject and verb.

Although the defendant had not come to a full stop at the official stop sign, he had slowed to less than five miles per hour and was not accelerating at the time of the accident.

Use auxiliary verbs carefully to shade your meaning. For example, you may use *did* to counter an argument.

The plaintiff did provide adequate warning.

You may use *can* to remind the reader that some action is possible under the law, or *must* to remind the reader that it is required.

Intent can be inferred from the defendant's actions.

The driver must come to a complete stop.

For more about this technique, see VERBS, AUXILIARY.

(b) Use specific words.

Specific and concrete words create clearer images in the reader's mind than general, abstract ones, and those clearer images are more memorable. For example, a *1965 black Stingray* is more memorable than *vehicle*. This tool is especially useful in drafting fact situations for briefs, because you can use concrete words for facts that favor your client and abstract ones for facts that you want to de-emphasize. For example, if you are de-emphasizing the illness of a testator and the medications she was taking, you might write the following.

Because Julia Easley had a history of arthritic and cardiovascular diseases, she was taking a variety of medications.

If, however, you were trying to emphasize the illness and the medications, you might write the following.

Julia Easley's health was poor. She suffered from excruciating tension headaches (R. 925), and during the past year she experienced increasing cardiovascular problems, cataracts, arteriosclerosis, and other problems (R. 928–53). She was also on a large and complex daily regimen of drugs (R. 454). Daily she took three kinds of barbiturates: Tuinal (R. 1115–16), Fiornal (R. 1113), and Fiornal with Codeine (R. 1113–14). Additionally, she took greater-than-normal daily dosages of Triavil (R. 114–15), a specialized compound tranquilizer formulated and normally prescribed for mental depression (R. 1148–49).

For related information, see COUNTERARGUMENTS, HOW TO HANDLE.

(c) Choose the most appropriate term of address.

This choice is related to the choice of concrete or abstract nouns. In a brief, if you have a situation where your client is a sympathetic figure and the opposition is not, use names such as *Ms. Jones* or *Julia Easley*, for both parties. This will gently remind the reader of the real people involved here. If the facts are not sympathetic to your client and you are making an argument based more on the impersonal logic of the relevant law, then use generic terms, such as *Plaintiff* and *Defendant*. Use the same kind of term for both sides, however; using *Ms. Jones* for the defendant but then using *Plaintiff* would be too confusing and too obviously biased, even if it seemed appropriate.

(d) Repeat key words.

If you want to emphasize a word, repeat it. This is most often useful in the argument section of a brief.

The defendant <u>abused</u> the privileges offered him; he <u>abused</u> the procedures designed to protect him.

When repeating a term, however, make sure that the idea represented by the term is indeed one you do want to emphasize. For example, repeating *clearly* will create a distraction, not effective emphasis.

Also remember that the effect of a repeated word grows exponentially, rather than linearly. That is, if you use a word twice, it is given perhaps four times the emphasis, not just two. So do not overdo it. This is a place where reading it aloud may work a disservice; you may hear yourself repeating a theme like the master orator Martin Luther King did, but your reader, not hearing your impassioned pauses and intonations, may instead find it amusing. Let your eye and common sense guide you.

(e) Repeat sentence or phrase structures.

This tool is particularly useful when analogizing cases (see COMPARISON) but is also useful and subtly dramatic in conclusions and sometimes in fact sections. Repetition of structure creates a sense of rhythm and anticipation. To some extent, it telegraphs to the reader what is coming, so that the reader gets a sense of completion when the expected information arrives.

At best, the City confused its argument by trying to do too much without a full explanation. At worst, the City contradicted itself by misapplying the law.

But this expectation can turn to boredom, so again avoid overdoing it. See also REPETITION.

(f) Adjust sentence length.

Short sentences are emphatic. Therefore use them for points you want to emphasize, but do not use them for unimportant points. This tool is particularly useful in fact situations, where tools involving word choice are often limited.

Julia was uniformly described by all the witnesses who had personally known her as a strong-willed, positive, and independent woman. <u>The plaintiff himself called her "independent and abrupt."</u>

It is also useful in Arguments.

The major purpose of the trial court's established procedures is to give the litigants a fair opportunity to address their claims and have them resolved by a court of law. <u>These petitioners had eight years of opportunity.</u> Therefore, their current procedural arguments . . . .

Several short sentences in a row create a choppy, rather impatient or angry tone. Sometimes this can have a useful effect.

> **The major purpose of the trial court's established procedure is to give the litigants a fair opportunity to address their claims and have them resolved by a court of law. That purpose was met here. <u>The litigants had eight years of opportunity. In this context, their arguments on appeal are particularly specious.</u>**

Three sentences are about as far as you should push the series. Any more and the court might sense an intemperate tirade. After a series of short sentences, return to sentences of normal length and make a scrupulously objective statement of your reasoning. See also SHORT SENTENCES.

(g) Insert information into a sentence with care.

If you want to use a point to set the stage for a punch line, put that point in an introductory phrase at the beginning of a sentence.

> **<u>Despite the difficulty of this test</u>, the gravity of the situation required that it be done.**

This technique becomes more dramatic when the introductory phrase is relatively long and the main clause is rather short.

> **Frightened by the approaching figure and seeing no means of escape, she fired.**

If you want to de-emphasize a point, put it in an added phrase at the end of the sentence, like an afterthought.

> **The minority arrived at the same conclusion, <u>although for different reasons.</u>**

When you do this, make sure that the word at the end of the sentence is not one you want to de-emphasize. For examples and more details on this technique, see SENTENCE STRUCTURE, subsection 7.

(h) Place key phrases at the beginning or end of a paragraph or a sentence.

In general, words at the beginning or end get more attention than those in the middle. In legal writing, things at the beginning have a slight edge because you are never sure the busy and often-interrupted legal reader will finish reading your document with care. While revising, scan your topic sentences to see if the first half-line of each paragraph includes the key terms of the paragraph. Avoid starting a paragraph with dates or case names unless you have a reason to emphasize that date or name.

> **<u>Evidence of this concern</u> showed up in the defendant's letter dated January 12, 1980, which stated** . . . .

rather than

On January 12, 1980, the defendant wrote a letter that showed evidence of this concern when it stated . . . .

For related information, see POSITIONS OF EMPHASIS.

(i) Use subtly emotional language, rather than overly emotional.

Emotional language should persuade, not lose, the reader. Therefore choose words precisely to fit the persuasive approach you are taking. Emotional words are not just positive or negative; instead, each word falls somewhere on a continuum between extremely positive and extremely negative. For example, one person who decided to maintain a position on an issue could be described as *ever-faithful, steadfast, unwavering, unchanging, stubborn*, or *pig-headed*. In legal writing, choose words that fall closer to the center of the continuum to color your meanings and avoid the extremes. For example, if trying to show that someone was overmedicated and thus not capable of making a will, write the following.

Julia Easley was on a large and complex daily regimen of drugs, including . . . .

rather than

Julia Easley was drugged into a vegetative state daily.

Also avoid overly emotional language because it draws the reader's attention to the emotional level of the writing itself, rather than to the content of the persuasive argument. For example, many extremely emotional words, such as *blockhead* or *disaster*, can impair the writer's credibility in court, where another lawyer can point out the silliness of the overstatement.

Finally, avoid overly emotional language because it may be limited by the constraints of legal writing. For example, many words with emotional overtones, such as *derelict* or *nuisance*, are also terms of art that must be used with precision, whether or not the emotional overtone is appropriate.

(j) Play one persuasive technique against another.

As you are applying these tools, you may find some contradictions; applying one principle means you violate another. Practices playing these techniques against each other to get just the effect you want.

(k) Avoid overdoing.

Any of these persuasive techniques can be overdone. If you tend to overdo, use Marilyn Monroe's technique to solve the problem. This may be apocryphal, but it has been said that Marilyn tended to over accessorize when she dressed up. To compensate for this, she kept a full length mirror in her entry. Before she left the house, she would walk away from the mirror and then turn quickly to look at her image. She would then take off the first accessory that caught her eye. Similarly, as you read over your last draft of a persuasive piece, take out the most obvious persuasive tools you have used. After all, it worked for Marilyn. Few would have called her over-dressed.

PHENOMENA OR *PHENOMENONS*?

Most dictionaries list either as the acceptable plural of phenomenon, but *phenomena* is preferred.

PHRASES

A phrase is a group of words working together, such as prepositional phrases, *in this case*; noun phrases, *the experienced supervising attorney*; and verb phrases, *had been reviewing*. In contrast, a clause is a phrase that includes both a subject and verb.

S   V

The supervising attorney had been reviewing the case.

For an explanation of the use of phrases, see SENTENCE STRUCTURE and SENTENCE, PARTS OF, subsections 6 and 7. For related information, see CLAUSES.

PIE CHARTS

See GRAPHICS, WHICH FORM TO USE, subsection 1.

PINPOINT CITATIONS

See CITATIONS, PINPOINT.

PLAGIARISM

Plagiarism is copying someone else's ideas or words and claiming them as your own. In legal writing, this is as unacceptable as it is in any other kind of writing. Using someone else's phrases, sentences, paragraphs, or organization in place of your own writing is plagiarism. Using the same components from cases and legal sources is, however, essential to legal analysis because these components build reasoning. But do cite every source specifically each time you use it, including a pinpoint citation to the particular page where the cited language appears.

Similarly it is perfectly permissible to paraphrase someone else's words, that is, to put their ideas in your own words, but only when you specifically acknowledge the source of that idea. Thus you may paraphrase and then cite to the authority for any holding, proposition, rule, quotation, or point of law. You may also quote passages from law review articles verbatim, but they must be marked as quotes and cited. For related information, see PARAPHRASE and QUOTATIONS, HOW TO PUNCTUATE.

PLAIN ENGLISH

In legal writing, plain English is English that is simple, clear, and readable. Many states require plain English in any kind of consumer document. If the document is not drafted in plain English, the consumer has grounds to sue for malpractice against the drafter of the document. Check your jurisdiction for its specific laws on plain English, but in general free your writing of jargon, legalese, and any undefined terms that will send a reader scurrying to a dictionary. For ways to revise for plain English, see READABILITY, subsections 3, 4, 7, and 8. See also SIMPLICITY, ELEGANT VARIATION, PLAIN MEANING and UNOBTRUSIVE DEFINITIONS.

PLAIN MEANING

Plain meaning is a TERM OF ART referring to a method of construing statutes that interprets each term by its dictionary meaning. This is a very literal interpretation and is often the point of departure for interpretation of a statute. For example, when a court is interpreting a statute for the very first time and there is little or no legislative history, the court may resort to the dictionary meaning of each word in the statute in order to apply the statute to the facts before the court. Therefore, as it relates to legal writing, plain meaning becomes important in drafting legislation. It also is often important in consumer contracts, which may be required by law to be written in plain English. Be sure that each term you use in drafting the statute stands up under the dictionary's scrutiny. See LEGISLATION.

PLEADINGS

Legal pleadings serve varied purposes. Common pleadings include complaints, answers, and cross complaints. For example, a complaint may start the litigation process, frame a dispute, encourage the opponent to negotiate, or stop the running of the relevant statute of limitations or perform a combination of these purposes. An answer may help the parties see what facts are at issue, which are not debated by either party, and what strategy the other party is developing. A cross-complaint may introduce a new party to the action or put the original plaintiff on the defensive.

Whatever purpose your pleading serves, following these steps will help you produce an effective document.

When prewriting, do each of the following.

1. Record deadlines on your calendar and schedule enough time to consider thoroughly the substance and strategy of the case. For more on this, see TIME MANAGEMENT.

2. Clarify your goals and strategy early in the writing process, so you include all needed information in your pleading while omitting unnecessary details.

3. Research your facts and law thoroughly to avoid costly errors. Allocate enough time for this, because you need to think through the case to the appeal level before you draft the pleadings. For more on this, see RESEARCH STRATEGY CHART.

Be sure to consider the following two questions at some time during your writing process, although it may be in prewriting, writing, or rewriting. See WRITING PROCESS.

4. Does the pleading include enough information to withstand adverse motions?

5. Does it include all information needed, so that no likely arguments are waived?

When rewriting, ask the following questions.

6. Does the pleading make only one point per paragraph?

7. Is it organized inductively, so that paragraphs asserting the evidence to support an element precede the paragraph stating that the element has been established? For examples, see COMPLAINTS and ANSWERS.

When revising, consider the following questions.

8. Is each paragraph worded specifically enough to withstand adverse motions, yet generally enough to maintain some flexibility later in the legal process?

9. Are all assertions free of ambiguity?

When polishing, do the following.

10. Check caption, signatures, and all other parts to make sure all court-required forms and conventions are followed.

11. Are all dates, numbers, names, addresses, and other particulars accurate?

12. Check spelling, punctuation, and other grammatical and mechanical concerns. For more detail on this, see POLISHING.

PLURALS OF NAMES

When making a name plural, add an *s*.

There are three Marys in the firm.

When the name ends in *s*, add *es*.

The Joneses are tenants in common.

Resist any urge to create any other variation by analogy from other common nouns.

The Zimmermans have both reviewed the will.

The Olympuses are joint tenants.

The Chanticleers all have equal shares in their company.

The wording of the will is ambiguous because the family includes two Jameses.

rather than

The Zimmermen have both reviewed the will.

The Olympi are joint tenants.

The Chanticleer all have equal shares in their company.

The wording of the will is ambiguous because the family includes two James's.

P.M.

It is written *p.m.* and in business writing is used only after a number, as in *7:15 p.m.* When it appears at the end of a sentence, only one period is used, as in the previous sentence.

POINT HEADINGS

Point headings, also known as argument headings, are conventions in argumentative writing designed both to tell the reader the legal point made in a section of the Argument and to outline the reasons supporting that legal point. Point headings also appear in the tables of contents of appellate briefs. The point headings, when read together, should give the reader an outline of the writer's argument.

1. Content and format for point headings.

Main point headings correspond to the issue statements. They provide the answer to the legal question asked in each issue, and so there should be a point heading for every issue. Use capital letters, single space, and use a roman numeral. Include the legal point and the reason if there are no subheadings or multiple reasons; include only the legal point if subheadings will indicate the reasons.

I. **THE TRIAL COURT ABUSED ITS DISCRETION WHEN IT AWARDED CUSTODY TO AN ALCOHOLIC MOTHER.**

or

I. **MR. SMITH HAS NO RELEVANT EXPERIENCE THAT QUALIFIES HIM TO RENDER AN EXPERT OPINION IN THIS CASE.**

Include enough legally significant facts to make your Argument specific to this case, but avoid cluttering the point heading with so many facts that it becomes too long. For related information, see ISSUE STATEMENTS and LEGALLY SIGNIFICANT FACTS.

Subheadings are used to give more specific reasons for the main legal point. Usually a paragraph or two of summarizing text follows a main heading, and then the first subheading follows that text. In subheadings, you may indent and capitalize the first letter of each main word, as in a book title; add underlining or bold face if it is customary in your jurisdiction. Or you may use some other graphic device that distinguishes it from major headings, sub-subheadings, and the rest of the text.

A. Mrs. Davis' History of Alcohol Abuse Demonstrates She Cannot Act in the Best Interests of the Children.

Sub-subheadings give particulars of the Argument under the subheading, and appear most often in appellate briefs. Use sub-subheadings to highlight important points in your Argument, but limit them to six at the most. Overusing them may make the brief look more like an outline than a cohesive argument.

Indent the sub-subheading and capitalize only the first word. Precede it with an arabic numeral.

1. Mrs. Davis has been arrested repeatedly for drunken driving.

2. Techniques for writing point headings.

(a) Make one legal point in each heading.

(b) Use a strong, accurate connecting word, such as *because*. See TRANSITIONS.

(c) Include a summary of the reason for the main legal point.

I. THE TRIAL COURT ERRED IN DENYING PLAINTIFFS' JURY INSTRUCTION ON DEFECTIVE BRAKES BECAUSE SUBSTANTIAL EVIDENCE INTRODUCED AT TRIAL SUPPORTS THIS THEORY OF PLAINTIFFS' CASE.

(d) Use persuasive writing, concentrating on strong subject–verb combinations and eliminating unneeded modifiers. For more detail, see PERSUASIVE WRITING, subsection 4(a).

(e) Make the point heading no longer than four single-spaced lines, if possible.

(f) Use parallel structure in all main headings and in all subheadings.

POINT OF VIEW, OBJECTIVE OR PERSUASIVE?

Point of view in legal writing travels along the spectrum from objective to persuasive. The writer's point of view tends toward the objective, or neutral, in memos, opinion letters, correspondence that gives information, and law review articles that synthesize or summarize information. Using a more objective point of view allows the writer to remain detached from the decision while informing the reader of the law and predicting any outcome or change in trends.

The point of view tends toward the persuasive in memoranda of points and authorities, pretrial briefs, trial briefs, appellate briefs, some law review articles, and some general correspondence letters. The purpose of using the persuasive point of view is to persuade the audience to accept the writer's argument.

After you have chosen the appropriate point of view, remain consistent throughout any given piece of writing. For advice on ways to establish these points of view, see OBJECTIVE WRITING and PERSUASIVE WRITING. For related information, see MEMORANDUM OF POINTS AND AUTHORITIES and AUDIENCE.

POLICY

Policy refers to the goals and reasons behind the law. These goals and reasons are rooted in the values of the general culture, the reasons we have laws in the first place. Policy precedes the law, gives rise to the law, and helps readers to interpret the law. It thus goes beyond a literal reading of the law. Policy may include factors such as social change, economic conditions, or unjust results from a literal interpretation of the law. Policy is often used to help interpret the meaning of the law. For example, if a state introduced laws for uninsured motorists but in the process created a gap in protection against under-insured motorists, attorneys might argue to the court that, as a policy matter, consumers should be protected from all improperly insured motorists and not just a subgroup. Often policy questions arise in arguments when one party desires the law be reinterpreted in response to changing social or economic values. For a broader context, see DISCUSSION SECTION, LEGAL ANALYSIS, and APPLICATION. For related information, see EQUITY.

POLISHING

Polishing, the last step in the WRITING PROCESS, includes checking for citation, grammatical, and typographical errors. Always polish your documents. The legal reader is concerned with detail, so failure to polish the presentation can undermine the legal writer's credibility and can erode the document's meaning. To insure time for polishing, work backward from the deadline and give yourself a reasonable amount of time to polish smaller details. For example, for a brief, allow an hour; for a memo, thirty minutes; for a short letter, ten.

Develop your own system for polishing, but make sure each aspect gets enough time. You might try the following system.

1. Read the document sentence by sentence from front to back, checking for each of the following in turn.

(a) omission of any words, such as *not*;

(b) punctuation; and

(c) incomplete sentences and other subject and verb problems, such as *none of the many options here are workable.*

2. Read each citation from back to front for correct citation form.

3. Read just for spelling and errors that a spell checker will not catch, such as incorrect or missing words. For related information, see MIS-SPELLINGS, HOW TO AVOID.

4. Reread for any problem peculiar to your own writing, such as dangling modifiers, overuse of *however*, or improper use of semicolons.

5. Read with a ruler, read aloud, read in small out-of-order pieces, or find some other way to read carefully so you will concentrate on every word to ensure its correctness.

POLISHING CHECKLIST

As you polish, ask practical questions of yourself. The following list can help you identify the questions you need to ask. You may want to check only one thing at a time because this often makes the polishing process more effective and less overwhelming.

1. Have I divided the polishing tasks so I do not try to do everything at one time?

2. With longer documents, have I divided the document so I can polish individual parts rather than the whole document at one time?

3. Have I checked all cites according to the BLUEBOOK, or the assigned source for citations?

   (a) Are CITATIONS complete, accurately ordered, and accurately punctuated?

   (b) Are pinpoint citations used for specific propositions, rules, holdings, quotes? See CITATIONS, PINPOINT.

   (c) Are case names spelled accurately?

   (d) Are page numbers and years accurate?

4. Have I checked spelling?

5. Have I also read each section for wrong words and words left out? For techniques, see POLISHING.

6. Have I checked headings, lists, tables, and similar components for consistent formatting and grammatical structure?

POSITIONS OF EMPHASIS

Positions of emphasis are locations in a written text that get more attention than the text in general. They include the beginnings and ends of sentences, paragraphs, sections, and entire works. Use these positions of emphasis to convey major legal points and arguments; all the points you want to emphasize should be in positions of emphasis, with less important or unfavorable information placed in between.

> **The best interests of children are of paramount concern to courts in custody disputes.**

rather than

> Most courts consider <u>the best interests of children</u> in <u>custody disputes</u> to be of paramount concern.

> **Although the trespassers caused much physical damage, their purpose was not to cause <u>mental anguish</u>.**

rather than

> The trespassers caused much physical damage, but causing <u>mental anguish</u> was not their purpose.

For related information, see SUBJECT–VERB COMBINATIONS. For ways to adjust your verbs to me more persuasive, see VERBS, AUXILIARY.

POSSESSIVES

In the law, possessives become important to PRECISION, such as *daughter's half or daughters' half* of an estate, so make sure you follow these rules.

1. Add an apostrophe and an *s* to make a singular noun possessive.

John's = belonging to John.

plaintiff's = belonging to a plaintiff.

statute's = belonging to a statute, as in *statute's language*.

2. Add only an *s* to singular pronouns to make them possessive.

its = belonging to it. **It's** = it is. *Its'* is never correct.

yours = belonging to you.

hers = belonging to her.

3. Add only an apostrophe to singular or plural nouns ending in *s* already.

Jones' = belonging to one Jones.

Joneses' = belonging to all the Joneses.

plaintiffs' = belonging to all the plaintiffs.

Some authorities allow adding an apostrophe and an *s* to plural nouns, such as *Jones's*. Whatever your choice, be consistent.

4. Add an apostrophe and an *s* to a plural noun that does not end in *s*.

women's = belonging to women.

For related information, see APOSTROPHES.

PRECISION

While accuracy means the reader can understand your meaning, precision means your reader must understand it. This control of meanings makes precision especially important in legal writing. Precision involves taking care in five components: (1) planning, (2) word choice, (3) consistency, (4) sentence structure, and (5) presentation.

1.   Precision in planning.

Include only needed content. This will help you control the meaning in your document. Select carefully the materials and reasoning you will use in your document. The temptation is great to include everything you find in your research, every section from all the form contracts you read, every fact that seems sympathetic to your client. But resist. Instead, carve your materials precisely by asking what each piece of content contributes to the document's goal, its message, or with the analysis itself. Use your understanding of varied purposes and audiences to decide what is needed. Resist the urge to *throw something in just in case.* Then include everything that's needed; nothing more and nothing less.

2.   Precision in word choice.

Overly broad legal terms are also a common source of imprecision, so use words that are no broader in meaning than you intend. For example, use *motorized vehicle rather* than *vehicle* if you did not mean to include horse-drawn carriages. Make sure your topic sentences, headings, issues, and other key sentences are focused precisely. Similarly, focus each part of your Question Presented or issue.

> **Under Missouri's assault law, which requires a showing of intent, <u>was a child capable of intending</u> assault when the child was only five years old and the child's act consisted of pulling a chair out from under a woman as she was sitting down?**

rather than

> Under tort law, <u>did assault occur</u> when a five-year-old pulled a chair out from under an elderly woman?

In the more precise issue, the law is focused on assault rather than all of tort law and identifies the relevant jurisdiction. The question, by using *capable of intending*, refers to the specific legal question being asked. The facts include all the information needed to understand both why intent may not be present (the age of the child and the indirectness of the act) and why it may be assault (the fact that the woman was just sitting down when the child pulled out the chair.).

In point headings, use appropriate terms of art and avoid vague words.

> **IN FAILING TO SUPPRESS THE EVIDENCE, THE TRIAL COURT ABUSED ITS DISCRETION BECAUSE THE GUN**

WAS PRODUCED AS THE RESULT OF AN ILLEGAL SEARCH.

rather than

THE TRIAL COURT ERRED BECAUSE THE SEARCH WAS IMPROPER.

In general, use concrete and specific words rather than abstract or general ones.

The defendant said that he had a gun as he grabbed Ms. Delaney's arm and poked her in the back.

rather than

The defendant said he was armed as he accosted the victim.

Use the latter version only if you mean to obscure the facts. For related information, see EMPHASIS, PERSUASIVE WRITING, and ABSTRACT NOUNS.

Also avoid ambiguous wording. While overly broad terms include more meaning than is intended, ambiguous terms include two or more different meanings. For example, avoid using *promised* in a contract when the readers could debate about whether this term created a contractual obligation or was a non-contractual statement of existing fact. Finally, check numbers and cross references, where a mistake can be both difficult to see and expensive to miss.

3. Precision through consistency.

When you have identified the precise content and words needed in a document, check your document carefully for their consistent use. This polishing detail, which is desirable in legal writing generally, becomes essential in drafted documents where a misstatement can have substantial ramifications. Whether you are drafting complaints, contracts, or briefs, use TERMS OF ART that unify the document and appear wherever appropriate throughout the document. Particularly if you are using excerpts from past samples, inconsistencies are likely to appear. Read the document specifically to make those terms consistent.

4. Precision through sentence structure.

Avoid ambiguous sentence structures. For example, your topic sentences should include a subject and verb that are focused on your main point and subordinate phrases that add the detail relevant to that particular point.

The issue that the appellant raises on this appeal is whether the trial court erred in applying the statute when it summarized its findings in only one sentence.

Trial court erred in applying the statute refers to the error raised on appeal, and the statement *in only one sentence* highlights a legally

305

significant fact in this case. For more help, see SUBJECT–VERB COMBINATIONS, and ISSUE STATEMENTS.

5. Precision in presentation.

In the midst of making many large decisions, you may forget the small ones. You may use inconsistent formats for headings, fail to conform to local format requirements, or use a curt tone in a business letter. These small imprecisions can undercut your credibility as well as your effectiveness. These matters deserve attention. Especially in letters, be precise about what tone you select, and be sure you stay consistent throughout. If you are following a form within your jurisdiction, check for conformity as to page length, spacing, and other details. If you are putting dates in the document, double check that the dates are accurate. Use pinpoint cites for any rule, holding, proposition, quotation, or specific reference.

> **An implied duty exists not to make changes in the work that would render the work a false attribution. Williams v. ABC, 938 F.3d 14, 16 (2d Cir. 2007).**

Just as all parts of your presentation should unite to send one overt and consistent message, your precision in presentation sends the more subtle message that you have taken meticulous care in preparing the document.

PREDICATE

See SENTENCE, PARTS OF.

PREFIXES, WHEN TO HYPHENATE

See HYPHENS, EX-, and *SELF-* OR *SELF*?

PREPOSITIONAL PHRASES

A prepositional phrase is a group of words that work together to show the relationship of a noun or pronoun to the rest of the sentence. This noun or pronoun is called the object of the preposition. A preposition, which is always the first word in a prepositional phrase, shows how the rest of that phrase is logically related to the sentence. Examples of prepositions are *of, to, on, off, between, through, in, at, without, over,* and *under.* The following examples of prepositional phrases illustrate the variety of information they can convey.

> **He built the house with his own hands.**

> **All nonresidents living in Illinois for more than three months of a calendar year must complete the following section.**

> **The contract will have been signed by that date.**

> **The settlement seems reasonable in light of the facts.**

For more information, see PREPOSITIONS.

PREPOSITION, ENDING A SENTENCE WITH

Style books allow ending a sentence with a preposition. The rule against it originated with an eighteenth century grammarian, perhaps because of the popularity of Latin at that time. Now the rule is archaic, even in the law. Ending with a preposition may sound too informal for some legal situations, but it is not technically incorrect. So revise the sentence when ending with a preposition creates inappropriate informality or awkward phrasing or when it will distract your AUDIENCE.

The witness was absolutely sure of these facts.

rather than

The witness stated that these were the facts he was absolutely sure of.

Do not, however, revise the sentence if the revision is more awkward than the original. Such fussiness is also called *hypercorrection*.

This is a rule I will not put up with.

rather than

This is a rule up with which I will not put.

PREPOSITIONS

Prepositions go before nouns, pronouns, or phrases working as nouns (that is the *pre-*), and show the relationship of that noun, pronoun, or phrase to the rest of the sentence (that is the *position*). Prepositional phrases thus begin with a preposition and end with a noun or pronoun.

in the car, beyond the cost, of this litigation, without his testimony

The noun or pronoun at the end of the phrase is called the object of the preposition. Prepositional phrases are useful and necessary, but watch for three problems when using them.

1. Avoid using many in a row. Prepositional phrases have a rhythm something like that of a slow waltz, and many of them in a row can waltz your reader right off to sleep.

The department is required to submit a written explanation if its income deviates substantially from predictions for 2005.

rather than

The department is required to submit a written explanation in the case of deviations of substantial size from the predictions of income for the calendar year of 2005.

2. Avoid using a prepositional phrase when a shorter grammatical phrase could do as well.

If the hearing is delayed, ...

rather than

In the event of the occurrence of a delay of the hearing, ...

See CONCISENESS and NOMINALIZATIONS.

3. Use the objective case (such as *me, us, him, her,* or *them*) of a pronoun that ends a prepositional phrase.

This written contract between <u>you</u> and <u>me</u> should help us avoid any confusion in the future.

rather than

This written contract between you and I should help us avoid any confusion in the future.

PRESENT PARTICIPLES

See VERBS, TENSES, subsections 2 and 3.

PRESENT PERFECT TENSE

See VERBS, TENSES, subsection 3.

PRESENT PROGRESSIVE TENSE

See VERBS, TENSES, subsection 2.

PRESENT TENSE

See VERBS, TENSES, subsections 1–3.

PRETRIAL BRIEFS

A pretrial brief is any brief written in support of or opposition to a pretrial motion. A pretrial brief uses persuasive writing to inform the reader of the law and to persuade the reader to accept the client's position, and it is usually filed with the Notice of Motion and Motion or shortly thereafter. For related information, see MEMORANDUM OF POINTS AND AUTHORITIES, NOTICE OF MOTION, and MOTIONS.

Check your jurisdiction for the particular format requirements. See BRIEFS for a sample format.

PREVIOUS TO

Usually you can substitute *before* for greater readability and conciseness.

PREWRITING

Prewriting includes all work done before writing the first substantial draft of a document. According to many successful legal writers, clear thought and focused effort at the prewriting stage will save hours of time later in writing, revising, and polishing. In a research project, prewriting includes the first five steps of your research strategy, taking notes on the research found, and thinking about your ORGANIZATION. Organization can include thinking and outlining or some other means of organization. See WRITING PROCESS, PREWRITING CHECKLIST, and PROCRASTINATION.

Organization is the key to successful prewriting. As soon as possible, categorize the sections and subsections of your problem so that the work can be done in compartments. For example, if you are writing a three-issue appellate brief, you might organize your prewriting by those three issues and work on only one issue at a time. Some writers prefer to begin the writing process by writing a very rough preliminary draft as soon as possible, rather than beginning with other prewriting activities. If you are one of these writers, you may apply the techniques below after your preliminary draft.

If you are comfortable with prewriting activities, be careful not to stay in this stage so long that the later stages of writing, rewriting, and revising are short-changed. The following techniques can help make your prewriting stage successful.

1. Think before you go to the library. In particular, do some version of the first five steps of the Research Strategy Chart first. (See RESEARCH STRATEGY CHART.)

2. Make the library work to your advantage by planning your research the way you might plan a trip to the grocery store: before you go, list the books you want to use and order the list.

3. Have your system of note-taking ready to go before you go to the library. See NOTES and READING.

4. Allow yourself to think about the problem even when you are not writing notes; if a good idea comes to your head, jot it down so you can easily file it with its issue.

5. Try to list or outline the important points that you want to make under each issue. Even though this list may be flawed, it will help you focus your research. See OUTLINES.

6. Allow yourself always to make your own comments and commentary as you take notes, to help you pull the pieces together in your own mind.

7. Pull all the pieces together by letting the law itself dictate the organization; resist using a pre-programmed organizational scheme, but instead respond to the organization of the law. For example, you might discover several elements to a rule and use them as subdivisions. Or you might have only one test to be applied to the facts in one unit.

PREWRITING CHECKLIST

Use the following list of questions to provide a starting point for clarifying and refining your writing process, modifying the list to suit your individual needs.

Overarching Concerns

1. Have I taken effective notes from the assigning attorney, supervisor, or other AUDIENCE?

2. Do I have a clear understanding of the document's PURPOSE?

3. Have I considered the document's scope?

Practical Concerns

4. Do I have a clear sense of the client's needs and budget?

5. Have I checked for in-house resources, such as similar documents produced in the past or people with experience in the area?

6. Have I written down a research strategy that is designed specifically for this project, my experience level, my client's budget, and my library's resources? See RESEARCH STRATEGY CHART.

7. Have I coordinated dates and duties with any collaborators? Have I scheduled and recorded interim and final deadlines?

8. Have I scheduled and recorded interim and final deadlines? As you immerse yourself in the process, periodically remind yourself of the overall concerns in writing. For example, ask yourself the following question.

9. Have I planned and written down the issues or thesis statement? Do I return to these periodically to keep my FOCUS and PURPOSE clear?

PRINCIPLES OF GOOD LEGAL WRITING

Writing is complicated and non-sequential; it is easy to feel lost among the details. The following broader principles, however, can help you remember the forest as well as the trees. They fall into three main areas: priorities, process, and product.

1. Priorities

Good legal writing must always communicate your meaning accurately and should always be easy to read. Whenever possible, it should also be appealing to the reader, a pleasure to read. These three qualities—accuracy, readability, and appeal—form a ready guideline to help the legal writer assess the importance of various writing tasks.

Relative importance cannot reliably be assigned to such qualities as complete research, good organization, precise wording, elegant sentence structure, or correct spelling. Rather, their importance depends on the effect on the reader. The following table lists examples of various errors and the type of effect they might have on the reader.

Sample Writing Problems That Vary in Their Seriousness

Area Problem Affects	Large-Scale Organization	Small-Scale Organization	Sentence Structure	Word Choice
		Aspects of Writing		
Accuracy and Thoroughness	Discussion of law is organized around cases without identifying overarching issues.	Discussion section is missing needed parts of the analysis.	Sentences are so hard to read that the meaning is lost.	The wrong word is used for a legal term of art.
Ease of Use	Subissues are commingled rather than divided.	The parts of the analysis are presented in an inconsistent or confusing order.	Sentences often need to be reread to be understood.	Various terms are used for the same idea or legal concept.
Appeal	A long discussion lacks any headings or clear transitions between main sections.	Information is repeated unnecessarily.	Sentences, although clear enough, are structured so important points do not stand out.	Some wording is overly formal, while other wording in the same passage is too casual.

Thus, for example even the small omission of a punctuation mark can be critical, as in the situation where *ten foot-long rods* was written in a purchase order instead of the correct *ten-foot-long rods*. The order was for uranium rods, and the cost of the error ran into the millions. Sometimes a mediocre-but-serviceable organization in a contract is not such a serious error as the omission of a critical clause.

So the legal writer needs to measure the importance of various writing qualities by the effects they have. Thus evaluate the importance of writing tasks based on their effect on accuracy, thoroughness, ease of use, and appeal.

3. Process

A healthy writing process involves a rhythmic alternation between two contradictory subprocesses: creation and critique. Like a breath, a heartbeat, or a footstep, both subprocesses are needed to complete the task, but those subprocesses cannot be undertaken simultaneously. A breath requires both expansion, to take in air with its needed oxygen, and contraction, to expel carbon dioxide and unneeded components of the air. Similarly, writing requires the expansive act of creation, considering and laying out various possibilities, and the contracting act of critiquing, which eliminates possibilities that are not workable. Many writers have problems writing because they are either trying to complete these contradictory tasks simultaneously or they are alternating too frequently between the two tasks, which adds stress to the writing process.

These two aspects of the writing process must alternate efficiently, at a pace that is optimal for the individual writer. Some writers will perform better when they write a complete rough draft of a section before stopping to revise any details within the section. Other writers will perform better stopping to revise after a few paragraphs or sentences. A few writers will even be comfortable alternating quickly between creating and critiquing, editing as they write. Whatever the rate of alternation, any writer will benefit from understanding the process and adjusting it as needed to enhance his or her overall writing process. The following list provides an overview and starting point for refining your own process.

(a) PREWRITING.

At this stage, focus on framing your issues, gathering your materials, and deciding how to design something appropriate for your AUDIENCE. Develop the document's PURPOSE, decide on the appropriate SCOPE, and choose a STANCE. Once you have gathered the materials, think about several possible ways to assemble them to meet your purpose. Reflect long enough to make a decision based more on the reader than on your own taste. Remember that good writing is good thinking, so make sure you have done enough of the second before you start the first. See also OUTLINES and ORGANIZATION FOR THOSE WHO CAN'T OUTLINE.

(b) WRITING.

At this stage, focus on getting it written, not getting it right. Let your thinking flow onto the page in the first draft, without stopping to edit.

(c) REWRITING.

Do not hesitate to rework main ideas and large-scale organization. Add content if necessary. When allocating your time, assume you will need to rework something. Few writers hit it right the first time. See PARAGRAPHS; ORGANIZATION, LARGE–SCALE; and ORGANIZATION, SMALL–SCALE.

(d) REVISING.

Reconcile yourself to the fact that it will take several passes to get the text right. If you focus on what is needed, however, this need not be an onerous task. Revise for ACCURACY, READABILITY, CONCISENESS, TONE, and EMPHASIS. In particular, revise POINT HEADINGS, ISSUE STATEMENTS, TOPIC SENTENCES, and CONCLUSIONS, because your reader will pay special attention to these parts of any legal document.

(e) POLISHING.

Use whatever technique works for you: moving from back to front, reading through separately for each kind of revision needed, reading aloud, or working section by section. Check such things as COMMAS, spelling, and FORMAT. Check especially for errors you know you commonly make.

3. Product.

Before you release your document to your audience, consider the following questions. Doing so can help you lift any document from mediocrity to excellence.

(a) Is the document tailored to your audience and purpose?

Make sure that you have made the best decisions about purposes and audiences, and that you have understood the practical constraints involved, the document's context, its historical setting, and its scope. Here you can also check your stance or point of view, to make sure it is consistent throughout. For related information, see AUDIENCE, PURPOSE, and PROFESSIONAL POSTURE.

(b) Is the document unified by one message?

Whether the document is answering one legal question, advancing one theory, or building one transaction, it has a message to which every part must contribute. Check the main message to make sure its language is precise; then check for consistency and support throughout the document, probably using the same terms.

(c) Does the document contain appropriate materials?

Law, facts, arguments, counterarguments, contract provisions, policy statements—all provide materials for legal documents. Cull from the possibilities those materials essential to the document's purposes and audiences. Include legally significant facts but not the entire background; use mandatory law first, going to persuasive only when necessary; use only contract provisions that apply to this transaction; and include all steps in your reasoning, not just the beginning and the end. Your materials are the key to the document's structure.

(d) Does the document use a coherent structure?

Because there are so many possible permutations and combinations of the components of legal analysis, the choices are many. Here reasonable minds often differ about how best to present the components. When choosing between competing approaches, choose the structure that will appeal to most of your readers. For example, while the structure may make sense to you because it follows the elements of a statute, your readers may be unpersuaded by such a dry presentation, even though you think it is inherently logical. Perhaps the elements should be rearranged to put the most persuasive ones first or to reflect a policy shift. When an audience resists your structure, it usually means it is not coherent enough. To make it more coherent, you can use your message to unify the document and then make sure the order flows from that message. To keep that flow, place your important points in POSITIONS OF EMPHASIS, such as headings, topic sentences, and conclusions. Keep working at it until any legal reader cannot misunderstand the structure.

(e) Does the document use appropriate proportions for each section?

Part of the document's message lies in the amount of text devoted to each section. Usually, the longer the text, the more important the reader assumes it is. Similarly, if there is heavy citation, the reader assumes the section is important. What confuses the reader is when much text is devoted to a small point or when an important point goes by too quickly. The proportions should reflect the relative importance of the components.

(f) Do substance and sentence structure match?

Readers also look for messages not just from word but also from the sentence structure, or syntax, within which those words reside. Use cohesive devices that reinforce the meaning, such as TRANSITIONS, REPETITION of a word or structure, and other verbal connections between sentences and within a paragraph. (For relevant techniques, see COHERENCE, PARAGRAPHS, and CONNECTIONS, MAKING THEM.) Finally, match substance and syntax by using dependent clauses for dependent ideas, PARALLEL STRUCTURE for parallel ideas, and main clauses for main ideas. Use semicolons to show two ideas are more closely related than if a period separates them. For related information, see PARAGRAPHS and SENTENCE STRUCTURE.

(g) Is the document polished?

Your credibility is linked to your attention to detail. Readers often believe that, if there is a typographical mistake, there is probably a research mistake, too. Even those jurisdictions who purport to relax about citation form or those supervising attorneys who say, "Just give me what you've got," do not tolerate typographical errors, citation mistakes, misspellings, and grammar miscues. Build credibility by polishing the document to the last dot. For more detail on these seven questions, see Jill J. Ramsfield, The Law as Architecture: Building Legal Documents (2000).

PRIOR TO

Prior to sounds a bit stuffy and can be ungrammatical. To avoid *prior to*, use *before*.

Before the accident, he ran three miles each morning.

rather than

Prior to the accident, he ran three miles each morning.

Or use *to*.

To receive this summary of past complaints, the consumer must file . . . .

rather than

Prior to receiving this summary of past complaints, the consumer must file . . . .

PROCEDURAL OR *SUBSTANTIVE?*

Use these terms precisely, because the distinction between them is critical in legal writing. *Procedural* refers to legal process, or the legal machinery for carrying on a suit. This machinery includes pleading, evidence, process, and similar practical matters. For example, the question of whether a court has jurisdiction over a particular suit is a procedural question; the question of whether post-verdict motions were filed on time is also procedural.

Substantive refers to the law itself, which regulates and defines the rights and duties of parties to the suit. For example, a defendant's right to be represented by counsel is a substantive right; a party's right to bring an action for wrongful death is also a substantive right.

Often substantive rights are referred to as the merits of a case. For example, to say *The judge is ready to make a decision on the merits* is to say that all the procedural matters have been settled so that the court may judge the remaining issues on the basis of the parties' duties and rights. Following this philosophy, often procedural issues must come early in the organization of briefs and memos, before substantive issues.

PROCESS AND PRODUCT COMPARED

The writing product is the document itself, which is subject to scrutiny and evaluation by your AUDIENCE and those who evaluate your performance, whether supervisors, clients, judges, or professors. To assist and even impress them, your product must exhibit ACCURACY and CLARITY, regardless of the constraints imposed on you by less-than-ideal conditions.

In contrast, your writing process is your personal way of getting the job done. It includes every aspect of your work, such as your time allocations for different tasks, your order for doing these tasks, and your style of interacting with others involved in the project. It is affected by your habitual ways of completing all the tasks involved in your writing process, such as ordering your research strategy, writing by dictating or typing, and proofreading. It is also affected by external factors that vary with the situation, such as your client's demands, your supervisor's agenda, and your energy level on the day you write.

Although your process is not generally scrutinized by others, it deserves your personal scrutiny because it can dramatically affect the product. Refining your legal writing process, particularly noting how it may differ from nonlegal writing processes, also has personal benefits; it can make you more effective, efficient, and confident. For ways to make this evaluation, see WRITING PROCESS.

PROCRASTINATION

Procrastination works if it is incubation, fails if it is empty postponement. To make procrastination work for you, do the following.

1. Start early.

Do short prewriting tasks early and then think. For example, write the Questions Presented as soon as you begin working on a memo and then think about them. Alternatively, you can gather the research, read it, and then think about it. If you are working on a contract, gather samples of previous contracts and study them to help you determine what components your contract needs to include.

2. Keep going.

Complete your research, draft some of the more standard contract sections, or take whatever notes work for you. Let the problem sit a while to let it breathe, turn over, move about in your mind. Then jot down ideas as they come to you and put them in your files. See BRIEFING CASES and NOTES.

3. Create a design or plan.

Set a time for completing the research and writing an outline. However cursory this outline may be, this step will usually force the procrastinating to end and the organizing to begin. This is the hardest step to take, but you must take it; skipping it can ruin worthwhile incubating. See OUTLINES or ORGANIZATION FOR THOSE WHO CAN'T OUTLINE.

4. Use the calendar.

Similarly, set a time to have each early draft completed, even if you are the only one who knows the deadline. By putting interim deadlines on your calendar and tying them to another person or task, you force yourself to avoid further procrastination by sheer embarrassment. If you do your own typing, try to find someone who will be a listener or a reader for your paper at a specific time, again so you have a deadline tied to another person.

5. Use interim deadlines.

Finally, schedule small interim deadlines instead of just one final deadline and stick to your schedule. This will break down your temptation to postpone.

For related information, see TIME MANAGEMENT, WRITING BLOCKS, GETTING STARTED, and WHEN TO STOP.

PROFESSIONAL POSTURE

Professional posture is the image you project of yourself and your role through a written document. You always want to leave the reader with a good impression, even though you must retain your focus on your document's purpose, and audience. You can create a good impression by communicating an appropriate professional posture in the document. That posture includes your professional responsibility and your personal style.

1. Professional responsibility.

Your professional responsibility varies as the particular situation and legal document vary, so take time to ascertain your responsibilities in each situation; then make sure you meet them. For example, in an opinion letter, you have a duty to remind the client that the choice is finally up to him or her, even though you recommend one particular course of action. Therefore, take care to explain with equal clarity both the reasoning behind your advice and the limits of your role as advisor. Explain clearly and completely so your reader could make an informed decision either way. For example, when you write a brief, you have a duty in most jurisdictions to acknowledge a precedent that seems unfavorable to your case. To meet that duty, cite the case but also argue that it is distinguishable based on different facts or reasoning.

2. Personal style.

Besides meeting your professional responsibility, you may want to communicate a personal style. For example, compared to other attorneys, you may be more formal or informal, more personal or impersonal, more impassioned or unemotional. You will probably adjust this style somewhat in each document you write, just as you adjust your manner of speaking when talking to different people. For more on this, see AUDIENCE. For ways to communicate your personal style, see TONE.

PROGRESSIVE TENSES

See VERBS, TENSES.

PRONOUN REFERENCE

See AMBIGUITY, WAYS TO AVOID, subsection 2.

PRONOUNS

Pronouns take the place of nouns, and they have many uses.

He is the officer who gave me a ticket.

Without it, they have no case.

The plaintiff must take the responsibility upon himself.

Each of you should write to your senator.

That may not be the most effective support for her position.

Four common questions arise about using pronouns include the following:

(1) when to use commas with relative pronouns,

(2) when to use *who* or *whom*,

(3) when to *use he, she,* or *they*, and

(4) when to use *we*.

1.   When to use commas with relative pronouns.

Relative pronouns, one subcategory of pronouns, deserve special attention because they are used frequently in legal writing and their proper use is often crucial to ACCURACY. Relative pronouns include *who, whose, that, which, whoever, whichever,* and *whatever*. These relative pronouns introduce subordinate clauses, or groups of words that include a subject and verb but cannot stand by themselves as sentences.

Your car, which was still in the lot at midnight, was towed.

This issue was resolved by the court in Barker v. Holmes, which stated....

Any nonresident who has lived in the state for more than three months must fill out this portion of the form.

All cars that remain in the lot after 10:00 p.m. will be towed.

All operators <u>whose</u> licenses expire this month must show the supervisor their renewed license.

Sometimes a subordinate clause adds extra information to the sentence but is not essential to the accuracy of the sentence. To punctuate this clause correctly, place commas before and after the subordinate clause.

Your car, which was still in the lot at midnight, was towed.

Sometimes, however, a subordinating clause is essential to the meaning of the sentence because the clause narrows the subject, or restricts the meaning of the subject. In this situation, removing the subordinate clause would make the sentence inaccurate. To punctuate this kind of subordinate clause correctly, do not put commas before or after the clause.

All cars [ ] that remain in the lot after 10:00 p.m. [ ] will be towed.

Any nonresident [ ] who has lived in the state for more than three months [ ] must fill out this portion of the form.

All operators [ ] whose licenses expire this month [ ] must show the supervisor their renewed license.

For related information, see THAT OR WHICH?

2. When to use *who* or *whom*.

Use *who* as a subject, *whom* as an OBJECT. First, use *whom* as the object of a PREPOSITION.

To whom did you present the question about the gun?

Second, use *whom* as the object of a verb.

Whom did you see on the night of the incident?

This use also applies to clauses that are inserted within another sentence, as in the following example.

Defendant is the person whom the plaintiff saw on the night of the crime.

Whom is needed here because it is the object of the verb *saw* in the clause explaining *person*.

Use *who* as a subject of a sentence or of a clause.

Who took my shoes?

You are the person who called me yesterday.

For an explanation of related terms, see SENTENCE, PARTS OF, subsections 3–6.

3. When to *use he, she,* or *they*.

Use *they* only when referring to a plural noun. Use *he or she* when you are referring to one person but do not know the sex of the person. For more on this question, see SEXIST LANGUAGE, WAYS TO AVOID.

4. When to use *we*.

We is a special problem in legal writing because you may, by using *we*, inadvertently speak for your whole law firm or organization, possibly creating legal obligations. Never use *we* when you really mean *I*; use *we* only when you are speaking officially for the organization of which you are a part, as one judge may do when drafting an opinion for the whole bench.

PROOFREADING

See POLISHING and POLISHING PROCESS CHECKLIST.

PROPER NOUNS

Proper nouns are names of specific persons, organizations, publications, and other such entities. *Helen Harris, American Bar Association, Texas Law Review*. Capitalize them.

PROVIDED THAT

Replace this phrase with *if* for greater CONCISENESS and CLARITY.

Our client has the contractual right to reject any shipment if she notifies Norcross of her decision within forty-eight hours of receiving that shipment.

rather than

Our client has the contractual right to reject any shipment, provided that she notifies Norcross of her decision within forty-eight hours of receiving that shipment.

Sometimes *provided that* may have been used to introduce something that will most likely happen; then you may replace it with *when*.

The transfer of ownership will occur at closing, when the seller provides the title and the buyer pays the full purchase price.

rather than

The transfer of ownership will occur at closing, provided that the seller provides the title and the buyer pays the full purchase price.

PUNCTUATING LISTS

See LISTS, STRUCTURE OF.

PUNCTUATION

Punctuation rules are critical to accuracy. For ways to punctuate sentences, see PERIODS, SEMICOLONS, COLONS, EXCLAMATION POINTS, and QUESTION MARKS. For ways to punctuate phrases within a sentence, see COMMAS, DASHES, SEMICOLONS, and CO-LONS. For ways to punctuate lists, see LISTS, STRUCTURE OF. For ways to punctuate quotes, see QUOTATIONS, HOW TO PUNCTUATE. For punctuation marks used within words, see HYPHENS, BRACKETS, and APOSTROPHES.

PURPOSE

Establish your document's overall purpose before you get too far along in the writing process. Although you may brainstorm a first draft or some notes, take time to think about why you are writing as well as what you want to say and to whom you will say it. Take time to be honest with yourself about your purposes: there may be many. For example, you may be writing to impress a new boss as well as to advise on a decision. This honesty often does not mean you state these purposes explicitly in the document, but it will nevertheless make your writing more effective and more efficient. You may want to write out your primary and secondary purposes. Then you can focus on meeting those purposes throughout writing, rewriting, and revising.

Your AUDIENCE will help you to determine your purpose. A supervising attorney may want a quick, direct answer; a worried client may want a long, gentle explanation. Thus your purpose is also linked to SCOPE; once you decide on your purpose, you will have a more definite idea of how long your document should be. The following list may help you more clearly define your purposes.

- Advise a client
- Organize a meeting
- Complete a transaction
- Soothe hard feelings
- Impress your boss
- Create a paper trail
- Collect a bill
- Answer a question
- Present a new legal theory

For more information on how to develop your purpose, see GETTING STARTED, OUTLINES, ORGANIZATION FOR THOSE WHO CAN'T OUTLINE, and AUDIENCE.

PURSUANT TO

Avoid this phrase when you can, because it is usually less clear than the alternative. Also avoid it because it is legalese.

In preparation for our meeting on estate planning, I am enclosing a questionnaire to help you collect the relevant information.

rather than

Pursuant to our meeting regarding estate planning, I am enclosing a questionnaire to will help you collect the relevant information.

To conform to this new regulation, we are revising our administrative procedures.

rather than

Pursuant to this new regulation, we are revising our administrative procedures.

QUALITY AS A MODIFIER

In formal legal usage, *quality* is still a noun, not an adjective. Technically, you can use *quality* as an adjective to mean *excellent*, but avoid doing so if it creates ambiguity.

He did an excellent job arguing in front of the jury.

rather than

He did a quality job in front of the jury.

Quality needs a modifier, such as *high*, *poor*, or *questionable*. Standing alone, it does not automatically mean *high* quality. So, write,

The product is of high quality.

rather than

This is a quality product.

QUESTION MARK OR PERIOD?

See QUESTION MARKS.

QUESTION MARKS

You know to use question marks with questions. The problems occur with sentences like the ones that follow.

The question is whether federal taxes on this investment must be paid through January 15 of this year.

Here a period, not a question mark is used, because the main subject and verb, *the question is* make a statement. But in the following sentences, use a question mark.

The court asked defendant's attorney, "Are you saying that federal taxes on this investment must be paid through January 15 of this year?"

The boy, when confronted by the clerk, said only, "Who, me?"

When a question mark comes at the end of a sentence, no period is used after the question mark. A question mark can be used mid-sentence, after the question, but a period is still used at the end of the sentence.

Can taxes on this investment be deferred? is the question.

This structure is rare and thus looks odd to most readers; try rewording the sentence whenever you can to avoid putting a question mark in the middle, even if it is grammatically correct to do so.

The question is, "Can taxes on this investment be deferred?"

On rare occasions, you may choose either a question mark or a period.

May we hear from you within one week.

Here the choice between a period and a question mark is a tactical one. When you are asking a question but implying a demand, you may use a period. This is not particularly advisable, however, because of the tone it creates. For handling question marks and quotation marks together, see QUOTATIONS, HOW TO PUNCTUATE, subsection 4.

QUESTIONS PRESENTED

The lens of the legal analyst's camera, the Question Presented focuses on the specific question to be answered in a legal memo. This term is used by many attorneys to differentiate it from the issue statement in a persuasive piece of writing, though the latter is also sometimes called a Question Presented. In its objective form, the ideal Question Presented can outline the memo because it can have three parts: (1) the general rule of law governing the question, (2) the legal question to be answered in this situation, and (3) the legally significant facts necessary for the analysis.

General law

Under Fed. R. Civ. P. 4(d)(1), <u>Summons: Personal Service</u>,

Legal question

was a notice effective

Legally significant facts

when it was delivered to defendant's wife and defendant did not reside at his wife's address?

These three parts are combined and written in either question form or *whether* form. The *whether* form enjoys common use among established lawyers, but it is grammatically incorrect because it is an incomplete sentence. The *whether* form also implies a statement rather than a question and can add extra words.

In either form, keep subject and verb close together to increase readability.

Whether notice was effective under Fed. R. Civ. P. 4(d)(1), <u>Summons: Personal Service</u>, when it was delivered to defendant's wife and defendant did not reside at his wife's address.

or

Under Fed. R. Civ. P. 4(d)(1), <u>Summons: Personal Service</u>, was a notice effectively delivered when it was delivered to defendant's wife and when defendant did not reside at his wife's address at the time?

You can put the legally significant facts at the end of the Question Presented so that the reader is focused by moving from general to specific. Placing the legally significant facts at the end also helps keep the question readable because it places the list at the end of the sentence. For related information, see LISTS, STRUCTURE OF.

Check with your reader to see if the particular facts of your case should be included in the Questions Presented, which will focus the questions on the client's situation. Your reader may prefer that the facts be stated in general terms so the memo is easier to use as a reference in future cases. For related information, see ISSUE STATEMENTS.

QUOTATION MARKS

Use quotation marks for quotes of forty-nine words or less. Also use quotation marks to indicate that you are referring to a word itself, rather than the thing the words stand for, as in the following example.

"Hearsay" refers to a statement, other than one made by the declarant while testifying at the trial or hearing, offered in evidence to prove the truth of the matter asserted.

For related information, see QUOTATION MARKS OR INDENTED QUOTES? and QUOTATIONS, HOW TO PUNCTUATE.

QUOTATION MARKS IN LEGISLATION

See LEGISLATION.

QUOTATION MARKS OR INDENTED QUOTES?

See QUOTATIONS, HOW TO PUNCTUATE, subsections 1 and 2.

QUOTATIONS, HOW TO PUNCTUATE

These rules are picky and extensive but worth observing. It is important to be accurate in legal writing, and particularly important to be accurate when quoting. These rules include

(1) when to use quotation marks,

(2) when to indent, sentence structure

(3) when to use a comma before a quote,

(4) how to use other punctuation marks with quotation marks,

(5) when to use single quotation marks,

(6) when and how to underline parts of a quote,

(7) how to mark changes in a quote,

(8) how to mark omissions from a quote, and

(9) how to maintain credibility when editing a quote.

1.   When to use quotation marks.

Use quotation marks to mark any direct quote. When the quote is forty-nine words or less, put it in quotation marks.

The court reasoned that "any error must in this situation be material."

Also use quotation marks to indicate that a word is being used to refer to the word itself, rather than to the meaning of the word. Thus, put quotation marks around a word when you could insert *the term* or the *word* before that word.

The court focused on "reasonable" when interpreting the meaning of this clause in the contract.

Avoid using quotation marks to indicate slang, sarcasm, irony, or anything other than direct quotes or words used as words. The precision of legal writing requires the precise use of punctuation, including quotation marks. If you feel uncomfortable using a word because it is informal or ambiguous, change the word rather than putting it in quotation marks.

The attorney's complaint about the secretary's typographical errors cannot be considered slander.

rather than

The attorney's complaint about the secretary's "typos" cannot be considered slander.

2.   When to indent.

When the quote is longer than forty-nine words, indent it and use single spacing. Put the citation on the first line of text following the quote, rather than within the indented quote itself.

In this case, mutuality required the court's closer scrutiny.

> **Despite the defendant's emotional plea regarding the centrality of upholding contracts to the free working of a democracy, we cannot ignore the plaintiff's complaint. In this case, the court must intervene because the issue of mutuality, not to mention that of duress, requires that**

the court examine both the contract's wording and the parol evidence surrounding the signing of that contract.

<u>Hartman v. Legler</u>, **986 F. Supp. 192 (S.D. Ind. 2007). Mutuality emerged from the contract's wording because**....

3. When to use a comma before a quote.

    Use a comma if the phrase before the quote introduces it.

    She said, "I killed him."

If the quote is an integral part of the larger sentence, do not use a comma.

He said "killed," not "stabbed."

4. How to use other punctuation marks with quotation marks.

    In the U.S., quotation marks go outside commas and periods, even if the comma or period is not part of the quote.

    The term on which we must focus is "mutuality."

This rule is the same for both double quotation marks ("—") and single ones ('—'). The rule is not meant to reflect logical concerns, but rather historical ones. Periods and commas on early U.S. presses kept breaking, so they moved them inside the quotations. One exception to this rule is legislation, where periods and commas are generally treated like all other punctuation marks. As always, check and follow your jurisdiction's rules. Another exception is British English, which also puts commas and periods outside the quotation marks when they are not part of the quote.

All other punctuation marks go inside the quotation marks if they are part of the quote, outside if they are not.

Common law recognized a defense to a privacy action where "the incident was a public concern and record"; however, the statutory policy had in effect eliminated this defense.

The semicolon is not part of the quote, so it goes outside the marks.

Smith reports "a majority of the jurors thought 'infer' meant 'assume'!"

The exclamation point is part of the quote, so it goes inside the quotation marks. *Infer* and *assume* refer to the words as words, rather than the concepts the words describe, and so are put in quotation marks. Single marks are used because the words are within another quote. For related information, see EXCLAMATION POINTS.

5. When to use single quotation marks.

    In the United States use single quotation marks only for quotes within other quotes.

    The defendant said, "He told me to 'get lost.'"

6. When and how to underline parts of a quote.

Underline to add emphasis to the key phrase in quotations long enough to be indented and single-spaced in the text. Underlining may encourage the legal reader to read the long quote by making it more visually pleasing. When you underline, add *(emphasis added)* after the citation.

As this court itself has stated,

> **[T]he court must intervene because the issue of mutuality, not to mention that of duress, requires that the court examine <u>the parol evidence surrounding the signing</u> of the contract. Such an intervention often illuminates the intentions of the parties, the nature of the contract, and the level of commitment to the agreement. Without the intervention, the parties might not be able to resolve the conflict.**

<u>Durant v. Colt</u>, 945 F. Supp. 641 (D.D.C. 2000) (emphasis added).

When the quote is indented, put the cite and *(emphasis added)* on the first line of text following the indented quote, not within the indented quote itself. For limits to this technique, see EXTENDED QUOTES.

7. How to mark changes in a quote.

In general, use brackets to mark any changes you make in the wording of a quote.

(a) If you are changing or adding a word to a quote to make it fit grammatically into your sentence, put brackets ([ ]) around that word.

> **As the court explained, "Despite the defendant's emotional plea regarding the centrality of upholding contracts to the free working of a democracy, [the court] cannot ignore the plaintiff's complaint."**

changed from the original

> Despite the defendant's emotional plea regarding the centrality of upholding contracts to the free working of a democracy, we cannot ignore the plaintiff's complaint.

(b) If you are adding or changing a letter within a word, put brackets around the part of the word changed. Even if all you do is change a letter from lower case (a) to upper case (A), you must put brackets around the change.

> **The court made this explicit when it said, "[W]e cannot ignore the plaintiff's complaint."**

changed from the original

> Despite the defendant's emotional plea regarding the centrality of upholding contracts to the free working of a democracy, we cannot ignore the plaintiff's complaint.

(c) If you are adding *sic*, put it in brackets. Add *sic* when you want to inform the reader that the error in the text was in the original, rather than being an error you made when copying the quote.

> **"In this cause [sic], Ms. Hofner did not realize she was waiving this right."**

8.   How to mark omissions from a quote.

In general, use ellipses to mark any omissions you make in a quote. An ellipsis is a series of three periods with spaces between them (...). To be accurate, you must not only use ellipses to mark any omissions; you must also use accurate spacing and punctuation before and after the ellipses, as the following rules explain. These rules are intricate, but important and useful to the careful reader. If ellipses are used accurately, the reader can tell exactly what changes you made in the original without having to look up the source.

(a) If you are omitting a word or words within one sentence, put a space before and after the ellipsis.

> **"The issue of mutuality ... requires that the court examine both the contract's wording and the parol evidence surrounding the signing of the contract."**

changed from the original

> The issue of mutuality, not to mention that of duress, requires that the court examine both the contract's wording and the parol evidence surrounding the signing of the contract.

(b) If you are omitting the rest of an entire sentence, put a space before the ellipsis and a space and period after the ellipsis. This fourth period represents the period at the end of the original sentence.

> **"There can be no negligence without duty.... "**

changed from the original

> There can be no negligence without duty, and in this case there is no duty.

(c) If the sentence quoted ended with a question mark or exclamation mark, use that mark rather than a period after the ellipsis.

> **"The jury thought 'imply' meant 'assume' ... !"**

changed from the original

> The jury thought "imply" meant "assume" in this situation!

> **"Did the defendant take all reasonable precautions ... ?"**

328

changed from the original

> Did the defendant take all reasonable precautions before starting up the mower?

(d) Similarly, if you are omitting the rest of one sentence and then continuing the quote at the first of the next sentence, put a space before the ellipsis, and a space and period after the ellipsis. After the fourth period, add two spaces and then begin the next sentence, just as you would after the period at the end of any other sentence.

> **"The court cannot base its decision on sympathy**.... **There can be no negligence without duty**.... **"**

changed from the original

> The court cannot base its decision on sympathy, no matter how great that sympathy may be. There can be no negligence without duty, and in this case there is no duty.

Again, if the sentence you are editing ended with a question mark or exclamation point, repeat that mark instead of the fourth period.

(e) If you are quoting the end of a sentence, omitting one or more sentences, and then continuing the quote with a later sentence, do the following. First, put a period, question mark, or exclamation point immediately after the last word of the quoted sentence right before the ellipsis, just as you would have done if you were not omitting sentences. Second, put in one space and then the ellipsis. Third, space once and then begin the next quoted sentence.

> **In this case, the court must intervene**.... **The issue of mutuality, not to mention that of duress, requires that the court examine both the contract's wording and the parol evidence surrounding the signing of that contract.**

changed from the original

> In this case, the court must intervene. Despite the defendant's emotional plea regarding the centrality of upholding contracts to the free working of a democracy, it cannot ignore the plaintiff's complaint. The issue of mutuality, not to mention that of duress, requires that the court examine both the contract's wording and the parol evidence surrounding the signing of that contract.

(f) If you are quoting the end of a sentence, omitting one or more sentences, and then continuing the quote mid-sentence, follow the same procedure explained in subsection (e), but also put brackets around the first word after the ellipsis if you are changing that letter from lower case to upper case.

> **In this case, the court must intervene** .... **[M]utuality requires that the court examine both the contract's**

wording and the parol evidence surrounding the signing of that contract.

changed from the original

> In this case, the court must intervene. Despite the defendant's emotional plea regarding the centrality of upholding contracts to the free working of a democracy, it cannot ignore the plaintiff's complaint. The issue of mutuality requires that the court examine both the contract's wording and the parol evidence surrounding the signing of that contract.

(g) Never use an ellipsis at the beginning of a quote, even if you have omitted the first word or words of the quoted passage. The ellipsis is unneeded because the fact that the first word of the quote was not originally capitalized is sufficient to indicate that words have been omitted.

[T]here can be no negligence without duty.

rather than

> . . . there can be no negligence without duty.

changed from the original

> As the defense so aptly argued, there can be no negligence without duty.

9.   How to maintain credibility when editing a quote.

Avoid extensive editing of a quote, even though you now know how to do it accurately. If you use ellipses and brackets too much, the reader will find the quote awkward to read and will probably suspect that you are misrepresenting the original idea. The solution in this situation is not to omit ellipses and thus sacrifice ACCURACY; it is to PARAPHRASE or to find another quote that fits the situation without needing such extensive surgery.

The court stated that it must intervene in this case to resolve the issue of mutuality despite the emotional pleas for freedom of contract.

rather than the extensively edited version

> Despite the . . . emotional plea regarding . . . upholding contracts to the free working of a democracy, [the court] cannot ignore the plaintiff's complaint. . . . [T]he court must intervene; the issue of mutuality . . . requires that the court examine both the contract's wording and the parol evidence. . . .

changed from the original

> Despite the defendant's emotional plea regarding the centrality of upholding contracts to the free working of a democracy, we cannot ignore the plaintiff's complaint. In this case, the court must intervene; the issue of mutuality, not to mention that of duress, requires

330

that the court examine both the contract's wording and the parol evidence surrounding the signing of that contract.

QUOTATIONS, LONG

See EXTENDED QUOTES.

QUOTATIONS, WHEN TO USE

Use quotations if the particular phrasing is central to your issue, such as phrases including terms of art or key passages from the applicable statute. Otherwise use quotes only if the answer to each of the following questions is *yes*.

1. Does the quotation contain information directly pertinent to the point?

2. Is the quotation no longer than one long paragraph, unless content requires all of it?

3. Does the quotation communicate the information more clearly than you could, even in an accurate PARAPHRASE? Alternatively, does this quotation communicate the information more eloquently than you could in a paraphrase?

On rare occasions, you may have a senior partner who wants you to cut and paste extensive quotes into your documents. Although this will not create a readable or attractive document, remember your practical situation and do the best you can. See also QUOTATIONS, HOW TO PUNCTUATE and EXTENDED QUOTES.

QUOTE WITHIN A QUOTE

See QUOTATIONS, HOW TO PUNCTUATE, subsection 5.

RAMBLING

To avoid this problem, see ORGANIZATION, and PARAGRAPHS.

RE

You may use *re* in subject lines for letters or memos, but do not use it in the text of the letter or memo. Instead use *regarding*.

READABILITY

Many factors work together to enhance the readability of a document. Here is a checklist of some of the most useful ones.

1. Use shorter sentences.

Check to make sure that your sentences do not habitually run more than three-and-one-half lines. One easy way to do this is to put a slash after each period in the draft. You can do this without actually reading the text; just skim for the periods. Then, looking at where the slashes fall, check for places where there are several long sentences in a row. Divide at least some of these into shorter sentences.

> **You may decide that the testimony of one witness is entitled to greater weight than that of another witness, or even of several witnesses. In weighing the evidence, you may consider your own knowledge, observations, and life experiences.**

rather than

> In weighing the evidence, you may consider the testimony of one witness as entitled to greater weight than that of another witness or several others, your own knowledge, what you have observed, and the experiences you have had in life.

If a sentence contains a list at the end, it may not need to be divided. For ways to handle the list, see the next subsection.

2. Use clear and logical lists.

Careful structuring of lists greatly increases readability. First, always make sure that the elements of your list are both logically and grammatically parallel.

> **The defendant moved his car into the left lane to pass, lost control on the snow-packed pavement, slid back into the right lane, and collided with the plaintiff's truck.**

rather than

> The defendant moved his car into the left lane to pass, was losing control, slid back into the right lane, and caused injury to the plaintiff when he hit her truck.

Then structure your sentence so that the list comes at the end. Additionally, when the list is long or complex, use signals, such as parenthetical numbers or tabulation, to help the reader see immediately the structure of the list.

> **To justify the exclusion of expert psychiatric evidence, the court discussed (1) maintaining the integrity of the bifurcated trial procedure, (2) avoiding allowing the guilty to go free, and (3) preserving the defendant's right against self-incrimination.**

rather than

> The court discussed maintaining the integrity of the bifurcated trial procedure, avoiding allowing the guilty to go free, and preserving the defendant's right against self-incrimination to justify the exclusion of expert psychiatric evidence.

For more detail about ways to do this, see LISTS, STRUCTURE OF.

3. Use familiar words.

Use words that your reader will understand without having to resort to a dictionary.

> **Counsel, by using apt wording and artful presentation, minimized this weak point in her argument.**

rather than

> Counsel, by applying her verbal acumen and felicitous propensity for oratory, accomplished a feat of legerdemain regarding this conceptual proposition.

Unusual words, even if the reader does know what they mean, force the reader to stop and think. Busy legal readers usually will not stop mid-thought to ponder the nuances of an individual word, and so your meaning may be lost. For more information, see FLOWERY LANGUAGE and JARGON.

4. Use consistent wording.

Use the same term for the same concept throughout the document; do not change it just for VARIETY.

> **The defendant <u>proposes</u> that his repair of the water heater was adequate. This <u>proposal</u>, however,....**

rather than

> The defendant <u>proposes</u> that his repair of the water heater was adequate. This <u>suggestion</u>, however,....

Using consistent terms aids readability by helping the reader know immediately that you mean the same thing. For more on this point, see REPETITION.

5. Keep the subject and verb undivided and focused on your point.

Keep the subject within seven words of the verb and make sure the subject and verb state the main point of the sentence.

> **If this case were retried, the <u>result would be</u> different because of the combination of the numerous defects in the proceedings below and the newly discovered evidence.**

rather than

> The total <u>effect</u> of the numerous defects in the proceedings below, which in combination with the newly discovered evidence referred to above creates a miscarriage of justice, <u>would</u> if this case were to be retried under optimum circumstances <u>produce</u> a different result.

In the second example, the subject (*effect*) is divided from the verb (*would produce*) by twenty-four words, and the two words of the verb (*would* and *produce*) are divided by ten words. By the time readers finally find the verb, they will forget the subject and have to re-read the sentence several times to find it. For more ways to restructure sentences, see SENTENCE STRUCTURE.

Additionally, precision is lost when the subject and verb do not clearly state the writer's point. In the previous example, *effect would produce* does not state the reader's main point. Moving the subject and verb together would have exposed this problem to the writer, who could then revise it to *the result would be different*. For more on this see SUBJECT–VERB COMBINATIONS.

6. Use precise transitions.

Use transitions that convey exact connections. For example, use *nevertheless* only when *nevertheless* is the logical connection between the two thoughts.

> **The litigation may cost more than the amount our client could recover if she wins the suit. Nevertheless, she has chosen to pursue her claim.**

rather than

> The litigation may cost more than the amount our client could recover if she wins the suit, although she has chosen to pursue her claim.

In the second example, using the wrong transition confuses the reader. For more on this and for a list of transitions, see TRANSITIONS.

7. Use consistent word signals.

If you use *second*, make sure that you used *first* earlier. Similarly, if you used *not only*, use *but also* later. Without these parallel signals, the skilled reader is left frustrated, like the waiting listener who hears one shoe drop but never hears the second. For related information, see CONNECTIONS, MAKING THEM.

8. Accurate and adequate punctuation.

Punctuation marks are the road signs of legal writing, and inaccurate punctuation can lead to wrong turns. Revise once just for accurate punctuation. For more information on punctuation needed but often omitted, see COMMAS and SEMICOLONS. For ways to spot these problems, see REVISING.

READER

See AUDIENCE.

READING

Your writing is affected by your own critical reading of others writing. Also, because reading is a large part of what you do as a lawyer, you want to gain the most benefit from that reading. The following ideas may help you accomplish this.

1.   Establish your purpose before reading.

Consider your purpose and then read accordingly. You may be reading for background information because you are new to the subject, for procedural information regardless of the substantive issue, for support for an argument, or for a thorough treatment of every current case in the jurisdiction. If you are reading to collect information for a memo, you will read more thoroughly than if you are skimming cases to see if there are any decisions at all on the topic. If you have more than one purpose, prioritize them.

2.   Take notes according to your purpose.

Take notes on information related to this purpose and mover more quickly over the rest of the material. If you are collecting all current law on a narrow topic, you may need to put your notes on index cards or the software equivalent. If you are taking notes on cases for three legal issues, you may need to write on separate legal pads, one for each issue. Or you may be able to assimilate background information on a web you draw on one page.

3.   Decide what relationship the source has to your issue.

If you are reading for research, decide how the source answers your question or redefines it. If you are reading for class, decide why the case is in that section of the book. Note also where it falls in the syllabus and connect it accordingly to the cases around it. Connect your source to the issue substantively by seeing what theme or sub-theme it suggests.

4.   Be aware of the source's context.

Nothing is written in a vacuum. Make a note of the source's year, its legal or policy context, its reaction to previous authorities, or its innovative elements. This context can offer tools for interpreting the source's subsequent impact. If a statute is codifying case law, it validates prior cases and makes them still good law. If a case is reacting to legislation, it may be invalidating the legislation or reshaping it for policy purposes. If a treatise is summarizing law from several states, it may be restating it too generally for application in your particular jurisdiction. Read the source not only for its literal, legal statements, but also for their context so that you glean information accurately.

5.   Note the source's internal elements.

A statute will have varying sections; decide what they are, why they are there, and how they interrelate. A case may ramble or be divided into sharply defined sections; use a case brief template to analyze what each part says. An article may be structured to have a certain impact. Step back, note the structure, and analyze it. By noting not just the substantive nuggets, but also the structure itself, you read thoroughly and safely. For related information, see OPINIONS, READING THEM.

6. Relate those elements to similar elements in other sources.

As you read, note any patterns you see among sources, any themes emerging, any fallacies in argumentation being repeated, and any contract sections that occur in every example. Analyze why those elements exist by comparing and contrasting them. Doing so allows you to, in turn, explain these patterns to your reader, who wants to know how sources relate to each other.

7. Read for use of terms of art.

Note how the source uses the terms of art you have defined in your question. Are they the same or different? Does use of the term vary within the document or among various sources? Your reader will want consistent definitions, so you need to harmonize usage of terms of art.

8. Note the source's construction.

As you read for content, also notice the writing itself. You may want to determine whether it is coherent and readable, whether the reasoning is logically based, or whether the writer has manipulated the reasoning to arrive at particular results. Such a critical reading of the source's own integrity heightens both your ability to use the source accurately and your ability to integrate your document and write well for another reader.

READING OPINIONS

See OPINIONS READING THEM.

REALLY

Really means *in reality* or *indeed*. It is overused, so avoid it unless it accurately conveys your meaning. Because *really* is used frequently and loosely in informal speech, it is probably best to replace the word with *in reality* in formal legal writing.

REASONED

See FIND, HOLD, OR REASONED?

REASONING, PRESENTING IT

Reasoning is the analytical process that moves a reader from an original idea or premise to a conclusion. In the U.S. legal community, reasoning takes many forms. The common law system fosters a traditional form of analogical reasoning; statutory law often lends itself to deductive reasoning; legal process suggests a sequence of points; and legal realism replaces literal interpretations of the law with sociology and empiricism. All of these forms of reasoning are based in our culture's history, traditions, and sense of logic and fairness, and they are just a few of the choices you have in reasoning.

The U.S. legal reader is particularly interested in seeing each step of the reasoning process you choose. Therefore, whatever form you choose, explain your reasoning step by step. Although obvious steps may be covered concisely, they should not be omitted.

Design the form of your reasoning to match your theme, your research, and your desired conclusion. Then lay that reasoning out step by step. For example, if you choose traditional analogical reasoning, you must (1) establish a basis in legal rules, (2) apply those rules to your situation by demonstrating how your situation is similar to or different from legal precedent in some relevant aspect, and (3) prove your conclusion by showing why your situation falls closer to one type of precedent than to another. This requires you to (4) organize carefully and consciously. In creating this traditional reasoning, then, consider the following concepts. While they offer a rudimentary starting point, they cannot offer a formula for every situation because reasoning is a complex process, unique to each problem.

1. Establishing the legal rules.

Provide a thorough yet concise presentation of the general rules. For example, if the entire statute is necessary for analysis, include the entire statute at the beginning of the reasoning process, but if only a few sections of the statute are necessary, include those sections only. If several cases must be synthesized to present one general rule, include them all; if only one or two cases are sufficient, limit the section to those two. If there are any relevant exceptions to the rule, include those. Resist the temptation to include any authority just because you found it. Select carefully according to your document's purpose, your audiences' needs, and your issue's scope. See LEGAL ANALYSIS.

Explain the rules precisely. Make sure you focus on the particular phrases and terms of art that express the concepts you will be using later in your application. Each case will contain various important legal terms and concepts. You need to select the few key terms to present; avoid including more language than needed because it will diffuse the focus of your argument. Synthesize the terms that are relevant to your issue, rather than reporting on all the details discussed in the statutory or case law you are using. See TERMS OF ART.

When using a case as a source of your rule, explain the relevant reasoning used by courts in applying that rule. Stating the rule and a few relevant facts from the case is not always sufficient. The reader needs to know why the court saw those facts as relevant. For example, emphasize terms like "unequal bargaining power" and link them to relevant facts if the court emphasized them in a precedent case and if that reasoning is relevant to your client's situation. Beyond just stating the relevant terms, you need to identify the aspect of those terms that made them significant to the outcome of the case. Because you will be applying the law to your client's situation, the reader needs to understand the whole relevant meaning of that law.

Explain the legally significant components of the source being analyzed. For example, the components of a case include the facts, reasoning, policy, or other elements of the case that, if changed, would change the outcome. This may not include all the components that were significant in the original case, so edit as is appropriate. As you explain these components, show how they fit under the rules.

2. Applying the rules.

In traditional analogical reasoning, your decisions are driven by similarity between many aspects of your client's situation and your sources. When the law you are citing applies because the holdings are favorable, your reasoning will synthesize those holdings. When you find a case that has legally significant facts very similar to yours, your reasoning will present those facts, probably in more detail than when you are using only a rule or a holding. When, however, the reason you are using this case is because the policy is relevant, then you will emphasize the court's discussion of policy. Your choices of emphasis and order are then essential parts of the reasoning.

Application, however, involves more than a simple comparison of fact to fact or holding to holding. You must also convince the reader that the similarity you present is legally significant. To do this, explicitly explain how the component is relevant to the reasoning, purpose, or other relevant legal concept. This is easier to do when your rule has been set up properly, because you will have already presented this connection in your presentation of the rule, when you explained the way the rule was applied in the precedent case. In your application, you will now echo that earlier reasoning, reapplying it to your client's case. Thus, to be most effective, the explanation of the rule and the application of that rule must be carefully coordinated and unified. As you use similar wording and even sentence structures when you now apply rules you presented earlier, you can create this coordination, unifying the whole analysis around your theme.

As you explain the strengths of your argument, also address the potential weaknesses in your position. To make your reasoning complete, anticipate the barriers in your audiences' way. To be fully informed, your readers need to know all aspects of your situation. If they are not aware of the counterarguments, bad news, or other scholarly positions, they are less likely to believe your position is sound. Such omissions in turn affect your credibility. For help in how to lay this out, see COUNTERARGUMENTS, HOW TO HANDLE.

Explain how the relevant information is of use in your case. To make these decisions, you must look both to your research and to your situation. In comparing the two, you will see various possible ways in which you can reason to your conclusion. You can then select both your information and your order accordingly, that is, both what to include and where to put it.

3. Completing the reasoning.

Complete your reasoning by explicitly connecting to your client's situation those concepts that emerged as important. This part of your reasoning may seem obvious to you and, if you've done a good job, you may think it will be obvious to your reader. Nevertheless, you must say it specifically in most settings. To do this, you often refer to the key concept or the term of art that is the focus of your rule, such as *unequal bargaining power*, and tie this concept to one of your client's legally significant facts, such as *high school dropout* and *certified public accountant*. The cord that binds the facts to the key legal concept is another phrase that is narrower than this concept but broader than the facts themselves, such as *greater education and financial experience*. Often you will not find this phrase verbatim in either your facts or the law itself. The concept will instead be implied through the pattern of application and through the facts the courts choose to emphasize in precedent cases. You must craft this phrase yourself, and crafting it correctly is the heart of the legal reasoning process.

When you do complete your reasoning, your reader will be grateful to be led away from the trees and reminded of the forest. This completion justifies your journey by reminding both you and the reader why you engaged in this reasoning in the first place.

4. Organizing the presentation.

What you include in your presentation depends on what contributes to your reasoning. You may want to emphasize any one of the following, for example: policy, the procedural posture, the holdings, the facts, or the equities. What you select depends on your overall message, the strengths and weaknesses of your situation, and the match between your situation and your sources. When you make this selection, you will use it to guide you in your presentation of the rule and its application to the facts. Thus the message runs like a bright thread through the fabric of your analysis, guiding the reader along your line of reasoning. The selection of your content is not driven exclusively by a prescribed format, but is driven by your understanding of the law, the facts, and the logical thread that runs through all this information.

Organize in a way that matches your overall purpose. When organizing your reasoning, remember that where you include information also depends on the relationships among sources and your situation. Therefore, sometimes the decisions of *what* and *where* are interrelated. Allow for several good organizational possibilities; then you can select the best. For example, when you see elements that suggest an element-by-element approach, you may want to follow them as the statute presents them. Do not, however, make that decision automatically. If it turns out that the first two elements are unfavorable as compared to your situation, you may want to begin with element three, which is more favorable. You have holdings in five previous cases to go with element three, four of which are favorable and one of which is unfavorable. You can decide, then, to rearrange the elements to begin with element three and synthesize the four favorable holdings to set up a favorable comparison with your case. You are selecting a reasoning pattern based on putting most favorable dispositions first. You can also group together the two neutral elements and put them at the beginning to get past them. Or you may decide that your audience will be confused by any departure from the statute's order, so you distinguish the first two elements strongly under one heading.

For related information, see RULES, LEGALLY SIGNIFICANT FACTS, SYLLOGISMS, DISCUSSION SECTION; LEGAL ANALYSIS; and ARGUMENT SECTION. For more suggestions on how to build reasoning, see Pierre Schlag and David Skover, Tactics of Legal Reasoning (1986) and Jill J. Ramsfield, The Law as Architecture: Building Legal Documents (2000).

RECOMMENDATIONS

Recommendations are appropriate in a memo's conclusion when the memo's purpose is to analyze the law and to predict the outcome in the context of pretrial discovery. Often the reader, another person in the same office, has assigned the writer the job of analyzing the law so that the reader can make a decision about a particular pretrial activity. For example, a partner might assign an associate to write a memo on whether or not the partner should move for summary judgment in a case. The associate should make the recommendation as specific as possible, after explaining the reasons in the discussion section.

Similarly, an attorney might recommend certain action in an opinion letter. This recommendation may be located wherever it is most logical: in the opening paragraph or the closing one, or under a separate subheading. Wherever it appears, the recommendation should be within the realm of professional, not personal, advice. See MEMOS, OPINION LETTERS, and OPINION OR ADVICE?

RECORD, CITING TO IT

Cite to the record in the statement of the case in pretrial, trial, or appellate briefs. As you cite, be scrupulous about using pinpoint references so the reader can quickly locate exact passages. For the reader's convenience, also refer to the record in the argument section if the reader might need to verify sources as an integral part of the argument.

Check your jurisdiction for the appropriate format for these citations to the record. Some prefer parentheses, *(Tr 38)*, some use none, *CP 19*, and others use periods, *R. 76*. For related information, see CITATIONS and CITATIONS, PINPOINT.

RECUR OR *REOCCUR?*

The difference in meaning between these two words is slight, but in some contexts it is important. *Recur* implies that the event happens repeatedly; *reoccur* implies that the event is repeated only once.

REDUNDANCY

See CONCISENESS. For related information, see REPETITION.

REFERENCES

See CITATIONS; FOOTNOTES; and RECORD, CITING TO IT.

REFERENTS

See ANTECEDENTS.

REGARDLESS OR *IRREGARDLESS?*

Regardless, always.

REJECTION LETTERS

See BAD NEWS, SOFTENING IT and BAD NEWS, GIVING IT, subsection 1.

REOCCUR OR *RECUR?*

See *RECUR* OR *REOCCUR?*

REPETITION

Repetition by careful design works in legal writing. Rather than avoiding repetition absolutely, avoid it only when it does not have one of the following uses.

1. Use repetition when it is needed for accuracy.

If you mean *contract*, do not shift to *document* or *agreement*. Changing terms confuses legal readers, who will think that you must mean something else if you changed terms. For more help, see ACCURA-CY, subsection 1.

2. Use repetition when it is needed for readability.

For example, repeating the same first word at the beginning of each item in a list can be very helpful to the reader when each item in the list is long.

> **Any proposed method for reducing marital status discrimi-nation <u>must</u> reflect the statutory complexity creating dis-crimination, <u>must</u> avoid reproducing the undesirable effects of the current taxation structure, and <u>must</u> show awareness that compromising one or more important policy goals is necessary in any tax scenario.**

For more on this technique and others, see LISTS, STRUCTURE OF, subsection 6 and READABILITY, subsections 4 and 7.

3. Use repetition as a transition to connect, or dovetail, two sentences or paragraphs.

> **Environmental Impact Studies could be handled similarly without <u>delaying</u> the hearing. Even if there were some <u>delay</u>,** . . . .

Repeating a key word from a previous sentence or paragraph shows how the idea that word represents fits in with the idea of the new sentence of paragraph.

4. Use repetition to create emphasis.

Sometimes the very fact that a repeated word gains attention can be an advantage. For example, you may repeat a word or structure that states a dramatic or important point.

> **The defendant <u>stated</u> this intention to his girlfriend. He <u>stated</u> it to his coworkers. He <u>stated</u> it to the cabdriver who took him to the airport.**

For a broader context, see EMPHASIS.

5. Use repetition when it is required by format or convention.

It is appropriate to repeat content from the main text in some circumstances. For example, when you write conclusions and introductions, which summarize the body of a text, you must by definition repeat key terms and major themes. Similarly, you will necessarily need to repeat some information when you write captions for appendices, graphs, or tables.

REPETITION OF SOUNDS

See ALLITERATION and ASSONANCE.

REQUESTS FOR PAYMENT

There are four do's here.

1. Do consciously decide what you want.

If you want money, focus on that and set aside your moral outrage at the way your client has been treated. In contrast, if you really want to express your moral outrage, do so in temperate language. Realize, however, that this expression may not do much to help you get money for your client.

2. Do consider your reader's motivations.

It is always useful to remember the possible motivations your reader may have and try to employ those motivations to get what you want. Choose not what persuades you, but what will persuade your reader. For example, if you are trying to persuade a party to settle out of court, do not use threats when you think the party would view that threat as a challenge and submission as a weakness. In that situation, you might instead explain that the cost of litigation would exceed the cost of settlement. Similarly, if you think that the reader is someone motivated by certain values, try to explain how the action you recommend is consistent with those values. For example, you might argue that paying a bill is essentially the same as keeping a promise. In short, try to explain how the action you recommend is consistent with some goal the reader has. Try to help the reader feel good, or at least not defeated, about taking the action you recommend.

3. Do consider tone.

Consciously decide what tone you want to create. For example, do you want to be nice, giving the reader the benefit of the doubt, or do you want to be tough? If you want to be nice, you may use kind opening and closing paragraphs. For more on this, see BAD NEWS, SOFTENING IT. If you want to be tough, you may use shorter sentences and impersonal language. For more on this, see TOUGH, SOUNDING THAT WAY. For related information, see TONE IN LETTERS AND EMAIL.

4. Do retain accuracy.

Make sure what you say is literally correct. Satiric comments or broad hints can be misread easily and can lead to further delays in getting the results you want. Do not resort to diatribe, even if your anger is completely justifiable. Lay out in objective language the facts, the options, and the results. Similarly, do not make empty threats; if your reader knows or finds out that one threat is empty, he or she may assume that later ones are empty too. See EMOTIONAL LANGUAGE.

RESEARCH AS WRITING

Legal research is more than just a gathering of materials. It is part of the analytical process itself. As you gather, read, sort, and assess your content, you also begin to design your document. If you write out your thoughts, you reap multiple benefits from your research, in effect writing at the same time.

1. Research to refine issues.

Whether or not you have a precise idea of your issue when you begin your research, each source you find may help define or redefine the issue. Ask, "How does this source answer, amend, or advance the issue?" and take notes accordingly. Note how the source addresses your issue, namely, how it uses particular verb phrases to respond to the issue, uses specific language that refines or amends your issue, or uses reasoning that expands or advances the issue to a different level. Decide how the material supports, undercuts, or distracts from your analysis. Although you focus on your issue and your client's desired outcome as you gather the materials, you must also account for analytical problems and obstacles. You want to do this as you research, minimizing your research of unessential sources you will subsequently discard.

Use your research time to cull and sort. Research actively, not passively. Gather your sources intentionally. Rather than researching like the hungry impulse shopper, research like the chef who knows what courses must be served and whose guests arrive within a few hours. Make a list, as suggested in THE RESEARCH STRATEGY CHART, and research accordingly.

2.   Research to analyze.

Each source is connected in some way to another. As you read, you are deciding (a) what those connections are and (b) whether or not those connections are pertinent to your analysis. As you take notes, sort the information into categories and decide how the sources connect in relation to your issues. You may not be able to sort and identify all the connections as you read the first time, but you will start to see patterns develop. Your sorting decisions will not be final, but they reveal possible ways of explaining what you are reading.

Review your document's purposes and your audience's needs to make final decisions on sources. If you are informing, you need to include all relevant law. If you are delivering bad news, you need enough accurate information to explain the results. If you are completing a contract, you need enough research to make sure the desired contract provision stands. If you are unsure about where a source may fit into your analysis, you may want to include it until you make your final design decisions.

3.   Research to design.

As you see the analytical connections among your sources, your facts, and your document's purposes or your audiences, your design possibilities also emerge. Those possibilities come from the variety of ways in which you can connect the analytical components. Those connections come from the component's relationship to your theme.

When you read a source, you often know whether or not it will be significant in answering your question and delivering your message. You may want to number yours sources accordingly, from 1–10. If you know it is essential and will appear often, it gets a "1." If it is related, will probably be important, perhaps it gets a "3." If not related at all, it gets a "10," and so on. You may add a sentence or two at the top of the source that shows its relationship to the issue and to any other sources. You may change your mind as you complete the cycle of reading, so allow for that. This system, or one like it, allows you to go back and do so.

If you are a visual learner and you see patterns emerging, you may want to draw a web that connects the ideas or Venn diagrams or boxes within boxes. If you are a linear learner, you may see an outline emerging. If you are an audio learner, you may want to dictate the overall contours of the analysis.

Make sure you allow for several possible designs. As Steven Spielberg says, "Always allow for the second idea, which may be better." Or the third or fourth. Often your first design is writer-based, a report on your research. This design explains what you have found—to yourself. If you need to do such a plan, do not consider it a draft of the final project. Instead, consider it as preliminary notes that you can later reshape to suit your purposes and audiences. Your best design, analysis, and writing springs from original research, carefully followed as your mind wraps itself around the problem. With attention on your issue, your sources' connections to one another, and your design possibilities, you will gain the most from your time researching. See also RESEARCH STRATEGY CHART.

RESEARCH PROCESS CHECKLIST

The following checklist is meant to provide you with a starting point for evaluating and improving your own researching process. It is not meant to be a rigid list of requirements.

1. Have I researched effectively?

    (a) Have I developed a flexible strategy?

    (b) Have I avoided becoming overly rigid, instead adapting my research strategy when the sources dictate a change?

    (c) Have I allotted time for each step and each source?

    (d) Have I avoided tangential research?

2. Have I taken effective notes?

    (a) Have I recorded the date of the source and of my notes?

    (b) Have I written down the full citation, in whatever form required in the final version of this document?

    (c) Have I related my source's information to my issues?

    (d) Have I kept track of all the sources I checked, even if they were unfruitful, so I will not repeat any research?

    (e) Have I updated my sources?

    (f) Have I reflected on my sources to synthesis an overall understanding of the relevant law?

3. Have I organized effectively for the readers?

    (a) Have I begun translating my research into an outline?

    (b) Have I connected my research with my outline in my notes, with cross-references or other indicators?

    (c) Have I tried other organizational approaches, so I know I chose the best approach?

(d) Have I checked with my AUDIENCE about the overall organization, where appropriate?

(e) Have I organized my materials for ready access?

RESEARCH STRATEGY CHART

The following ten-step Research Strategy Chart is designed to help you maximize your research efficiency and effectiveness. You will need to adapt your strategy to each research project, however, because research is a product of multiple factors: your experience on the topic, available sources, time, the client's budget, the supervising attorney's suggestions, and so on. Your efficiency depends on your ability to take these factors into account. Your credibility depends on your ability to find exactly what is needed. To achieve this credibility, develop a research ethic of seeking the mandatory authority quickly. As part of this ethic, use your projects to familiarize yourself with all possible legal research sources, not just the comfortable ones.

Any research strategy begins at your desk, so take the first five steps before you begin to research. That way, you can decide what sources you should go to first, second, third, and so on. This saves the time spent wandering from one source to another. Fight the temptation to go online or run to the library without having completed this portion of the strategy. Write down your strategy. The writing will assist you in remembering the search and omitting repetitive start-up time if you get interrupted. The preliminary issue statement is particularly important because it helps you focus your research from the very beginning.

For further elaboration on each step, see the specific pages cited to in Christopher Wren & Jill R. Wren, The Legal Research Manual: A Game Plan for Legal Research and Analysis (2d ed. 1992). These cites are noted by *LRM*, followed by the specific page number.

Before you look at sources

1. Collect the facts.

Just as a journalist does, make sure you know the *who*, *what*, *when*, *where*, *why*, and *how* of the facts. You can collect the facts by reading the complete file or transcript, taking notes during a client interview, doing your own discovery, and talking directly to the client. *LRM* 30.

2. Analyze the facts and create search terms.

Using whatever system you prefer or have, group the facts into their general categories. If you do not know enough about the area of law to identify all these categories, consult a secondary authority to provide the needed background and terms. The West Group originally used the categories of *Parties, Objects, Basis, Defense,* and *Remedy.* Lawyers' Co-op used *Things, Acts, Persons,* and *Places.* You can invent your own, depending on the kind of law you practice. Give each category a page or column. Transfer your facts from Step 1 to these columns. Then brainstorm synonyms and antonyms for the facts in each column. These terms become your search words.

3.   Formulate a preliminary issue statement.

This can be done before you know the law by following a format that goes from general to specific, using the key words *under, did,* and *when,* as follows:

General Law [as specific a category as you can without doing any research]

Under Missouri assault law,

Legal Question

did Fred assault Harvey

Legally Significant Facts

when he waved an unloaded gun in Harvey's face?

The first part of the question tells you what sources to use, such as the Missouri Statutes Annotated index or the Missouri state database. The second part tells you what topic to finds or what search terms to use, such as *assault.* The third part tells you how to filter through the summaries of the sources you read if you are looking for factual comparisons. For example, you would look for sources involving a loaded gun or an unloaded gun waved in the vicinity of someone or in someone's face. You can eliminate those cases whose summaries do not indicate a similarity to these legally significant facts or to related principles.

To organize the research, put the issues in a preliminary order of importance. For example, put threshold issues such as *standing* first because if your research reveals a lack of standing, you may not need to research any other substantive issues. See *LRM* 37.

4.   Verify jurisdiction.

Make sure you know whose law applies. You can look at court papers in a case to make sure you know what court or even what judge is hearing the case. If there is a potential conflict of laws question or a question about whether federal or state law applies, make resolving the jurisdiction question the first issue when you begin your research.

5.   Make a three-part research plan.

Map out where you will go first, second, and third. You may want to go to several more places, but make sure that you go to at least three sources. Rather like the Mercedes symbol, legal research requires a look along three lines before the circle is complete. For example, if you begin on Lexis, check Westlaw and a regional digest. If you begin with A.L.R., check a looseleaf source and the statutes annotated, and so on. It is crucial to think this through before you start researching to avoid wasting time wandering from shelf to shelf or from database to database at the computer. For example, after you look through the Missouri statutes, you might plan to go to the Missouri Digest, then to the Missouri Patterned Jury Instructions, and then to an updating source.

As you research

6. Find the law.

The purpose of this step is to make sure you find all relevant primary sources, provisions, statutes, regulations, and cases. If you were given a statute or case name, for example, you might start with A. If you were not given a known authority, you might start with B. And if you are completely unfamiliar with the area of law, you might start with C.

(a) Known authority.

- Statute or regulation. See *LRM* 51.
  - Go to the statutes or regulations annotated for that jurisdiction.
  - Update.
  - Check looseleafs if researching administrative regulations.
  - Check a secondary source for related authority.
  - Update again, using a different updating service.
- Case. See *LRM* 53.
  - Find the case and review the headnotes.
  - Choose the headnotes that are pertinent and note the topic title and key or section number.
  - In Westlaw, put the key number in to retrieve the sources that cite that topic.
  - Update.

(b) Descriptive word or fact word.

- Statute or regulation. See *LRM* 46.
  - Take the list developed in Step 2 and look up those words in the index to statutes or regulations to see if there is a statute or regulation on that subject.
  - If so, follow steps listed under *statute or regulation* above.
- Case. Have I allotted time for each step, each source? See *LRM* 49.
  - Find the appropriate digest for that jurisdiction.
  - Take the list developed in Step 2 and look up those words in the index to the digest.
  - Move from the index to those topics in the digest.
  - Check pocket parts.

348

- Use the words from your list to write a query and search the computer database.

(c) Encyclopedias, treatises, and other sources useful for your own background. *LRM* 65.

- Check the *A.L.R.* Quick Index. Use descriptive words; you may find a gold mine here if there is an annotation on your topic.

- Check the *Index to Legal Periodicals* and the *Current Resources Index* for law review articles. Also check *C.J.S., Am. Jur.*, and the *Restatements*.

- Check your library book catalogue for treatises on relevant topics.

7. Read the law (before you print it).

(a) Evaluate internally. *LRM* 79.

- Statute.

  - Evaluate the language of the statute itself.

  - Is there a general factual similarity to this case?

  - Is there ambiguity in the legislative intent that favors this case?

  - Does the statute's context give it a focus applicable to this case?

  - Does the statute's legislative history illuminate its meaning?

  - How do the canons of construction augment the statute's meaning? *LRM* 87–88.

- Case.

  - Is there a factual similarity to this case?

  - Is the RULE pertinent and useful?

  - Is there a general similarity that is useful if the facts are recharacterized?

  - Does the POLICY provide a useful basis for argument?

(b) Evaluate externally. (See 8 below.) *LRM* 89.

- Current status.

  - Has the statute been invalidated, repealed, or amended?

  - Are these subsequent interpretations of cases useful to this case?

- Extend the law.

  - Can a new rule or innovative twist be formulated?

- Is the statute a codification or a departure from previous rules?
- Has a novel policy or doctrine emerged?

8. Update the law.

(a) Use WESTLAW'S KeyCite or Shepard's on LEXIS. See UPDATING THE LAW.

(b) Check the pocket parts and supplements.

(c) Check the looseleaf reporter services.

(d) Check other possible sources, such as newspapers, for recent opinions or references to the source.

9. Take effective notes.

(a) Have a system and write out the plan. See NOTES. *LRM* 123.

(b) Reread your preliminary issues periodically to maintain your focus.

(c) Record full CITATIONS in proper form.

10. Ask or call.

Sometimes information is not easily available in print or your library does not have it. You may then find it more useful and efficient to ask esoteric questions of your librarian, the supervising attorney, another associate who has worked on similar cases, or an expert in the field. You may also find it more efficient to call sources, such as agencies that have set up a number for asking questions.

RESPONDENT

Respondent can be used as either a proper noun or a generic description, like *Appellant, Defendant,* and *Plaintiff.* When used as a proper noun, it should be capitalized and used without an article.

Respondent objects to Appellant's characterizing the case as a simple one.

When used generically, it should not be capitalized, and the article should be used.

The respondent filed the brief well within the time limits.

Lawyers use *respondent* both ways, so check the conventions of your office or particularly of your audience. If your readers have no preference, choose whatever you prefer, but be consistent throughout the document. Avoid choosing the proper noun solely for conciseness; omitting *the* will shorten your document slightly but may create a telegraphic or harsh tone.

RESTRICTIVE PHRASES

See THAT OR WHICH?

350

REVISING

Revising, as defined here, occurs after REWRITING in the WRITING PROCESS. During rewriting, you settled the document's content and organization; during revising, you are free to concentrate on the expression of that content. Revising includes refining small-scale organization, SENTENCE STRUCTURE, TRANSITIONS, PARAGRAPHS, GRAMMAR, and PUNCTUATION.

There are three things to remember about revising.

1. Do not revise while you write.

Trying to combine both tasks slows down both the writing and the revising processes. When you are writing, concentrate solely on expressing your ideas, no matter how unpolished your writing may seem. Revise later.

2. Do not revise while you rewrite.

Rewriting involves adding, deleting, and moving content. Revising before you rewrite often means you spent time refining a passage you later end up deleting. Work out your organization and get everything in place before you start revision.

3. Revise in stages.

It is exhausting and inefficient to try to revise on every level at once. For help with this, see REVISING PROCESS CHECKLIST.

REVISING CHECKLIST

The following list may seem long, but each step can move quickly. And, when you have completed the process, you can have confidence that your document has moved several notches higher in quality.

1. Have I ensured accuracy?

   (a) Is the content accurately stated? Could any points be misinterpreted because of ambiguity? See AMBIGUITY, WAYS TO AVOID.

   (b) Are TERMS OF ART and key terms used correctly?

   (c) Is each PARAPHRASE used accurately?

   (d) Is the name and status of each party correct?

2. Does the structure match the content?

   (a) Can the audience see how the content of sentences is connected? Do clear and precise transitions connect paragraphs and sentences? See CONNECTIONS, MAKING THEM.

   (b) Do HEADINGS, when read apart from the text, present the message and structure of the document?

   (c) Do topic sentences give the overall message of each paragraph, usually appearing at the beginning of the paragraph? See TOPIC SENTENCES and SUBJECT–VERB COMBINATIONS.

(d) Do topic sentences, when read consecutively and without the intervening text, reveal the progression of the document's logic to the readers?

(e) Are paragraphs coherent? See PARAGRAPHS and PARA-GRAPH BLOCKS.

3. Is the document easy for any prospective audience to read?

(a) Are subjects and verbs close together?

(b) Is there more active voice than passive voice?

(c) Is the text free of excessive quotations, string citations, and JARGON?

(d) Are sentences free of unnecessary nominalizations?

(e) Are unnecessary modifiers eliminated, such as *clearly* and *obviously?*

(f) Is sentence length appropriate throughout? Is it varied for interest?

(g) Are lists clearly structured? See LISTS, STRUCTURE OF.

(h) Are sentences free of unnecessary prepositions and prepositional phrases?

(i) Is the text generally concise? See CONCISENESS.

4. Is the point of view unified throughout the document?

(a) Is that wording echoed throughout the document in key places, such as headings and topic sentences? Are the headings parallel in meaning and structure? See SUBJECT–VERB COMBINATIONS, PARALLEL STRUCTURE, and POSITIONS OF EMPHASIS.

(b) Is the tone and level of formality appropriate and consistent?

(c) Is VOICE unified throughout the document?

5. Are all criticisms from reviewers systematically incorporated throughout the paper, changing PARAGRAPH STRUCTURE, SEN-TENCE STRUCTURE, WORD CHOICE, TONE, and overall STYLE appropriately?

6. Have I mercilessly critiqued my own writing?

REVISING THE WRITING OF OTHERS

See EDITING and MANAGING WRITERS.

REWRITING

It is useful to distinguish rewriting from revising, because each task deserves its own attention and requires a different focus. Rewriting, as defined here, follows the writing stage in the writing process. When rewriting, you focus on matters of content, large-scale organization, logic, and coherence. This is the stage where criticism takes over from creativity and the text starts moving from a writer-oriented first draft toward a reader-oriented final draft. Unlike revision, at this stage you are still concerned primarily with the document's legal aspects and ideas rather than their final expression. Revision focuses on making sure that the document is correct, complete, and coherent.

Rewriting should be separated from the other stages in the writing process so you can concentrate on criticizing the content, not its expression. The most common mistake many writers make, one that costs hours, is to write, rewrite, and revise simultaneously. Some writers even try to polish while writing the first draft. This approach forces the id of creative thought to clash with the super-ego of correction, an impossible and insufferable pairing. The result is often writer's block. No wonder.

Give rewriting its own time. Do any major shifting of large sections, focusing on priorities appropriate for the document. (See PRINCIPLES OF LEGAL WRITING.) Check the document to make sure it

- fulfills its purpose,
- answers the audience's questions,
- includes all relevant law and facts,
- states all the steps necessary in the legal analysis,
- encompasses the appropriate scope, and
- uses logical organization.

These checks should help you make sure your document is correct, complete, and coherent. For specific questions to ask yourself, see REWRITING PROCESS CHECKLIST. See also ORGANIZATION, LARGE–SCALE.

The following techniques can help you ask the right questions. Check the headings, subheadings, and positions of emphasis to make sure that each indicates how that part factors into the whole. Move paragraphs or sections as needed until the order is logical and the headings reflect that order. Read the first sentences of each paragraph aloud, omitting the supporting information in the rest of each paragraph, to make sure that the presentation flows smoothly from step to step. Make sure each opening sentence is specific enough to make the paragraph's subject clear. Also make sure the sentences are worded so that the reader can see how each paragraph's ideas either connect to the previous paragraph or clearly indicate any departure from a previous topic. Often the topic sentences will echo terms of art used in headings or in the previous topic sentence, and this communicates your message throughout the document. This check allows you to not only refine your large-scale organization but also to insure that someone speed-reading your document will not miss your message. Read aloud any sections that are not working. Listen for shifts in wording, organization, or ideas that would be jarring to reader. You may hear problems that you cannot see.

In summary, concentrate on the large-scale organization and on content. Avoid revising at this stage. Instead, when you are satisfied that everything needed is present and in an overall logical order, then move to revising.

REWRITING CHECKLIST

1. Have I made final decisions about the theme or message?

2. Does the organization match this message?

   (a) Is this ORGANIZATION still working? Does it match the PURPOSE and the AUDIENCE's needs?

   (b) Is the structure congruent with the substantive law as it applies to my client's facts?

3. Is the order of the points coherent?

   (a) Can any legal reader follow the order?

   (b) Is there a reason for creating this order? Will the reader understand that reason? Is that reason related to the document's PURPOSE?

   (c) If used, are threshold issues first?

   (d) If writing persuasively, have I organized the issues in the most persuasive order?

   (e) Have I used POSITIONS OF EMPHASIS well to guide the reader?

4. Have I filled in all holes?

   (a) Have I included all needed facts? For details see BACKGROUND FACTS, EMOTIONALLY SIGNIFICANT FACTS, and LEGALLY SIGNIFICANT FACTS.

   (b) Have I included all relevant legal issues?

   (c) Is the law correct and complete? Have I included all relevant constitutional provisions, statutes, cases, regulations?

   (d) Have I included strengths and weaknesses of all arguments?

   (e) Have I explained why some legal points are stronger than others?

   (f) Have I included all steps in the reasoning?

   (g) Have I connected the points in my analysis throughout the document so that the audience understands the reasons I reached my conclusions?

   (h) Have I included the prediction, remedy, result, practical steps, where appropriate?

5. Have I omitted tangents?

6. Have I kept my VOICE consistent throughout the text?

RHETORICAL QUESTIONS

Avoid them in legal writing. Rhetorical questions, which have either an obvious answer or no answer, usually irritate legal readers and invite them to question your point. Ask questions only in your ISSUE STATEMENTS or QUESTION PRESENTED; give the answers to those questions in your ARGUMENT SECTION or DISCUSSION SECTION. To make a rhetorical point, state it in declarative sentence form.

RHYMES

Avoid them in legal writing unless you intend to be humorous and the humor is appropriate to the content and AUDIENCE. For related information, see ALLITERATION.

ROUGH DRAFTS

See WRITING and WRITING PROCESS.

RULES

Legal rules are statements of law that provide the basis for legal analysis. They are often general principles that can be applied to several situations, such as constitutional provisions or statutes. Sometimes they are derived from cases, where a judge has used a common law principle as the basis for the analysis. When a rule derives from cases, the writer must often determine that rule by looking at the court's foundation for its reasoning. When a rule is not explicitly stated, the writer must formulate a statement, often synthesizing holdings from multiple cases to establish the general rule.

In the broader sense, *rule* refers to the law that you will be applying in a given situation, rather than to a particular statement. For related information, see SYLLOGISM, SYNTHESIS, and HOLDINGS.

Rules fall into a hierarchy of authority. Thus, if a constitutional provision is involved in your issues, it is usually discussed first because the constitution supercedes all other law. If a statute is involved, it often comes next, or first if no constitutional provision is involved. Case law usually comes last because it provides the rules when there is no statute covering the issue, or it provides the definitions of terms in the constitution or statute.

Consider the following in presenting the rules.

1. Present rule structure early.

When legal rules provide the structure for your analysis or argument, present the rules early. This overview of the rules foreshadows the structure of your analysis.

> **All citizens are protected from unreasonable searches not only in their homes, but wherever they have a right to be. Wash. Const. art. I, § 7.**

> **The Plaintiff's recovery is barred when the plaintiff's negligence exceeds the defendant's negligence. Or. Rev. Stat. § 18.470 (2007).**

> **Jury misconduct occurs when a juror supplies information to other jurors that is outside the recorded evidence of the trial and not subject to the protections and limitations of court proceedings. Salverson v. Anderson, 99 Wash. 2d 746, 752, 913 P.3d 827, 830 (2007).**

Legal readers need to know the sources from which you have drawn the rules, so cite thoroughly and accurately. It is not usually sufficient to cite extensively from one source and put only one citation at the end of a paragraph, because that leaves the reader guessing about how much of the information is attributable to the cited source. Instead, cite after each relevant statement that provides new information. Often, this means you will include a citation after every sentence when presenting a rule unless a statement directly follows another in the source itself.

2. Decide whether case law presents a rule.

You may find a rule from case law in any of three ways.

(a) A case may explicitly state the definitive rule; if so, you may cite the case singly as the source of that rule.

(b) Several cases may be synthesized to form the rule; if so, you must cite those cases separately, each standing for a proposition that contributes to the rule.

(c) Several cases may provide a rule plus exceptions; if so, you should cite the case giving the rule first, with the cases giving exceptions after.

3. As you construct your rule from cases, synthesize when needed.

Synthesizing a rule means pulling pieces from several cases together to explain the rule for the particular issue. Courts do not always state these general rules because they decide specific factual situations and thus do not need to pull the larger rule together. You must therefore synthesize it yourself. To do this, step back from the pieces and try to see the larger picture. (For help with this, see REASONING.) Then characterize that picture in your own words as a topic sentence. (See TOPIC SENTENCES.) Follow this sentence with the sections of the cases that create this picture, and give appropriate citations. Then explain enough about each case to show the reader how that piece fits into your big picture of the rule.

4. When constructing a rule from cases, include exceptions.

Remember that any rule may have exceptions so, after making sure that the rule and its source are clear to the reader, follow with the exceptions. If you know that the opposing side will raise a question, you know you must deal with it. For ways to address these points in persuasive writing, see COUNTERARGUMENTS, HOW TO HANDLE.

5. Check for accuracy and logical links.

Your presentation of the law outlines the structure of your entire analysis, argument, or explanation, so make sure the rules are accurately presented. Check for logical links between subparts, so that the reader knows exactly how the rule works when applied. Then you are ready to follow this logic in applying the rules to the facts of your analysis.

SAID

Substitute *this, that,* or a more detailed description.

This document was signed by the plaintiff.

rather than

Said document was signed by the plaintiff.

Arcane legal language includes *said* as an adjective; do not use it that way. Similarly, *said* was once used in legal documents to say, *I mean the one mentioned above, in contrast to any mentioned below or elsewhere.* But often no other one was mentioned, so *said* was nonsensical. When you need to distinguish one item from another, simply repeat the designation used earlier.

the 2004 contract

rather than

the said contract

For related information, see SUCH.

SALUTATIONS

The salutation is the line beginning with *Dear* that traditionally introduces the text of a letter. Salutations are often included in email, too. There are three common questions about salutations: (1) whether to include them, (2) how to write them when you do not know the sex of the reader, and (3) whether to punctuate them with commas or semicolons.

1. Including or omitting the salutation.

In general, include the salutation in letters. Include the salutation in email to create a more courteous, formal, or businesslike effect. Some writers omit the salutation in business letters, substituting instead a subject line, and this is not technically wrong. Omitting the salutation, however, makes the letter or email seem rather abrupt and impersonal, which is not the tone you usually want in either. For more on this generally, see TONE IN LETTERS AND EMAIL.

2. Writing non-sexist openings.

If you do not know the sex of the person to whom you are writing, substitute the name without a title of *Mr.* or *Ms.*

Dear D. A. Young:

Dear Terry Holmes:

If you do not know the name, use the person's title or some appropriate generic term if you are writing a letter.

Dear Administrator:

Dear Client:

If you cannot come up with a generic term, you may use the following in a letter, but you risk sounding too formal in an email.

Dear Sir or Madam:

Use *Dear Sir* only when you are sure the reader is male.

3. Choosing commas or colons.

Use colons in writing formal or business letters or email. If you are writing something that is a social courtesy, such as a thank you note or an expression of congratulations, use a comma. A colon would also be appropriate, except in a note that is much more personal than business-like in tone.

SARCASM

Do not use sarcasm in legal writing; it is too easy for the reader to take it literally. Even if the reader catches your sarcastic tone, that tone is usually inappropriate in legal writing. In general, sarcasm is only effective when writing to readers who already whole-heartedly agree with your position. Dry humor may occasionally be used, because the content will still be literally correct. Many of your readers, however, will miss the humor altogether, so you risk losing them or having them misinterpret your meaning.

SAYING NO

Saying *no* to requests to do additional work may be hard for you, as it is for many lawyers. But maintaining a good quality to your writing will require you to learn how to do it. Taking on all requests eventually forces you to do mediocre work, which will damage your credibility and reputation. In contrast, saying *no* when appropriate keeps the quality of your work high and may win you respect. To help you know when you cannot take on more tasks, stay aware of your deadlines and workload.

Depending on the professional posture you choose to project, you can refuse gently *(I would love to, but I don't think I can do a good job ...)*, firmly *(I cannot do that for you. I'm sorry.)*, with limits *(Yes, I can do that for you but not until six weeks from now.)*, or you can flatter *(Of all the people I enjoy working with, you are the one I enjoy most. But I cannot do it for you this time. Please ask again.)*.

If you know that your refusal will cause you problems or create tension, try asking to be used as a back-up *(This is very inconvenient for me right now. Can you find someone else? If not, then get back to me.)* or give along-term *no (I will do this last project for you, but I cannot be called upon with such short notice in the future.)* Find ways that work best with your personality and that of your associates. For related information, see TIME MANAGEMENT and PROFESSIONAL POSTURE.

SCARCELY

Scarcely is an adverb that means *barely* or *assuredly not*. It has a negative meaning, but is not as obvious as *no* or *not*. This makes it easily misread, and thus it is best to avoid this term. Because *scarcely* has a negative meaning, it should not follow another negative.

The defendant could scarcely deny the charges.

rather than

The defendant couldn't scarcely deny the charges.

Place *scarcely* just before the word or group of words that it modifies.

The defendant heard the pronouncement of sentence with scarcely a change in demeanor.

rather than

The defendant heard the pronouncement of sentence scarcely with a change in demeanor.

SCHOLARLY WRITING

Writing a scholarly paper usually requires you to use a different writing process. This happens because scholarly writing differs from other kinds of legal writing in

    (1) audience,

    (2) purpose,

    (3) scope,

    (4) technical details, and

    (5) footnotes.

The following subsections help you adapt to these differences. For a checklist of qualities needed in scholarly writing, see SCHOLARLY WRITING CHECKLIST. For ways to adapt your personal writing process, see SCHOLARLY WRITING PROCESS. For related information, see PROCESS AND PRODUCT COMPARED.

1. Audience.

Readers of scholarly writing expect a thorough treatment of the topic. Beyond that, your readers differ, including any of the following:

- experts in the field who expect accuracy and exhaustive research,

- practitioners who want practical answers to specific questions,

- judges who want to be brought up to date on this topic,

- nonlawyers who want to understand this topic,

- prospective future employers looking for excellent analysis and good writing,

- faculty committees evaluating your for tenure, who also require innovative thought, and

- future scholars looking for examples of creative analysis and thorough research.

Keep these diverse readers in mind as you identify your purpose and synthesize the substance of the paper. To do this, you might try to imagine all your potential readers gathered in one room; then create the tone, organization, style, and thesis that will satisfy both the most confused and critical readers' needs. For related information, see AUDIENCE.

Alternatively, you may choose one primary audience and write for that audience through the first draft and first stages of rewriting. Then, in later stages of rewriting, adjust your organization to accommodate your other, secondary audiences. Thus in rewriting you might

- insert paragraphs that answer questions these readers may raise;

- replace technical terms or add definitions of some terms of art; or

- move some extensive technical details to tables, footnotes, or subsections so the readers who want to can easily skip over this detail and still follow your article.

2. Purpose.

Just as a scholarly paper is read by several audiences, it may also serve several purposes. For clearer focus, decide which purpose is uppermost. Write it down and then use that statement to maintain your focus as you research, write, revise, and work through footnotes. As the following list illustrates, some of the purposes of your paper may be

- to organize a confusing array of issues;

- to expand a field of knowledge by offering a new direction;

- to predict developments in the law;
- to suggest changes in the law or advocate a plan of action; or
- to secure tenure or clients.

After you clarify your purpose, remember it. As you write, keep in mind the question, *so what?* This question will help you can relate each point to the overall purpose.

3. Scope.

When you have determined the paper's overall purpose, consider the scope that your purpose dictates. Write down a target page length; that number may help to keep your message manageable. Then ask yourself whether or not you can achieve your stated purpose in this amount of space. As you rewrite, narrow or broaden your topic accordingly, so your audience will easily comprehend your message, the relevance of your research, and the originality of your commentary.

4. Technical Details.

Before you begin researching, become familiar with your citation guide's current edition. This will enable you to record the full citations correctly as you find them. Having to return to the sources solely for citation information is time-consuming and irritating.

5. Footnotes.

If you are doing traditional scholarly writing, use footnotes for any of the following three purposes:

- to cite authority for all unoriginal propositions,
- to expand on authority by offering several other sources, or
- to add supporting details.

For a more complete list of how to use footnotes, see SCHOLARLY WRITING CHECKLIST.

Avoid using footnotes to write another paper within this text, to argue with yourself, to record irrelevant sources, or to substitute for deciding where to put some information or analytical point. Footnotes should enhance the paper, not salve the writer's frustration at researching an unused source. Above all, do not diminish the impact of your analysis by making footnotes longer than the content justifies. For additional information on scholarly writing, see Elizabeth Fajans and Mary R. Falk, Scholarly Writing for Law Students (2d ed. 2000). For other relevant information, see EMPHASIS and IMAGERY.

SCHOLARLY WRITING CHECKLIST

As you refine your scholarly paper during REWRITING and REVISING, create your own checklist for the document, perhaps with the help of your editors or some of your readers. Use the following questions to get started.

SCHOLARLY WRITING CHECKLIST

1. Audience.

   (a) Does the paper include information needed by all intended audiences? For information on various readers, see AUDIENCE, CONTEXT–INDEPENDENT WRITING, and SCHOLARLY WRITING, subsection 1. See UNOBTRUSIVE DEFINITIONS.

   (b) Does the paper account for your readers' backgrounds and how much knowledge they already have?

2. Purpose.

   (a) Is your overall purpose evident throughout the paper? Does it relate directly to a precise and explicit thesis statement? See SCHOLARLY WRITING, subsection 2, and THEME.

   (b) Is the paper original, analytical, and creative, and not just descriptive?

   (c) Is the purpose explained early enough to satisfy the reader?

   (d) Is the document's point of view clear at the outset? Is it primarily persuasive or informative? Something else? (See POINT OF VIEW.)

3. Content.

   (a) Is the research thorough enough to support the thesis statement and to be useful to the reader?

   (b) Have all legal materials been accurately synthesized?

   (c) Do all parts of the paper support the thesis?

   (d) Is extraneous or unhelpful material omitted?

   (e) Are all relevant views on the topic presented accurately?

   (f) Do footnotes function properly? For example, does each do one of following:

   - cite authority for all unoriginal propositions;
   - expand on one authority by offering other, related sources where appropriate;
   - add detail, explanation, or definitions needed by the uninitiated reader;
   - add detail for the reader using the paper as a scholarly tool; or
   - give the text of a statute, regulation, quote, or specific source being discussed?

4. Organization.

   (a) Does the structure flow from substance?

   - Are the parts of the whole congruent with some logical rationale? For example, do they use one of the following:

- parts used in previous cases,

- parts used in a statute,

- parts used in other legal documents,

- parts of an overall process, or

- different causes of one effect?

- Is the paper's organization consistent and unified throughout the document?

- Is each section internally logical?

  - Do paragraphs within each section connect to each other? See TOPIC SENTENCES and CONNECTIONS, MAKING THEM.

  - Is each paragraph logically structured, whether deductively, inductively, or in some other pattern?

  - Are sentences organized logically, e.g., subordinate ideas are subordinated, main ideas appear in main clauses, and PARALLEL STRUCTURE is used to present like ideas?

(b) Is the structure obvious to any reader?

- Will any reader, at any point, not misunderstand the writer? For ways to keep the paper unambiguous, see AMBIGUITY, WAYS TO AVOID.

- Does the introduction present a blueprint for the paper?

- Is each section's relationship to the thesis statement clearly reflected by its order in the organization?

- Is each section connected accurately and clearly both to the thesis and to previous and subsequent points?

- Is the paper written in layers, using headings, footnotes, or paragraph blocks so that the reader can easily identify each part's role in the whole? See HEADINGS and ORGANIZATION, LARGE–SCALE.

5. Clarity.

(a) Will the reader, at any point, not misunderstand the content? For related information, see AMBIGUITY, WAYS TO AVOID.

(b) Is phrasing clear?

- Is word choice precise?

- Is plain English used, jargon and legalese omitted?

- Do the subject-verb combinations carry your message, remind the reader of the thesis?

(c) Is text readable?

- Is there only one main point per sentence?

- Are topic sentences generally the first sentences of paragraphs?
- Are subjects and verbs close together?
- Is passive voice avoided unless needed?
- Are nominalizations minimized or avoided?

(d) Does phrasing emphasize key points?

- Are key points made in positions of emphasis?
- Is repetition used effectively where appropriate?
- Does parallel structure reveal parallel ideas?
- Do short sentences make emphatic points or catch reader's attention? See SENTENCE LENGTH and SENTENCE STRUCTURE, subsection 1.

(e) Do all wording changes flow together to create an eloquent whole?

- Are all emphatic techniques reinforcing the content, rather than distracting from it?
- Are no phrases or techniques overused, so that they draw the writer's attention to the phrase itself?
- Is emphasis focused on key points, rather than invoked too much or indiscriminately?

6. Mechanics.

(a) Is grammar correct?

(b) Is punctuation correct?

(c) Are citations correct?

(d) Has it been proofread for wrong words?

SCHOLARLY WRITING PROCESS

When working on a scholarly paper, your writing process will likely change; this happens because the purpose, scope, audience, and deadlines for a scholarly paper differ from those used in legal practice. You will often have much longer period of time to write a scholarly work than to write practical documents. You may not be given a topic, so you will need to add a step in the process for preliminary research to identify your topic. Thus your research will be more comprehensive, your writing will include more detail, and your rewriting may require more reorganization because of the paper's broader scope.

Further, you will need to make sure that a scholarly paper is creative and thorough. Your scope may be broader or deeper and your audience more diverse in experience. To adapt comfortably to these differences, you might want to include the following steps in your process.

Prewriting

1. Set your deadlines.

Set both your final and interim deadlines, and write them on your calendar. Take time to consider how this project will blend with your other work; keep balance in your schedule. When setting interim deadlines, you might include the following steps.

    (a) Getting started
- Topic selected
- Preemption check completed

    (b) Prewriting
- Research completed
- Notes completed
- Outline drafted

    (c) Writing
- First draft completed, with footnotes
- Further research completed

    (d) Rewriting
- Draft rewritten for organization, content; matched to topic, purpose, audience, scope
- Draft to editor, or other reader

    (e) Revising
- Draft Revised
- Second to the Last Draft Completed

    (f) Polishing
- Footnotes Checked for Accuracy and Citation Form
- Final Draft Completed

2. Select a topic.

Check the subject index in a secondary finding source such as an index to legal periodicals, a news service, or a specialized source. Read for a general understanding of a topic that interests you, and take notes on specific ideas that catch your interest. Narrow your topic until it fulfills a scholarly purpose and is timely, useful, and interesting. See SCHOLARLY WRITING, subsections 1–3, and SCHOLARLY WRITING CHECKLIST, subsections 1 and 2.

If you have not done so already, state the topic in one sentence, even if you do not use this exact statement in the paper. This theme will help you retain your focus throughout the process and should prevent you from going too far afield in your research. For more ideas, see THEME.

3. Do a pre-emption check.

If you wish to publish the paper or if your reader expects originality, check to make sure your topic has not been preempted by another writer. You must do an exhaustive search of scholarly materials. Plan for a sufficient amount of time to do this, knowing it will be well invested. The search will complete the research you started in your topic search and begin the research you will use in your paper.

If someone has come close to your topic, modify it so it adds something new. For example, you may have to create a theory, propose a statute, or offer a new synthesis. If you cannot add anything new, abandon the topic and try another.

4. Reconsider purpose and scope.

When you have secured and sufficiently modified your topic, identify more specifically your purpose and scope. See SCHOLARLY WRITING, subsections 2 and 3. List several possible purposes and decide which is uppermost; relate your ideas to your list throughout the process. Then identify the scope you expect to cover on your topic, and the page length. Similarly remind yourself of scope as you develop the project so you can adjust the topic if it becomes too narrow or broad.

5. Take accurate notes.

In particular, note terms of art, phrases that contribute to the development of your proof or criticism, and arguments that need refutation. Use the terms you capture in your notes to develop and refine the language of your thesis sentence.

If you are comfortable doing so, sketch an outline as you take notes. The outline should combine an accurate picture of your topic with your original idea about it. As you sketch, build logical connections between the research and your message, keeping the purpose and scope in mind. See ORGANIZATION. This is a good time in your process to get feedback, so you might want to go over the outline with your editor or professor.

6. Make a drafting plan.

You may want to draft in pieces, concentrating fully on each piece, or draft in one sitting. For example, if you have a historical background section, you might want to draft that in one sitting. Or if you are developing your argument, you might want to draft that without stopping. You may even want to draft the whole article all at once so you are forced to synthesize the document fully. Your topic can change so much that it loses its force and integrity, so be flexible enough to change your plan to suit the paper but realistic enough to meet your deadline.

Writing

7.   Begin drafting well ahead of a first draft deadline.

Because of its detail and length, scholarly writing requires more time. For example, you will need more time deciding what to include because you will have so many sources. When in doubt, include it. Allow yourself to overwrite at this stage as needed to keep your mind free. You can edit for conciseness and unity in later stages of the process. Beware of procrastination at this point. If you are having trouble writing, see WRITING BLOCK, WRITING, PERFECTIONISM, and PROCRASTI-NATION.

Rewriting

8.   Plan for multiple redrafts.

Keep aware of the final deadline and pace yourself so you can redraft as much as necessary to explore the topic comfortably. You may need several drafts during rewriting, for example, to get the content and organization to fit your purpose and message. You may need as many drafts for revising to capture tone and voice.

9.   Decide how to use your footnotes.

Some writers are comfortable including the full citation and writing the whole footnote as they draft, which a strong outline will permit. Others add footnotes when rewriting or in the early stages of revising. Avoid the other extreme of writing all footnotes after you have complet-ed the draft; they will take too long to write and may be analytically divorced from the main text. See SCHOLARLY WRITING, subsection 5.

Revising

10.   Ask for comments and criticisms on the paper.

To gain specific advice, you might want to send a cover memo with the paper asking questions about the draft and how to handle particular-ly troublesome places. The reader, by responding to your specific ques-tions and adding other comments, will offer valuable evidence of audi-ence reaction. Then you can adjust the draft to make it clearer. If you have more than one reader, compare suggestions and pay special atten-tion to the common points. Attend to the problem the readers see; if you disagree with their solutions, fashion one that is better. Criticism from many readers should strengthen your paper, make it more accessible to a variety of readers, and offer you more writing techniques. For ideas on how readers may react, see EDITING.

Polishing

11.   Read the paper once just for technical details.

Refresh yourself on accurate citation usage and make sure that every citation is accurate and correct. You might want to work backward or on the second half of the paper first, where there are usually more mistakes. For more techniques, see POLISHING. For additional information on scholarly writing, see Elizabeth Fajans and Mary R. Falk, Scholarly Writing for Law Students (2d ed. 2000).

SCOPE

Scope describes what your document covers, its length and depth. You can measure scope in part by content and page limit. Scope in content refers to the amount of material and the level of detail you use. For example, you may be analyzing a narrow tort issue within one state, so your scope is derived from that state's mandatory authority on that issue, your discussion about that mandatory authority, and its application to your situation. If the mandatory authority is not sufficient to address the issue, you will expand your scope to include persuasive authority from another jurisdiction.

Scope in page limit refers to either the official page limit to a document, such as a brief, or to the unofficial page limit generated by the circumstances. If you are writing a brief on that tort issue, the court may have a limit on the number of pages you can write. You will limit your analysis accordingly, concentrating on the mandatory authority and legally significant facts, adding salient points about persuasive authority only if necessary. If you are doing a memo on the tort issue, you may discuss the mandatory authority in more detail and add a small range of persuasive authority showing how other states assess the situation. The challenge in doing this occurs because many legal issues lend themselves to the proportions of a scholarly article. Your could, for example, discuss each bit of mandatory authority in great detail and add persuasive authority from dozens of states, all of which might have something to say about that tort issue. That is usually too much.

Scope is interrelated with AUDIENCE and PURPOSE. Before you begin researching, assess the appropriate scope for the situation, determining as closely as you can how much your reader will read and what purpose you want to achieve. You may even ask your audience directly. The answer can determine how much research you do and how you design the document. While the scope of the document discussing in OUTLINING may seem logical and appropriate, it may be too long for some audiences and for the purpose of obtaining the children for the mother. So, before you write, you may regroup the presentation to show what elements are not in dispute, then focus in one section on the elements most favorable to the mother, and demonstrate in another section how the father cannot meet the best interests standard. This will shorten the document and heighten its persuasive impact. As you research and rewrite, reassess scope periodically; most readers appreciate conciseness in design, perhaps more than conciseness in sentences.

368

SECTION

Section should always be spelled out when it begins a sentence. In text, also spell out *section* except when referring to a U.S. Code provision or a federal regulation. Use the symbol § in footnotes and cites. Use *s.* or *sec.* only if your jurisdiction permits.

SELF– OR *SELF?*

Use *self-* when adding it as a prefix to another noun: *self-interest, self-serving,* and *self-sufficient.* Use *self* as the first syllable in words such as *selflessness, selfish,* and *selfsame.* For related information, see HYPHENS.

SEMICOLONS

Semicolons have two uses: (1) as an end mark between two clauses and (2) as a super comma.

1.   As an end mark between two clauses.

You may use a semicolon instead of a period between two sentences if those sentences are closely related logically but could each stand as complete sentences.

> **The Plaintiff did not intend to destroy another's property; he broke the window only because he saw flames inside the house.**

Avoid, however, allowing yourself to use semicolons without clarifying the logical relationship of your points.

> **This action violated Tremont's rights to both freedom of speech and due process.**

rather than

> This case involves not only freedom of speech, but also due process; each of these issues indicates that Tremont's rights were violated.

Do not use a comma between two independent clauses unless a conjunction such as *and* follows the comma. This error occurs frequently when *however* connects the clauses.

> **Cutts denied being at the scene of the crime; however, he admitted having been there two hours earlier.**

rather than

> Cutts denied being at the scene of the crime, however, he admitted having been there two hours earlier.

2.   As a super comma.

You must use a semicolon, instead of a comma, at the end of each element in a list if a comma occurs within any one element in the list.

> **The Company warrants for one year that its compressors (1) are free from defects in material and workmanship; (2) have**

the capacities and rating set forth in the Company's catalogs, provided that no warranty is made against corrosion, erosion, or deterioration; and (3) meet all relevant federal safety standards.

The Company is not liable for any delay in performance due to any of the following:

(1) any act of God, including but not limited to floods, epidemics, fires, storms, or earthquakes;

(2) any acts of others beyond the reasonable control of the Company, including but not limited to strikes or other labor disturbances, riots, wars, acts of civil or military authority, or acts of the Customer; and

(3) any cause beyond its reasonable control, including but not limited to delays in transportation, inability to obtain necessary materials or components, or labor shortages.

The semicolon helps the reader see where each item on the list begins and ends.

Do not use a semicolon at the end of each element in a list solely because the list is tabulated rather than run in text. Commas are still sufficient if there are no commas within any of the items listed.

"Remanufacturing equipment" included the following processes:

(1) disassembly to a predetermined standard established by the Manufacturer for each model,

(2) cleaning,

(3) refinishing,

(4) inspecting and testing to new machine test standards,

(5) installation of all retrofits, and

(6) operational testing.

For related information, see TRANSITIONS; HOWEVER; and LISTS, STRUCTURE OF.

SENTENCE FRAGMENTS

Sentence fragments are phrases that could be part of a sentence, but as worded do not make up a complete sentence. To be a complete sentence, the phrase must have a subject and verb, which makes it a clause.

        S   V

Any vendor who supplies the University must file this document.

rather than

Any vendor who supplies the University.

                                  S   V —   V

Even if the work is derivative, parts of it may still be copyrightable.

rather than

Parts still copyrightable.

If there is a sentence fragment, most legal readers will assume you have not polished the document. Some will assume that you did not know better. Although fragments can be used for emphasis, their effect in legal writing can be summed up as follows.

Probably too dramatic.

The previous fragment may have caught your attention, but it is too informal for legal writing. Thus, even in persuasive writing, be careful. Make sure your fragment is unambiguously intentional if you use it. While you could use the following version if you are beginning a paragraph that leads directly to it,

Not so here.

you might better preserve your credibility by writing,

That is not what happened here.

For other ways to create emphasis, see EMPHASIS.

SENTENCE LENGTH

In general, avoid making sentences longer than three-and-a half lines of text. The one exception to this is sentences containing lists, which are easier to read because of their more obvious structure.

A doctor may forego disclosure to his patient if any of the following situations occur: (1) if the patient is unconscious, incompetent, or otherwise incapable of understanding the information; (2) if the patient is a minor; (3) if in the doctor's opinion the information would have a disproportionately adverse reaction on the patient's ability to make a rational decision; or (4) if an emergency exists which allows no time to safely consult with the patient.

One handy way to check sentence length is to scan several pages of your text and draw slashes after each period, which you can do without actually reading the text. Then look at the slashes. If you see several sentences in a row that run more than four lines, try to shorten at least one.

Similarly, if you see several sentences in a row that are only one line long, see if you should combine two of them or make some other changes to avoid a choppy tone. Occasionally, however, you may want this choppy effect.

> **The major purpose of the trial court's established procedure is to give the litigants a fair opportunity to address their claims and have them resolved by a court of law. That purpose was met here. <u>The litigants had eight years of opportunity</u>. <u>In this context, their arguments on appeal are particularly specious.</u>** . . .

For related information, see SENTENCE STRUCTURE; REVISING CHECKLIST; and TOUGH, SOUNDING THAT WAY.

SENTENCES, PARTS OF

Knowing the parts of a sentence can help you understand sentence structure, which in turn can help you write sentences that convey your meaning emphasize your points effectively. If you have trouble identifying such things as verbs or indirect objects, this quick overview may help.

1. Verb.

Each sentence has at least one verb. The verb expresses either an action, such as *hit* or *received*, or a state of being, such as *is* or *seemed*. The verb may be one word, such as *signed* or *appeared*, or more than one word, such as *must complete* or *will have been signed*. When the verb contains more than one word, it is called a *verb phrase*.

The following verbs express an action.

> **Faulkner <u>signed</u> a waiver of rights.**

> **All nonresidents living in Illinois for more than three months of a calendar year <u>must complete</u> the following section.**

> **The defendant <u>agreed</u>.**

> **The contract <u>will have been signed</u> by that date.**

> **The trial court <u>determined</u> that the defendant's statements <u>were</u> voluntary and <u>admitted</u> them at trial.**

The following verbs express a state of being.

> **The settlement <u>seems</u> reasonable in light of the facts.**

> **The plaintiff <u>is</u> a former employee of Stills, International.**

> **In this case, nevertheless, the problem <u>exists</u>.**

For common problems, see VERBS. For more information on specific kinds of verbs, see VERBS, TENSES; VERBS, AUXILIARY; VERBS, IRREGULAR; VERBS, LINKING; VERBS, MOODS; VERBS, PARTICI-

PLES; VERBS, TENSES; DIFFERENT TENSES IN THE SAME SEN-
TENCE; and VOICE, ACTIVE OR PASSIVE?

2.   Subject.

Each sentence has at least one subject. The complete subject is the
person, thing, or idea about which the verb speaks, and may be one word
or many.

Faulkner signed a waiver of rights.

**All nonresidents living in Illinois for more than three
months of a calendar year** must complete the following
section.

The defendant agreed.

The contract will have been signed by that date.

The trial court determined that the defendant's statements
were voluntary and admitted them at trial.

The settlement seems reasonable in light of the facts.

The plaintiff is a former employee of Stills, International.

The defendant's statements were voluntary.

The *simple subject* is the main word in the *complete subject*.

All **nonresidents** living in Illinois for more than three
months of a calendar year must complete the following
section.

3.   Predicate.

Each sentence has a predicate. The predicate is the part of the
sentence that says something about the subject.

All nonresidents living in Illinois for more than three
months of a calendar year **must complete the following
section**.

The defendant **agreed**.

The trial court **determined that the defendant's statements
were voluntary and admitted them at trial**.

The contract **will have been signed by that date**.

The settlement **seems reasonable in light of the facts**.

The plaintiff **is a former employee of Stills, International**.

The defendant's statements **were voluntary**.

Every predicate includes at least one verb, and it may include any or all
of the following: direct objects, indirect objects, prepositional phrases,
and participial phrases.

4. Direct Object.

A direct object is the person, object, or idea receiving the action of the verb.

The plaintiff built <u>the house</u> with his own hands.

Faulkner signed <u>a waiver</u> of rights.

The defendant's action destroyed <u>that right</u>.

All sentences have a subject and predicate, but not all have a direct object.

5. Indirect Object.

An indirect object receives the direct object, rather than the action of the verb.

The plaintiff gave <u>the defendant</u> the house when she agreed to cohabit.

Here, *the defendant* received the house, and thus is the indirect object. *The house* is the direct object, because it was the object of the verb, *gave*. Not all sentences have an indirect object.

6. Prepositional Phrase.

A prepositional phrase is a group of words that work together to show the relationship of a noun or pronoun to the rest of the sentence. This noun or pronoun is called the object of the preposition. A preposition, which is always the first word in a prepositional phrase, shows how the rest of that phrase is logically related to the sentence. Examples of prepositions are *of, to, on, off, between, through, in, at, without, over,* and *under.* The following examples of prepositional phrases illustrate the variety of information they can convey.

He built the house <u>with his own hands</u>.

All nonresidents living <u>in Illinois for more than three months of a calendar year</u> must complete the following section.

The contract will have been signed <u>by that date</u>.

The settlement seems reasonable <u>in light of the facts</u>.

7. Participial Phrase.

A participial phrase is a group of words that work together to show the relationship of some action to the rest of the sentence. A participle, which is always the first word in a participial phrase, is either the *-ed* or *-ing* form of a regular verb, (*followed, following, covered, covering*) or the past tense or *-ing* form of an irregular verb (*held, holding*). The following examples illustrate how participial phrases can be used in a sentence.

The boat, <u>built by Mr. Tremat,</u> should not be considered community property.

The attorney focused her argument on this issue, <u>building carefully on these fact</u>s.

<u>Covered by snow</u>, the edge of the ditch was not visible.

The statute <u>covering this issue</u> is unambiguous.

This right, <u>held inviolate since the founding of our country</u>, must not now be extinguished.

Any court <u>holding on this issue</u> must address the elements of the statute.

8. Clause.

A clause is a group of words that includes both a subject and a predicate.

      subject   predicate

<u>The trial court</u> <u>determined this issue.</u>

In contrast, a phrase does not necessarily include both a subject and a predicate.

a case of first impression

determining this issue

There are two kinds of clauses: independent (or main) and dependent. An independent clause can be set off as a sentence by itself.

The defendant knew or should have known this.

The company gave a free water heater to residential customers.

Every sentence must include at least one independent clause.

A dependent clause cannot by itself form a sentence because it is logically dependent on an independent clause.

that the plaintiff would not be aware of the stock market usage of the phrase "passed its dividends"

who installed electric space heating

This logical dependence is signaled by the conjunction that introduces the dependent clause, which is called a subordinating conjunction. For related information, see SUBORDINATION.

Make sure all dependent clauses are part of a larger sentence including an independent clause.

The defendant knew or should have known that the plaintiff would not be aware of the stock market usage of the phrase "passed its dividends."

rather than

The defendant knew or should have known. That the plaintiff would not be aware of the stock market usage of the phrase "passed its dividends."

The company gave a free water heater to residential customers who installed electric space heating.

rather than

The company gave a free water heater to residential customers. Who installed electric space heating.

For related information, see SENTENCE STRUCTURE.

SENTENCES, MAIN

See TOPIC SENTENCES.

SENTENCE STRUCTURE

Mastering the basics of sentence structure provides a valuable tool for effective writing. After you learn how to change the structure of a sentence, you can use that skill to emphasize or de-emphasize points, to increase readability, to change tone, and to clarify transitions between paragraphs and sentences.

What follows are explanations of four basic sentence structures (subsections 1–4) and examples and explanations of ways you can exploit those basics to create sentences that are both readable and effective (subsections 5–7). For help identifying the grammatical parts of a sentence, see SENTENCE, PARTS OF.

1. Simple Sentence.

Grammatically, this sentence includes only one set of subjects and verbs, although it may have many modifying phrases.

             S   V
This case addresses three issues.

             S   S   V
Mr. Smith and his attorney will confer on the matter tomorrow.

             S   S   V   V
The defendant and his wife ransacked the house and took items worth $3,000.

Strategically, use a simple sentence that has only a few words, usually fewer than ten, if you want the dramatic impact that a simple sentence can have.

The Court of Appeals refused to consider this argument because it "was not properly ... presented to the trial court." The court did not elaborate.

2. Compound Sentence.

This structure includes two or more independent clauses joined by a conjunction, semicolon, or colon. An independent clause could be set off as a sentence by itself.

    S   V   conjunction

There can be no negligence without duty, and in this case
   S   V
there is no duty.

    S   V   semicolon

There can be no negligence without duty; in this case, no
   S   V
duty exists.

                         S   V   Colon

In this case, one element of negligence is missing:
   S   V
there is no duty.

This structure can create a one-two punch. This effect will be stronger if the second of the joined sentences is short. For related information, see SENTENCE, PARTS OF; SEMICOLONS; and COLONS.

3. Complex Sentence.

In a complex sentence, one or more dependent clauses have been inserted into another sentence, which is the independent clause.

      dependent clause

Because more married women entered the labor market as second earners,

      independent clause

more married couples were subject to the tax penalty.

The independent clause includes the main subject, verb, and object of the sentence. Because this is the structural heart of the sentence, you want to put your main information here.

More married couples were subject to the tax penalty.

Often you will want to use dependent clauses to add some background information, elaboration, or other less important points to the sentence. A dependent clause cannot by itself form a sentence because it begins with a subordinating word, and thus it is logically dependent on an independent clause.

because more married women entered the labor market as second earners

The complex sentence is useful because it allows the writer to show the logical interrelationship of two or more points while giving more

377

emphasis to one point. As a result, the complex sentence is common in legal writing. To use it effectively, however, you must keep the complex sentence readable and logically structured.

> **This court interpreted this statute broadly in previous cases, when it applied the statute to parents of minor children, trustees of the estates of handicapped adults, and foster parents.**

rather than

> This court, when it in previous cases applied the statute to parents of minor children, trustees of the estates of handicapped adults, and foster parents, interpreted this statute broadly.

Avoid using complex sentences exclusively; also exploit the strengths of simple and compound sentences. Too many complex sentences make the text less interesting. For a related topic, see VARIETY. If all your sentences are complex, try restructuring some important points into simple sentences.

Also avoid overdoing the complexity of the sentence. In general, do not insert more than two dependent clauses in one sentence; doing so gives the reader a bite too big to chew. If you decide you must show the logical interrelationship of more actions, try putting those actions in separate sentences and using a connecting word or phrase that explains that logical interrelationship.

> **Waivers of constitutional rights not only must be voluntary; they must also be knowing, intelligent acts done with sufficient awareness of the relevant circumstances and likely consequences. Breckenridge v. United States, 900 U.S. 321, 323 (2007). Furthermore, waiver of the right to counsel cannot be presumed from a silent record. Kelstad v. Karney, 969 U.S. 506, 516 (2007).**

For more on the use of the complex sentence, see subsection 7. For help connecting two sentences, see TRANSITIONS and CONNECTIONS, MAKING THEM.

4. Inverted sentence.

One final structure you can use occasionally is the inverted sentence. In this structure, some part of the predicate, such as the object of the verb, comes before the subject.

> **Imprudent it was, but not illegal.**

rather than

> It was imprudent, but not illegal.

In the inverted version of this sentence, the predicate adjective *imprudent* is placed before the subject *it*, rather than after the linking verb *was*. The inverted sentence is dramatic precisely because the parts of the sentence are out of their usual order. It is so dramatic, however, that it is hard to find an occasion to use it in legal writing without sounding self-conscious, as would be the case if someone said, *While coming to work today, an old friend I saw.*

5. Using subjects and verbs effectively.

Put your main point in the main subject and verb in your sentence. Conversely, de-emphasize points by putting them in dependent clauses. For example, the following sentence emphasizes *he had slowed and was not accelerating* by making that the main subject and verb.

> **Although the defendant had not come to a full stop at the official stop sign, he had slowed to less than five miles per hour and was not accelerating at the time of the accident.**

6. Choosing the best sentence structure.

In general, vary your sentence structure. This variety should come naturally, however, out of the logical structures needed by your content. Never use a sentence structure that goes against the logical structure of your content. To do so is tantamount to signaling that you plan to move to the right lane on a freeway and then moving to the left lane instead. Even if the reader manages to keep up with you, that reader will be distrustful and unhappy. For more help in determining what structure fits your content, see subsection 7.

7. Inserting information in a sentence.

Although the unmodified, simple sentence is strong and effective, you will usually need to add more to the sentence because you need to add more information. There are three places where these extra phrases can be inserted.

(a) Insert extra phrases after the independent clause.

> **This inflationary effect was especially marked for two-earner married couples, <u>whose income is aggregated for tax purposes</u>.**

> **Triavil offered no treatment or cure for tension head-aches, <u>as testified by Dr. Paul Wyles</u> (R. 1159).**

> **The minority arrived at the same conclusion, <u>although for different reasons</u>.**

This structure is the mainstay of communication because it is the easiest for the reader to follow. For example, in the following sentence you understand the point immediately because you get the independent clause right away, before getting the elaboration.

> **I saw an old friend while coming to work today.**

As such, this structure is useful for presenting routine information that needs no special emphasis.

> **This inequity affected more people in the early 80's when more married women entered the labor market.**

It is also useful for presenting information that is complex and thus must be presented in a simple form.

> **Unmarried individuals paid substantially greater taxes than married individuals between 1948 and 1969, in some cases more than 40% in excess of a married individual's tax on an identical income.**

(b) Insert extra phrases before the independent clause.

> **<u>Until recently</u>, others have supported inserting legislative veto provisions in statutes covering most agency rulemaking.**

> **<u>Despite the difficulty of this test</u>, the gravity of the situation required that it be done.**

This structure, a mainstay of storytellers, is useful when you want to create a touch of suspense. For example, after reading the following sentence, you expect more after hearing the introductory phrase.

> **While coming to work today, I saw an old friend.**

The change in structure alone tells the reader that this is the beginning of a story. You might use this touch of suspense to present either facts or an argument.

> **Pointing the gun at the teller, the defendant ordered her to fill the bag with cash.**

> **Because there was no timely notice, this opportunity for hearing provided no opportunity at all.**

Additionally, placing information before the independent clause is a useful way to provide a transition at the beginning of a paragraph. In the following example, the information placed at the beginning of the paragraph both reminds the reader of the topic of the previous paragraph and shows the reader how that topic relates to this paragraph.

> **Environmental Impact Studies could be handled similarly, without delaying the hearing.**

> **<u>Even if there were some delay</u>, that delay would present no procedural difficulties.**

Finally, placing a dependent clause before the independent clause can signal to the reader that the added information is less important than the independent clause.

> **Although there are three kinds of marital status discrimination, this comment focuses only on the marriage penalty.**

This structure can be useful when you need to include an unfavorable fact and you want to make that fact seem as unimportant as possible.

> **Although Mr. Allerton was in the room during the signing of the will, he was there only because it was his habit to sit in the living room while reading the evening paper.**

(c) Insert extra information in the middle of the independent clause.

> **Anorexics, <u>by failing to eat,</u> passively expose themselves to harm.**

This structure, a tool of orators, creates a very formal tone. For example, the following sentence sounds rather stuffy.

> **I, while coming to work today, saw an old friend.**

This structure is harder to read because to understand the main point the reader must remember the first part of the sentence, read the interrupting clause, and then reunite the last part of the sentence with the first in his or her memory. Therefore, avoid using the structure in sentence after sentence; give the reader breathing space between these difficult sentences. Also, avoid allowing the interruption to exceed seven or eight words. If the interruption is longer, the reader would have to reread the sentence to get the point.

> **The burden is on the defendant to show, not just that the tax is excessive, but also that the defendant was taxed for more than its fair share.**

> **These issues, controversial but crucial, must be resolved by this court.**

> **Dr. Yu, who attended the plaintiff immediately after the accident, has testified that her internal injuries were caused by the faulty seatbelts.**

For information in problems associated with long interruptions, see AGREEMENT, SUBJECTS AND VERBS.

SENTENCES WITH *AND*

See SENTENCE STRUCTURE; AND, subsection 2; and LISTS, STRUCTURE OF.

SETTLEMENT LETTERS AND EMAIL

A settlement letter is written to encourage a party to settle a case. It is usually written by one client's attorney and directed to the other client's attorney. A settlement letter is designed to inform the reader of the writer's argument and to persuade the reader to accept that argument. While this kind of action can be taken by email, the ramifications are so great that many lawyers prefer the paper form. Check with your colleagues to determine the correct medium. Consider the following in writing either a letter or email intended to settle a case.

1. Choose the approach you think is most likely to influence the other attorney.

For example, if you think the attorney and client can be persuaded gently, you might want to begin with a friendly opening, show you have considered the other side, and then build your argument, leading to the settlement offer. If you think this attorney and client would be more convinced by a stronger opening, start with the offer of settlement. For related information, see AUDIENCE.

2. Make sure the attorney knows that you understand the other client's position.

For example, if the client and attorney have already offered a settlement, remind them that you are aware of that offer, of how much it was, and that you are grateful for the offer.

3. Choose a tone appropriate to the method of persuasion.

This tone might be tough if you expect unreasonable opposition, or friendly if you want them to be convinced that your offer is fair. For more information, see TONE IN LETTERS AND EMAIL.

4. Follow a format that includes the following, adjusting the order and content to suit your purpose, tone, and audience:

(a) a heading,

(b) a salutation,

(c) an introduction that identifies the purpose of settling,

(d) your terms for settlement and the reasoning behind them,

(e) a course of action on the settlement matter,

(f) a specific directive to the attorney to call you or answer your offer of settlement,

(g) a closing. For help here, see CLOSINGS FOR LETTERS AND EMAIL.

See also GENERAL CORRESPONDENCE LETTERS AND EMAIL and PERSUASIVE WRITING.

SEXIST LANGUAGE, WAYS TO AVOID

The first thing to remember when avoiding sexist language is that it is legitimate and even desirable to use *he* or *she* when you are talking about a specific person, as you usually are in briefs or memos. Sexist language here would be to use *he* when referring to a woman or *she* when referring to a man.

Sometimes, however, you will be discussing general principles that apply to all persons. When a singular pronoun is needed in that situation, use *he or she*, or *she or he* if you prefer. If you find yourself awash in *he or she*'s, you can use any of three techniques to avoid the pronoun problem.

1. Reword the phrase to omit the pronoun.

Anyone desiring a position with this firm should submit a résumé at the interview.

rather than

Anyone desiring a position with this firm should submit his or her résumé at the time of his or her interview.

2. Substitute *one* throughout the text.

One cannot apply for a loan if one does not have collateral.

rather than

A person cannot apply for a loan if he or she does not have collateral.

This technique, however, is hard to use gracefully. It often creates phrasing as awkward as the original *he or she*.

3. Refer to people in the plural so that you can substitute *they* for *he or she*.

All attorneys must adjust their trial strategies in response to this ruling.

rather than

Each attorney must adjust his or her trial strategies in response to this ruling.

This is often the best approach when discussing broader ideas, as is common in scholarly articles. Do not, however, resort to using a plural pronoun to refer to a singular noun.

Anyone desiring a position should submit a résumé.

rather than

Anyone desiring a position should submit their résumé.

This use of the plural pronoun is still considered grammatically incorrect by most authorities. It is also dangerously ambiguous in legal drafting. For example, *each child shall inherit an equal share of the land as long as they live* could result in confusion about what happens if one of the children dies.

Do not resort to using *s/he*. It is convenient for the writer but not for the reader, who will stumble slightly over the term, substituting *he or she* to read the sentence. Always write with the reader's convenience in mind, rather than your own.

If you find that nothing you try sounds graceful, choose the accurate *he or she* rather than the inaccurate *he*. In legal writing, a conflict between accuracy and elegance should always be resolved in favor of accuracy. For avoiding sexist language when beginning a business letter, see SALUTATIONS, subsection 2.

SHALL

In all legal writing except LEGISLATION, use *must* instead of *shall* to state that something must be done; use *may* when stating something that may be done. Legislation traditionally treats *shall* as establishing a requirement, and therefore *shall* is not ambiguous in that context. The general public, however, does not necessarily give *shall* this more specific reason. To them, *shall* is often an archaic or fancy version of *will*. They also may read *shall* as meaning either *must* or *may*, and thus it can be ambiguous.

I shall attempt to go over Niagara Falls in a barrel.

For this reason, *must* is usually the more precise choice.

S/HE

Resist the temptation. Use *he or she*, or *she or he* if you prefer. *S/he*, besides looking funny, is hard to read aloud, and anything that is hard to read aloud is hard to read silently. Write for the reader's convenience; the reader will be grateful. If *he or she* seems cumbersome to you, see SEXIST LANGUAGE, WAYS TO AVOID for other tactics. If you need to provide a place for the reader to line out the inappropriate option, use *he/she*.

SHEPARD'S CITATIONS

See UPDATING THE LAW.

SHORT SENTENCES

Short sentences provide one of the most effective ways to emphasize a point.

This was an error.

He failed to do so.

The Court of Appeals refused to consider this argument because it "was not properly ... presented to the trial court." The Court did not elaborate.

Several short sentences in a row also create a clipped, no-nonsense tone.

My client, Ms. Ambrose, does not intend to pay this bill. She has no reason to pay this bill. She did not receive any software from your company. She did not order any software from your company. Until receiving your bill, she did not know your company existed.

Avoid creating any unintended emphasis by avoiding short sentences for unimportant points or using several short sentences in a row, unless you want a clipped or exasperated tone. For related information, TOUGH, SOUNDING THAT WAY and PERSUASIVE WRITING, subsection 3(f). For a broader context, see SENTENCE STRUCTURE.

SHOULD

Should has several meanings, and thus can create some ambiguity. In the following sentence, for example, it could mean *ought, must,* or *may*.

The affidavit should be in our office at least five days before the scheduled hearing.

In general, legal writing needs the meaning of *must*; use *must* whenever that is your meaning.

The affidavit must be in our office at least five days before the scheduled hearing to insure the proceeding going forward.

Should can be useful when you want to imply that something was not done that should have been.

The police should have read him his <u>Miranda</u> rights before searching his car.

Should is sometimes used to imply doubt that something will happen in the future. But avoid this use, because this implication is ambiguous and thus may not be inferred by the reader.

The contract should arrive in our office by next Thursday.

You may consider using *should* for tact when the statement is an indirect request, although *ought* may actually be the precise choice.

To insure the proceeding going forward, the affidavit ought to be in our office at least five days before the scheduled hearing.

The safer route may be to make a direct request.

Please send the affidavit to our office at least five days before the scheduled hearing to insure the proceeding going forward.

When the statement is a comment on what may happen, use *may* rather than *should*.

The affidavit may arrive in our office several days before the actual hearing.

To increase readability, avoid using *should* at the first of a sentence when you really mean *if*. While *if* is precise because it can only mean that what follows is an *if* ... *then* situation, *should* is less precise because it can introduce either a question or an *if . . . then* situation. For related information, see VERBS, AUXILIARY.

SIC

This is a Latin word that means *thus* or *so*. Use it within quotations to inform the reader that the error in the text was in the original, rather than an error you made when copying the quote. *Sic* is surrounded by brackets.

The police read defendant his <u>Mirenda</u> [sic] rights.

When the error is minor and obvious, as in the previous example, consider whether just correcting it would be a courtesy to the original writer. This might be appropriate when citing a case to the court who wrote the case, for example. For related information, see QUOTATIONS, HOW TO PUNCTUATE.

SIGNALS

Signals are used before CITATIONS as shorthand to indicate their exact use. As such, signals replace unnecessary text, such as *the court held that* or *another court also agreed that*. Signals may be used as the verbs or ordinary sentences, in which case they are not italicized. When signals are used as verbs, matter that would be included in a parenthetical explanation should be made part of the sentence itself. For specific instructions on how to use signals, check your citation manual. For related information, see CITATION TABLE.

SIMPLE SENTENCE

A simple sentence includes only one set of subjects and verbs, although it may have many modifying phrases.

       S   V

This <u>case</u> <u>involves</u> three issues.

  S   S   V

<u>Mr. Smith</u> and his <u>attorney</u> <u>will confer</u> on the matter tomorrow.

          S   S   V   V

The <u>defendant</u> and his <u>wife</u> <u>ransacked</u> the house and <u>took</u> items worth $3,000.

Strategically, use a simple sentence that has only a few words, usually fewer than ten, if you want the dramatic impact that a simple sentence can have.

The Court of Appeals refused to consider this argument because it "was not properly . . . presented to the trial court." <u>The court did not elaborate.</u>

For related information, see SENTENCE STRUCTURE and SHORT SENTENCES.

SIMPLICITY

Simplicity has gained status in legal writing over the years, mostly because of the universal overload under which lawyers and judges operate; most legal readers want to finish the job and go home. Confine your presentation to the information essential to your case, nothing more and nothing less. Achieving the delicate balance between thoroughness and simplicity in your writing will win you respect and credibility.

To achieve simplicity, concentrate on

- using terms of art and other key terms in subjects and verbs,
- focusing issues specifically,
- using clear and logical organization,
- revising for conciseness, and
- using plain English, rather than legalese or flowery language.

For specific suggestions, see CONCISENESS, REPETITION, PARAGRAPHS, WORD CHOICE, and READABILITY, subsections 3 and 4.

SINCE OR *BECAUSE*?

See *BECAUSE* OR *SINCE*?

SINGLE QUOTATION MARKS

Although writers in some other countries conventionally use single quotes ("___") instead of double quotes ("___"), lawyers in the United States use double quotes. Single quotes are used only for a quote within a quote. For related information, see QUOTATIONS, HOW TO PUNCTUATE.

SINGULAR OR PLURAL?

When deciding whether to use the singular or plural form, always use the one that is grammatically accurate, even if it seems wordier or less smooth.

Each petitioner must sign his or her full legal name.

rather than the slightly less precise

All of the petitioners must sign their full legal names.

Use consistent numbers throughout.

Each petitioner must sign his or her full legal name.

or

Petitioners must sign their full legal names.

rather than

> Each petitioner must sign their full legal names.

When you may accurately use either singular or plural, consider the following guidelines. Use the plural *they* for any of the following three reasons.

1. You want to distance the reader from the idea or persons the term represents.

> **Injured plaintiffs must file their claims before the statute of limitations runs.**

2. You need to avoid using *he* or *she* too much.

> **Attorneys must file their complaints by the fourth day of the month in which they are requesting a hearing.**

rather than

> An attorney must file his or her complaint by the fourth day of the month in which he or she is requesting a hearing.

3. The point you are making applies logically to a class of people or a concept, rather than an individual.

> **The asbestos victims in this class action request monetary damages for several reasons.**

Use the singular *he* or *she* for any of these reasons, when doing so does not cause distracting repetition.

4. You want to pull the reader closer to the idea or persons the term represents.

> **Each defendant must be held accountable for his or her part in this tragedy.**

5. The point you are making applies logically to a concern for an individual rather than a class of people or a concept.

> **Unlike an older child, a toddler cannot describe a parent's abusive actions. But he or she can feel the results of the abuse, and may be permanently harmed.**

For related information, see S/HE and SEXIST LANGUAGE, WAYS TO AVOID.

SLANG

Avoid using slang in legal writing because it is too informal, too emotional, and often too imprecise.

SLANTED LANGUAGE

See EMOTIONAL LANGUAGE.

SLASH

The only time you should use a slash (/) in legal writing is when you are writing a form in which the person signing is to mark out the inappropriate word, as in *Mr./Ms./Mrs./Miss*. For related information, see AND/OR and S/HE.

SMOOTHNESS

See COHERENCE, EMPHASIS, LOGICAL LINKS, and READABILITY.

SO

So has several different meanings and thus must be used carefully to avoid potential ambiguity. For example, when used as a conjunction, *so* can introduce a clause stating a consequence of the point stated before *so*.

The defendant was in the hospital at the time, so he could not have been at the meeting.

When *so* introduces a clause stating a consequence, substitute *and as a result* if *so* could be ambiguous.

The defendant was in the hospital at the time, and as a result he could not have been at the meeting.

So can also introduce a clause stating the purpose of the point stated before *so*.

Mrs. Williamson asked for the check to be mailed to her mother's home so her husband could not intercept it.

To avoid ambiguity, substitute *so that* when you are introducing a clause stating a purpose.

Mrs. Williamson asked for the check to be mailed to her mother's home so that her husband could not intercept it.

So may also intensify an adjective or adverb.

So serious was the oversight that, had it not been caught by Ms. Abrahams, it would have cost the company millions of dollars.

The car moved so slowly that it created a traffic hazard.

SOMEBODY

Use *someone* instead in formal legal writing because *somebody* sounds informal. Like *someone*, *somebody* is singular and takes a singular verb.

Somebody claims to have seen defendant elsewhere that night.

SOMEDAY OR *SOME DAY?*

Someday means at *some future time*; *some day* means a *day in the past or the future*.

SOMEONE

Someone is singular and uses a singular verb and a singular pronoun.

If someone needs to contact me, he or she should call this number.

SOMETIME OR *SOME TIME?*

Use *sometime* to refer to an indefinite point in time.

This question will reoccur sometime in the future.

Use *some time* to refer to an indefinite quantity of time.

We need to spend some time identifying all the options we have when the question does arise.

SO WHAT?

You may have encountered this comment on your paper, or you may be feeling it about a point you are trying to make. Most legal readers ask, *So what?* whenever they read legal documents. Those readers have been taught to question each authority, each premise, and each idea. They expect explanations, yet they also expect no extraneous information.

So what? usually indicates that the opposite has occurred: the reader has encountered an idea that is not fully developed or is extraneous. Or it may only seem so because it is inadequately connected to the overall message, to the previous point, or to the next point.

Make *So what?* work for you. Ask yourself that question during prewriting, as you decide what to include; during rewriting, as you decide what is and is not essential to the analysis; and during revising, as you check your expression for accuracy. Answering the question throughout the document will ensure that no one in your audience will have to ask it. See REVISING. For a broader context, see WRITING PROCESS.

SPECIFICITY

See PRECISION.

SPELLING PROBLEMS

See MISSPELLINGS, HOW TO AVOID.

SPLIT INFINITIVES

An infinitive consists of *to* plus the verb. Some readers believe a split infinitive is grammatically incorrect; it no longer is, but avoid splitting an infinitive when writing for readers who may still think it is a grammar error.

to move afterwards

rather than

to afterwards move

On rare occasions, however, a split infinitive will avoid ambiguities.

The mayor agreed to only suggest the alternative if the matter came up in committee meeting.

In this case, putting *only* before *to* would communicate that this was the only thing to which the mayor agreed.

The mayor agreed only . . . .

Putting *only* after *suggest* would communicate that this is the only alternative the mayor would suggest.

suggest only this alternative . . . .

When forced to make a choice like this, choose the clarity of the split infinitive over the elegance of the ambiguous unsplit version. You may often find, however, that you can avoid the problem by restructuring the sentence altogether.

The mayor agreed that she would only suggest the alternative if the matter came up in the committee meeting. She would refrain from requesting it.

This is the safest route; your revised version will offend no one and still avoid ambiguity. If you choose to boldly split with this tradition, consider whether this minor rebellion will cost you CREDIBILITY with your reader, and then decide. For related information, see PRECISION and AMBIGUITY, WAYS TO AVOID.

SQUINTING MODIFIERS

A squinting modifier could be called shifty-eyed, because its gaze shifts indecisively between two different terms. Because it could be modifying either term, it creates ambiguity.

The point the appellant is making logically applies to the Fourth Amendment claim.

Logically, as it is currently placed, could modify either *making* or *applies*. Often the phrase's position creates the ambiguity, and reordering solves the problem.

The point the appellant is making applies logically to the Fourth Amendment claim.

At other times clearer verbal signals may be needed.

The point, which the appellant has logically presented, applies to the Fourth Amendment claim.

STANDARD OF REVIEW

The standard of review is the standard by which appellate courts measure errors made by trial courts on specific legal issues. When writing an appellate brief, make sure you state the standard of review for the issue you are appealing. You can place the discussion of the standard of review at the beginning of each main section, right after the point heading, or weave the standard into your argument. In some jurisdictions, you can use a separate section for the standard of review. The standard of review differs for each legal issue and must therefore be discovered by researching that specific subject matter.

One way to think about standard of review is to see it on a spectrum from most restrictive to least restrictive, as illustrated here.

```
                    gross abuse                    clearly
                    of discretion    de novo       erroneous
most restrictive- - -I- - - -I- - - - - -I- - -I- - - - -I- - - -I-least restrictive
                    arbitrary and                 abuse of          erroneous
                    capricious                    discretion
```

At the left are the standards that give the reviewing court the least amount of leeway when reviewing a decision below. That is, only if they find that the decision below was arbitrary and capricious will they overturn, as in reviewing administrative agency decisions, which are more technical. At the right are the standards that give the most leeway. Under the *de novo* review, the court may review all aspects of the case below, as in constitutional cases that affect rights.

Derive the specific definition of the standard of review for your issues by examining each case in that subject area and determining the exact circumstances under which the court was willing to reverse the trial court. Pay attention to your jurisdiction. In a similar case in another jurisdiction, the appellate court might reverse the lower court only if the lower court *manifestly abused* its discretion.

STARE DECISIS

Stare decisis, which means *to stand by decided matters*, is the legal doctrine that requires similar situations to be treated similarly in common law. For example, if a five-year-old child is found in one case to be incapable of forming intent to commit a tort because of his age, a five-year-old child in another case must similarly be found incapable of forming intent because of his age. This doctrine enables common law to be somewhat predictable.

Stare decisis thus describes a legal concept. It does not, however, replace the need for an explanation of legal reasoning. Thus, when explaining how a line of common law applies to a new case, do not assume that you have supported your case adequately just because you have used the term, as in the following example.

> Under *stare decisis*, this five-year-old child is incapable of forming any intent.

Instead, explain your reasoning fully. For help doing this, see ANALYSIS and REASONING.

Conceptually, *stare decisis* also presents at least two other problems. First, there are rarely exactly similar cases, so the practice of common law is to analogize, which is often the weakest form of argument, according to some. Thus a six-year-old may be similar enough, but a nine-year-old may not. Much of the reasoning in traditional common law focuses on whether or not a new situation is similar enough to an old one to warrant a similar outcome. Second, legal analysis is in the process of pulling away from *stare decisis*, beginning with the legal realism movement in the early twentieth century and continuing through post-modern legal analysis in the early twenty-first century. Courts use *stare decisis* as only one of several ways to analyze a problem, so outcomes are less predictable and more complicated. Lawyers have a greater array of analytical choices now, which allows more possibilities for designing arguments and assisting clients.

STATEMENT OF FACTS

The Statement of Facts is one section in an objective memo or brief. Its purpose is to explain concisely the facts that gave rise to the legal issues, so the Statement of Facts tells the reader why the document exists. It may be placed either after the caption; after the Question Presented and Brief Answer in a memo or the Issue in a brief; or as part of the Introduction to a brief or memo.

1. What to include.

The Statement of Facts must contain all the legally significant facts, those facts that, if changed, would change the outcome of the analysis. The Statement of Facts must also include any background facts or emotional facts needed to orient the reader to the information being analyzed in the memo. The reader should not encounter any new facts in the other parts of the memo.

Generally it is difficult to determine precisely what the Statement of Facts should include until you have finished writing the issues and discussion section. For that reason, either wait to write the Statement until you have completed the analysis or argument or plan to revise your Statement after completing the other parts of the memo. Check to be sure that all the facts you used later in the memo do indeed appear in the Statement of Facts.

Despite this need for completeness, the Statement of Facts should be concise. Thus, after you have checked for completeness, revise the facts again for conciseness. Omit any facts that you now see as unneeded. Beyond those deletions, do not remove content. Instead, use more concise phrasing and reduce lengthy transitions. For ways to do this, see CONCISENESS.

2.   How to organize.

You may organize the facts in any way that assists your analysis or argument. Two common ways people think of organizing facts are chronologically or topically. When the factual sequence is legally significant or when the facts are simple and the issues unified around one area of law, you may organize chronologically. Often, however, chronological is not the best solution.

Many readers prefer topical organization because it often matters little when something occurred, just that it did. Grouping together facts that give rise to specific legal issues allows the reader to plan for the analysis while reading the facts. When the procedural history is complex, you may combine these two organizational patterns, pulling facts into several topical groups of paragraphs and then organizing chronologically within that group. When the events leading to the case occurred at several different locations or involve several distinct concerns, you may group the facts by those locations or concerns and organize chronologically within those groups. If the facts are extremely long and complex, you may even add sub-headings. You can modify a straight topical or chronological organization by adding an opening paragraph that overviews the situation or presents a central event before launching into the strict chronology.

Whatever organization you choose, remember that you are explaining how the client has reached this point and how these issues arose. Remembering this can help you explain or advocate naturally and directly, and the reader will be grateful. For related information, see LEGALLY SIGNIFICANT FACTS, EMOTIONAL FACTS, BACKGROUND FACTS, CHRONOLOGICAL ORGANIZATION, and TOPICAL ORGANIZATION.

STATEMENT OF THE CASE

The Statement of the Case is a section in persuasive legal documents that crafts the facts to make the reader see the common-sense justice in the client's position. The Statement of the Case, or its equivalent, appears in such legal documents as Memoranda of Points and Authorities, pretrial briefs, trial briefs, appellate briefs, and settlement letters. Judges and litigators agree that it is a crucial part of any brief, and some believe it is the most important part. The Statement of the Case should leave the court wanting to find in favor of your client, while the Argument should leave the court believing that such a finding is legally justified. The Statement of the Case is written persuasively and contains legally significant facts, relevant background and emotional facts.

The Statement of the Case needs to be clearly organized without becoming lifeless. Begin by dividing the procedural details from the facts leading to the trial. Then you can prepare your fact statement in three steps.

1. Present the procedure.

You may want to emphasize certain aspects of the procedure. If you represent the Appellant, you may emphasize aspects of the procedure that were in error, perhaps tying in the effect of this error to the outcome. This may work best in a topical organization. If you represent the Respondent, you may want to explain how the procedure worked as it should. Often this works best in a chronological organization, with an air of normalcy and with little particular emphasis. Sometimes you may want to emphasize aspects of the procedure that compensated for the error and made it harmless, if you cannot directly show that no error occurred. Choose the organization that best suits your persuasive goals. In appellate briefs, this section may be quite detailed and may need to be set apart with a separate heading, such as *Procedural History*.

2. Present the facts.

How much you emphasize particular facts leading up to the trial depends on your brief's purpose. If the merits of the case favor your client but some procedural anomalies occurred, then you may want to emphasize the facts so that the judge is less eager to let a procedural technicality upset the judgment. If, however, the facts do not favor your client, you may want to state them more generally, allowing the procedural facts to become the clearer picture in the judge's mind.

Group the facts chronologically if the story is simple or the chronology itself is legally significant or compelling. But you may find it most effective to group the facts topically if the events occurred at several different locations or involve several distinct concerns. Within each group of events, you can then organize chronologically. If the facts are extremely long and complex, you may even add sub-headings.

3. Revise for emphasis.

After your basic organization is in place and you have drafted your Argument, revise the facts for emphasis. This revision will breathe life and drama into your Statement of the Case. After reviewing for completeness and conciseness (for help here, see REWRITING and REVISING.), choose two or three facts that you want to emphasize. These facts should be the ones that you want to stay in the reader's mind throughout his or her reading of your brief, the facts that are most likely to make the reader want to find in favor of your client. When you have chosen these facts, revise your sentence structure to make them stand out in the statement. Rather than emphasizing every fact you can, focus the reader's attention on these key facts. For techniques to achieve this, see EMPHASIS.

When you have restructured these emphasized facts, revise the rest of the statement so that the emphasized facts fit in smoothly and naturally. Build around these facts just as a composer builds music around the dramatic highlights of a symphony. For help doing this, see READABILTIY and SENTENCE STRUCTURE, subsections 6 and 7. For related information, see PERSUASIVE WRITING, LEGALLY SIGNIFICANT FACTS, EMOTIONAL FACTS, BACKGROUND FACTS, CHRONOLOGICAL ORGANIZATION, and TOPICAL ORGANIZATION.

STATISTICS

Whenever you use statistics, be sure they are logically connected to your legal reasoning, are well documented, and advance the point you are making. Do not allow them to distract from your main purpose.

Statistics are most often useful to support an explicit contention. For example, you could support an assertion that a faulty taillight rarely causes injury with statistics on the number of accidents in which a faulty taillight was cited as a cause. To make its significance clear, you would then explain the significance of the statistic to your case. Thus statistics are usually best placed in the middle of a paragraph or paragraph block. Unless their significance is striking and intuitively clear, statistics are not as effective as opening or summary sentences.

Also consider your audience and its particular reaction to statistics, if you can predict it. Statistics stir varied responses in readers. Although some readers revere statistics, others have a reaction similar to that credited to Disraeli: "There are three kinds of lies—lies, damned lies, and statistics." Thus their persuasive power is uncertain. For information related to presenting statistics, see GRAPHICS, WHEN TO USE and GRAPHICS, HOW TO USE.

STATING CONDITIONS

See CONDITIONS, STATING THEM and ON THE CONDITION THAT.

STATUTE DRAFTING

See LEGISLATION.

STRING CITES

See CITATIONS, STRING.

STRUCTURE

See SENTENCE STRUCTURE or ORGANIZATION, LARGE-SCALE.

STUFFY LANGUAGE

See PLAIN ENGLISH, FLOWERY LANGUAGE, and TONE.

STYLE

Style is used to refer to three different concepts:

(1) choices made in writing, including syntax patterns, word choice, verb phrases, usage, methods of presentation, and other choices;

(2) level of objectivity or persuasiveness; and

(3) conformity to or violation of standard rules.

1. Choices made in writing.

Your personal writing style is communicated through the habitual choices you make in your wording, sentence structures, paragraph structures, sentence rhythms, and other structural facets of writing. As clothes reflect your personal tastes, so your written product inevitably reflects your personal level of formality, your choice of tone, and your patterns of organization. For example, you may use active voice, and short sentences for emphasis. You may use long introductory phrases to build the reader's anticipation, or you may use particular sentence rhythms, such as long-long-short-long. To illustrate the effect of style, consider the following three versions of the same opening to a paragraph.

> **Section III(c) is still more illogical and unsound. In devising a new monthly fee for the company, the government arbitrarily assumed that the company included thirty-five minutes each of peak and off-peak air time in its proposed monthly fee access.**

> **Even more surprising is Section III(c). There, the government's new monthly fee plan is based arbitrarily and mistakenly on a false assumption: that the company included thirty-five minutes each of peak and off-peak air time in its proposed monthly fee access.**

> **In devising a "new" monthly fee for the company under Section III(c), the government arbitrarily assumed that the company included thirty-five minutes each of peak and off-peak air time in its proposed monthly fee access, an assumption not based in fact, law, or practice.**

Your personal legal writing style will develop over time. To develop a style you like, study the syntax and writing patterns used by other writers. Keep a list of the kinds of phrases, syntax patterns, word choice, and overall structures that appeal to you and why. Determine which techniques are appropriate in different contexts. Experiment with different techniques as you liberate your legal writing voice. Study, imitate, experiment, and discover. Using your observations, build your own style repertoire.

To actively change your personal style, focus on one aspect or incorporate one new technique at a time until become comfortable with it. Begin with the basics components of style: sentence structure and word choice. As versatility develops with these basics, add other skills. Gradually, these skills will merge into a pattern that is your own style.

Do not, however, become preoccupied with the problem of developing or losing your personal style. Instead, focus on mastering the various aspects of good writing. From this seed of individual mastery, your personal style will blossom naturally and inevitably.

You will need to vary your style according to your document's purpose. You may choose a quiet, standard legal style for form letters or email. You may choose an elaborate style for a short appellate brief, or a blunt style for a trial brief. For a discussion of aspects of writing that frequently influence your style, see WORD CHOICE, POSITIONS OF EMPHASIS, SENTENCE STRUCTURE, TONE, and VERBS, TENSES. For more information on components of style and how to recognize and imitate them, see Chapter 6 of Jill J. Ramsfield, The Law as Architecture: Building Legal Documents (2000).

2.   Level of objectivity or persuasiveness.

Objective and persuasive writing are more like points on a continuum than separate categories. Depending on your audience and your purpose, you will place each document at a different point along this continuum. Legal research memos, for example, are usually written in an objective style. This means that they focus equally on the strengths and weaknesses of any particular argument. The memo's purpose is to provide the reader with all the information he or she needs to make a decision, more than to advocate for a particular decision. In contrast, briefs written to a court are written in a persuasive style. Although these briefs often do address weaknesses in the writer's position, they do so only to explain how those weaknesses do not defeat the writer's purpose, which is to persuade the reader to make a particular decision in favor of the client.

Many documents fall closer to the mid-point of the objective-persuasive continuum. For example, an opinion letter that answers a client's question may explain why one action is preferable to another, but it always fully informs the client of his or her options. The opinion letter finally leaves the decision to the client. Similarly, a Complaint filed with a trial court presents facts rather than making persuasive arguments. Nevertheless, the purpose of the Complaint is to establish to the judge that the Plaintiff does indeed have a claim for which legal relief exists.

For concerns related to objectivity or persuasiveness, see the entry for the particular document you are writing, such as APPELLATE

BRIEFS, BRIEFS, GENERAL CORRESPONDENCE LETTERS AND EMAIL, and PLEADINGS. See also OBJECTIVE WRITING, PERSUASION, TONE IN LETTERS AND EMAIL.

3. Conformity to or violation of standard rules.

Legal writing, or English for Legal Purposes, is generally more formal than other kinds of English. As part of that formality, it is more conservative in its observation of rules, as discussed throughout this book. And it is dangerously unreadable when created without attention to style details. So study the writing within your legal community for patterns, norms, and expectations. Once you have mastered those, experiment with how much you can stretch within those rules, or stretch the rules themselves. For example, a deliberately fashioned sentence fragment may draw attention to a critical point in trial brief. Or a short, thematic sentence may set a dramatic tone in the opening of a Summary of Argument. Contractions may be appropriate in an informal email. Make sure you know the rules before you break them; then break them for calculated and successful effect. For concerns related to standard rules, see BENDING THE RULES for a general discussion. For help with particular rules, see the entry for the relevant topic, such as SEMICOLONS, VERBS, or SUBJECT–VERB AGREEMENT.

SUBHEADINGS

See POINT HEADINGS and HEADINGS.

SUBJECT

See SENTENCE, PARTS OF, subsection 2.

SUBJECT LINE

The subject line offers a good opportunity to make sure your reader gets your message, no matter how hurried the reader may be. This is true whether the subject line appears in an email, a research memo, or a letter. To make the most of this opportunity, phrase your subject line to include the specific essence of your content. For example,

in email, use

Mtg today at 1

rather than

important!

in a research memo, use

H.   Jakobsen Workers' Comp Claim against McGinnis Manufacturing

rather than

Workers' Comp Claim

399

in a letter to a client, use

RE: Proposed estate plan for you and your spouse

rather than

RE: response to your request

SUBJECT–VERB AGREEMENT

Sometimes, when the subject and verb are far apart in a sentence, the writer accidentally uses a plural verb with a singular subject, or a singular verb with a plural subject.

In the interviews, <u>each</u> of the many therapists currently finding their practice restricted by these recent holdings is [not <u>are</u>] less likely to be willing to treat these patients.

If you receive any comments about agreement from your readers, take the comment seriously. Take steps immediately to remedy the problem. Even though it may happen only occasionally, subject-verb agreement is considered a basic language skill in English, and even occasional errors in this area substantially erode the reader's opinion of the writer's ability.

To check your subject-verb agreement, underline the subject and verb in each sentence throughout your document or a section that has been giving you trouble. Then read just those subjects and verbs. You will then expose any agreement problems immediately, and you can fix it. One good way to avoid making these errors is to avoid putting more than seven words between your subject and verb. This will not only help you avoid agreement problems, but will make your writing more readable. See READABILITY, subsection 5.

SUBJECT–VERB COMBINATIONS

Subject-verb combinations help move the legal reader along when they are specific and concrete; they halt the reader when they are vague and abstract. Because the subject and verb are the main part of the sentence, try to place important information in your subjects and verbs; often this information is best expressed by terms of art and key facts. Do not waste subjects and verbs on information that is unimportant to the reader.

        S   V

The <u>show-up I.D. negated</u> the effect of capturing the defendant one block from the crime.

rather than

        S   V

The <u>court stated</u> that the show-up I.D. negated the effect of capturing the defendant one block from the crime.

400

In this example, the legal point is more important than the narration that the court stated it. Use a citation to give that information.

Minimize use of combinations like *it is, there is,* or *there were.* Use nouns instead of those pronouns, specific verbs instead of those verbs of being.

S   V

False imprisonment occurs when a person is restrained without his or her consent.

rather than

S   V

There is false imprisonment when a person is restrained without his or her consent.

For related information, see TERMS OF ART; KEY FACTS, CONCISENESS, subsection 4; and READABILITY, subsection 5.

SUBJUNCTIVE TENSES

See VERBS, MOODS.

SUBORDINATING CONJUNCTIONS

See CONJUNCTIONS and SUBORDINATION.

SUBORDINATION

You are subordinating information when you make one point in a sentence depend structurally on another point.

Although our client did not look both ways immediately before stepping into the street, this fact alone is not enough to constitute contributory negligence.

The writer here subordinates a fact that works against his case by placing it in a dependent clause beginning with *although.* Similarly, the following sentence downplays an unfavorable fact by putting it in a dependent clause beginning with *even though.*

Even though he had not come to a full stop at the stop sign, the defendant had slowed to less than five miles per hour and was not accelerating at the time of the accident.

See also SENTENCE, PARTS OF, subsection 8 and EMPHASIS.

SUBSTANTIVE OR *PROCEDURAL*?

See *PROCEDURAL* OR *SUBSTANTIVE*?

SUCH

Avoid using *such* as an unnecessary adjective, which is sometimes used in arcane legal writing. Substitute *this, that*, or a more detailed description.

This document was signed by three witnesses.

rather than

Such document was signed by three witnesses.

SUMMARY OF THE ARGUMENT

The Summary of the Argument is a separate section used in long briefs to state the gist of the writer's arguments without referring to specific authority. The section appears just before the Argument. The purpose of this section is to pull together the writer's arguments without stopping the flow with references to details of authority. Thus at one glance the reader can understand the writer's argument.

A general guide for writing summaries is to use one paragraph per issue. Make sure you state the Summary of the Argument in your own words, as if you were making an oral presentation, rather than solely quoting. For related information, see PARAPHRASE.

As a process matter, writing a Summary of the Argument can be a good way of getting started. Even if this summary is not included in the final product, it can help you focus issues, answers, and explanations. For related information, see BRIEFS and APPELLATE BRIEFS.

SUPPORT

The legal reader generally does not believe any assertion unless it is backed by authority such as case law, statutes, or regulations. Therefore, support your assertions more thoroughly in legal writing than you might in other situations. In a brief, for example, if you are illustrating why your client should have been able to breach a restrictive covenant, give examples of cases where others have breached a restrictive covenant and show the legal, factual, economic, or policy similarities that explain why the same legal principles should apply in your case.

When stating your rule, show the legal reader that you have stated each rule correctly by including pinpoint cites to the page in a case where the rule is stated. (For help here, see CITATIONS, PINPOINT.) When explaining what a rule means, show that your reasoning is valid by paraphrasing the court's reasoning and again giving pinpoint cites. (For help here, see LEGAL ANALYSIS.) When including a case that you believe is relevant to your client's situation, prove your point by telling the reader the relevant aspects of the precedent case. (For help here, see RULES.) When synthesizing the rule from various sources, make sure the connections among the sources are evident. (For help here, see SYLLOGISMS and SYNTHESIS.) When explaining how that case applies to your client's situation, prove your point by explaining the common qualities or common legal issues your case and the precedent cases share. (For help here, see REASONING.)

Do not expect your reader to fill in the gaps for you. When rewriting, make sure you have not made assertions that are not connected to authority, to your issue, and to each other. For other related information, see REWRITING, REVISING, and PARAGRAPHS.

SYLLOGISMS

A syllogism is a form of deductive reasoning that consists of a major premise, a minor premise, and a conclusion. It moves from general to specific.

Major premise

All men are mortal.

Minor premise

Socrates is a man.

Conclusion

Therefore Socrates is mortal.

Syllogisms in some form are used in legal writing when the analysis proceeds from the general to the specific. The major premise is derived from the law itself, and it states the rule governing the specific situation, such as the general rule that *All men are mortal*. The minor premise expresses the intersection of the rule, *man*, and the facts of the situation, *Socrates*. The conclusion is validly derived when, among other things, the term in common, *men-man*, appears in the first two premises and not the last. In legal writing, the conclusion states the logical outcome of applying the rule to the situation. That conclusion may be a prediction, as in a memo; a holding, as in an opinion; or a request for relief, as in the argument section of a brief.

You may find the syllogism a useful reference for designing your document's structure because you can use it as a device to expose each step in your reasoning. More often, you may find it helpful for reading other documents and trying to test the validity of their reasoning. Your notes may look like this.

Major premise

Delay between the commission of an offense and the initiation of prosecution is a violation of defendant's due process rights.

Minor premise

The conduct of the State is a delay between this defendant's commission of the robbery and the State's initiation of prosecution.

Conclusion

Therefore, the conduct of the State is a violation of defendant's due process rights.

or

Major premise

A party entitled to judgment as a matter of law is a party who can receive a directed verdict.

Minor premise

This party is entitled to judgment as a matter of law.

Conclusion

Therefore, this party is a party who can receive a directed verdict.

Remember that few legal propositions present themselves so neatly. Instead, the premises in legal arguments are often in dispute, so analyze those premises first. And most legal reasoning involves a complex interaction of premises, each of which must be untangled and analyzed, as in the following examples.

First level of reasoning about lack of consent.

Major premise

Entries into a home without evidence establishing consent are entries into a home without consent. [*Not explicitly stated by the court*]

Minor premise

The officers' entry into defendant's home was entry into a home without evidence establishing consent.

Conclusion

Therefore, the officers' entry into defendant's home was entry into a home without consent.

Second level of reasoning about lack of consent renders entry illegal.

Major premise

Entries into a home without consent are illegal entries.

Minor premise

The officers' entry into defendant's home was entry into a home without consent.

Conclusion

Therefore, the officers' entry into defendant's home was an illegal entry.

Third level of reasoning about late consent as unreliable.

404

Major premise

Consents to searches given after illegal entries are consents that are not reliable.

Minor premise

Defendant's consent was consent to search after an illegal entry.

Conclusion

Therefore, defendant's consent was a consent that was not reliable.

Fourth level of reasoning about unreliable consent requires warrant.

Major premise

Searches made pursuant to consents that are not reliable are searches that require warrants.

Minor premise

The officers' search was a search made pursuant to consent that was not reliable.

Conclusion

Therefore, the officers' search was a search that required a warrant.

Fifth level of reasoning about warrantless searches as illegal.

Major premise

Searches that require warrants that are conducted without warrants are illegal searches.

Minor premise

The officers' search was a search that required a warrant conducted without a warrant.

Conclusion

Therefore, the officers' search was an illegal search.

Sixth level of reasoning about evidence from illegal search as inadmissible.

Major premise

Evidence gathered pursuant to an illegal search is evidence that cannot be admitted into court.

Minor premise

The evidence gathered by the officers was evidence gathered pursuant to an illegal search.

Conclusion

Therefore, the evidence gathered by the officers is evidence that cannot be admitted into court.

When reading cases, make sure that you yourself understand the connection among all three parts of the syllogism and the interconnection among the syllogisms. If the connections are faulty, these holes in the reasoning may allow you to distinguish the case from your client's situation; you can then fill the holes according to your own reasoning and perhaps reach a different result.

When writing, make sure your reader understands the connection among the parts of each syllogism and the interconnection of the syllogisms. Make sure that, if you are looking for syllogisms or trying to create them, you account for other types of reasoning, such as inductive reasoning, policy-based reasoning, law and economics arguments, and narratives. For more suggestions on how to build reasoning, see Pierre Schlag and David Skover, Tactics of Legal Reasoning (1986) and Jill J. Ramsfield, The Law as Architecture: Building Legal Documents (2000). For writing techniques that help show the connections, see CONNECTIONS, MAKING THEM. For general help, see LEGAL ANALYSIS, ARGUMENT SECTION, and RULES.

SYMBOLS IN EMAIL

Keep your use of symbols to a minimum in professional email. Resist the urge to use happy faces, sad faces, or any other symbols used to communicate emotions in informal email to friends. Also avoid using any stylistic symbols that may not translate correctly when opened by your reader's email server. For example, tabulations, bullets, italics, and even underlining often create unreadable messages, when they are received by another email system, especially when they occur in attachments. For this reason, keep all formatting simple and minimal in email.

SYNTHESIS

Synthesis describes the putting together of several disparate elements into a whole. This term is often used to refer to the process of common law analysis where several holdings or other components of previous holdings are combined to form a current rule or synthesis of the law. In a strictly common law analysis, this synthesis often appears at the beginning of an analysis in a Discussion or Argument. In statutory analysis, several holdings are often synthesized to define statutory terms. To synthesize accurately, recognize the themes and connections among the components you are synthesizing. Use your own language to demonstrate the connections among the parts so that the reader understands how the pieces make a whole. For related information, see LEGAL ANALYSIS, REASONING, and TRANSITIONS.

TABLES

See GRAPHICS, WHICH FORM TO USE, subsection 5.

TACT

See BAD NEWS, SOFTENING IT; TONE; and TONE IN LETTERS.

TAKING NOTES

See NOTES.

TENSES

See VERBS, TENSES.

TERMS OF ADDRESS FOR COURTS

See JUDGES, HOW TO ADDRESS.

TERMS OF ART

Terms of art are those terms used specifically in the law to describe legal theories, rules, or doctrines. They are the words that carry the most weight in legal writing and the words on which the legal reader focuses. Because of their importance to the legal reader, terms of art should often be used as subjects and verbs in the sentences in which they appear.

> **The Parol Evidence Rule prevents admission of this evidence.**

Terms of art should also be placed at positions of emphasis, such as the beginnings or ends of sentences.

> **Plaintiff brought an action under the theory of res ipsa loquitur.**

> **The police escaped the strict requirements of the search and seizure rule by claiming that they were operating under exigent circumstances.**

> **Washington is one of a minority of states to use the Family Car Doctrine.**

Terms of art should generally be used in the legal questions of questions presented or issue statements. Make sure they are used precisely as intended under the authority specific to them. If you are quoting key language from a statute, you may want to identify that fact by putting the term of art in quotation marks.

> **Under the exigent circumstances exception to the Fourth Amendment, were police in "hot pursuit" when defendant had sold drugs to an undercover officer four hours before the search and had not left the premises?**

Under Washington <u>tort</u> law, can a five-year-old commit an "intentional tort" when he pulls a chair away from an elderly lady who is in the process of sitting down?

Use Latin terms when they are terms of art, such as *res ipsa loquitur*. Do not, however, use them when they can be replaced by plain English. For example, use *before* rather than *a priori*. Similarly, terms such as *hereinafter* or *aforesaid*, are legalese, not terms of art. For related information, see POSITIONS OF EMPHASIS, RULES, LEGALESE, QUESTIONS PRESENTED, and ISSUE STATEMENTS.

TEXT MESSAGING AND INSTANT MESSAGING

Avoid using these systems for business communication. In legal writing, speed can be an enemy as much as a friend. Legal firms have experienced problems caused by faxing offers and other documents back and forth quickly between parties because the lawyers lacked the time they needed to consider all the ramifications of the offer. Young attorneys have lost jobs because they have sent hasty, ill-advised email. Text messaging and instant messaging present the same opportunities for disaster, perhaps offering an even greater risk of saying something that should not be put in writing. For your professional safety, restrict your use of these systems to personal, non-work-related communication. For related information, see VOICE MAIL

THAT NEEDED?

Omit *that* only if doing so will not confuse the reader.

Mr. Salovar agreed he would pay the overtime costs.

or

Mr. Salovar agreed that he would pay the overtime costs.

But retain *that* when needed.

The court decided that the ruling was an abuse of discretion.

rather than

The court decided the ruling was an abuse of discretion.

The confusion occurs when the noun after the verb could be a direct object, as would be true with *the key* in the following sentence.

The prosecution found the key here was the defendant's own admission.

That is needed to avoid the temporary confusion, as an aid to readability.

The prosecution found that the key here was the defendant's own admission.

In the following example, however, *his safety procedures* could not be the direct object of *believed*, so *that* may safely be omitted.

The defendant believed his safety procedures were adequate.

For related concerns, see *THAT* OR *WHICH?*

THAT **OR** *WHICH?*

In legal writing, especially legal drafting, it is useful to maintain a distinction between *that* and *which*. This remains true even though many writers in other fields do not bother to use these terms carefully.

1.   Use *that* when you are adding a phrase to narrow the range of items covered by a word.

All cars that remain in the lot after 10 p.m. will be towed.

[R]emain in the lot after 10 p.m. narrows the range of cars under discussion, so *that* should introduce the phrase. Do not put commas before or after this narrowing phrase, called a *restrictive phrase*. This punctuation rule is important because even general writing still observes this distinction.

2.   Use *which* when you are adding a phrase that does not limit the range of items covered by the word it modifies, called a *nonrestrictive phrase*.

Your car, which was still in the lot at midnight, was towed.

The range included in *your* car is not limited by the following phrase, so *which* is the correct word to begin the phrase. Put commas both before and after a *which* phrase. The commas work like parentheses, showing that the phrase could be lifted from the sentence without changing the essential meaning. Another way to think about the distinction is that if you need commas, use *which*; if you do not need commas, use *that*.

3.   For ACCURACY, use both commas and *which* to distinguish nonlimiting phrases from limiting ones. If you do not, your sentences may suffer from AMBIGUITY.

The taxes, which have been paid, should not appear on this statement.

or

The taxes that have been paid should not appear on this statement.

rather than

The taxes which have been paid should not appear on this statement.

In the first version, all the taxes have been paid. In the second, some of the taxes have been paid. In the last version, however, you are not sure if all or part of the taxes have been paid.

4.   *Which* can be substituted for *that* when two *that's* appear in a row.

That which is good is not always pleasant; that which is pleasant is not always good.

rather than

That that is good is not always pleasant; that that is pleasant is not always good.

When possible, however, revise to avoid *that which*, which is rather awkward to read.

THE

Do not omit *the*, *a*, or *an* solely to gain conciseness.

The owner of the car gave the keys to Hendricks, who was supposed to move the car to a legal parking spot.

rather than

Owner of car gave keys to Hendricks, who was supposed to move car to legal parking spot.

Omitting these articles will give the text an abrupt tone, like a telegram, and will decrease the text's READABILITY.

THEIRS OR *THEIR'S?*

Theirs, always.

THEME

The theme of your document is the message you intend to convey. It is the document's essence, the idea unique to that document. It should tell your reader the *what* and *why* he needs to know.

Laffon violated Barker's moral right because he altered the sculpture so significantly that any reasonable viewer would misinterpret Barker's original message.

Current ethics rules are inadequate to handle conflicts that arise in public interest practice.

The democratization of Taiwan has forced the Nationalist Party and the Chinese Communist party to leave the zero-sum game of dominance in order to explore other options that benefit all parties.

Usually you can state the theme in one sentence, although you need not include that exact sentence in your document. If you cannot contain it in one sentence, you may have too many sub-themes instead of one overarching message. In memos, the theme is usually in the brief answer; in briefs, it is in the opening paragraph or Summary of Argument; in email or letters, it is usually in the opening paragraph.

Draft the theme to assist yourself in getting started on your draft; the theme is sometimes clearer before you research or draft. Adjust the theme as you work on your issues and Questions Presented; there the theme emerges as you match question and answer. Finally, use the theme to test your document's coherence. Write the theme and make sure it is the message you wish to convey. As you rewrite and revise, note where you state the theme and sub-themes and how you relate them to each other. Alter the theme if you need to do so to unify the document. For related information, see ISSUES, QUESTIONS PRESENTED, and SCHOLARLY WRITING.

THEREBY

Avoid using this term unnecessarily because it is legalese.

The judge sentenced the defendant to seven years, and so closed the case.

rather than

The judge sentenced the defendant to seven years, thereby closing the case.

For related information, see LEGALESE.

THERE IS OR *THERE ARE?*

The answer to this question depends on the word that follows the verb, the PREDICATE adjective. If it is plural, use *are*.

There are <u>twelve members</u> on each jury in this state.

If it is singular, use *is*.

There is <u>one alternative</u> we have not yet discussed.

Sometimes the choice is not so obvious with more abstract nouns. For example, either of the following sentences is correct.

There are <u>precedents</u> for this line of reasoning, although they address different factual situations.

or

There is <u>precedent</u> for this line of reasoning, although the cases establishing this precedent address different factual situations.

If you use this phrase frequently, consider more concise alternatives. For more on this, see SUBJECT–VERB COMBINATIONS. For related information, see SINGULAR OR PLURAL? and NONE, SINGULAR OR PLURAL?

THERE ARE ... THAT

See THERE IS ... THAT.

411

THERE IS ... THAT

Omitting this phrase when you can do so creates a more concise sentence.

No cases address this issue directly.

rather than

There are no cases that address this issue directly.

Similarly, revise to omit *it is ... that* and *there are ... that*. For more examples, see CONCISENESS, subsection 10.

THEY OR *HE OR SHE*?

When choosing between the plural or singular form, first determine whether one of the two forms is required for ACCURACY.

If a member chooses to go forward with a grievance, he or she must explain that grievance in writing.

rather than

If members choose to go forward with a grievance, they must explain that grievance in writing.

The second version could be read to exclude an individual from bringing a grievance, and so would be unclear.

If accuracy does not limit you, you may use the plural form to avoid using *he or she* too much.

The members had the opportunity to air their concerns at the November meeting.

Whichever number you choose, use it consistently throughout the text. For related information, see SINGULAR OR PLURAL?

THIS

This frequently creates ambiguity because it can refer to any idea or object and because it often starts a sentence. To avoid ambiguity, add the noun after *this* when it begins a sentence.

You must ultimately make a judgment about the weight of the evidence. This judgment will help you decide what the verdict should be.

rather than

You must ultimately make a judgment about the weight of the evidence. This will help you decide what the verdict should be.

In the second version, it is not clear whether *this* refers to *judgment* or *evidence*. For related information, see AMBIGUITY, WAYS TO AVOID, subsection 2.

THOUGH OR *ALTHOUGH*?

See *ALTHOUGH* OR *THOUGH*?

TIME MANAGEMENT

Writing well often involves managing your time, particularly when you have several projects to finish. For many writers, if the load becomes unmanageable, it often reduces the quality of personal life. But when you develop a more efficient approach to time management that is realistic given your own writing process, then you can enhance your ability to meet professional demands without sacrificing personal life. To increase your writing efficiency and effectiveness, follow three important rules:

(1) compartmentalize,

(2) concentrate, and

(3) condense.

1. Compartmentalize.

Pull together similar tasks, such as researching several short projects, drafting your email, or polishing outgoing documents. As much as you can, do similar tasks in one block of time. For example, set aside time for reading email and responding and filing them, rather than reading them any time they come in. Allocate some time periodically throughout your day to check email, so you respond quickly enough, but avoid allowing email to consume too much of your time. Allow enough time to sort them, respond in priority, and file attachments or the email itself. Then set aside a different compartment for drafting the Argument of a brief, holding meetings, and so on. This approach eliminates unnecessary changeover time, and your mind can remain focused on each type of task.

2. Concentrate.

Having compartmentalized tasks, devote all of your attention to the compartment in front of you. You should find that your mind works more easily and quickly when you give it only one type of task at a time.

3. Condense.

After you have created compartments and increased your concentration, try to decrease the quantity of time you spend without jeopardizing the quality of the product. Unmonitored researching or writing will expand to fill any amount of time available. Sometimes changing the medium will help; you might dictate letters rather than write them by hand, or revise on paper rather than on the screen. Conversely, you may find that your first draft is more concise and organized if you write the theme and sub-themes by hand. Become more alert to ways that increase speed without causing unnecessary stress. When reviewing email, scan the names and subject lines to determine which mail to open when. When time is short, perform triage; open important email and leave others to be opened later.

When you have taken command of these three tasks, you can then move on to improve your overall approach to managing your time. For example, you may want to add some of the following goals to your list.

4. Write down directions.

If you have had trouble understanding what is wanted of you, try writing directions down when you receive them. Then, if you have a question, you can refer to your notes rather than contacting your supervisor or retracing your steps. Take your laptop with you to meetings and initial assignment discussions. Similarly, if you give directions, send them by email. Then, when you are busy, the person to whom the task has been delegated can continue to work without having to interrupt you. Writing precise directions can save hours of volleying between attorneys. It also saves start-up time reminding yourself where you should be going on the project.

5. Touch each document or email only once.

Try to avoid shuffling documents too much. When dealing with email, try to sort it as you read: delete, save in a separate file, respond now. If you must, save any email that needs a complex response for another compartment of time. When reading your email, then, you can address these in that triage. Use your hard drive to store documents in subdirectories and files, which may make finding them faster and easier.

When dealing with the miscellaneous papers that cross your desk, decide what to do with each and avoid letting them pile up. That way, you will not feel overwhelmed by the sight of more paper adding to the papers you are producing. For example, as you read each day's paper mail, try to discard on the spot what you can, dictate or write needed responses, and take action or give directions for the action to others. Try to give each paper a home by filing it immediately, marking a deadline on it, or forwarding it to the person who should take action.

6. Say *no*.

Know your own capacity as a researcher and writer, and try to decline projects that will overwhelm you or interfere with the quality of other projects. If you are under particular pressure from a supervisor, choose a gentle way to say *no* or set aside time to meet with that person in the future to discuss reasonable workload. See SAYING *NO* for specific suggestions.

7. Delegate whenever you can.

Ask others to do tasks that they can, and save your time for matters only you can do. This can be a hard adjustment to make, especially if you are used to doing everything for yourself. For ways to do this, see EDITING and MANAGING WRITERS.

8. Percolate, don't procrastinate.

Rather than putting a project aside when you receive it, try to begin immediately, even if you are only collecting the ingredients and turning on some energy. Take a few minutes to gather facts, hypothesize some issues, and note a possible research strategy. Write it down, so you will not wonder later what that inspiration was. Then stop; leave those ideas while you work on another compartment. Percolating usually allows your mind to create better ideas than doing the project all at once does. In fact, it is often necessary to good legal analysis because it allows time for your ideas to steep. See PROCRASTINATION and PERFECTIONISM.

9. Use the calendar and the clock.

Know your major deadlines and pace yourself accordingly. Use the clock as a helpful friend who reminds you when the mind is wandering unnecessarily, when the meeting you are conducting is going too long, or when you are tempted to research longer than you should. Writing tasks often take longer than you anticipate, so set a realistic ending time before you begin.

10. Choreograph your day.

Use your high energy times for the most critical tasks or those you like least; use your low energy times for the least critical or those you like most. When your energy wanes, answer calls, hold meetings, or do other activities that will keep you awake. Then your day will become more even, rather than clustered around least favorite and most favorite moments.

Although you may see many changes you want to make in managing your writing time, implement changes gradually. This minimizes upset to either your own balance or that of your associates. You might start by changing your approach to one major writing project or by trying one new technique for a period. At the end of that project or period, assess the success of the change and revise your writing process as needed. If the change worked, try it next on two projects at once. Gradually, you can fold your new techniques into your schedule, and give yourself a year or more to transform yourself into an efficient and effective writer.

TITLES OF JUDGES

See JUDGES, HOW TO ADDRESS.

TO ALL INTENTS AND PURPOSES

Find a shorter way to say this idea or omit the phrase. If the sentence needs something more, try to find one word that makes your point.

Therefore my client is innocent.

rather than

To all intents and purposes, my client is innocent.

TO BE

To be, in its various forms, communicates a continuing state of being. When used appropriately, this verb does not add unnecessary words to the language. Additionally, the past tense of *was* is also a useful linking verb and is not in itself PASSIVE VOICE. Therefore do not try to avoid using *was, were, are*, or *is*; instead avoid their overuse. *To be* has three main uses: (1) as a linking verb, (2) as a helping verb, and (3) as a statement of existence.

1. As a linking verb.

This is its most recognized use, where it often is the only verb in the sentence.

Strict interpretation of this statute <u>is</u> essential to the preservation of this doctrine.

The problem with using this and other linking verbs is that they create a sentence without action. When used frequently, the writing itself stagnates and becomes uninteresting to read. To avoid this problem, use action verbs whenever it is logical to do so.

The motor stalled immediately after the plaintiff engaged the gear.

rather than

The motor was immediately inoperable after the driver engaged the gear.

2. As a helping verb.

Used as a helping verb with the *-ing* form of another verb, a form of *to be* shows that an action occurred over a period of time.

The witness <u>was</u> operating a lawn mower at the time he reported hearing the scream.

Often this communication of relative time is legally significant. This use of *to be* is needed, not wordy; it is also past progressive tense, not passive voice, so you need not avoid it for that reason.

To be does create the passive voice, however, when used as a helping verb with the *-ed* past participle form of the main verb.

The lawn mower <u>was</u> operated by the witness.

Passive voice is harder to understand and requires more words, so use it only when it is needed. For more on this, see PASSIVE VOICE.

3. As a statement of being.

This is the use seen least in legal writing.

She <u>is</u>.

It may occasionally be useful, however, for EMPHASIS in PERSUASIVE WRITING.

The witness has repeatedly testified that, since the attack, she is terrified by sudden noises. She is.

For related information, see VERBS, TENSES.

TONE

Tone communicates the writer's point of view or attitude toward the reader and the subject matter. Choose a tone appropriate for the medium, such as objective for office memos, persuasive for briefs, friendly for informative client letters, or stern for tough settlement letters. Then choose words and sentence structures to convey that tone.

Tone is established and conveyed through attention to details of word choice and sentence structure. As the following subsections explain, you can convey tone through

(1) word choice

(a) by choosing the appropriate subjects, verbs, and modifiers;

(b) by choosing appropriate terms of address;

(c) by choosing words that have the appropriate emotional overtone and level of formality;

and through

(2) sentence structure

(a) by making effective use of active and passive voice and positions of emphasis, and

(b) by choosing appropriate sentence length, subject–verb combinations, and various kinds of sentence structure.

1. Conveying tone through word choice.

(a) Choose appropriate subjects, verbs, and modifiers.

For example, in memos, when you want to convey an objective and businesslike tone, use terms of art as subjects and verbs to keep the text focused on the issue being analyzed rather than the people involved.

The Family Car Doctrine holds parents liable for their child's negligence.

Keep modifiers to a minimum, and then use only factual, specific information. This creates a businesslike, unemotional tone.

Jamison grasped Hendricks by the arm and led him to the door.

rather than

Jamison rudely grasped the unfortunate Hendricks by the left arm and inexorably led him slowly to the battered wooden door.

For related information, see MODIFIERS and TERMS OF ART.

In briefs, when you want to convey a persuasive and more assertive tone, retain terms of art as subjects and verbs to help the reader focus on your point. But also use stronger subjects and verbs when stating favorable facts, that is, subjects and verbs that give the reader a vivid picture of those facts.

Jamison grasped Hendricks left arm and pulled him slowly toward the door.

When stating unfavorable facts, use weaker, more abstract subjects and verbs.

The defendant then took Hendricks by the arm and moved to the door.

Also use modifiers with subtle emotional connotations that favor your position.

Muttering threats, Jamison grasped Hendrick's bruised arm and pulled him toward the door.

But do not overdo, or you may hamper your credibility. For more specific information, see PERSUASIVE WRITING.

(b) Choose the appropriate terms of address.

In a memo or brief, you want to avoid terms of address that refer to yourself or the reader because the focus should be on the legal issues and the parties rather than on the attorneys or judges.

Granting a summary judgment is not justifiable in this case.

rather than

You must not grant a summary judgment because we think these facts preclude it.

In an email or letter to a client, however, you will often want to refer to yourself and the reader because you are indeed speaking as one person to another.

At our meeting on Tuesday, April 11, you asked me to give you a legal opinion on whether . . . .

rather than

In response to the request made on Tuesday, April 11, for an opinion on whether . . . .

If you avoid all personal references in email and letters, you create a distant, cold tone. You may want to use this cold tone occasionally, as in a tough settlement letter, but it is not wise to use it with your current clients. For related information, see TOUGH, SOUNDING THAT WAY and TONE IN LETTERS.

(c) Choose the appropriate level of formality.

In general, use more formal language in official documents, such as briefs or opinion letters, because you want to sound respectful and serious. Use less formal language in other writing, such as memos or general correspondence letters, where you want to be readable and avoid being stuffy. Be careful of becoming too informal in email. For example, you might say the following in a conference with another attorney.

Helen Thomas bought her computer at the local Apex store.

But you might write it this way in a brief,

Ms. Thomas purchased her computer at Apex Computers, located at 417 Cherry Street.

or this way in an email.

You bought your computer at your neighborhood store.

Avoid creating a stuffy tone by using overly formal language, especially when describing everyday concepts.

the trash truck

rather than

the refuse management vehicle

2. Conveying tone through SENTENCE LENGTH and structure.

(a) For a clipped, no-nonsense tone, use shorter sentences.

My client, Ms. Ambrose, does not intend to pay this bill. She has no reason to pay this bill. She did not receive any software from your company. She did not order any software from your company. Until receiving your bill, she did not know your company existed.

(b) For a more conversational tone, use longer sentences with the subject and verb near the beginning of the sentence.

You asked me to research the possibility of recovering part or all of your down payment on a stereo you later decided not to purchase.

rather than

In our phone conversation, you stated that, after some consideration, you wanted to recover....

or

You asked me to research a question for you. Specifically, you want to know if you can recover part or all of a down payment. The down payment was made for....

For more information, see the entry for the specific kind of document you are writing.

(c) For a more formal tone, use some interrupting phrases in your sentence structure.

Anorexics, <u>by failing to eat,</u> passively expose themselves to harm.

This sentence structure is harder to read because to understand the main point the reader must remember the first part of the sentence, read the interrupting clause, and then reunite the last part of the sentence with the first in his or her memory. Therefore avoid using it in sentence after sentence; give the reader breathing space between these difficult sentences. Finally, do not allow the interruption to exceed seven words. After a longer interruption, the reader would have to reread the sentence to understand the point.

For related information, see TONE IN LETTERS; OBJECTIVE WRITING; and PERSUASIVE WRITING.

TONE IN LETTERS AND EMAIL

Tone is especially important in letters and email. As the tone of your voice creates an impression in the mind of the listener, so the tone of your correspondence creates an impression in the mind of the reader. Thus, although your tone may range from friendly to tough, it should always be within the limits of temperate, businesslike communication. A chatty tone will seem slightly unprofessional in all but purely personal email and letters. A tirade will also seem unprofessional, even in the toughest collection letter. A careless tone, even in an email, will send the message that the reader is not important. Within these limits, however, you must make your own choices, based on what is appropriate to the situation and what suits your personal communicating style.

Using tone effectively in letters and email involves three tasks:

(1) choosing the appropriate tone,

(2) creating that tone through word choice and sentence structure, and

(3) keeping the tone consistent.

1. Choosing the appropriate tone.

Before you begin writing, consider your relationship to the reader. For example, if your reader is a judge or your supervisor at work, you will probably want to use a tone that is both businesslike and respectful. This means that you will state your points as concisely as possible but will not omit appropriate opening and closing sentences, such as the following closing to an email requesting a favor.

Thank you for your help in this matter.

If your reader is a client or colleague, you may choose to be polite and businesslike or, if appropriate, you may choose a friendly tone.

Please call if you have any further questions.

Or even

I am looking forward to our next tennis match.

If your reader is your client's opponent or a client who has not paid you for three months, you may sometimes choose a tough, businesslike tone.

Please pay this bill promptly.

or

I trust this settles the matter.

2. Creating the appropriate tone through word choice and sentence structure.

Choosing your words carefully is one effective way to establish your tone. For example, if you want to create an informal and friendly tone, use less formal words, such as *talk* and *meeting*. If you want to create a more formal tone, use more formal words, such as *confer* and *discussion*. Avoid, however, using formal words to the point that your letter becomes hard to read or stuffy.

Regarding this question, I have conferred with Ms. Jamison's attorney, who explained that . . . .

rather than

In pursuit of this query, I have held consultations with counsel for Ms. Jamison, who elucidated the point by stating that . . . .

Another way to avoid a stuffy tone is to avoid inappropriately using the third person, such as *this attorney*, when the first person, *I*, is accurate. In general, email and letters are addressed from one person to another, and so the use of *I* is appropriate, or *we* if you are speaking officially for a group of people, such as a whole law firm.

You may also establish your tone by using appropriate sentence structure. For example, if you want to create a friendly, informal tone, use longer sentences rather than terse ones.

Thank you for your kind invitation to speak at your annual banquet honoring outstanding alumni from the law school.

rather than

Thank you for the invitation to speak at the law school alumni banquet.

Conversely, if you want to create a tough, no-nonsense tone, use short, rather choppy sentences.

> **My client, Ms. Ambrose, does not intend to pay this bill. She has no reason to pay you. She did not receive any software from your company. She did not order any software from your company. Until receiving your bill, she did not know your company existed.**

rather than

> My client, Ms. Ambrose, does not intend to pay this bill because she has no reason to do so. She did not receive or order any software from your company, and in fact did not know your company existed until receiving your bill.

3. Keeping the tone consistent.

Inconsistent tone occurs most often when an email or letter includes words that are noticeably more formal or informal than the rest of a letter. For example, a writer may use a formal phrase, such as *please be advised that*, in an otherwise informal letter. Or a writer may use a colloquialism, such as *ripped off*, in an otherwise businesslike letter.

Uneven tone also sometimes occurs when sentence structure changes markedly. For example, a reader might be taken aback by a series of three SHORT SENTENCES near the end of an otherwise friendly email. Similarly, a reader might be put off by a long, complex sentence in an otherwise informal email. Therefore revise your email and letters just for consistent tone.

For more help in choosing the appropriate tone, see the following more specific entries: GENERAL CORRESPONDENCE LETTERS; REQUESTS FOR PAYMENT; or TOUGH, SOUNDING THAT WAY. For related information, see WORD CHOICE and SENTENCE STRUCTURE.

TOPICAL ORGANIZATION

Topical organization refers to organizing the facts or the analysis by legal topic. In a memo, topical organization can be used in the Statement of Facts, the Discussion, or both. In a brief, it can be used in the Statement of the Case, the Argument, or both. For example, when an appellate brief contains both procedural and substantive issues, under topical organization the procedural and substantive facts would be presented separately. The Argument would then follow the same large-scale organization.

Use topical organization when the chronology of events is not as important as the legal character of the events themselves. For example, when a memo discusses two issues, such as one on *the Family Car Doctrine* and another on the *definition of a minor child under the wrongful death statute*, following the chronology of events would not be as important as organizing the events into two groups: those to which the Family Car Doctrine applies and those to which the wrongful death statute applies. To make this topical organization clear to the reader in longer descriptions, you may separate the topics by subheadings.

In contrast, see CHRONOLOGICAL ORGANIZATION. For related information, see ORGANIZATION, LARGE–SCALE; and REWRITING.

TOPIC SENTENCES

Topic sentences, or thesis sentences, deserve particular attention in legal writing because they convey the main points of paragraphs. Topic sentences are most effective at positions of emphasis. For example, use a topic sentence at the beginning of a paragraph to state the conclusion the paragraph supports. Alternatively, use it to create a question in the reader's mind and then explain the answer in the body of the paragraph. Thus the topic sentence sets up an expectation that the body of the paragraph fulfills.

Although the 1969 Act eased the singles penalty, it did so at the expense of married couples.

The questioning legal reader will ask, "Okay, so how exactly did the Act disadvantage married couples?" If this is the point the paragraph explains, the topic sentence has prepared the reader for the paragraph's content. Or use a topic sentence at the end of a paragraph to summarize or conclude; remember, however, that busy legal readers may skip the end or get impatient about any suspense created by waiting for the point.

For related information, see POSITIONS OF EMPHASIS and PARAGRAPHS.

TOTALLY

See COMPLETELY.

TOUGH, SOUNDING THAT WAY

Try the following techniques to sound tough.

1. Use shorter sentences, perhaps several in a row.

    This creates a clipped, no-nonsense tone.

    My client, Ms. Ambrose, does not intend to pay this bill. She has no reason to pay you. She did not receive any software from your company. She did not order any software from your company. Until receiving your bill, she did not know your company existed.

2. Use objective language.

    If you use emotional words (*unabashedly, horrendous, outrageous*), you will sound angry, but not tough. Tough people stay in control.

Persuade with careful use of POSITIONS OF EMPHASIS and SENTENCE STRUCTURE.

3.   If appropriate, explain the options the reader has and the results of those options.

This puts the responsibility clearly in the reader's lap. If the reader is at all inclined to feel guilty, this explanation makes the reader squirm. If the reader has no sense of guilt, the explanation will still make your position clear, so you have lost nothing.

4.   Never threaten idly.

The people with whom you most likely need to get tough are often those people who have heard many threats in their lives and have learned to ignore them. They may be experienced enough, however, to recognize a genuine threat that is well-presented. For related information, see LETTERS; GENERAL CORRESPONDENCE LETTERS; SETTLEMENT LETTERS; BAD NEWS, GIVING IT; and TONE IN LETTERS.

TRANSITIONS

One way to communicate the logical connection between two points is to use headings, sentences, phrases, or words. These devices signal the relationship between the content of one section, paragraph, or sentence to the next. To make these connections clear, choose accurate, exact transitions that reveal the nature of the connection. Use repetition of key words and parallel structure to convey the connection.

Use this technique in headings between sections.

I.   POLICE VIOLATED DEFENDANT'S FOURTH AMENDMENT RIGHTS FIRST WHEN THEY ENTERED HER HOME WITHOUT A WARRANT.

and

II.   POLICE VIOLATED DEFENDANT'S FOURTH AMENDMENT RIGHTS AGAIN WHEN THEY SEIZED EVIDENCE THAT WAS NOT IN PLAIN VIEW.

Use it to connect paragraphs with strong topic sentences.

Plaintiff was a holder in due course because she took the check in good faith.

and

As a holder in due course, Plaintiff is now entitled to the value of the check.

Use it to connect sentences within a paragraph.

Plaintiff was a holder in due course because she took the check in good faith. This good faith was evident in ....

424

When using transitional words between paragraphs or sentences, you may find that you use only one or two transition words most of the time, perhaps repeating one word three or four times on a page. This overuse can signal several problems. Sometimes, overuse of one transition signals organization problems. For example, if you use *however* frequently, check to see if you are combining points that could better be presented in separate paragraphs. Other times, overuse of one transition may mean that you are using the word out of habit rather than out of conscious choice. If so, some other word will probably be more precise. For example, *similarly* may be more precise for a comparison than *additionally*. To help you choose the most accurate transition quickly, consult the following list of transitions grouped by their logical functions.

1. Signaling similarity.

   - *similarly*
   - *analogously*
   - *as*
   - *accordingly*

2. Signaling contrast.

   - *not ... but, not only ... but also*
   - *but*
   - *in contrast, conversely, on the contrary,*
   - *however*
   - *nevertheless*
   - *on the one hand ... on the other hand*
   - *while, yet*

3. Introducing conditions

   - *although, even though, though*
   - *if, only if, but only if*
   - *provided that, unless,*
   - *when, whenever*
   - *while*
   - *whereas*

4. Introducing results.

   - *if ... , then; when ... , then;*
   - *accordingly, consequently*
   - *therefore, thus*
   - *as a result, hence*

- *so, so that*

5. Introducing reasons for a result.
    - *because*
    - *if*

6. Introducing examples or explanations.
    - *as if, as though*
    - *for example*
    - *specifically*
    - *namely*
    - *that is*
    - *such as*
    - *including, including but not limited to*
    - *i.e.*

7. Signaling a list.
    - *first, second, third, etc.*
    - *both … and*
    - *either … or, neither … nor;*
    - *and, also, additionally*
    - *furthermore*
    - *or, nor*
    - *last, finally, in conclusion*

8. Showing time relationships.
    - *after, afterward, later, once,*
    - *during, while, meanwhile, concurrently, at the same time*
    - *as, as long as, simultaneously,*
    - *before, earlier, since*
    - *then, until,*
    - *when, whenever*
    - *now*

9. Showing relationship of place
    - *where*
    - *wherever*
    - *near, nearby*
    - *beside, behind, before, in front of*

10. Summarizing
- *finally*
- *in conclusion*
- *in summary*

For other ways to make transitions, see CONNECTIONS, MAKING THEM.

TRIAGE

Borrowed from the medical field, *triage* describes an approach that is useful in writing emergencies as well as medical ones. When you find yourself with inadequate time to finish a document to the quality level you want, it is time to practice *triage*. To do this, create a comfortable system. For example, you can quickly write out a list of all the tasks remaining to finish the document to the quality you desire. Then determine why each task is needed. If the task is needed for ACCURACY or to make the document legally and functionally sufficient, label it with an *A*. If the task is needed to make the document more readable or easier to use by the reader, label it with an *R*. If the task is needed to add professional polish or for any reason other than those previously listed, label it with a *P*.

Then complete all the tasks labeled with an *A*. These must be completed before the document leaves your hands. When those are finished, begin working on the tasks labeled *R*. When those tasks are completed and if any time remains, begin working on the tasks labeled *P*. While this triage may not result in a perfect document, it is likely to give you the best results you can achieve given the time you have. More important, it is likely to prevent you from omitting any tasks that are necessary to avoid serious problems.

TRIAL BRIEFS

Trial briefs are usually filed with the court before the trial begins. They inform the trial court of counsel's theory of the case by presenting the applicable rules and the arguments constructed from the rules as they are applied to the facts. A trial brief should indicate what is to be proved, how it is to be proved, and what the outcome of the case should be. Each side files a trial brief so that the court has an idea of the structure of the trial before it begins. Except under extraordinary circumstances, both sides exchange trial briefs.

Check your jurisdiction for the specific requirements for format of a trial brief; in particular, consider your audience; if possible, check with someone who knows that judge. For the usual format for a trial brief, see BRIEFS.

A trial brief is a persuasive document that needs to convey the facts, issues, and arguments in a way that is factually accurate while still conveying a sense that your client's position is just. To accomplish this, see entries for the parts of the trial brief: ISSUE STATEMENTS, STATEMENT OF THE CASE, POINT HEADINGS, ARGUMENT SECTION, and CONCLUSION. Also see the general topics that are especially important in trial briefs: AUDIENCE, PERSUASIVE WRITING, LEGAL ANALYSIS, CITATIONS, and FORMAT.

UNCLEAR MEANING

This comment could be triggered by problems in any of several areas. For help, see MODIFIERS, DANGLING; PRECISION; and AMBIGUITY, WAYS TO AVOID.

UNDERLINING

Underlining has four specific uses in legal writing:

(1) to add emphasis to terms or phrases in quotes,

(2) to identify case names and components of a legal record, and

(3) to identify foreign words or phrases.

To avoid confusion,

(4) underlining should not be used solely to recreate the emphasis a word would be given in speech.

1. Adding emphasis to terms and phrases in quotations.

Underline to add emphasis to important terms in quotes, such as in a rule or holding. When you underline part of a quote, add (*emphasis added*) after the citation following the quote.

> **As this court itself has stated, "[T]he court must intervene because the issue of mutuality, not to mention that of duress, requires that the court examine <u>the parol evidence surrounding the signing</u> of the contract." <u>Durant v. Colt</u>, 945 F. Supp. 641 (D.D.C. 2006) (emphasis added).**

Similarly, underline to add emphasis to the key phrase in quotations long enough to be indented and single-spaced in the text. Underlining may encourage the legal reader to read the quote by making the single spacing more palatable. When you underline, add (*emphasis added*) after the citation on the first line of text following the indented quote, not within the indented quote itself. The phrase (*emphasis added*) within a quote would signal that that phrase was present in the original quote.

> **The court in this case addressed the issue of mutuality.**

> > **Despite the defendant's emotional plea regarding the centrality of upholding contracts to the free working of a democracy, we cannot ignore the plaintiff's complaint. In this case, the court must intervene because <u>the issue of mutuality</u>, not to mention that of duress, <u>requires that the court examine both the contract's word-</u>**

ing and the parol evidence surrounding the signing of that contract.

Holmes v. Cardozo, 945 F. Supp. 498 (D.D.C. 2007) (emphasis added).

2. Identifying case names and components of a legal record.

Underline cases in citations in text. Do not underline the comma.

Peabody v. Hart, 958 F.3d 391 (7th Cir. 2007).

Underline references to the record, if your jurisdiction so requires. Check for local practice about whether or not to underline the period.

Defendant failed to use his turn signal. Tr. 17.

3. Identifying foreign words or phrases.

Underline phrases from other languages if they are not commonly incorporated into English. Often, however, the phrase you use will have been incorporated, such as Latin phrases that are terms of art.

The court appointed a guardian ad litem.

but

In France, this right is known as the droit moral.

4. Not underlining to replace the emphasis of speech.

Do not use underlining to replace the emphasis you would give a word when speaking. This use of underlining is acceptable in casual writing, such as in an email to a friend or an informal memo to a coworker, but it is less effective in briefs or research memos for several reasons. First, the use of underlining can be confusing. Often the legal reader's first reaction to underlining is to assume you are highlighting a quote or indicating one of the other four specific uses of underlining in legal writing. Second, legal readers may think you are resorting to the obvious, which can make you seem less in control of the text. To avoid this problem, use positions of emphasis and sentence structure techniques instead of underlining. For ways to do this, see EMPHASIS. For related information, see QUOTATIONS, HOW TO PUNCTUATE and CITATIONS.

UNDERSTANDABILITY

See CLARITY and READABILITY.

UNDOUBTEDLY

Avoid the term. The point is probably not undoubted by all legal readers. If it is, you do not need to tell the reader this. If you must use *undoubtedly*, do not spell it *undoubtably*. See MODIFIERS.

UNINTERESTED **OR** *DISINTERESTED?*

See *DISINTERESTED* OR *UNINTERESTED?*

UNIQUE

Unique means that the item or idea referred to is the only one of its kind, or without an equivalent. *Unique* is not preceded by qualifying adverbs. For example, do not say *the most unique* or *rather unique* or *somewhat unique*. If it is unique, it is *unique*.

UNITY

See COHERENCE.

UNLESS

Use *unless* with care because it is easily misread. *Unless* is actually a negative, like *not* or *no*, but often readers do not realize this. As a result, readers may miss the negative and think the *unless* phrase means the opposite of what the writer intended. To avoid this ambiguity, substitute another word for *unless* when possible.

Come to the hearings <u>only if</u> you are subpoenaed.

rather than

Come to the hearings unless you are subpoenaed.

A signature on an absentee ballot must be notarized. The only exception to this is a military member's signature on an absentee ballot.

rather than

Notarize a signature on an absentee ballot unless the absentee voter is a member of the military.

UNOBTRUSIVE DEFINITIONS

Unobtrusive definitions are short, conveniently placed explanations of technical terms that may not be completely familiar to the reader. These definitions are helpful to include when you are not sure whether you should include a definition. The reader who understands the term can skip over the definition easily, because the definition is structurally identifiable as a definition. The reader who needs the definition, however, will read it and thus understand your point. There are three ways to include unobtrusive definitions:

(1) include an appositive,

(2) insert an explanatory sentence, or

(3) include a definition section.

1. Include an appositive.

Include an appositive, or a few words in a phrase inserted immediately after the term being defined.

430

The tortfeasor, or the person committing the tort, ...

For related information, see APPOSITIVES.

2.   Insert an explanatory sentence.

When a longer definition is needed, insert an explanatory sentence right after the sentence using the phrase.

At least 80% of the net tax should be paid during the tax year. Net tax is the tax remaining after all deductions have been included.

Sometimes these definitions are placed in parentheses. But avoid overusing parentheses because they can become a visual distraction to the reader. For related information, see PARENTHESIS.

3.   Include a definition section.

If you need to insert many definitions, you can include an alphabetical list of those definitions in a separate section, such as the definition sections in statutes, contracts, or trusts. Save this approach for times when it is absolutely necessary. Use a definition section only when needed because a separate section is inconvenient for the reader.

If you are afraid you will offend sophisticated readers by defining legal terms, reanalyze your text in relation to your audience. Readers are often more frustrated by undefined terms than by excessive definitions. For example, a judge may be frustrated by *a logic flow schematic of an example embodiment of the present invention* because she has not done patent cases for a while. Similarly, a client may be frustrated by *tortfeasor* because he is not sure exactly what the word means. When in doubt, give your audience the definitions for any key terms or terms of art that may be unfamiliar. For related information, see READABILITY, LEGALESE, JARGON, TERMS OF ART, and PRECISION.

UNTIL SUCH TIME AS

Substitute *until*; you will gain conciseness with no loss in precision.

UNTO

Just use *to*. *Unto* means *to*; it does not mean *onto*.

UPDATING THE LAW

There are four major ways of updating legal sources, all indispensable to thorough research.

1.   Use a legal computer research system.

Each computer research system used by lawyers to update has its own supplementary method of updating legal sources. These services not only update the sources but also help you to find other legal sources relevant to your topic. They are the main services you can use to determine whether the source you are using has been overturned, distinguished, endorsed, or modified in any way. In other words, these services let you know if your source is still usable. LEXIS offers an electronic updating service patterned on Shepard's Citations, which is the book form once indispensable for updating the law. WESTLAW offers a service called KeyCite, which performs many of the same services offered by Shepard's on LEXIS. The displays are similar, as is the information provided. Both services give researchers timely and accurate information regarding the history of legal sources. But be aware that both services use their own analysts and interpreters; the information they provide is their interpretation only. You must go directly to the sources they describe to verify their interpretations. When updating, follow these steps.

(a) Use *Shepard's* or *KeyCite*.

(b) At your terminal, after you have entered the system, enter your citation. If your case has parallel citations, you may enter any of the cites to access the same information.

(c) The service will provide you with the previous and subsequent history of your source, as well as references to other cases and secondary sources that cite your source. You can examine those cases and secondary sources directly from the display.

(d) Note if, according to that system's analysis, a case was subsequently overturned, distinguished from other cases, dissented from, and so forth. The notations differ for cases, statutes, regulations, law review articles, court rules, city charters, and constitutions. Inspect the display you are given for specific guidelines.

(e) If necessary, restrict the citations you are given. Restrictions include jurisdiction, headnote, positive or negative treatment, and type of citation, such as a case or a law review article.

For related broader contexts, see also RESEARCH STRATEGY CHART, step 8.

2. Use books.

(a) *Shepard's Citations*.

This set of books provides specific updating service for all cases, statutes, rules, and constitutional provisions. For specific instructions on using the books, see the books themselves. Many libraries have discontinued use of the book form of updating, so check with your local library. If you do use the books, check the entire set of books and supplements, not just the most recent ones.

(b) Pocket parts and supplements.

These print sources update volumes in the law, such as case digests, annotated statutes, treatises, legal encyclopedias, and the words and phrases book. Those volumes using pocket parts have them enclosed in a pocket within either the front or back cover. Those using supplements have the supplements stacked separately after the volumes on the library shelf. Whichever your volume uses, make sure to check both the main volume and the pocket part or supplement for the most current developments in that topic.

3. Use looseleaf services.

Looseleaf reporters cover specific areas of the law. These are useful for updating the law because they are specialized. You may find sources and analysis of a specific area of law before that information appears elsewhere. Each looseleaf service has its own system for use, so check the how-to-use section in each looseleaf you use.

UPON OR *ON*?

Upon means *on the surface*; *on* means *in support of*, among other things. While the words are sometimes interchangeable, in legal writing use *upon* for the literal and more formal meaning, and *on* for either the literal or the figurative.

He placed the exhibit upon the table in front of the jury.

but

Counsel assured the defendant he was on the defendant's side.

UTILIZE

Substitute *use*, which is precise, readable, and not suggestive of JARGON.

Please use this form to provide the information requested.

rather than

Please utilize this form to provide the information requested.

UTTERLY

Omit this word; in legal writing, it almost always strikes the reader as an overstatement that weakens the statement rather than strengthening it. To emphasize a point, try using a short, direct statement rather than adding utterly.

The plaintiff's statement is false.

rather than

The statement made by the plaintiff is utterly false.

For related information, see LITERAL MEANING.

VAGUE WORDS

See AMBIGUITY, WAYS TO AVOID, subsection 3; PRECISION, subsection 2; and WORD CHOICE, subsection 6.

VARIETY

The word *variety* is sometimes used as a noun meaning a *collection of various things*. As such, it is too general to be useful in legal writing. If there is a variety, that variety will usually have to be explained.

In legal writing, avoid varying nouns or verbs solely for the sake of variety. Legal readers look for consistency, particularly in terms of art and key terms. For more on this, see KEY TERMS, TERMS OF ART, and ACCURACY, subsection 1.

Do vary sentence length and sentence structure, but let this variety arise naturally from the logical relations of your content. For ways to achieve this, see SENTENCE STRUCTURE and EMPHASIS. Also vary your choice of transition words by using those that reflect the precise relationship of ideas. For help with this, see TRANSITIONS. For related information, see CONNECTIONS, MAKING THEM.

VERBAL OR *ORAL?*

See *ORAL* OR *VERBAL?*

VERBOSITY

See CONCISENESS.

VERBS, EFFECTIVE USE OF

Verbs, which are words expressing an action or a state of being, focus the legal reader more than any other part of speech. In legal writing, verbs play a particularly important role in outlining the contours of legal analysis. When the verbs are right, the whole analysis falls into place. The following five guidelines can help you use verbs effectively. For grammar guidance related to verbs, see VERBS, TENSES and SENTENCE, PARTS OF. For more information about specific kinds of verbs, see VERBS, IRREGULAR; VERBS, LINKING; VERBS, MOODS; or VERBS, PARTICIPLES.

1. Make sure subjects and verbs agree.

Sometimes when the subject and verb are far apart in a sentence, you may accidentally use a plural verb with a singular subject, or a singular verb with a plural subject. One good way to avoid having this happen is to avoid putting more than seven words between your subject and verb. This will not only help you avoid agreement problems, but will also make your writing more readable.

Each of the therapists interviewed *had become* less willing to treat these patients after finding their practice restricted by these recent holdings.

rather than

> In the interviews, *each* of the many therapists currently finding their practice restricted by these recent holdings *were* less willing to treat these patients.

For related information, see READABILITY, subsection 5.

2. Use specific verbs.

Verbs move the reader through the text when they are specific, but halt the reader when they are vague. Try to state important action in the verb, rather than wasting this part of the sentence on information less important to the reader.

> **The show-up I.D. <u>negated</u> the effect of capturing the defendant one block from the crime.**

rather than

> The court <u>stated</u> that the show-up I.D. negated the effect of capturing the defendant one block from the crime.

In this example, the legal point is more important than the fact that the court stated it. Use a citation to give that information.

Avoid abstract combinations like *it is, there is,* or *there were.* Use nouns instead of those pronouns, specific verbs instead of those verbs of being.

> **False imprisonment <u>occurs</u> when a person is restrained without his or her consent.**

rather than

> There <u>is</u> false imprisonment when a person is restrained without his or her consent.

For related information, see THERE IS ... THAT.

3. Use active voice.

Active voice describes an action done by the subject.

> **<u>The court decided</u> that freedom of association was not an issue.**

rather than

> <u>It was decided</u> that freedom of association was not an issue.

Active voice is easier to read and more concise. It also adds precision because it makes clear who did what. Therefore, use active voice unless the writing requires passive voice for effect. For more help here, see ACTIVE VOICE and PASSIVE VOICE.

4. Use the auxiliary verb that best expresses your shade of meaning.

Careful use of auxiliary verbs can clarify the exact meaning of your verb. For example, if you wanted to communicate that the defendant had the capacity to do something but did not, use *could.*

The defendant could have set the emergency brake.

Conversely, if you want to communicate that the defendant had good reason for not setting the brake, use *would have*.

The defendant would have set the emergency brake had he not been rushing to assist the people in the other car.

For specific information about this use of verbs, see VERBS, AUXILIARY.

5. Split infinitives only when required for accuracy.

The standard wisdom here has been to avoid splitting infinitives at all times.

to move afterwards

rather than

to afterwards move

Because many of your readers will be of that school, you should avoid splitting infinitives when possible.

On rare occasions, however, a split infinitive will avoid ambiguities.

The mayor agreed to only suggest the alternative if the matter came up in committee meeting.

In this case, putting *only* before to would communicate that this was the only thing to which the mayor agreed.

The mayor agreed only....

Putting *only* after *suggest* would communicate that this is the only alternative the mayor would suggest.

The mayor agreed to suggest only this alternative....

When forced to make a choice like this, choose the clarity of the split infinitive over the elegance of the ambiguous unsplit version. You may find, however, that you can avoid the problem by restructuring the sentence altogether.

The mayor agreed that she would only suggest the alternative if the matter came up in the committee meeting. She would refrain from requesting it.

This is the safest route; your revised version will offend no one and still avoid ambiguity. For related information see ONLY, WHERE TO PLACE. For a definition of infinitives, see VERBS, TENSES.

VERBS, AUXILIARY

Auxiliary verbs, or *helping verbs*, are added to the basic verb to change verb tenses and to add specific shades of meaning. Choosing the correct auxiliary verbs, therefore, can help you be more precise and persuasive. The following list explains how to use specific auxiliary verbs.

1. Should.

Should implies that some action was preferable, but was not in fact taken. For example, it can be useful for suggesting a breach of duty.

The defendant should have set the emergency brake.

2. Could.

Could implies the capacity to do something, but suggests that the action will not or has not been done.

The defendant could have set the emergency brake.

3. Would.

Would implies that an action would have been taken had conditions been different.

The defendant would have set the emergency brake had he not been rushing to assist the people in the other car.

4. Can.

Can implies capacity to do something, although the action has not yet been taken.

When weighing the evidence, the jury can take into account the witness's apparent intelligence and the clarity of the witness's memory of the event.

5. Might.

Might implies possibility.

The district attorney might prosecute.

Often *might* suggests *if facts were otherwise*.

6. May.

May implies permission to do something.

If the Seller fails to comply with the nondiscrimination clauses of this contract, the Seller may be declared ineligible for further government contracts....

May also implies the possibility of something happening.

The grand jury may subpoena you.

Because it has two possible meanings, watch for potential ambiguities when using *may* in drafting. Sometimes, but not always, the meaning of *may* will be clear in context. When ambiguity is possible, use *might* for possibility and add some phrase like *if he or she chooses* for permission.

7. Must.

Must implies a requirement to do something or to refrain from doing something.

437

The Seller must not in any manner advertise the fact that the Seller has contracted to furnish goods to the Buyer without first obtaining the Buyer's written consent.

8. Shall.

Shall can imply a requirement, and is used to mean this in legislation.

All Petitioners shall file . . . .

But in general writing *shall* also implies the future tense.

The Williams opera shall premiere in December, if all goes as planned.

Therefore *shall* can be ambiguous; whenever ambiguity is possible, use *must* for requirements and *will* for future tenses. For related information, see SHALL.

9. Do.

Do adds emphasis. It often indicates a positive answer when a negative one is expected.

On the contrary, I do plan to attend the hearings.

10. Do not.

Do not denies an action.

My client does not know of any such plans.

11. Am, are, is, was, were, has, had, have, and been.

These auxiliaries combine with the main verb to form other tenses.

I am meeting with the client today.

We are considering the matter.

The defendant is planning to testify.

We were considering the matter, but decided it was not worth further pursuit.

The defendant was planning to testify before this evidence came to light.

Ms. Wiley had considered settling out of court.

Both attorneys have filed pretrial motions.

They have been planning this banquet for months.

For an explanation of how tenses are formed, see VERBS, TENSES.

VERBS, IRREGULAR

Irregular verbs are verbs that do not form their past participles in quite the same way that regular verbs do. The future tense, however, usually does not vary in its form.

438

Regular verb

Present: **I finish, you finish, it finishes**

Past: **I finished, you finished, it finished**

Future: I will finish, you will finish, it will finish

Irregular verb

Present: **I am, you are, it is**

Past: **I was, you were, it was**

Future: **I will be, you will be, it will be**

Common irregular verbs are *to be, to go,* and *to have.* For more information, see VERBS, PARTICIPLES and VERBS, TENSES.

VERBS, LINKING

Linking verbs, such as *to be* or *to seem,* link a subject and a predicate but show no action. They are roughly equivalent to equal signs. Avoid overusing linking verbs, because they are not as emphatic, interesting, or precise as active verbs.

The court reasoned that . . . .

rather than

The court's reasoning was that . . . .

Use linking verbs, however, when they accurately state the point. Often linking verbs are needed when TERMS OF ART are the subjects of the sentence.

Awarding custody to the mother is in the best interests of the children.

The standard of care is higher here because of this fiduciary duty.

For a clarification of active and passive voice and linking verbs, see VERBS, ACTIVE OR PASSIVE?

VERBS, MOODS

Mood refers to changes made in the form of the verb to indicate whether or not the action described by the verb happened in fact. These changes in the form of the verb are called inflections, and create four moods. These moods are important conveyors of meaning in legal writing.

1. Indicative.

The indicative mood refers to actions that have in fact happened, are happening, or will in fact happen. This mood is used most often in legal writing, and can be used with any tense.

The defendant filed a motion for failure to state a claim.

The buyer <u>is agreeing</u> to assume this responsibility.

The legislature <u>will consider</u> the matter in the next session.

2. Subjunctive.

The subjunctive mood refers to actions that will not necessarily happen, but are being discussed hypothetically.

If I <u>were</u> you, I <u>would</u> file a claim.

If the defendant <u>were</u> younger, such an assault <u>might have been</u> possible.

The subjunctive mood can be used with any verb tense, as the following list illustrates.

(a) Past Subjunctive.

If the legislature <u>intended</u> for the law to exempt owner-operated bars, it <u>should have stated</u> so in the law itself.

(b) Past Progressive Subjunctive.

If the legislature <u>had been planning</u> to exempt owner-operated bars, documentation of that plan <u>would</u> surely <u>have appeared</u> somewhere in the legislative history of the law.

(c) Past Perfect Subjunctive.

If the legislature <u>had intended</u> for the law to exempt owner-operated bars, it surely <u>would have stated</u> so in the law itself.

(d) Future Subjunctive.

If the legislature <u>were to exempt</u> owner-operated bars, it <u>would create</u> a suspect classification.

(e) Future Progressive Subjunctive.

If the legislature <u>were planning</u> to exempt owner-operated bars, local bar owners' associations <u>would</u> surely <u>be made aware</u> of that plan.

(f) Future Perfect Subjunctive.

If the legislature <u>were to have exempted</u> owner-operated bars, they certainly <u>were not aware</u> of that intention when they drafted the law.

For related information, see VERBS, TENSES.

3. Imperative.

The imperative mood states commands directly to the reader.

In preparation for this meeting, please <u>complete</u> this questionnaire and <u>bring</u> it with you to the meeting.

This direct address creates a more personal tone, and so it must be used appropriately. For example, direct address is natural for a request in a letter.

> **For our next meeting, please (1) <u>bring</u> all documents relating to the previous sale of your house and (2) <u>collect</u> all tax information for 1992.**

You could also naturally use it in a written request to someone you supervise.

> **When researching the DuBois case, <u>check</u> the statutes for any provisions relating to previous sales.**

But it is not used in formal court documents, such as a pleading. There, use the third person.

> **The plaintiff respectfully requests that this court overturn the trial court's ruling.**

It may also be inappropriate in a note to a superior or colleague, for reasons of TONE. In that situation, use the question form if adding *please* is not sufficiently deferential.

> **Could you please provide me a copy of the client's letters that address his preferences for the will?**

4. Emphatic.

The emphatic mood is formed by adding *do* to the verb. Some sources call this use of *do* by other grammatical names, including classifying it as a tense. Whatever its classification, you may use the emphatic mood to underscore a positive or negative response.

> **He <u>does plan</u> to pursue the matter.**

> **She <u>does not consider</u> this offer acceptable.**

VERBS, PARTICIPLES

Participles are the forms of verbs that combine with auxiliary verbs to form different verb tenses. There are two kinds of participles: present and past.

1. The present participle ends in *-ing*, such as *deciding, continuing, being, losing*, and *going*.

It is used to form progressive tenses.

> **The trial is <u>continuing</u> to draw much attention from the media.**

> **The children were <u>playing</u> near the pool when the accident happened.**

> **The Court will be <u>deciding</u> this issue next month.**

In contrast, this *-ing* form is called a gerund when it is used as a noun. (Also see GERUND.)

Seeing is believing.

2. The past participle of regular verbs ends in *-ed*, such as *decided* and *continued*.

The past participles of irregular verbs such as *been, lost*, and *gone*, do not end in *-ed*. Past participles are used to form past and perfect tenses.

The attorneys had already <u>decided</u> how to proceed when the settlement offer came.

The defendant has <u>lost</u> on appeal, but is going to pursue other possible actions.

Participles can also be used to introduce phrases, which are then called *participial phrases*. These participles modify a noun, so make sure that noun is in the main clause or you risk creating ambiguity.

<u>Discouraged</u> by this lack of response, Allen decided to leave the organization.

The defendant tried to put out the flames with a blanket but was forced back, <u>coughing</u> and <u>gasping</u> for air.

For more on using participles accurately, see MODIFIERS, DANGLING and MODIFIERS, SQUINTING.

VERBS, TENSES

Verb tenses tell the reader how the actions in the text relate to each other. The rule about using verb tenses is to be accurate, not just to use the same tense throughout a document. You will usually need to use different tenses to communicate how actions relate to each other. Do not, however, shift tenses without a logical reason for doing so. Verb tenses can also be used to add shades of meaning, as long as accuracy is not lost.

Depending on the grammar source you read, English has between three and a dozen tenses. The following list takes a moderate approach, listing nine tenses, and the infinitive form. The following subsections also explain ways you can use tenses to your advantage in legal writing. For more on similar techniques, see VERBS, AUXILIARY.

1. Simple Present Tense.

Use the simple present tense for a current or habitual action.

I <u>handle</u> all the estate planning in the firm.

Its main use in legal writing is for referring to statutes or other rules currently in effect.

False imprisonment <u>occurs</u> when ....

This statute <u>requires</u> all nonresidents to ....

Do not use the present tense in situations where you do not want to imply that this is a habitual action. Instead, use the present progressive tense.

Our client is complaining that the Jones Corporation ....

rather than

Our client complains that the Jones Corporation ....

2. Present Progressive Tense.

Use the present progressive tense for actions currently in progress. This tense is formed by *am, are,* or *is* and the *-ing* participle.

The client is suing the Jones Corporation.

Also use the present progressive tense for actions going on during or in the context of some present action.

Even as we are debating the issue here, the courts face the same issue in Colson v. Perry.

3. Present Perfect Tense.

Use the present perfect tense for actions now completed but related to a current action. The present perfect tense is formed by *have* or *has* plus the past participle.

After the testator has executed the will, the will becomes valid.

When used in context with another action, that action is usually stated in the present tense, as in the previous example. The present perfect tense is useful for showing that a current action is logically subsequent to a previous recent action.

Once the offeree has relied to his detriment upon the offer, the contract is enforceable.

4. Simple Past Tense.

Use the simple past tense for actions completed before the current writing.

The court decided to review the case.

The past tense is useful for suggesting an action is finished and cannot be changed.

The Supreme Court resolved this issue in ....

5. Past Progressive Tense.

Use the past progressive for actions completed before the current writing but going on over a period of time in relation to some other past action.

Mr. Jones was changing a flat tire when Mr. Smith's car struck him.

The past progressive tense is formed by *was* or *were* and the present participle, or the *-ing* form of the verb. When used with another action, the other action is usually stated in the past tense, as in the previous example.

The past progressive tense is useful for showing the context in which some past action happened, and thus it can suggest mitigating circumstances.

So bad was Julia's health that, even though he <u>was battling</u> cancer at the time, Colonel Hart insisted that Julia never be left alone.

6. Past Perfect Tense.

Use the past perfect tense for actions completed before some other past action took place.

Because Anderson <u>had accepted</u> the original offer, the contract was legally valid.

The past perfect is formed by *have, had,* or *has* and the past participle. When used in context of another action, that other action is usually stated in the past tense, as in the previous example.

The past perfect is useful for expressing a previous past action that logically led to a subsequent past action.

Since the tenant <u>had given</u> the landlord permission to enter the apartment to repair the faucet in the kitchen, the landlord assumed he could also repair the broken latch on the bedroom closet door.

7. Simple Future Tense.

Use the future tense for actions not yet done.

We <u>will send</u> you a draft of your new will so that you can review it before our next conference.

The future tense is formed by *will* and the same form of the verb that would go after *to* in the infinitive verb, such as *send, finish*, or *be*.

The future tense suggests that the action will in fact happen, even though it has not yet happened. It is useful for suggesting a result is certain.

Judge Roland Hausler <u>will win</u> re-election.

8. Future Progressive Tense.

Use the future progressive tense for actions that will be going on over a period of time in the future.

This action <u>will be pending</u> for many years before the court reaches a decision.

The future progressive is formed by *will be* plus the present participle, or *-ing* form of the verb. When used in the context of another action, that action is usually stated in the present tense, as in the previous example.

9. Future Perfect Tense.

Use the future perfect tense for actions that are not yet completed but will have been completed before some other action.

> **The company <u>will have bound</u> itself legally to the contract when it accepts the offer.**

The future perfect tense is formed by *will have* and the *-ed* form of the verb. When used in the context of another action, that other action is usually stated in the present tense, as in the previous example.

This tense is useful for showing the logical consequence of future possible actions.

> **If the court accepts the plaintiff's reasoning, then it <u>will have opened</u> the door to unharmed plaintiffs seeking to recover damages.**

10. Infinitive Verbs.

Although the infinitive is not technically a tense, it can be used to clarify sequence and meaning like a tense. The infinitive form is not tied to any person or time. It consists of *to* plus the verb, and often functions like a noun.

> **<u>To appeal</u> may be too expensive.**

It is useful when you want to suggest that the point you are making is always true, rather than focusing particularly on the present instance.

> **<u>To say</u> that one idea cannot be expressed in print is to say that all ideas are subject to potential censorship.**

VERB TENSES, DIFFERENT ONES IN THE SAME TEXT

The governing rule here is to use the accurate tense. Doing this will often require you to use different tenses within a passage of text and even within a sentence. Nevertheless, keep the verb tense consistent throughout your text when you can without loss of accuracy. For example, use simple past tense in both of the main verbs in the following sentences.

> **The trial court <u>found</u> that the defendant had made a good faith effort to inform the plaintiff of the impending problems meeting deadlines. The court also <u>stated</u> that the plaintiff had ignored the defendant's requests.**

rather than

> The trial court <u>found</u> that the defendant had made a good faith effort to inform the plaintiff of the impending problems meeting deadlines. The court also <u>states</u> that the plaintiff had ignored the defendant's requests.

Use of two different tenses within the same sentence is often necessary to keep the time relationship of two actions clear.

present perfect

Because the court <u>has determined</u> that state law applies

present

rather than federal, it now <u>can address</u> the question of jurisdiction.

past

Although the plaintiff <u>argued</u> his case under a theory of

present

restitution, he now <u>requests</u> what are in effect punitive damages.

In contrast, the following version, which uses a consistent tense, is inaccurate because the events did not occur at the same time.

past perfect

Although the plaintiff <u>has argued</u> his case under a theory of restitution, he

past perfect

<u>has requested</u> what are in effect punitive damages.

Thus in the previous example, two different tenses are used within each sentence: the simple past and the past perfect. The past perfect tells the reader that these actions (*had made, had ignored*) was completed before the other past actions (*found, stated*) began.

VERIFICATION

A verification is sometimes included at the end of a COMPLAINT, after the attorney's signature.

Plaintiff asserts that the facts stated above are true.

[Plaintiff's name typed under his or her signature]

Adding a verification helps drive home the importance of being truthful, which is useful especially when the attorney is taking the client's word for the truthfulness of key facts.

VERSATILITY

The legal writer must develop versatility for maximum effectiveness because lawyers must write to a non-legal as well as a legal audience and because the legal audience is varied in both background and needs. To develop this versatility, learn how different writing techniques work so you have the tools and understanding you need. For help doing this, study examples of others' writing, particularly those who are your primary audience. Exchange ideas with others about strategy, theory, and practical recommendations; then practice varying your approach to organization and style. For related information, see SENTENCE, STRUCTURE OF and HABITS.

Practice adapting to different audiences' needs. Your own writing will improve as you add to your repertoire the successful structures, approaches, writing patterns, and styles of others. If you are working for a supervisor who sees a different theory or structure to your document, try to compose the document that way, even if you disagree about why. Similarly, if you are working for a judge who prefers terse expression, or even a partner who demands flowery language, try imitating those styles. With these additions, you will become more adept and quick in your ability to choose the expression and approach you want. For related information, see AUDIENCE and STYLE.

VERY

Avoid overusing *very*. It adds little meaning, and often it detracts from the word it modifies, rather than emphasizing it.

This issue is crucial.

rather than

This issue is very important.

For related information, see MODIFIERS.

VIRGULE

See SLASH.

VIRTUALLY

Virtually means *essential to all purposes* or *in effect*.

It contrasts with *literally*.

The exceptions have virtually swallowed the rule.

Often *virtually* can be omitted with no loss of accuracy. Also see LITERALLY and MODIFIERS.

VIZ.

Viz., or *videlicet*, is unnecessary because there are clear English equivalents. Use *namely, that is,* or *that is to say* instead.

For related information, see LEGALESE.

VOICE

Voice is a literary term for the way you transmit an image when writing a particular document. Voice is created by many components:

favored sentence structures, levels of formality, preferred word choices, preferred organizational patterns, both large-and small-scale. Your voice is, then, a collection of your habits or preferences. As you develop your legal voice, you may expand or shift some of those preferences, depending on the context of your writing, just as your voice shifts when you talk to your spouse or your boss. As a legal writer, your voice might be that of a bill collector asking a client to pay an overdue bill, an advocate trying to change a judge's mind, or an apologetic bearer of bad news. But in all situations, the shift lies within a professional and temperate range.

Voice is alive and well in legal writing. From Holmes to Cardozo to Scalia, legal writers have carved out specific laws, persuaded readers, and stopped detractors short by the use of their voices. As you read and hear legal voices, you may accept or reject certain of their features. Eventually, you can combine features and generate others to create your own legal voice, which will develop over time. You need not lose your past writing voice because you have entered the law. You will, however, need to adapt the voice to the constraints of legal writing. To do this, analyze its features and decide what transfers well into legal writing. You will decide what to use or drop. You will also decide when to use your legal voice strongly and when, instead, to soften that voice for the sake of your audience. And there will be times when you need to imitate literally another's voice. See GHOST WRITING. For a discussion of various components of personal style, see TONE, SENTENCE STRUCTURE, and WORD CHOICE.

VOICE, ACTIVE OR PASSIVE?

Voice is a verb form that indicates the relation between the subject and the action expressed by the verb. In active voice the subject does the action; in passive voice the subject receives the action.

The boy hit the ball. [Active voice]

The ball was hit. [Passive voice]

The defendant assaulted the victim. [Active voice]

The victim was assaulted. [Passive voice]

The court held the identification evidence admissible. [Active voice]

The identification evidence was held admissible. [Passive voice]

For ways to identify passive or active voice, see ACTIVE VOICE, subsection 2.

1. Uses of active voice.

Using active voice instead of passive voice usually eliminates extra words. Using active voice also eliminates the ambiguity that might be caused by abstract verbs, such as *consists of* or *concerns* or *involves*.

Petitioner filed the motion on time.

Section 436 requires taxpayers to notify the IRS of any changes.

2. **Uses of passive voice.**

Passive voice is useful in four specific situations. In legal writing, use it consciously and for these reasons only; otherwise, use active voice instead.

(a) Passive voice is useful for de-emphasizing unfavorable facts or law. For example, the attorney for the defense might want to write the following.

> **The plaintiff was assaulted by the defendant**.

The attorney for the prosecution, however, might write the following.

> The defendant assaulted the plaintiff.

(b) Passive voice is useful for hiding the identity of the actor.

> **A decision was made to cut your salary.**

Here, passive voice avoids telling who made the decision.

> **It can be argued that the defendant assumed the risk.**

(c) Passive voice is also useful when the subject is very long. In this situation, passive voice creates a more readable sentence by keeping the subject and verb closer together.

> **This action is required by statutory law, by the common law principle of due care, and by a general sense of justice.**

rather than

> Statutory law, the common law principle of due care, and a general sense of justice require this action.

(d) Finally, passive voice is useful when the subject is much less important than the object.

> **Freedom of speech cannot be encumbered by concerns of propriety**.

rather than

> Concerns of propriety cannot encumber freedom of speech.

VOICE MAIL

When you need to leave someone a message that is best not put in writing, consider using the phone rather than email. Even though voice mail is recorded, it is not easily forwarded to dozens of other people, as is email. Of course, it is still recorded, so do think before you speak, and use the same level of formality you would use when talking to the person face to face in your office. For particularly delicate matters, set up a face-to-face meeting.

WAS OR WERE?

See *THERE IS* OR *THERE ARE?* or SUBJUNCTIVE MOOD.

WE

We is a special problem in legal writing because you may, by using *we*, inadvertently speak for your whole law firm or organization. Never use *we* when you really mean *I;* use *we* only when you are speaking officially for the organization of which you are a part, as one judge may do when drafting an opinion for the whole bench.

We [the members of the firm] suggest you try to settle the case.

rather than

We [I, but I don't want to admit it] think the merits of the case are too weak.

or

We [who?] now move on to the next issue.

For related information, see PRONOUNS and ANTECEDENTS.

We can also be used in constructions where a verb is implied. For example, *as well as we* implies *as well as we are,* and *such as we* implies *such as we are.*

I am sorry to inform you that the defendant's firm is unwilling to discuss a settlement with lawyers such as we.

WELL OR GOOD?

See *GOOD* OR *WELL?*

WHEN AM I DONE?

See WHEN TO STOP.

WHEN OR IF?

Use *when* to refer to a relationship of time; use *if* to refer to a logical relationship. See also WHEN OR WHERE?

WHEN OR WHERE?

When indicates a point in time; *where* indicates a physical place. In Questions Presented and issue statements, often you should use *when* because it is more precise, describing events in time. Use *if,* however, when referring to a logical relationship rather than the relative timing of two different events.

450

WHEN TO STOP

The purpose of this section is to help you overcome any tendencies you may have to fiddle with a document forever, miss your deadlines, frustrate your coworkers and typists, or drive yourself crazy with uncertainty about your writing. Ideally, each document you produce would be perfect. Realistically, that is not possible. It is seldom possible to get even one document perfect, let alone all that you write. You therefore have to make some decisions about which documents are worth pushing closer to perfection and which must be turned in sooner.

The following guidelines can help you make these difficult decisions at each stage of the writing process. But also use your common sense and revise the list as needed to suit your circumstances. For related information, see WRITING BLOCK.

1. When to stop researching.

Stop when you keep finding the same sources. Stop when mandatory authority is sufficient to answer the question. Stop when you have the appropriate research to answer the question within the scope of the project. Save time by following the Research Strategy Chart and by completing all updating. Do not waste time looking for the fictitious smoking gun, or the case exactly like yours; concentrate instead on the sources that turn up repeatedly or appropriately address the question. For related information, see RESEARCH STRATEGY CHART.

Stop when you have the essential sources appropriate to the document's SCOPE. Although there may be numerous other sources to answer the question, your AUDIENCE may not need all of them. If you can, ascertain the appropriate level of detail necessary to answer the question before you begin researching. Then you can choose the essential sources and eliminate the others as you read. If you can answer the question using MANDATORY AUTHORITY, you may be able to stop; if not, you may need to use PERSUASIVE AUTHORITY.

2. When to stop PREWRITING.

If you tend to linger at this stage so long that you have inadequate time for the later stages of the writing process, stop when you have completed enough of an outline to give shape to your general ideas and when you have listed specific points under each general idea. In general, however, allow plenty of time for this stage; it will prevent time-consuming errors at later stages.

3. When to stop WRITING.

The critical factor here is to stop rewriting, revising, and polishing during this first draft. Let your ideas flow, unedited. If you sense holes in your reasoning, let them pass for now; fill them in later in the rewriting stage. If you sense awkward phrases, let them pass also; you can revise them later.

451

4.   When to stop REWRITING.

Stop when you have the large-scale ideas in place, the paragraphs in a logical order, the topic sentences in place, and all needed content and explanation in the text. Make sure the organization is correct, complete, and coherent enough to be followed by any legal reader. Also make sure any unneeded information is omitted. Then move on to revising.

5.   When to stop REVISING.

The key here is to do first things first. Ask yourself the following critical questions before you move on to those concerns that are desirable but not critical.

(a) Does each topic sentence state the point clearly and unambiguously? For help here, see TOPIC SENTENCES.

(b) Is every supporting sentence accurate and logically connected to the paragraph in which it is included? For help here, see ACCURACY and ORGANIZATION, SMALL–SCALE.

(c) Is all unneeded information omitted?

(d) Is the point of view consistent and appropriate?

Then, as you have time, revise the text further, asking yourself each of the following questions.

(e) Are the sentences readable? For help here, see READABILITY.

(f) Are POSITIONS OF EMPHASIS used effectively?

(g) Are EMPHASIS techniques used effectively?

(h) Is TONE consistent and appropriate?

6.   When to stop POLISHING.

When polishing, first ask yourself the following questions.

(a) Are all citations complete and written in accurate form? See CITATIONS, BASIC FORMS.

(b) Does the document meet all format requirements?

(c) Are all quotes letter perfect? See QUOTATIONS, HOW TO PUNCTUATE.

(d) Are all numbers correct, including such details as numbers in citations and dollar amounts?

(e) Are all names spelled properly?

Then proofread the text for typographical, grammatical, and punctuation errors. Make sure to incorporate on the list your own frequent errors. When this is done, if you have time left, you may go back and check any other concerns that you wish. If you have no time left, at least you can take comfort in the fact that you have avoided major writing errors.

WHERE OR *WHEN?*

See *WHEN* OR *WHERE?*

WHETHER

Whether is a subordinating conjunction that introduces a dependent clause.

Whether the court will address this question is unknown.

Therefore a *whether* clause by itself cannot be a complete sentence.

whether the court will address this issue

In legal writing, however, *whether* is often used to introduce QUESTIONS PRESENTED and ISSUE STATEMENTS. If you use the *whether* form of a Question Presented or Issue Statement, end it with a period, not a question mark.

To avoid writing your Issue or Question Presented as an incomplete sentence, see if you can reformulate it as a question, leaving out *whether*.

Did the trial court err in awarding custody of both children to a mother when ... ?

rather than

Whether the trial court erred in awarding custody of both children to a mother when....

WHETHER OR *WHETHER OR NOT?*

Use *whether*. The *or not* has been dropped in all but the most formal writing.

WHICH OR *THAT?*

See *THAT* OR *WHICH?*

WHOEVER OR *WHOMEVER?*

Use *whoever* as you would use *who*; use *whomever* as you would use *whom*. Thus, use *whoever* as the subject of a sentence, *whomever* as the object of a verb or preposition. Each means *any person whatever*, but the choice of where to place these relative pronouns depends on the word's grammatical placement, as with *who* and *whom*.

Whoever talked to the client on Tuesday neglected to report the details of the discussion to the partner.

and

I will give the tickets to whomever.

Some of the confusion occurs when the pronoun appears to be the object of a preposition, but is actually the subject of a dependent clause.

I will give the tickets to whoever calls first.

but

You may invite whomever you want.

WHO OR *WHOM?*

Use *who* as a subject, *whom* as an object. Thus, use *whom* whenever it is the object of a preposition.

To whom did you present the question about the gun?

Use *whom* as the object of a verb.

Whom did you see on the night of the incident?

Or use *whom* when it introduces a clause that identifies a person who is the object of a linking verb that acts as the direct object of the verb.

Defendant is the person whom the plaintiff saw on the night of the crime.

Use *who* as a subject of a sentence.

Who took my shoes?

Also use *who* as the subject of a clause.

You are the person who called me yesterday.

When you do this, use the verb ending that matches the word *who* replaces.

It is I who am interested in this matter.

It is he who is interested in this matter.

WILLS, DRAFTING

The principles for writing wills are much the same as those for writing contracts. As with contracts, you might want to use forms to help you get started. For help here, see FORMS, USE OF. In addition to the principles listed under CONTRACTS, DRAFTING, also focus on these important tasks.

1. Ascertain the client's needs and the jurisdiction's requirements.

Interview the client thoroughly, so that you are clear about his or her desires and concerns. Ascertain the details you need about matters such as assets, legal domicile, and beneficiaries and other relatives. Ask the client to identify alternative beneficiaries and personal representatives. But while concentrating on getting all the needed information, also pay attention to your client's sensibilities. For many people, preparing a will is an emotional event; the client will appreciate a sensitive interviewer.

Next, research your jurisdiction's statutory and procedural requirements for wills. If your jurisdiction's requirements are less stringent than other states, consider creating a will that conforms to the higher standards. For example, even if your jurisdiction requires only two witnesses to the will, include three witnesses so that the will would also be recognized in other states.

In your research, consider also the tax and property ownership consequences. Anticipate possible problems in transferring ownership of various properties. Consider what happens to debts incurred by the testator. Prepare for possible challenges to the will. Allow sufficient time for this critical planning.

2.   Choose and organize the document's content.

Generally, wills include at least the following parts:

(a) an introductory clause naming the testator,

(b) what to do with anything left over (the residuary clause),

(c) general and specific bequests,

(d) appointment of personal representatives,

(e) a place for the testator's signature (the testimonium), and

(f) a place for witnesses to sign, saying that the will was properly executed.

Some wills also include trust arrangements, instructions to pay burial expenses, instructions to pay just debts, statements of disinheritance, naming of guardians for minors, and other special clauses. Adding these special clauses can create problems as well as prevent them, depending on the specific circumstances. Therefore, make sure you have researched the ramifications of each provision you decide to include. Check your jurisdiction, rather than relying on this list alone.

3.   Revise the document for accuracy and clarity.

The will must stand up to legal scrutiny, but the client and executor must also understand all the particulars of the will. Rewrite and revise with these two goals in mind. As when drafting a contract, plan to make many passes through the document. On separate passes, check for consistent and unambiguous language, specific references, and absence of legalese. Identify all needed terms of art and make sure that you have explained them to the client. Never include a single word or phrase that you yourself do not understand. You must be able to explain this document to the client, so you must be able to answer any questions about it. Even more important, the document must stand under the ultimate scrutiny of a wide legal and nonlegal audience. For related information, see AUDIENCE, TERMS OF ART, and LEGALESE.

4.   Adjust language for tone if needed.

Use flowery language only if your client prefers this because of the seriousness of the situation. Never sacrifice precision. For more explanation, see FLOWERY LANGUAGE.

5.   Polish with great care.

Revise painstakingly for grammatical accuracy and correct punctuation. Mistakes in these areas can translate into thousands of dollars, as the following phrases show.

my daughter's share of the estate

or

my daughters' share of the estate

divided equally among my nephew, my son, my daughter and my son-in-law

or

divided equally among my nephew, my son, my daughter, and my son-in-law

6. Near the end of the process, look again at the will as a whole and make sure it accomplishes your client's wishes and is legally sound.

The detail work necessary to drafting can temporarily blind you to the effectiveness of the whole. For more detail about drafting wills, see Mary B. Ray & Barbara J. Cox, Beyond the Basics, a Text for Advanced Legal Writing, Chapter 16 (West 2d ed. 2003).

WOMAN, LADY, OR FEMALE?

Use *woman* unless the context requires one of the alternatives.

WORD CHOICE

Choose words carefully because every word counts in legal writing. The following list provides an overview of the major concerns involved in effective word choice.

1. Use specific nouns and verbs rather than abstract ones.

This will help focus the reader on your main points.

The defendant moves to dismiss the case under Fed. R. Civ. P. 12(b)(6).

rather than

This concerns the defendant's motion to dismiss.

For related information, see PERSUASIVE WRITING, subsections 4(a)–4(c) and EMPHASIS.

2. Use terms of art or key terms, but avoid unneeded verbiage, such as legalese. For definitions, see TERMS OF ART, KEY TERMS, and LEGALESE. For related information, see PRECISION and READABILITY.

3. Avoid unneeded modifiers; use only modifiers needed for essential information.

An <u>alcoholic</u> father cannot serve the <u>best</u> interests of <u>his</u> children.

rather than

> An <u>habitually</u> alcoholic father <u>clearly</u> cannot serve the best interests of his <u>unfortunate</u> children.

For related information, see MODIFIERS and CONCISENESS, subsection 7.

4. Use accurate transitions to convey the logical links between ideas.

> **The litigation may cost more than the amount our client could recover if she wins the suit. <u>Nevertheless</u>, she has chosen to pursue her claim.**

rather than

> The litigation may cost more than the amount our client could recover if she wins the suit, <u>and</u> she has chosen to pursue her claim.

> See TRANSITIONS.

5. Use consistent wording.

> Use the same term for the same concept throughout the document; do not change it just for variety.

> **The defendant <u>proposes</u> that his repair of the water heater was adequate. This <u>proposal</u>, however,** . . . .

rather than

> The defendant <u>proposes</u> that his repair of the water heater was adequate. This <u>suggestion</u>, however, ...

For related information, see ELEGANT VARIATION and REPETITION.

6. Use the most specific term possible.

> For example, do not say *vehicle* when you mean *school bus*. Use more general terms only when you need to be ambiguous for some reason, or the context requires them. For related information, see AMBIGUITY, WAYS TO AVOID, subsection 3. For a discussion of situations where you may need to be vague or ambiguous, see EMPHASIS, subsection 2.

7. Make sure all pronouns are unambiguous.

> For example, if two or more women are mentioned in a text, then *she* is likely to be ambiguous. Therefore, check each pronoun.

> **Ms. Jones did not ask Ms. Wilson to double check the amount because Ms. Wilson routinely checked all the amounts listed.**

rather than

> Ms. Jones did not ask Ms. Wilson to double check the amount because she routinely checked all the amounts listed.

Also make sure each *this* is unambiguous. *This* is the pronoun most likely to cause inaccuracies. *This* can refer to an idea or a thing, one word or a whole sentence; as a result, you must make sure that the reader always knows what *this* means. If there is any question, add the appropriate noun after *this*.

> **The court reasoned that the difference in the age of the fetuses was not the factor determining this issue. This reasoning** . . . .

For more examples, see THIS and AMBIGUITY, WAYS TO AVOID, subsection 2.

WORDINESS

See CONCISENESS.

WORDY PHRASES

For general information, see CONCISENESS. For a discussion of specific phrases, see the entries listed in the table below. For a quick fix, try the shorter phrase in the right column.

Wordy Phrase	Concise Alternative
at this point in time	**now, currently**
during the time that	**while**
at the time that	**when**
for the period of	**during**
in absence of	**without**
it is . . . that	**[Start with the word after *that*]**
possibility that	**if, whether**
prior to	**before**
there are . . . that	**[start with the word after *that*]**
until such time as	**until**
in question	**this**

Try omitting the following words and phrases.

Omit these words and phrases

as a matter of fact

of course

clearly

really

fact that, the

to all intents and purposes

the fact of the matter is

undoubtedly

it is said that

utterly

obviously

very

WOULD

Would implies that something should have been done but was not in fact done. Thus it can be useful in Statements of the Case when you are explaining the reason behind an unfavorable fact.

The defendant would have set the emergency brake had he not been rushing to assist the people in the other car.

It can also be useful in Arguments to express hypotheticals or dicta.

The assumption would be valid if the defendant had intended to purchase the property, thus showing some interest in its transfer. But he made no such purchase.

But do not use *would* if you mean to imply that something will be done or if you do not want to imply that it should have been done. For general information, see VERBS, AUXILIARY.

WRITER'S BLOCK

See WRITING BLOCK.

WRITING

Writing is a creative act, not a critical one. It involves capturing your ideas on paper. When you reach this stage of the writing process, try to write without stopping to correct anything: don't get it right, just get it written. At this stage, your ideas need to be unencumbered by revision concerns. The critical voice will have time to correct and revise later, in the rewriting and revising stages.

One way to do this is to keep your words flowing onto the page. If you get stuck on a point because you are suffering from writing block, either skip that part or break it down into smaller pieces, but try not to stop. If necessary, write out your frustration, such as, "I can't remember the source but I know it's here somewhere!" and keep writing. When you finish, leave the draft, and catch your breath. Let the draft breathe, too, before you begin rewriting. Then, when you return to your first draft, remember that rough drafts, although necessary, are not final drafts. Expect to rewrite and revise extensively.

Other ways to keep writing creative, rather than critical, include changing the medium you use to write, writing before you outline rather than after, and writing a middle section first rather than starting at the beginning. For example, you might try dictating rather than typing the first draft. You might write a draft as a means of brainstorming before you outline. Or you might begin by writing about the point most familiar to you.

There is no one right method to use; the right method is the one that helps you get the document written. For more help, see WRITING PROCESS, WRITING BLOCK, and GETTING STARTED.

WRITING BLOCK

Writers may suffer from writing blocks at any stage of the writing process, but usually the cause is that the writer

- feels overwhelmed by the task,
- believes the written product must be perfect,
- feels he or she is inadequate to the task, or
- experiences all of the above.

Almost all writers suffer from writing blocks occasionally; some endure them on almost every project. Fortunately, writing blocks can usually be overcome by using any or all of the following techniques.

1. Divide and conquer.

Break the writing task into smaller steps, and keep breaking it down until you see a step that does not look overwhelming. Never mind if the list of steps is pages long; each of those steps may go rather quickly. These small tasks may be boring, but they will not be overwhelming. Then order the steps and start doing them. To gain a sense of progress, check each one off as you finish. For example, if the whole project seems overwhelming, start by listing all the tasks involved, such as

(a) research,

(b) outline,

(c) write,

(d) rewrite, and

(e) revise.

Then break each one of those down. You might break *outline* into

(b) outline

- list all possible points,
- group those points somehow,
- summarize each group, and
- decide which group goes first, second, etc.

If this is still overwhelming, you can break *list all possible points* into

- list all possible points,
  - list all points that make sense to me,
  - list all points mentioned in any analogous cases, and
  - identify all points that occur on both lists.

2.   Start somewhere else.

If you are stuck on a particular writing task, set it aside and work on something else. For example, if you cannot decide how to organize the facts section of a memo, leave it and begin writing the issues. If you cannot write the issue, try writing the conclusion. You need to complete many tasks in any writing project, but you need not complete them in any particular order.

3.   Separate the essential from the desirable.

You do not have time as a legal writer to make everything perfect; you must focus on quality and adequacy, but not on perfection. For example, when revising, focus on essentials, such as accuracy and clear organization, before you tackle desirables, such as emphasis and tone. For help doing this, see WRITING PROCESS. If you are finding it hard to get started, see GETTING STARTED. If you are having trouble finishing, see WHEN TO STOP. For related information, see PERFEC-TIONISM, TRIAGE, and DEADLINES, MEETING THEM.

WRITING ON THE WORD PROCESSOR

See COMPUTERS FOR WRITING.

WRITING PROCESS

The writing process is the entire creative, analytical, and critical experience that begins with an idea or assignment and ends with a finished document. The process as we see it incorporates five stages: PREWRITING, WRITING, REWRITING, REVISING, and POLISHING. You can save a great deal of time and become much more effective throughout the process by understanding each of these stages. Your writing process is personal and should be comfortably fitted to your own temperament and work habits.

Your process must also be productive and effective, building on your strengths while compensating for your weaknesses. Thus you may want to evaluate your process and adapt changes that improve it. You may find it useful to write your own process out as a checklist, so that you can focus on one step at a time, which can be more efficient and less stressful. The key to success in streamlining your writing process is breaking it into pieces and fixing one piece at a time. Over time, your techniques will work into a smooth process that is strictly yours.

The following suggestions can help you make your writing process both more efficient and more effective.

1.   Identify the point in the process with which you are most comforta-ble.

For example, you might like research but hate revising, or you might feel comfortable correcting mechanics and citations but very uncomforta-ble in writing. You are probably fastest at that point where you feel most comfortable, so you can allocate the least amount of time for that step when you establish your schedule.

2.   Identify where you are least comfortable.

For example, you may dislike revising because you are not sure of grammatical structures and how to fix them, so you get bogged down in miscellaneous questions. Or you may dislike writing because you feel each sentence has to be perfect before you go on to the next one.

3.   Focusing on the least comfortable task, break it into subtasks and give your full attention to each subtask.

For example, if you dread writing the first draft, try to write without allowing yourself to delete ideas you think may be weak, reorganize sentences, check spelling, or revise awkward phrases. Trust yourself to edit the document for those concerns later. At this time, just get all your ideas on paper. Alternatively, if you dislike revising, try not to revise all of every sentence all at once. Instead, revise the whole text once just for sentence structure. Then revise it again just for transitions. Revise a third time for accurate word choice. These small read-throughs can be done in between other tasks during the day. Additionally, by giving them your full concentration, you can complete them effectively in a minimal amount of time. Separate the creative from the critical and decide if you are trying to do too many things at once. For help here, see WRITING and WRITING PROCESS CHECKLIST.

4.   Incorporate into your process your deadlines and the constraints they represent.

Start with your deadline and work backwards toward the starting point, setting interim deadlines for each stage of the process. By allocating the most time for the place that is the least comfortable and the least time for the place that is the most comfortable, you can set a more realistic schedule that you will be more likely to meet. For an example of organizing to meet deadlines, see DEADLINES, MEETING THEM.

5.   Re-evaluate your writing process periodically; you will probably find yourself outgrowing your old process as your experience and skill increase.

6.   Concentrate on breaking bad habits by conquering one bad habit in each major writing assignment that you have.

For example, if you are weak on transitions, concentrate primarily on transitions in the revision process on one paper. Keep working on transitions on subsequent assignments until you feel comfortable with them; then move on to another bad habit. For example, you might concentrate next on better sentence structure.

7. When you want to make changes in your writing process, work through your process chronologically, because improvement in the early stages of the process may change the later stages automatically.

The following checklist follows this chronology, and offers some questions to ask yourself as you complete this evaluation. For a starting point, see sample checklists under PREWRITING, RESEARCHING, REWRITING, REVISING, and POLISHING.

WRITING TO OTHER ATTORNEYS

You can often relax your correspondence style when writing to these readers, because they share your profession and may be personal friends. You may be able to include more legal terms and fewer definitions. Or you might dwell on analysis and interpretation more than description. Just do not relax so much that you lose accuracy or lessen your professional posture. Especially watch for the pitfalls of becoming too relaxed in email. For related information, se GENERAL CORRESPON-DENCE LETTER AND EMAIL and TONE IN LETTERS AND EMAIL.

The first subsection below outlines how writing for legal readers differs from writing for nonlegal readers in word choice, tone, and level of detail.

1. Word choice.

You may use technical legal vocabulary and terms of art more frequently with legal readers, as a shorthand way of expressing a point. But use a term only when you are sure the reader will understand it readily. For example, you might write the following sentence to another attorney in your firm.

> **Our client was probably a holder in due course because he took the check in good faith without any notice.**

In contrast, the following sentence, written for your client, would use fewer legal terms.

> **You are probably entitled to keep the check because you had no idea that Mr. Hobbs had forged it.**

2. Tone.

Tone conveys your relationship to the reader and the situation, apart from the literal content of the document. As that relationship varies, your tone will vary. For example, when writing an informational memo to a close colleague, you may use more personal phrases or more informal, direct language.

> **Jane, I'll be writing my first brief for Judge Chang next week. I know you have a lot of experience in his court—got any helpful hints about writing for him?**

In contrast, you may use a more formal tone to a colleague you do not know.

> **Dear Mr. Morton:**
>
> **You and I will be representing the plaintiffs in Carolet v. McCartney. To coordinate our strategies, I would like to meet with all the plaintiffs' attorneys. I suggest that the meeting be during the second week in February. Please call my office this week to arrange a mutually convenient time.**

3. Level of detail.

Include as much detail as your reader needs to understand your point. Beyond that, adjust the level of detail to make your reader comfortable. Some attorneys prefer that all memos be kept as brief as possible, while others feel uneasy if not fully informed of the thought or research behind a point. If possible, ask the reader whether he or she wants copies of cases, short summaries of legal conclusions, or the middle route of the standard memo. When beginning to write for a new employer, ask that employer if he or she has good examples you can review. The more you learn about your reader, the more effective, efficient, and comfortable writing will be for you. For related information, see AUDIENCE, WORD CHOICE, and TONE.

YET

Yet, a conjunction, can be used in legal writing to indicate *nevertheless* or *despite this*. Like *but, yet* can be an effective transition to show contrast and opposing ideas.

> **Plaintiff still claims my client is guilty, yet he has failed to meet his burden to prove that guilt.**
>
> **Most commentators rely on this reasoning. Yet none has provided adequate authority on which to base that reasoning.**

For related information, see TRANSITIONS.

YOU

Use the second person, *you*, to address the audience directly, when appropriate. For example, you may use *you* in GENERAL CORRESPONDENCE LETTERS AND EMAIL where you want to sound like you are talking to a person face to face.

> **You asked that I write to you about the legal consequences of your automobile accident.**

You may also use *you* in consumer contracts or other situations when you need to tell someone clearly what he or she can or cannot do.

> **If you choose to change attorneys, you must notify** . . . .

Do not, however, use *you* in BRIEFS to the court. In those situations you are focusing on the argument itself, rather than on a one-to-one conversation.

> **Equity requires consideration of this issue.**

rather than

You must consider this issue.

ZWEURGET

Zweurget (pronounced somewhat like *tsvoirgit*) is a rather esoteric noun that expresses the felling of confidence, accomplishment, and giddy exuberance one feels upon completion of any arduous, lengthy, and complex task. Thus it readily describes a writer's feeling at the end of any major writing project.

The authors basked in the zweurget they felt when they finished the manuscript.

While it aptly explains the feeling, *zweurget* is an unfamiliar term, and thus should be avoided in legal writing. You may, however, use it with your friends to let them know how you feel when you finish a project.

†